dying into life

The Yoga of Death, Loss and Transformation

This book is dedicated to the SIRI SINGH SAHIB YOGI BHAJAN who modeled to us how to live and die consciously.

And to all those who have felt the agony of loss and who have had the courage to grow and shine because of it.

Prayer

Give me peace so I can be graceful.
Give me strength so I should be serviceful.
Give me happiness that I can be loved.
Give me health, wealth, so I can give myself.
Give me tomorrow that I can take away somebody's sorrow.
Give me today that I can be kind, compassionate.
Thanks for the yesterday, and thanks for the life.
Give me all the strength to live and let live,
  so that in Thy Name I can live that grace
  which Thou has bestowed on me,
For Thy Name, for Thy sake, I ask Thee to be with me.

YOGI BHAJAN

dying into life

The Yoga of Death, Loss and Transformation

As Taught by Yogi Bhajan, Ph.D., Master of Kundalini Yoga and Meditation
Written by Guru Terath Kaur Khalsa Ph.D.

Guru Ram Das Books
PO Box 845
Santa Cruz, New Mexico 87567
gtkhalsa_2000@yahoo.com
www.guruterathkaur.com

FIRST EDITION

Book design, cover and layout by Sopurkh Singh Khalsa, GRD Design
Yoga and meditation photographs by Gurudarshan Kaur Khalsa

First Printing, November 2006

ISBN: 1-4243-1253-1

APPROVED BY THE KUNDALINI RESEARCH INSTITUTE
This book has received the KRI seal of approval which is granted only to those products which have been approved through the Kundalini Research Institute review process for the accuracy and integrity of those portions which embody the technology of Kundalini Yoga and 3HO lifestyle as taught by Yogi Bhajan.

Thanks to 3HO Foundation for permission to use previously published material.

Printed and bound by Versa Press Inc., East Peoria, Illinois

Guru Terath Kaur has also written the book, The Art of Making Sex Sacred, available at www.guruterathkaur.com, Ancient Healing Ways and Spirit Voyage.

Always consult your physician before beginning this or any other exercise program. Nothing in this book is to be construed as medical advice. The benefits attributed to the practice of Kundalini Yoga come from the centuries-old yogic traditions. Results vary with individuals.

Contents

ACKNOWLEDGEMENTS

WHERE DO I BEGIN? So much love, time, expertise, knowledge and care went into the making of this book. *Dying Into Life* was definitely the product of many talented and conscious people. I am honored to have worked with them all. I would first like to acknowledge the Siri Singh Sahib Yogi Bhajan for all of his teachings on death, without which this book would not exist. His knowledge on this topic makes this book the astonishing piece it is. Second, I want to thank my husband, Guru Terath Singh, who was my first editor, sounding board and cheerleader. He never questioned why or how long but patiently put up with me through the whole arduous process, even making late night trips to Wal-Mart for computer ink cartridges.

Next are those who helped me in the research stage of the book – Dr. Gurucharan Singh and Guruka Singh who clarified my copious questions, Siri Ved Singh, who helped me access hours of Yogi Bhajan materials, Indra Kaur, who accessed hard to find meditations and Guru Dev Singh, who gave me deeper meanings to the meditations. I extend a deep appreciation to Dr. Seva Kaur, who researched homeopathic remedies appropriate for the process of death, trauma and grief and to Dharma Singh from Germany, who opened his conscious funeral home to me, enabling me to see and write about a better way to care for the deceased.

To my editors, Sarb Nam Kaur and Ek Ong Kaar Kaur, who encouraged me to examine, expand and clearly articulate. Also, to my proofers, Dharma Kaur and Sarb Jit Kaur, whose hours of tedious and loving service was daunting. And, a thank you to Satya Kaur from KRI who diligently pushed to get the book KRI approved, especially the yoga sets, all done in a chair or bed, something never attempted before.

A very special appreciation to my team that put the book together in a beautiful form – GuruDarshan Kaur, who did the amazing photographs;

and Sopurkh Singh, who designed the cover (the mandala), the inner graphics and the layout of the book with Kirn Jot Kaur. And, to those yoga students and teachers, who gave their time to pose for the photographs – Bir Singh and Bir Kaur, Case Crenshaw (Agia Akal Singh), Devi Dyal Kaur, Emma Lopetegui (Hargopal Kaur), Margie Montoya (Sat Jagat Kaur), Sahib Simran Kaur, Arnie Nance (Ardas Singh), Dolores Balkey and Dolores Martinez. They gave personalities and humanness to the photographs, demonstrating that yoga and meditation are for everyone.

The heart of the book consisted of the incredible and meaningful stories, poems, songs and quotes from so many. – Yogi Bhajan, Guru Singh, Guruka Singh, Shakti Parwha Kaur, Har Nal Kaur, Guru Tej Singh, Guru Tej Kaur, Dr. Shanti Shanti Kaur, Hari Nam Kaur, Kirn Kaur, Ardas Kaur, Dr. Sewa Simran Siri Singh, Guru Simran Kaur, Hari Jiwan Kaur, Sat Kartar Kaur, Ram Das, Arlo Gutherie, Dr. Kartar Singh, Dev Saroop Kaur, Amritpal Singh, Swami Dev Singh, Hari Dharm Kaur, Guru Nam Kaur, Siri Amrit Singh, Devi Kaur, Narinyan Singh, Sat Kirn Kaur, Hari Kaur, Sat Jiwan Singh, Siri Pritam Kaur, Guru Dev Singh and the students of Miri Piri Academy – Atma Kaur, Guru Prakash Singh, Guru Karm Singh, Siri Radha Kaur, Sat Prakash Kaur, Simranjit Kaur, Guru Shabd Singh, Sat Santokh Singh, Fateh Singh and Amrit Singh.

The accompanying CD with the correct rhythm and pronunciations of the mantras is an invaluable tool to making *Dying Into Life* a user friendly manual. I especially want to thank Steve Chavez of Chavez Recording Studio and Guru Hukum Singh for his melodic and precise recitations.

May your blessings be manifold. Humbly, with deep gratitude, **GURU TERATH KAUR**

INTRODUCTION

LIFE IS AN UNPREDICTABLE JOURNEY WE ALL MAKE, with death being the ultimate unknown. As we venture on our river of life, we encounter many things – joys, tragedies, gifts and losses. Sometimes our way seems effortless, as though the current was carrying us with ease. Other times, the boulders in our way seem insurmountable and threatening. To bring meaning and try to make sense of this voyage, each of us has an ideology or boat to more efficiently navigate our course.

I was a World War II baby, born into an ideology with clear messages about life and death that were prevalent in Western Culture at the time. God was an external "Father" figure, to be respected and feared in the same breath. Even though there was a place called Heaven, where one could earn everlasting life depending on one's earthy deeds, the underlying message was understood – birth was the beginning and was a joyous welcomed occasion; death was the end, a dreaded occurrence one feared. Death was rarely talked about. It was only brought out of the closet when absolutely necessary. It was somewhat accepted, if one was old and had lived a long, full life. The premature death of someone with good qualities or the death of a child or a young person was looked upon as being a tragedy, a waste and somehow an injustice. For many, this ideology or some version of it is still widespread today. There is no right or wrong belief system. As the times change, our beliefs about life and death change as well.

Usually at some point in our life, we make an inner quest to examine our childhood ideology and formulate a new one, which fits our adult identity and its values. My inner search began during the social revolution of the 1960's. With the War in Vietnam and the Civil Rights Movement tearing our country apart, it was a period of tremendous unrest and disharmony. I felt alienated, confused and torn from just about everything. Then in 1970, a miracle entered my life – Kundalini Yoga as taught by the Yoga Master, Yogi Bhajan. I began taking classes, and my personal transformation was set in process. Along with the yoga and meditation, came a whole oriental philosophy about life and death. My consciousness changed; how I saw the world and responded to it changed as well. I began to feel my inner spirituality…yoga and meditation unveiled my soul. God was no longer a separate being…we were One. I was home.

The Siri Singh Sahib Harbhajan Singh Khalsa Yogiji, commonly known as Yogi Bhajan, was the Master of Kundalini Yoga. He was born and raised in Northern India, where he was trained by many masters of various spiritual disciplines and became a Master of Kundalini Yoga at the age of 16. Kundalini Yoga has been around for thousands of years. In India it was restricted to a few elite castes and was passed from generation to generation only through oral expression. Not only was the science of yoga very limited to a few, it carried an aura of mystery. Yogi Bhajan came from India to the West to teach this ancient technology in 1968. One of his greatest merits was unveiling the secrecy and myths surrounding Kundalini Yoga, making its techniques accessible to everyone.

He created 3HO, the organization for Healthy, Happy and Holy living, where tens of thousands of men, women and children from many different backgrounds have applied the technology of Kundalini Yoga to experience drug-free, healthy, balanced, happy and successful lives. He developed Yoga Centers in over 20 countries and most states in the US. He became widely recognized as a world leader and a champion of world peace and healing. He was the current Mahan Tantric, the teacher of White Tantric Yoga, a technique that helps remove subconscious mental blocks. He also earned a Ph.D. in

A little story, which took place in my early years as a yoga student: I remember sitting with some other yoga students talking with Yogi Bhajan. Yogiji, as we all called him, was talking to us about our lack of inner identity, values and commitment. Basically, he told us, all we had to do was know ourselves. "The inner self of the self is sitting, waiting for you to realize that self," (The Teachings of Yogi Bhajan, 1977). He made it sound so simple, like 'what's the problem?' Then, a fellow yoga student, Richie, spoke up and defended our unsophisticated ways. He reminded Yogi Bhajan that as a young Sikh boy growing up in India, he had all the Sikh Gurus and heroes to model inner wisdom. As Americans, our heroes at best were Batman and Mickey Mouse. Richie appealed to this holy man for his compassion and understanding. Nodding our heads in agreement, we all had a good laugh. Being a true Master, Yogi Bhajan's only response was, "If you want to be like me, follow the teachings."

Guru Terath Kaur

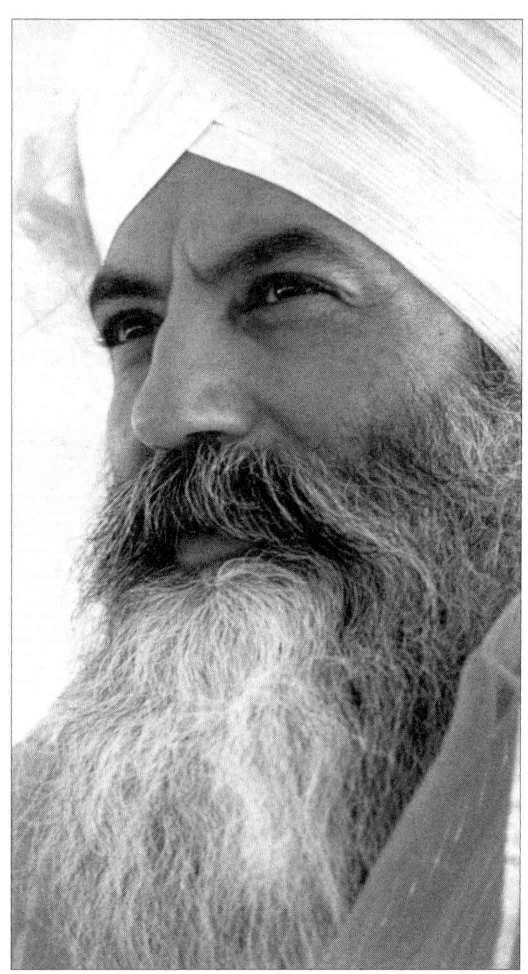

Yogi Bhajan

the psychology of communication. He published over 30 books, and his teachings are published in over 200 books and videos. From the beginning, he proclaimed that his mission was not to collect disciples but to develop Aquarian Teachers. His motto in life was – **If you can't see God in all, you can't see God at all.**

A lot has happened since the tumultuous time of the 60's, but we are still faced with much uncertainty in the world. More than ever before, death and loss are common occurrences in our lives. In the United States, over 50% of marriages end in divorce, with second marriages even more likely to fail. My father worked for the Pacific Telephone Company for 35 years. Today people may change companies and careers several times during their productive years, which means one's interaction with neighborhoods, friends, co-workers, churches, cultures and countries change as well. The evening news bombards us with stories of minute-by-minute accounts of tragedy and loss in living color and gory detail, all while we are eating our dinner. Above everything else, we are losing something, which is often too elusive to recognize – our sense of self and inner peace.

Just as we live in a time of great uncertainty, we also live in a time of tremendous hope and change. We are in the cusp period going from the Piscean Age – for the last three thousand years – to the Age of Aquarius (to begin in 2012). The Piscean Age was a period of individualism, where God was experienced as an external figure, and knowledge came from outside of ourselves. This transition involves nothing less than a complete shift in consciousness and world views. We will identify ourselves to be co-creators with God and will perceive God in everything and everybody, including ourselves. Wisdom will be an inner experience. This is where the technology of

Kundalini Yoga comes in. It will help us develop and experience this new consciousness from within.

Life teaches us that our journey cannot be mapped or controlled. But with training, we can prepare ourselves to view and respond to our challenges with more grace and inner serenity. *Dying Into Life* will give you such training. It is a yogic guide to life, death and transformation. Now, perhaps more than any other time in history, we need and are ready for the ancient teachings of Kundalini Yoga, as taught by Yogi Bhajan, a universal discipline that can benefit everyone, no matter what their religion or creed.

In the Piscean Age we said, 'I want knowledge; take me to where it is.' In the Aquarian Age we will say, 'I have the knowledge; now give me the experience.'
YOGI BHAJAN

Yoga literally means "union." It serves as a vehicle to unite our soul with our Creator. Kundalini Yoga is said to be the most powerful of the twenty-two schools of yoga, because it integrates all elements of yogic science. Included in the practice are sound and mantra, breathing techniques (*pranayama),* body postures (*asanas*), hand position (*mudras)* and meditation, which balance and strengthen all the systems of the body. Kundalini Yoga brings clarity to the mind and develops one's relationship to Infinity. This balance enables us to harness the energy of the body, mind and spirit, so that we can be in control of ourselves, rather than being controlled by our thoughts and feelings. As you journey through this book, you will have the chance to experience the vast benefits of Kundalini Yoga in relation to the cycle of life and death. **Be sure to refer to the accompanying CD for the pronunciation of the mantras. For your convenience the number by the mantra in this manual corresponds to the number on the CD.**

The philosophy and technology in this book may appeal to many populations. Whether you are looking for a personal guide, are a yoga teacher, are coaching a friend preparing for death, are a caregiver for someone seriously ill or you are just curious – *Dying Into Life* has something for you. For some, the Yogic Tradition may be totally new and seem strange. For others, it may be a cohesive collection of what you already believe and experience. Some of you may read it in one sitting; others may find that you need to take each chapter one at a time, slowly savoring the concepts and techniques. Benefiting from this book isn't an all or nothing situation. Embrace what makes sense to you for now, and leave the rest. You may wish to revisit *Dying Into Life* in the future.

We are not human beings having a spiritual experience; we are spiritual beings having a human experience.
YOGI BHAJAN

Keep in mind that while reading the pages of this book, we will go through a process together. Every aspect of you – mind, body, spirit and emotions – will be stimulated by the philosophy, yogic science and personal stories presented. Without a doubt, the book's greatest gift to the reader is its technology – Breathing, Yoga, Mantra and Meditation – because unless you have an experience, the concepts will be mere words. I may say something like –"The mind follows the breath" – but until you experience it for yourself, it is just an idea. For this reason, every chapter will have yogic techniques or "tools," which support the concepts presented. These techniques are your "personal tool kit" to get the job done. You are the carpenter, equipped with the needed resources to not only ease the journey but also change tragedies into opportunities for tremendous personal growth and transformation. With training and practice, we all can even prepare ourselves for our last great adventure – death.

My intention and prayer is that this book will be a catalyst for the story of your own journey to surface and be examined. Each chapter will end with Process Exercises. I highly recommend that you choose some to complete; knowing something will be accomplished by practicing it. May healing and blessings grace your inner quest.

The author, Guru Terath K. Khalsa Ph.D.
with Yogi Bhajan Ph.D., Master of Kundalini Yoga.

PART I The Foundation of Yogic Tradition

THE YOGIC TRADITION can symbolically be compared to a toy train set, with its tracks in the shape of a figure 8. The left side of the loop is marked *Life*, and the right side is marked *Death*. The intersection in the middle is the transition going from life to death and death to life. We are the train, the engine being our soul, with the attached cars as our accompanying physical body, mind and emotions for that lifetime. Also attached is our baggage or karmas for the trip. Making our way along the track, we encounter challenges along its course – opportunities for growth and erasing our karmas. If we pass the tests, we may be able to drop baggage/karma along the way. If not, we may need to pick up additional baggage. The only thing that is constant is the engine, our soul, going with us from incarnation to incarnation. The ultimate mission of the journey is to pay off one's karma, so the soul can consciously merge with the Infinite.

As you will notice, the shape of the figure 8 has no beginning or end, signifying the Yogic attitude of life and death. One naturally flows into the other. In this way, we could say we are "living into death and dying into life." One is a preparation for the other. In life, our goal is to connect to our individual infinity, which prepares us to experience it in death. With no end or beginning, the process continues until all karmas are completed and our individual consciousness merges with the Universal Consciousness – God. Keep this theme in mind, because like the train track, we will return to it again and again.

Imagine a mandala, with the contents of Part One as the nucleus, from which the rest of the book will grow. As we progress through the chapters, more and more aspects will be added, all reflecting back to this core. In these first chapters, we will examine three concepts: God exists within us; Breath is our link between life and death and our connection to the Infinite; and the Word or vibration is the basis of all creation. As the Yogic Tradition is based on philosophy supported by a yogic science and technology, we will also acquaint ourselves with the Kundalini Energy, the Eight Chakras, the Ten Bodies and the practices of Breathing, Yoga and Mantra. The foundation in Part One will give you the information and technology to more fully comprehend and benefit from the other Parts of the book. Everything presented supports our mission – "Living with grace, one will die with grace." Feel free to refer back to this foundation, as needed.

All of the practices in this book can be done either sitting on the floor in an easy cross-legged position (Easy Pose) or sitting in a chair with the feet flat on the floor. Many of the practices can be done lying on a bed. The spine is kept straight. You will find more about these positions in Chapter Five – *Yoga for Health and Healing*.

Before doing anything else, let's "Tune In"

Every Kundalini Yoga Practice begins with chanting the Adi Mantra: "***Ong Namo Guru Dev Namo.***" By chanting this mantra one is vibrating to the highest frequency for practicing Kundalini Yoga. Through the sounds of these syllables, you are dialing your mind to the channel that will give you the clearest reception to receive these teachings. Your consciousness is tuning in to the Divine Teacher. Chant this mantra before you practice any of the yogic techniques. Also, try chanting it any time you read this book, with the intention that its teachings will penetrate your consciousness at the highest frequency.

"***Ong***" is the infinite creative energy experienced in form – or God as Creator. To chant ***"Ong,"*** slightly pull in the navel (the "O" is pronounced as in "go") and vibrate the ***"ng"*** at the *Third-eye* (Ajna, the sixth chakra, seat of intuitive power, pituitary gland, a focus point during meditation) by slightly blocking the back of the throat with the back of the tongue.

"***Namo***" has the same root as the Sanskrit word Namaste, which means reverent greetings. It means bowing down or acknowledging. Together "***Ong Namo***" means "I call on the infinite creative consciousness."

"***Guru***" is the embodiment of the wisdom – the giver of the technology. "*Gu*" means darkness and "*ru*" means light, so Guru means "that which takes one from darkness to light." The first syllable, "**gu**" is short, the second, "*ru*," is long (pronounced together as "g'roo"). The "*r*" is rolled off the roof of the mouth, with a slight hard sound.

"*Dev*" means divine, in a non-material way (pronounced like "Dave"). "*Guru Dev Namo*" means, "I call on the divine teacher or the universal wisdom."

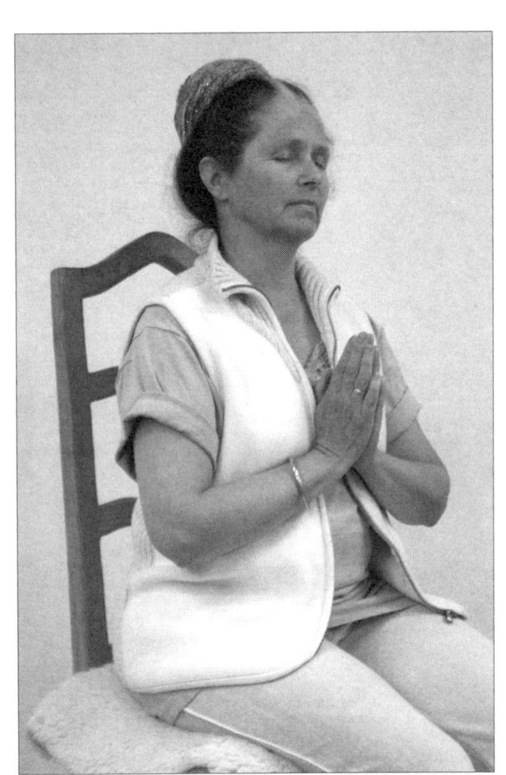

To Begin

Be sitting with a straight spine either in *Easy Pose* (legs crossed, sitting on the floor) or in a chair with the feet flat on the floor or lying straight on a bed. Put the hands in *Prayer Pose* by pressing the palms flat together, fingers straight and together, pointing up; then press the joints of the thumbs into the center of the chest, at the sternum. This is done to neutralize the positive (right, or male) and negative (left, or female) sides of the body. Inhale deeply. Your focus is at the *Third-Eye* point (between the eyebrows, ¼ inch up from the bridge of the nose). As you exhale, chant the entire mantra in one breath. If you cannot do this, take a quick breath after "*Ong Namo*" and then chant the rest of the mantra. Chant this mantra at least three times. (Refer to the accompanying CD for pronunciation – 1.)

Ong Namo Guru Dev Namo

CHAPTER 1

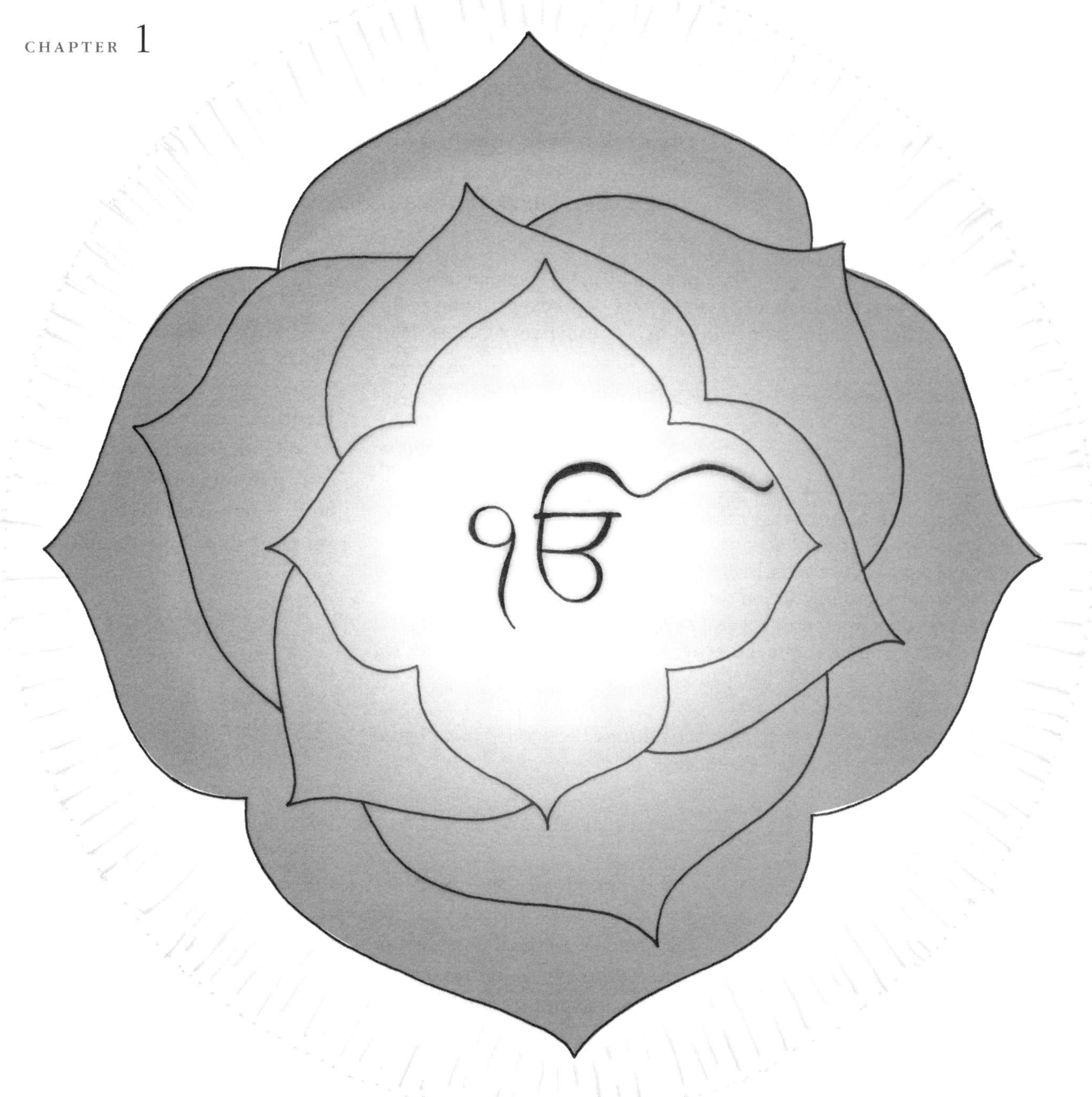

God Exists Within Us

THE BASE OF YOGIC PHILOSOPHY rests on the concept that God exists within us. God is not seen as a punishing or rewarding patriarchal figure outside of us, but an energy experienced within. In Yogic terms, we talk about a *"divine trinity"* – God, Guru (our own intrinsic inner wisdom) and Self. Instead of knowing the existence of God through "belief," a yogi knows the existence of Infinity through "inner awareness." In this way, we can identify ourselves as being co-creators with God. Our individual soul/infinity can communicate with the Supreme Soul. There is no higher or lower; God is not great and we are not small. We are God. All of yogic technology is designed to give its practitioners this experience. This basic concept of yogic philosophy has enormous implications in our daily life and in our preparation for death. Let's take a closer look at it.

With God's grace, we may be given the opportunity in this lifetime to meet a spiritual teacher. An actual spiritual teacher knows beyond a doubt his or her true identity and has the mission to guide others to experience that as well.

God gives you the teacher, and the teacher will give you God. It is a full exchange system.

YOGI BHAJAN

The job of the spiritual teacher is not to be a father, a mother or a friend. A spiritual teacher is a friend of your consciousness and chisels you until you are free of your past karmas. His or her job is not to become your crutch but to give you a technology so you can develop the ability to self-confront and thus access your inner wisdom and light. The end result is merging the Self with the One. A true spiritual teacher will also help you cross over at the time of death.

The teacher is an analytical sandpaper who scrapes away your attachments, so that your Self can reflect your essence.

YOGI BHAJAN

Our finite self is our physical body, mind and emotions, which will eventually wither and die. Our infinite self is experienced through our soul and is eternal. Our soul is the individual expression of spirit; it contains the basic nuclear energy of us, our core. Usually we base our identity on the finite. We attach ourselves to what is tangible about us, like our looks, our accomplishments and our roles in life. The problem is that these things are transient in life, and if we base our identity solely on them, we will suffer and restrict ourselves. Conversely, if we base our identity on our inner relationship with our soul, we can relax into the flow of God energy and use it to create wholeness in our life, even in times of great distress and loss.

Imagine a circle, representing you, with smaller oblong shapes coming from the center of it, representing aspects of your life, each labeled with things like – father, daughter, singer, religion, career, financial stability, youth, skinny, home and health. Now begin to take these pieces away. What happens? The circle is filled with holes in it. Symbolically, this is how we will feel – like something has been ripped from us, leaving us incomplete and empty. Now imagine the same circle with another smaller circle in the middle of it, labeled SOUL. When you take the other pieces away this time, how does it feel? There will be holes, we will feel the pain of the loss, but we will have our core to hold us together. Our identity will be based on our undying soul.

Finite self

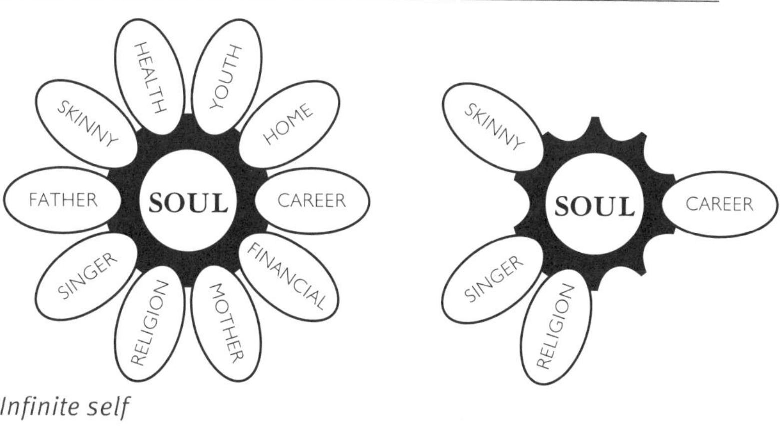

Infinite self

We were given the sensations of our physical or finite body to not only experience our external world but our infinity as well. One practitioner described this:

> *"While meditating in the early hours of the morning, I feel an explosion of energy within me, rising along my spine until I see colors at the point of my Third-Eye. I feel blissfully connected to my soul."*

Sometimes the sensations are much more subtle, coming in the form of tranquility, inner knowing and acceptance. These sensations are

Called or not called, God is always here.
Carl Jung

All my life I have prepared for one thing –that the day I meet God, I will meet Him as a part and parcel of Him, never as an individual. Never meet any individual as an individual to an individual. Meet that person always as a part and parcel of him or her, as if you are one. Because there is one God, and every creation of that one God is one. Learn this art of being one.
YOGI BHAJAN

You may choose to leave God, but God will not leave you.
YOGI BHAJAN

comforting, because they are all ours from within. They have not come from an external stimulus, which can be taken away or altered. Through this experience of God within, we never need to feel alone or abandoned. No religion or dogma or book or teaching or teacher or priest stands between Thou and us. In relation to losses or deaths in our life, we will always have a companion. That union or oneness is always there. We need only to allow its presence.

The soul expresses itself through the heart. This leads us to the realization that all living beings are One, connected through the same Cosmic Energy, called God. ***God And Me, Me And God Are One. God And You, You And God Are One. God And We, We And God Are One.*** We experience this godliness in others and ourselves through heartfelt actions of kindness, forgiveness and service. It may also be expressed through art, music, dance and healing – anytime our soul flows forth into external manifestations. We experience it through our sensations – the sight of a sunset, the smell of a rose, the touch of a newborn baby's skin or the taste of an orange. This awareness develops planetary citizens, equally concerned about all peoples and living things everywhere. It's as though the whole Universe is like an exquisite mosaic, with every person, tree, animal, insect and planet a piece of the whole – miraculously sustained and held together by God, our glue. Think about how this awareness can affect our attitudes about relationships, violence, hunger, education, health care and ecology.

If we know (through experience) that we are God, wouldn't it also mean that infinite potential lies within us? Usually we rely on our ego or personality – which is limited – to accomplish a task. But what if the limited 'I' got out of the way, allowing the 'higher self' to do the job?

Two of my heroes are Mother Teresa and Elizabeth Kubler-Ross. These women both worked with the dying and were legends in their own right. I had the blessing of meeting both of them. I was struck with how tiny in stature they were. How could someone so small accomplish things so big? I came to one conclusion – they weren't working alone. They had a whole team of Infinite players. God and Gurus and Angels and Divine Spirits were all guiding and carrying them. They inspired me to allow my own expansion.

Thinking about writing this book was overwhelming for me. How could 'I' do it? For months, in my morning meditation, a voice kept haunting me – *"You have to write that book."* I argued back with every excuse why I couldn't do it. The voice wouldn't leave me alone. Finally, we made an agreement. 'We' would write the book. Every morning in my meditation, I asked – *"What do you want me to write today?"* And this is basically how I run my life. The minute 'I' runs the show, I am bogged down with my insecurities and fears. But if 'I' allow 'WE' to do it, the potential is without boundaries. The challenge is getting myself out of the way. This is where meditation is my friend and tool.

The Five Sutras of the Aquarian Age

1 Recognize that the other person is you.

2 When the time is on you, start, and the pressure will be off.

3 Vibrate the Cosmos. The Cosmos shall clear the path.

4 There is a way through every block.

5 Understand through compassion or you will misunderstand the times.

YOGI BHAJAN

As you continue through the book, reflect upon these sutras. They will take on a deeper and deeper meaning.

My relationship to my soul gives me self-empowerment. Instead of feeling like a victim, at the whim of external influences, I know I have choices. I may not be able to totally control what happens to me, but I can control how I respond to it. For example, let's say out of a co-worker's insecurity, he degrades the project that you have just spent months developing. You have no control of the event; you do have control of how you respond to the event. If you come from your ego and personality, your reaction will reflect your own insecurities and "littleness," and you may create an unpleasant situation you'll have to deal with later. But if

Be practical, be real. God is within you, not outside. The moment you feel that God is in you, it will cover all your situations in life.
YOGI BHAJAN

If you check out your life, you will find that 100% of your problems are because you do not have a relationship with your spirit, your soul.
Yogi Bhajan

you come from your vast infinity, your solutions will be creative, neutral and expansive, uplifting the situation for everyone involved.
In circumstances like these, drink a full 8 ounces of cool water, which will help cool your nerves. Take some deep breaths and take a little walk. In Chapter Six – you will find a meditation – **Ten Steps To Peace** (pg. 99)– well suited for these occasions.

How does all of this prepare us for death? Experiencing our soul during life gives us a "knowing" that we are more than our mere physical body. The physical body, like an old coat, will be shed; the soul never dies. This experience of deathlessness takes the mystery, and thus fear, out of death.

We have all had experiences of our soul from time to time. What blocks us from living in that place all the time? Sometimes we get stuck in the different faces of our ego – a few being doubt, fear, guilt or apathy. What will pull us out? Taking the first step. Try some of the Process Exercises on the next page and reflect on your reactions. Then, keeping the concept of "**God and Me, Me and God are One**" as the base, continue to read on.

PROCESS EXERCISES

Take a few minutes to complete one or more the following activities and process your reactions.

1 Go back to the second and third paragraphs in Chapter One, talking about basing our identity on the finite vs. the infinite self. Thinking of the losses in your own life, complete the suggested exercise – drawing the circle with the oblong pieces labeled with identities applicable to your own life. How does it feel when you take those identities away? Now do the exercise again, this time putting the label of SOUL in the middle of the circle. How does it feel now? Did you feel any difference? Keeping in mind your own life, expand upon this idea. If so inclined, write about it.

2 Tune In (refer back to page 18 for instructions). Sit for a few minutes and chant some repetitions of – “God and Me Me and God Are One.” Chant the complete phrase in one breath, taking a deep breath in between each repetition.

3 Tune In. Complete the meditation – “I Am I Am,” found on the next page. How did you feel after you completed it? Did it help you connect to your soul? Be sure to read Chapter Five – Yoga For Health and Healing – which will give you the basics to begin a yoga practice.

4 Reflect upon and write about what’s blocking you from relating to your soul all the time.

5 Think about a time in your life when you did something from your ego v.s. your “Higher Self.” What was the difference? Which worked better for you?

6 Reread The Five Sutras for the Aquarian Age found on page 23. How do you interpret them? Considering what we discussed in this chapter, how does it apply to your life?

MEDITATION INTO BEING: "I AM, I AM"

Now is the time to live to this simple rule: "God is within me. I am, I am."
YOGI BHAJAN

This mantra connects the finite and infinite identities. The first "I Am" that emphasizes the "I" is the personal and finite sense of self. The second "I Am" that emphasizes slightly the "Am" is the impersonal and transcendent sense of the Self. All real mantras blend this polarity of the finite and Infinite in their internal structure and design. If you only say the first "I Am," the mind will automatically try to answer. "I am what?" This sends the mind on a search through all the categories and roles that hold the finite identities. If you immediately say the second part of the mantra, "I Am," the thought becomes "I Am what I Am." To be what you are is the essence of truth and will lead you to the nature of reality. The hand and the breath move in rhythm and strengthen your ability to maintain a sense of self as your awareness expands.

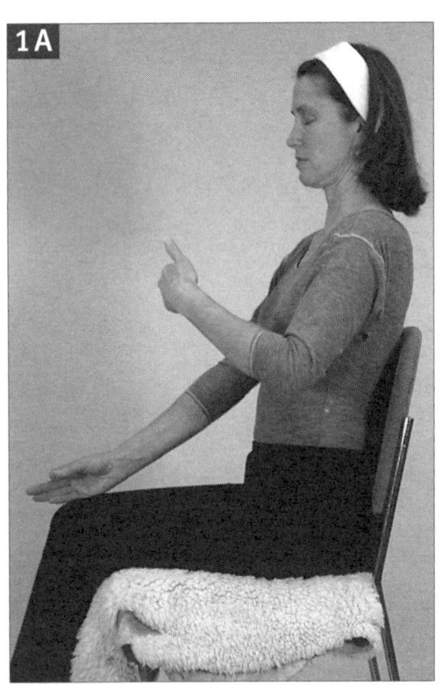

How to do it
Sit with a straight spine, either in a chair with the feet flat on the floor or in *Easy Pose* (legs crossed) on the floor. The neck is in a light *Jalandhar Bandh* or *Neck Lock. (Refer to The Bandhs in Chapter Four.)*

Eye position: Fix the eyes at *1/10th* open. The eyes look straight ahead through the eyelids. See page 47 for a full explanation.

Mudra (Hand position): Keep the spine straight. Place the right hand over the right knee. Keep the elbow straight and the hand relaxed in *Gyan Mudra* (the index finger tip on the tip of the thumb). Raise the left hand in front of the Heart Center. The palm is flat and faces toward the chest. The fingers point to the right.

Mantra: I Am, I Am

Breath and Movement: Start with the left hand 6 **inches** from the chest **(1A)**. Chant out loud *"I AM"* as you draw the hand close to the chest to a distance of about 4 **inches away from the chest (1B)**. Then chant *"I AM"* as you extend the palm straight away from the front of the chest to a distance of about 12 **inches (1C)**. Then take a short breath through the nose as you draw the hand back to the original position of 6 inches from the chest. Create a steady rhythm with the mantra and the breath.

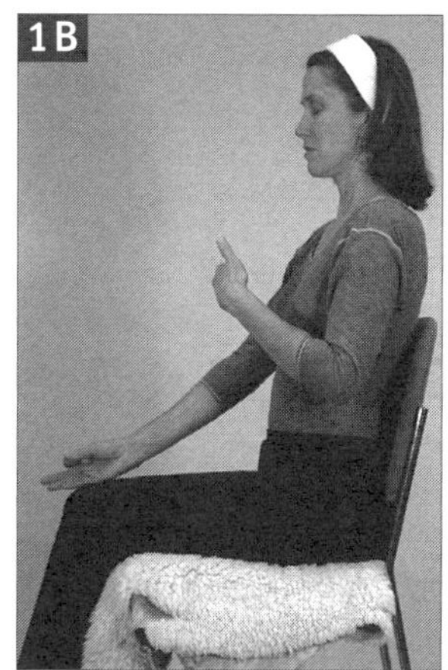

Time: Continue for 11–31 minutes.

To end: Inhale deeply, hold the breath and the posture (See page 32), and then relax completely.

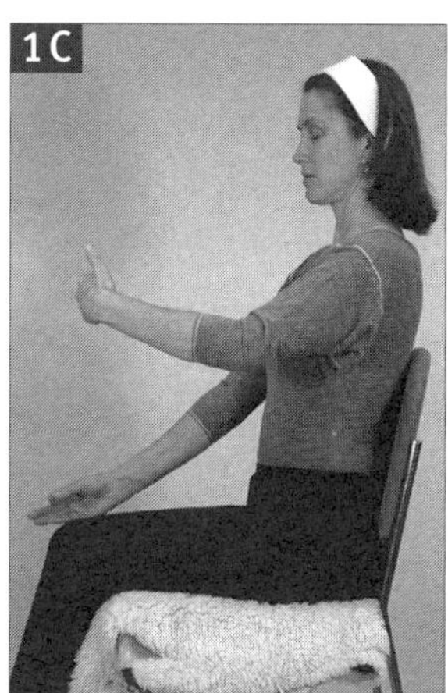

Comments: If we can develop the relationship between the finite sense of the self and the Infinite sense of the Self, the mind will more easily remember this identity when it starts to attach to a particular emotion or object. Shifting to the perspective of Infinity, the mind will automatically break the spell of momentary gratification and remind us of our True Identity, thus breaking the painful cycle of karma.

CHAPTER 2

The Breath of Life (Pranayama)

Meditation on breath is a meditation on life. It is very simple. This sound in you is an infinite sound, and so long as this sound of inhale and exhale continues, you are alive. They call it Anhat, ultimate mantra. If you don't chant this mantra, you cannot chant any others either. You have to chant this mantra in every religion before every God. Any moment that you cannot chant this mantra, you cannot exist. Do it gracefully, rhythmically and musically. It is known as pranayama, and it is very essential.

Yogi Bhajan

God exists within us. The next natural question is how do we have that experience for ourselves? The answer is actually quite simple – through the Breath. We are all a part of the creation, the finite, and every breath we take links us to the One who created us, the Infinite. There is nothing more sacred or basic to our existence than our breath. It is our connection to our life force (*prana*) – the link between life and death. If we fail to inhale, the life force will leave the body and we will be dead.

In Yogic Tradition, breath is so honored that life is not granted in days and years but by a given number of breaths. A finite amount of prana is given to you and you consume it everyday. Any activity in which your breath is shorter and lighter brings you closer to death than when your breath is deeper and softer. As normally no one knows how many breaths they will have, the ancient Yogis became masters of their breath. It only makes sense – breathing slower puts less strain on the body, enhances the quality of our life and thus lengthens our life as well.

Unfortunately, most of us in this era were not given the awareness of the sacredness of our breath, and therefore, were not trained in how to use its potential. It seems so easy. Don't we just take a breath in on the inhale and let it go on the exhale? Does it matter how we breathe? Yes, it actually matters a lot, because breath affects our physical, mental, emotional and spiritual well-being in a very profound way. We can lengthen our life and control the quality of our life by consciously breathing. The difference between "automatic" breathing and yogic breathing (*pranayama*) is awareness – the awareness to be able to manage our life with consciousness instead of whim.

On the physical level, *pranayama* holds the key to our energy reserves and vitality. Breathing deeply, inflating the lungs to their capacity, increases the oxygen in the blood, which nourishes all the cells of the body. Oxygen regenerates, heals and detoxifies the cells. Recent scientific research tells us that disease cannot survive in increased levels of oxygen. What potential! By learning how to increase our breath, we can give ourselves oxygen therapy

– exciting a lift in energy, preventing illness or stimulating healing. It's free, and it's self-regulating. (If you would like to learn more about Oxygen Therapy as an alternative healing modality, you will find much information on the Internet.)

Breath also plays a major role in the interconnection between the mind and body. Whatever the mind believes has a resonant effect in the body. The more erratic our breath, the more erratic our mind – and the body pays the price. Perhaps you have had self-destructive thoughts that played out in your body, like, 'What if I get sick?' All of us have occasional sleepless nights, lying awake, even though we are exhausted. Our mind is racing with thoughts about this and that, one of which is 'I can't get to sleep.' In such times it would be helpful to know a technique to slow down the breath. Remember, the mind follows the breath, and the body follows the mind – sleep happens. (See Left Nostril Breathing page 34.)

The mind is so powerful that it can also control our emotions and actions. Sometimes haunting thoughts seem to control our lives. The thought spirals out of control and our emotions follow the lead into self-destructive behaviors. Instead of being victims of our emotions, "reacting" impulsively to what life brings us, we can train ourselves to consciously "respond," for the betterment of all. At these times, controlled breathing can stop the cycle, because the slower we breathe, the more control we have over our state of mind. The mind becomes clear, calm and neutral. We experience a state of serenity in which inner Truth becomes reality, allowing us to neutrally evaluate all aspects of the situation. We don't need to look outside of ourselves for the answers to life; we can go within, the abode of real wisdom.

We are now ready to consciously learn different breathing techniques. Instead of breathing automatically, as we normally do, we will learn how to consciously breathe with intention and purpose. These breathing techniques will increase our awareness in life and thus enhance the quality of our life. This same awareness will enhance the quality of our death as well.

You are alive by your breath, you are a product of your breath, and your realization is through your breath. The moment you are in touch with your breath, the universe pours into you.
Yogi Bhajan

Holding the Breath in or out

At the end of a *pranayama* exercise or yoga posture, it is customary to *inhale then hold* and *exhale then hold.* Many times yoga students while holding the breath will tighten the neck and throat muscles and stiffen the tongue. This can create too much pressure in the eyes, back of the skull, heart and neck. Instead, as you inhale or exhale the breath is *suspended*, by relaxing the muscles of the diaphragm, ribs, abdomen and face. Breath suspension will make your body operate at a higher level of efficiency. Mastering this technique will give you control of the inflow and outflow of the life force itself. You will be able to remain calm under pressure.

The following breathing exercises can be done in a chair, the feet should be flat on the floor, with the spine straight, sitting a little away from the back of the chair. They can also be done lying down on the back in a bed. Be sure to put a pillow under the knees, to relieve any pressure on the lower spine. They can also be done sitting in an easy cross-legged position on the floor (*Easy Pose*) with the spine straight. To begin with, feel free to do the exercises for less than the times given, working up to the designated times. Be sure to **Tune In (See page 18).**

BREATH TECHNIQUES

Long Deep Breathing (LDB)

Not only does Long Deep Breathing give us all of the above benefits in life, it is an invaluable tool in preparing us for death. Death can be a very pleasant and blissful experience – we are going home to our Creator – we don't need to fight the process. At the time of death, the breath becomes slower and less frequent, which can be a frightening experience, causing panic and distress. If we are trained in how to take long, slow and deep

breaths in life, it will not be a foreign experience at the time of death. We will get the most out of each remaining breath and we will be better prepared to surrender to the natural process of *prana* leaving the body – allowing death to happen.

BENEFITS

Long deep breathing is our most basic Yogic Breath and is used in conjunction with many Kundalini Postures. It is very powerful and can:

- *Cleanse the blood*
- *Bring clarity and neutrality to the mind*
- *Calm and revitalize the body*
- *Clear mucus from the lungs*
- *Stimulate endorphins in the brain*
- *Manage physical and emotional pain*
- *Calm the mind and body for a restful sleep or in times of stress*
- *Expand the aura (electromagnetic field around the body)*

How to do LDB

Whether sitting on the floor in *Easy Pose,* in a chair with the feet flat on the floor or lying flat on a bed, have the spine straight. Place one palm over the lower abdomen, the other is resting on the chest. Inhale through the nostrils into the lower abdomen. Allow the breath to inflate the lower abdomen like a balloon. As the lower abdomen expands, it will push the palm up. Keep inhaling. The breath will automatically rise upward, expanding the lower rib cage, continuing, until it reaches the chest and throat, expanding this area as well and pushing the other palm up. Pause, holding the breath a couple of seconds. Then, exhale through your nose, reversing the process. The chest will lower all the way down to the lower abdomen. Pull the abdomen down. You should be able to hear yourself breathe. When you feel comfortable with this breath, if lying on a bed, relax your arms to your sides, with the palms facing up, or if in a chair, fold your hands in your lap. Practice this breath 1–3 minutes.

Millie, one of my yoga students in a retirement home, found long deep breathing to be very helpful when she needed to relax for a colonoscopy procedure. Normally when she had medical procedures, she was so tense and nervous that she needed maximum doses of sedatives and anesthesia. Using long deep breathing, she eventually needed only small doses of medication. She was very proud of her ability to manage her own relaxation and pain. Her doctor was also impressed.

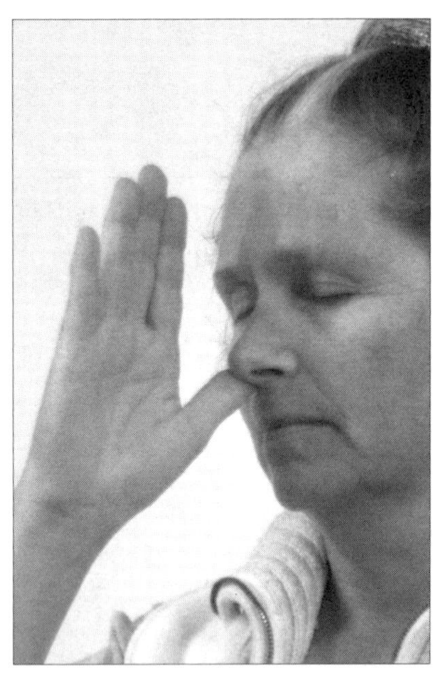

Left Nostril Breathing

Left Nostril Breathing is a calming breath. It is especially helpful when one is tense, nervous or upset. It is also effective in helping to go to sleep.

To practice left nostril breathing, sit with a straight spine or lie down. Block the right nostril with the right thumb and inhale and exhale deeply through the left nostril. Breathe as long and slow as you can for 1–3 minutes. To end, inhale, hold, exhale and relax.

At times of sleeplessness, lie on your right side, block off the right nostril and breath only through the left nostril until you find yourself getting drowsy. It works.

Right Nostril Breathing

When you need an energy boost, do Right Nostril Breathing. Right Nostril Breathing is done in the same way as Left Nostril Breathing, except you block off the left nostril and inhale through the right nostril, exhaling through the right nostril.

Cooperation Between the Nostrils

Did you know that air does not flow through both nostrils equally at the same time? Every 2 ½ hours more air is either passing primarily through the left nostril or the right. Believe it or not, this inequality greatly affects your energy. When the air is predominately passing through the left nostril, you are accessing the moon energy of the body, which is calming, cooling and relaxing. On the other hand, when the air is passing more through the right nostril, the sun energy is stimulated, which is hot, energetic and active. Knowing various breathing techniques are wonderful tools to be able to access the energy you need.

Alternate Nostril Breath

To balance the energies, left and right, moon and sun, calming and energetic, do this breathing technique. Have the spine straight, either sitting in a chair or lying on a bed. Block the right nostril with the thumb of the right hand, the index and middle fingers are pointing up, keeping the ring finger free. Inhale through the left nostril long and slow. Block the left nostril with the ring finger and exhale through the right nostril, long and slow. Now this is very important and the key to the breath, keeping the left nostril blocked, inhale through the right nostril, then block the right nostril and exhale through the left nostril. Keeping the right nostril blocked, inhale through the left nostril and exhale through the right nostril. Do you see a pattern here? The nostril you exhale out of is the same nostril you inhale through. Keep this pattern going for 1–3 minutes.

4/4 Part Breath to Energize

The next time you need a pick-me-up, instead of grabbing a cup of coffee or a coke, do this breath technique. It will revitalize and energize you physically and mentally in just a few minutes. Whether you are a caregiver needing extra energy to keep up in your demanding job or someone struggling with fatigue from a serious illness, try this breathing technique for 1–3 minutes and notice the difference in how you feel.

Sit with a straight spine either in a chair with the feet flat on the floor or lie on your back on a bed. Put the palms together at the center of the chest, with the fingers pointing up (Prayer Pose) with the thumbs pressing against the sternum. A continuous pressure against the palms should be maintained throughout the breathing. Powerfully inhale through the nose in four equal parts (like sniffs) and exhale in four equal parts. The lungs should be completely filled at the end of the fourth inhale and empty at the end of the fourth exhale. As you inhale, the stomach expands out. As you exhale, the stomach is pumping in. Eyes are focused at the Third-Eye. To maintain mental focus, you can mentally chant a four-syllable positive affirmation, like 'I am happy,' or 'I am healthy.' Continue for 1–3 minutes. To end, inhale, hold the breath ten seconds, exhale and relax.

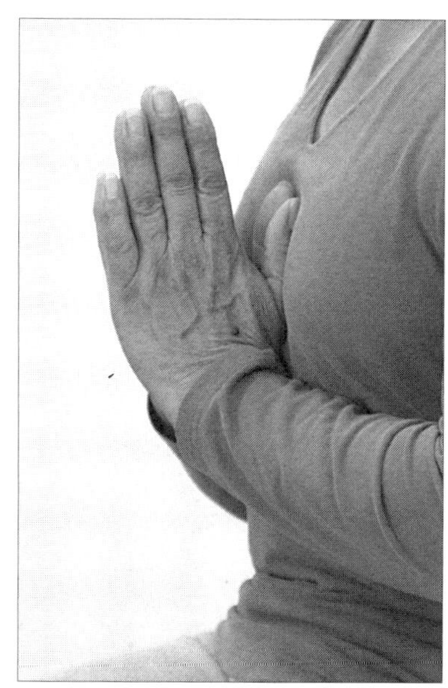

SITALI PRANAYAM

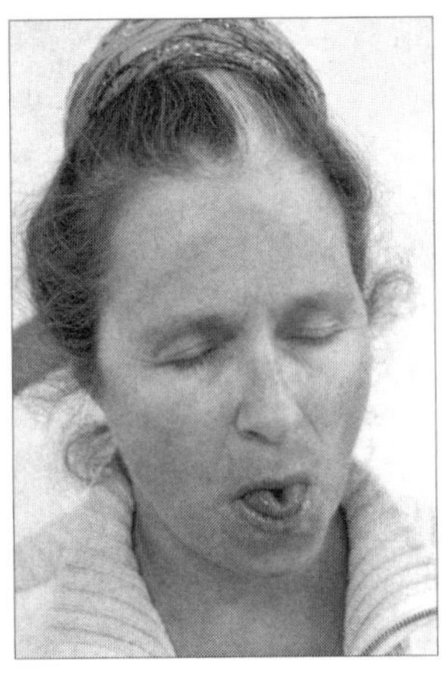

Sitali Pranayam is known to soothe and cool the spine in the area of the fourth, fifth and sixth vertebrae, which balances the sexual and digestive energies. It is often used for lowering fever. When practiced regularly, this breath can aid detoxification and rejuvenation. Often the tongue may taste bitter at first, a sign of toxicity. As you continue to practice, the taste will become sweet.

How to do it

Sit or lie with a straight spine. Curl the tongue lengthwise. Inhale deeply and smoothly through the curled tongue. Exhale through the nose. Continue for 3–5 minutes. To end, inhale, hold. Pull in the tongue. Exhale and relax. This can be repeated for two more 3–5 minute periods. Note: If you cannot curl the tongue lengthwise. It's fine; it's genetic. Just do the best you can.

CANNON BREATH

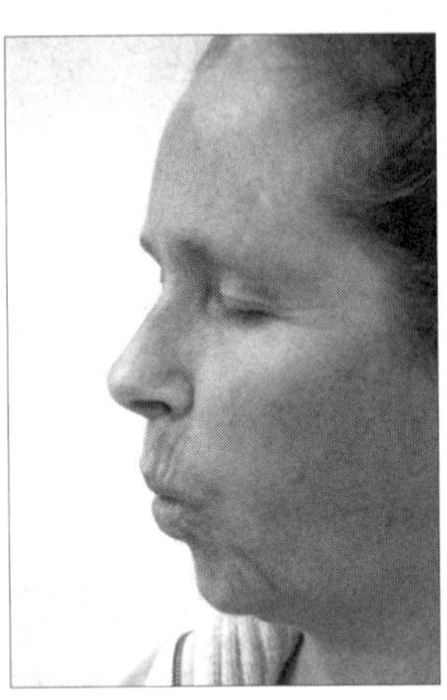

Cannon Breath cleanses and strengthens the parasympathetic nerves and adjusts the digestion. Cannon Breath is Breath of Fire (See page 37) done through the mouth. Often Yogi Bhajan would call for a powerful Cannon Breath exhale to end an exercise.

How to do it

The mouth forms a firm "O" shape. Mouth should not be too puckered, nor should the lips be limp. The pressure of the breath is in the cheeks and over the tongue, although the cheeks should not bulge.

BREATH OF FIRE (BOF)

This is an energetic, rhythmic breath powered by the navel point and solar plexus. It is fairly rapid, practiced through the nose (2–3 breaths per second). It is continuous with no pause between the inhalation and exhalation.

To begin

Sitting or lying with a straight spine, powerfully exhale through the nose, pulling the navel point and solar plexus back toward the spine. Feel the diaphragm contract upwards. As you inhale, relax and release the inward pull of the navel to allow the breath to automatically return to the lungs; the diaphragm extends down. When learning Breath of Fire, it is helpful to put a palm flat on the navel to feel the stomach pushing the hand out on the inhale and in on the exhale. It is a common mistake for beginners to reverse the breath, pushing the navel in on the inhale and out on the exhale, (can cause hyperventilation). Begin slowly, making sure that you are breathing properly, picking up the pace once your body is trained to the correct rhythm. Begin by practicing for 1–3 minutes.

Breath of Fire is not hyperventilation. Hyperventilation occurs when one is breathing rapidly in the chest or reverses the breath pattern. To avoid hyperventilating, concentrate on completely exhaling. If you feel dizzy or nauseous while doing Breath of Fire, temporarily discontinue. These sensations can be part of the detoxification process or the body adjusting to the added oxygen. As one practices, these sensations will subside. It is important to have a light stomach when practicing breathing techniques.

Benefits of Breath of Fire

- *Expands the lung capacity.*
- *Strengthens all 72,000 nerves in the body, to resist stress.*
- *Releases toxins and deposits from the lungs, mucous linings, blood vessels and other cells.*
- *Repairs the balance between the sympathetic and parasympathetic nervous systems.*
- *Strengthens the navel point.*
- *Increases oxygen delivery to the brain, facilitating a focused, intelligent and neutral state of mind.*
- *Boosts the immune system, helping to prevent disease and illness.*
- *If called for in the instructions of the exercise, doing BOF with most Kundalini Yoga exercise enhances the effectiveness of the exercise.*

Author's Note: BOF may be too cleansing for someone who is seriously ill. Start cautiously and see how you feel. If you become dizzy or ill, slow it down or stop altogether. 4/4 Part Breath may be a better choice. BOF is a good choice, though, for caregivers, who need extra energy and endurance. You can even do it as you walk around.

MEDITATION TO PREVENT FREAKING OUT

What it will do for you

This meditation will alter your energy by changing your nostril breathing. You can't get out of your body, but you can change its energy. If you are thinking something neurotic and find out that you're breathing through your right nostril, start breathing through your left nostril instead. This will change your energy from agni (fire) to sitali (cool).

If you are irritated, depressed or in a weird mental state, start breathing from the right nostril. In 3 minutes you will be a different person. This ability to change nostrils in breathing should be taught to our children within their first 3 years. Exercising this ability can prevent nervous breakdowns.

Mastering this technique is good training for the time of death. At death it is best to be breathing equally through both nostrils at the same time. This meditation will give you that awareness.

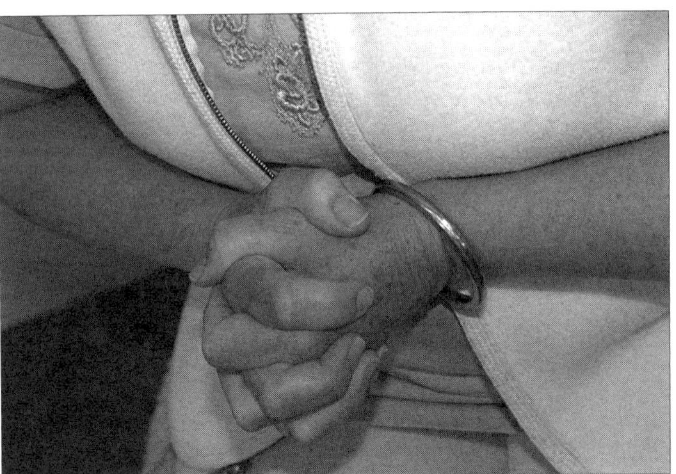

How to do it

Sit in a comfortable meditative posture with your spine straight. Interlace your fingers with your right thumb on top. Place your hands at the center of your diaphragm line, touching your body.

Close your eyes. Concentrate on your breath at the tip of your nose. See from which nostril you are breathing. Within 3 minutes you should know. Then change it. If you are breathing primarily through your left nostril, consciously change to your right nostril. Be sure to keep your shoulders completely relaxed. You should have a pressure at your hands, but none at your shoulders.

Practice changing this breath back and forth for as long as you like. Start with 5–11 minutes.

It almost seems too easy to work, doesn't it? Don't take my word for it. Try these breathing techniques and experience the effects for yourself. It is better to practice them on a regular basis and then when the need arises, you will automatically know what to do. We train for all kinds of things. This is training as well, training on how to live and die with awareness.

PROCESS EXERCISE

Use yourself as a laboratory. Do a little self-research. Choose one of the breathing techniques in this chapter and practice it every day for one week. Notice any changes in how you feel. Then, choose another technique and practice it for the next week. Continue until you have tried all of the techniques. Reflect on how you can use these tools in your life. The next time you feel nervous, irritable, low in energy or tense, apply one of these techniques and notice how you feel. Share a technique with a friend.

Inhale and hold the breath, and talk to your breath: 'O my breath, you are the source of life. When you leave me and join the Universal Breath, give life to all.' Let it go. Inhale again, and hold this breath of life and talk to it: 'O my breath, you are responsible for my living and enjoying this life on this Earth. When you leave me and join the Universal Breath, see that all live in coziness.' Let it go. And then inhale deeply again, and talk to your own breath: 'O my breath, without you, nothing can exist in me. Now, as you leave me and join the Universal Breath, give life to all.' Let it go. These are the three great charities of prayer.

YOGI BHAJAN

CHAPTER 3

The Word

If your words have the strength of the infinite in them and you value them and they are virtuous, you are the greatest of the great. If you do not value your words, you have no value. Your own word is your value as a human being. Your word is your value. In the beginning was the Word and the Word was with God and the Word was God.
YOGI BHAJAN

NOT ONLY IS THERE AN INTIMATE CONNECTION between the Creator and the breath, this relationship also extends to sound or the Word. In scriptures it is said that God spoke and the world was created. Or perhaps it was – God vibrates and the whole creation evolves. Everything in the universe has a vibratory frequency. By vibrating a particular combination of sounds, in combination with the breath, we can tune our individual consciousness into various levels of intelligence, or consciousness. The universe will respond back.

In Kundalini Yoga, a combination of divine sounds, called sound current, is used in the form of mantras (*"**man**" means mind, "**tra**" means to tune*), which consist of energy having a definite effect on the human psyche. The creation of these sounds, by massaging the tongue over the 84 meridian points on the upper palate, stimulating the hypothalamus, thalamus and pituitary, creating a chemical environment in the brain whereby infinite wisdom is experienced. As it removes the constrictions and distortions of the ego, one's Truth can be felt, and God is experienced from within. Our pain and "bondage" in life is felt when we forget Infinity. Mantra is a powerful tool and is accessible to anyone who uses it.

There are many kinds of mantras. Each one will invoke a different vibratory effect, according to its purpose. Whether it's for developing intuition, releasing anger, increasing prosperity or preparing for death, the enormous wealth of mantras can be used to bring about positive change in one's life. No intellectual understanding is necessary. If we merely use them, the results will speak for themselves.

Mantra helps people faced with a terminal illness to connect to their souls…gives them their vastness…clarity of understanding. I worked with a woman diagnosed with cancer, who would recover and then kept having reoccurrences. She had done Kundalini Yoga many years. This illness put her through a crisis in faith. 'Why did I get sick? Haven't I done everything right over the years? Aren't I a healthy person, who has lived a healthy lifestyle?' Finally, she was able to understand that illness and death are a part of life. It was not because she was a bad person, because she failed in some way…or that her spiritual practice failed.

As a healthy, fit person, being debilitated was very challenging. She didn't have the energy to do Kundalini Yoga, but she found that chanting, combining mantra with breath, energized her. It gave her a sense of calmness and equilibrium…so much so that others thought she must be in denial. It's a misconception that you have to "work" Kundalini Yoga. It can be very subtle and very powerful. In the end, she had a very peaceful death, which she could convey to family and friends, helping them to accept her death.

Meditation gives perspective. Illness, death and loss deepen our understanding and acceptance that they are a part of the whole human experience.

Shanti Shanti Kaur Khalsa,
Director of Guru Ram Das Center for Medicine and Humanology

The universe is created by sound and spirit. What is the frequency at which you want to create? What is the energy, which you put into the creating? How sweet are you? How simple are you? How secure are you? That decides your life.
YOGI BHAJAN

I am including here a very powerful mantra used to cut through the negative cycle of the mind. To each negative thought, the mantra brings a positive thought and inner balance is achieved. The mantra is, ***"Ek Ong Kaar Satgur Prasaad, Satgur Prasaad Ek Ong Kaar"*** (One God has created the creation, and is realized by the Grace of the True Guru). Chanting this mantra five times will stop the negativity of the mind and reverse it. (Refer to accompanying CD for correct pronunciation – 2.)

Throughout the book, you will find various mantras to enhance aspects of your life. As we progress into the chapters addressing issues on death, the mantras will reflect those needs. Mantra is a friend and tool to aid us on our journey in life and toward death. They help us live our lives to the fullest, finishing our karmas and manifesting our destiny. They prepare us for death by giving us an experience of the Infinite. And when death calls us Home, they give us a "key" to leave with grace and serenity. (Refer to the accompanying CD for proper pronunciation of mantras.)

Hari Kaur is a Kundalini Yoga Teacher Trainer in New York. She had a near death experience. *Shabd Guru* (See sidebar on next page) helps her recapture the bliss of that experience.

I was under a lot of stress, working long hours as an advertising executive and directing plays on the side. I had a history of bad migraine headaches. On an off day in my apartment, I felt dizzy and hit my head. I could feel my body leaving, but I had a strong survival instinct. I pulled myself along the carpet with my fingernails until I reached the phone. I called my roommate's work place. Even though I had lost my nervous system and couldn't form words, the people on the other end recognized my grunts.

When the paramedics arrived, there was no breath, heartbeat, or signs of life. In the hospital, I saw my own body below on the table. 'Oh, there I am.' 'What are they doing down there,' I innocently wondered? I was floating high, not in the physical body. I was completely comfortable, humorous and happy, looking around like a kid. Suddenly I got what was happening. At that exact moment, I took off really, really fast, like a comet or something.

I spiraled through a tunnel of white light. Instead of seeing people from my past, I felt sensations of them. I also felt sensations of darkness and light, and of earth, air and water. I felt my pleasure and pain as well as that of the whole universe – like all of the polarized manifestations of Infinity. There was no time. There is no way to explain how good it felt – like a million orgasms.

There were a few little lights starting to twinkle. I was going so fast that I started to arc as I traveled, then the speed stopped. It was like the blackest, blackest sky with no stars. There was nothing, but I wasn't feeling or seeing it. I was it. I had no thoughts or body sensations any more. I felt one with a Super Consciousness of light and vastness – free of time and polarities. There was no resistance. It felt like "home"... ecstasy... being one with God.

Then, I had a profound conversation out there – "Uhuh"..."NO." I didn't hear or feel it – it just was. It was so clearly heard, but I didn't have ears... so clearly understood but I didn't have a mind...so clearly felt but I didn't have a body. I couldn't stay. I wasn't happy

Guru Nanak, born in 1469 A.D. in a small village, which is now in Pakistan, was a humble man of God consciousness and universal awareness. A prolific poet, saint and prophet of peace, love and truth, he was centuries ahead of his times. Going against the norms of the times – when spirituality was only for the elite castes – Guru Nanak made spiritual knowledge accessible to everyone. He sang Divine songs, saying that God prevails through everyone, and that we are all instruments of Divine Wisdom.

Guru Nanak's songs are based on the Shabd Guru, written in Gurmukhi, with its origins in Sanskrit. Shabd Guru – "Shabd" means sound, "Guru" means teacher or knowledge that transforms you – consists of a combination of Divine sounds, based on the power of Naad, the Sound Current, which alters our consciousness and dissolves the ego that obstructs our inner truth.

All of the mantras in Kundalini Yoga are based on this science. His most beloved and recited song is Japji, the Song of the Soul. It is made of forty paurees or stanzas, which can liberate one from the cycles of birth and death. From his teachings, the Sikh Religion began, with Japji being the basis for the Sikh Scriptures, the Siri Guru Granth Sahib, which Sikhs revere as their living Guru. For a better description of Japji and some of its Paurees, refer to Appendix II.

about it. When I was kicked back, I went really fast. There was a lot of resistance. The communication guided me to take a yogic breath. I had not started yoga yet. I remember the moment my mouth opened, the breath went right through the crown of my head.

When I got back into the body, the pain was more

excruciating than anything I have ever experienced. I was trying to talk to the doctors, but I had no nervous system. I couldn't coordinate the right body part to move on command. It was as if I had been put together incorrectly. As closely as the doctors could estimate, I had had a stroke and had been dead for approximately 30 minutes. I remember laughing so hard that I threw up all over the doctors. I found this whole thing to be so funny – all of this commotion about life and death. I was so high. I was a different person. The nurse leaned over to me and said, 'Something really happened to you out there, didn't it? Don't doubt yourself.' Since then, I have had only one more migraine headache.

A near death experience is so powerful that it's unquestionable. You can't make up this experience. It has had a profound effect on the way I look at life and death. I have no fear of death. Life is pretty relaxed if you're not afraid of death. I still have to make mistakes, but now everything is relative. Life is so short you might as well go for it. I have a fair amount of back pain. This experience has helped me deal with the pain, because I know that the physical body is only one reality. Shortly after my "death," I left advertising and found Kundalini Yoga.

I try to get the experience back. Meditation, especially chanting the Shabd Guru with devotion, (mantras and the sound current) get me the closest to it. It is one way we can break through the polarities. My mission in life, now, is to help others live life to the fullest and die fearlessly.

PROCESS EXERCISES

1 Think about the power of the word. When has someone else's words profoundly affected you? When have your words manifested something in some situation or person? Can you acknowledge the significance of your words – that they have a powerful vibratory effect?

2 Think of a negative situation in your life. Sit down and chant the mantra given for negativity (See page 43). When completed, how do you feel?

COMPONENTS TO MEDITATION

(More About Meditation in Chapter Eight)

Besides mantra, meditation may contain other components – eye focus, breath, and hand mudra (positions). This description is to aid you with meditations in this book.

Eye Focus

There are various places to focus the eyes, depending upon the meridians and parts of the brain to be stimulated.

Third-Eye Point

Unless otherwise specified, focus the eyes at the *Third-Eye Point* – midway between the brows, one-half-inch above the eyebrows and one-half-inch beneath the skin. Locate this point by closing your eyes and gently rolling the eyes up and in. Focusing at the *Third-Eye Point* stimulates the pituitary, the seat of intuition.

Tip of the Nose

The eyes can be 1/10 open or closed, focused down at the tip of the nose. Considered the highest lock, it stimulates the pineal gland, the frontal lobe and new energy pathways in the brain. Meditating here will elevate you.

Moon Center

The eyes are closed, focusing down at the tip of the chin. This produces a calming and cooling effect. You will clearly perceive your Self. Meditating here will control all your emotions – good, bad, right, wrong.

Crown Chakra

The eyes are closed and rolled upward toward the top of the head. This stimulates the pineal gland and energy of the Crown Chakra. Meditating at this point is a good practice for death, because this is the point from which you will exit.

1/10th Open

The eyelids are relaxed and 1/10th open. Instructions of the meditation vary. The eyes may be focused straight ahead or down to the tip of the nose. This eye focus slightly stimulates the optic nerve, is calming and develops intuition.

HAND MUDRAS

There are numerous hand mudras or positions that lock and guide the energy flow and stimulate different areas of the brain. Each finger relates to a planetary energy and the quality that each planet represents. The thumb relates to the persona of the individual (the ego). You will be learning many mudras in the meditations incorporated in this book. The more commonly used ones are included below.

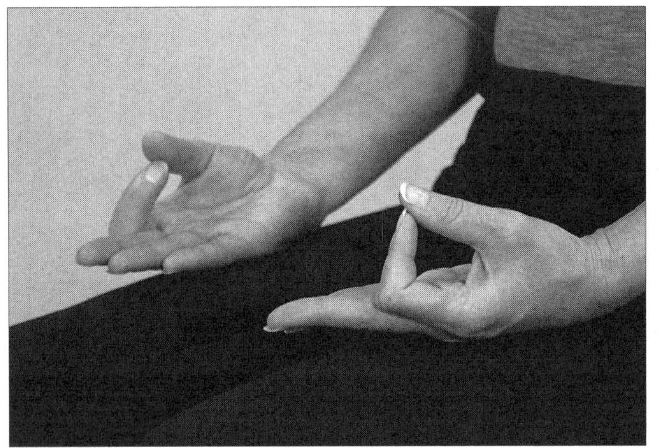

Gyan Mudra – SEAL OF KNOWLEDGE

To form *Gyan Mudra*, put the tip of the thumb together with the tip of the index finger. The other fingers are straight but relaxed. The energy of the index finger is associated with Jupiter, representing knowledge, wisdom and expansion. Using this mudra stimulates receptivity, inner wisdom and calmness. It is one of the most commonly used.

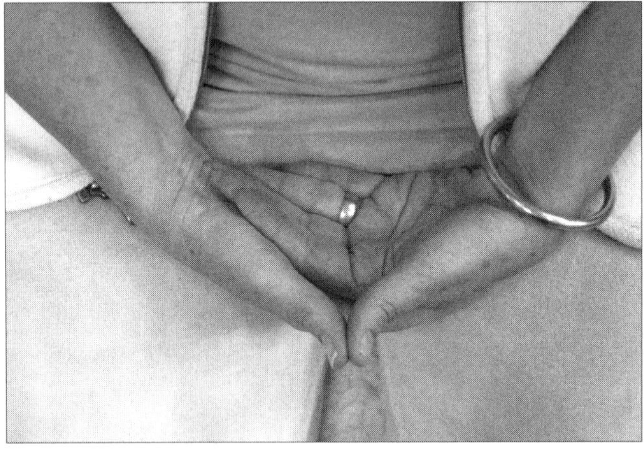

Buddha Mudra – HANDS IN THE LAP

For a woman, rest the right palm facing up in the lap with the left hand palm up on top of it. Put the thumb tips together. The hand positions are reversed for a man.

Venus Lock

It connects the positive and negative sides of the Venus Mound – the fleshy area at the base of the thumbs (associated with the planet Venus). This mudra channelizes the sexual energy and promotes glandular balance. When placed in the lap during meditation, it can facilitate concentration and focus.

How to do it

Place the palms facing each other. For men – interlace the fingers with the left little finger on the bottom. Put the left thumb tip just above the base of the right thumb on the webbing between the thumb and the index finger of the right hand. The tip of the right thumb presses the fleshy mound at the base of the left thumb (see photo). Reverse the entire sequence of alternation the fingers for women, so the left forefinger is on top, and the right pinky is on the bottom.

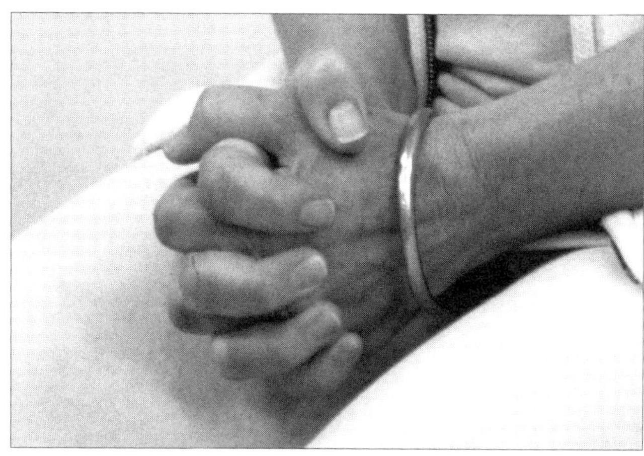

Male representation of mudra.

Bear Grip

Place the left palm facing out from the chest with the thumb down. Place the palm of the right hand over the left facing the chest. Curl the fingers of both hands so the hands form a fist. This mudra is used to stimulate the heart and to intensify concentration.

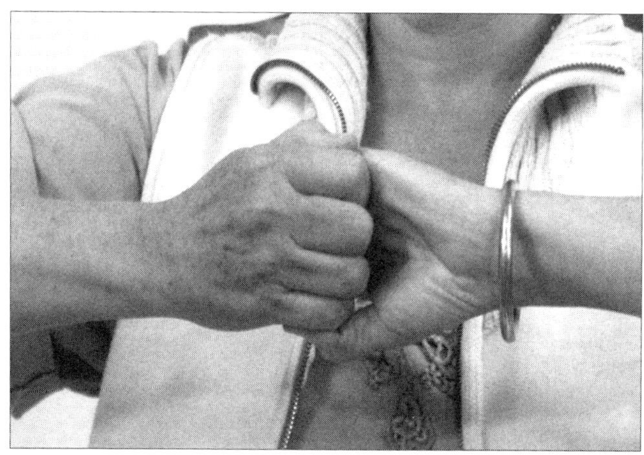

CHAPTER 4

Understanding Yogic Science

Kundalini Yoga is a science, which works on the seven chakras, the arcline (the 6th body) and the aura (the Eighth Chakra). It works directly on the total energy, and that flow of energy has one simple way: either you sway it or it sways you. Either you are above the energy and ride it, or you go below the energy and it rides you. That is where Kundalini Yoga fits in; you will learn to ride your energy, to experience it and penetrate any given situation to attain a balance.

YOGI BHAJAN

KUNDALINI YOGA is based on *"Yogic Science."* An appreciation of some of its basic principles will help us understand how yogic technology moves and balances the energy in the body and thus determines our consciousness. Some of you may find this information boring and dry and will rely more on your experience and intuition. Others of you will find this information fascinating and useful in your practice. Whichever way is your style, this chapter can be used as a resource and will be a foundation in understanding many concepts presented in subsequent chapters.

Yogis explain that there are two major forces in the human. One is *prana*, the life force of the atom – the motion and coding of life energies through the realms of the mind and body – located in the *"upper triangle."* The other is *apana,* the eliminating force of the body and is located in the *"lower triangle." Prana* flows through channels called *nadis*. There are 72,000 *nadis,* of which 72 are vital. Of those 72, three major nadis are important for the understanding of Kundalini Yoga: *ida, pingala* and *sushmuna.* The *Ida Nadi* ends at the left nostril and represents the negatively charged energy (*apana*) of the moon. It eliminates body wastes and has a cooling, soothing and healing effect on the mind and body. The *Pingala Nadi*, ending in the right nostril, corresponds to the positively charged energy (*prana*) and brings in the stimulating, energizing and heating energy of the sun. The central nerve current in the body, the *sushmuna*, originates at the base of the spine where the three *nadis (ida, pingala* and *sushmuna*) meet and runs through the center of the spinal column to the top of the head. The aim of the yogi, or one who wants to experience "the union of heaven and earth," is to have "energy" run through the *sushmuna* nerve current. This is the *"Kundalini"* energy.

Kundalini means "the curl in the lock of the hair of the beloved." It is a poetic description of the uncoiling of our essential consciousness, our creative potential. It has been described in Yogic mythology as a serpent coiled 3 1/2 times, with its face downwards in the First *Chakra* at the base of the spine. No *samadhi* (bliss) is possible without its being awakened.

The practice of *pranayama* (breath exercises), yoga positions and meditation stimulates the sleeping *Kundalini*. *Prana* is directed down to the *Navel Chakra*, while the *apana* is drawn upward from the *Root Chakra* to the *Navel Center*. The mixing of these two forces at the *Navel Chakra* creates tremendous heat, *(tapa),* which stimulates the *sushmuna* and thereby raises the *Kundalini* up the six chakras until it reaches the top of the head. Symbolically the *Kundalini* hisses like a serpent beaten with a stick and enters the hole of the *sushmuna*. When it travels from chakra to chakra, layer after layer of the mind becomes open and one experiences an elevated consciousness or bliss.

Kundalini Yoga makes the self pure. Then you do not have to depend on anybody, you are independent – walking tall and carrying God in your heart.

YOGI BHAJAN

THE EIGHT CHAKRAS

We have eight Chakras – wheels that take in and distribute energy and information. These centers reflect our state of consciousness and well–being. The **First Chakra** represents the earth element and is located in the rectum. Its concerns have to do with elimination, security, survival and confidence. The **Second Chakra** has to do with the water element and is located in the sex organs. This center of consciousness reflects our creativity and relationship with sexuality. The **Third Chakra** represents the fire element and is located in the navel point, where all 72,000–nerve endings meet. The concerns here revolve around digestion, projection, control, personal power and identity.

These first three chakras are often referred to as the *"Lower Triangle,"* because they mainly deal with issues of worldly life and physical needs. The Fifth, Sixth, and Seventh Chakras are known as the *"Upper Triangle,"* with the Fourth Chakra, the Heart Chakra as the point of balance between

Death is nothing but a good sleep. A Sikh (Seeker of Truth) looks at death as union with the Beloved Creator. It is a time of joy because the soul has longed for this moment of Ultimate Yoga (which means union). Sadness at this time is an experience of one's individual loss for the departed. Sikhs regard this time as an opportunity to love and accept God's will and sing His Praises.

YOGI BHAJAN

them. When one's energy is in the "*Upper Triangle,*" one's consciousness is universal and expansive.

The **Fourth Chakra,** called the "Heart Center," is the air element and is located at the center of the chest. It is here where one's experience shifts from "me to thee," or from "me to we." Unconditional love, sacrifice, compassion and kindness are projected from this center. The **Fifth Chakra** is located at the throat and is ruled by the element ether. This energy center has to do with the power and impact of one's speech and expression. The **Sixth Chakra** (Ajna Chakra), is located at the center of the forehead, slightly above the eyebrows, and is sometimes called the "Third-Eye Point." It is from this center that we can access our intuition and universal knowledge. The **Seventh Chakra,** located at the top of the skull, is also referred to as the "Tenth Gate," "Crown Chakra," or "Gate of Salvation." When the Kundalini energy raises to the seventh center, one experiences oneness with the Infinite and a state of blissfulness. The **Eighth Chakra** is the magnetic field or aura of the human being. It normally extends up to nine feet in all directions around the person. If the aura is strong, the person will feel powerful and protected; if it is weak, the person will be vulnerable and ineffective, open to disease and negative forces.

In Kundalini Yoga, the objective is to balance the energies of all the chakras. If we only lived in our upper triangle, we would not be able to relate to the physical world. To put it bluntly – for example, we'd be constipated. Yogi Bhajan has often said that a holy man is one who knows how and when to use his nine holes. Learning how to direct the energy through the chakras is like knowing how to use the gears of a car. We can use the technology of Kundalini Yoga, to choose which chakra is appropriate in a particular situation. For example, if I am giving a presentation, I will not only want my chakras to be balanced, but I will also want certain ones to be stimulated – my Navel Center for confidence; my Heart Center and Throat Center, so that my communication is direct and heartfelt; my Third-Eye, so I can intuit what's needed in this setting.

The chakras also serve a crucial function at the time of death. If practiced during life, one will be able to direct the energy up the chakras at the time of death, the soul leaving through the Tenth Gate. We will discuss this in more detail in Chapter Ten – *Rehearsing Death*. Starting on page 58 you will find two meditations – **Sat Kriya** (a Kriya is a set of one or more exercises for a particular purpose) and **Seven-Wave Meditation,** both which balance the chakras and stimulate the Kundalini Energy. In the next chapter, the Bandhas or Body Locks will be presented – very powerful techniques to direct the energy up the chakras.

Benefits of Kundalini Yoga

- *Balances and strengthens the glandular and nervous systems – expands the lung capacity and purifies the blood*
- *Improves one's general physical and mental well-being*
- *Increases flexibility; tones and strengthens*
- *Helps to de-stress and relax*
- *Trains the mind to think positively and be in control of thoughts and attitudes*
- *Manages pain*
- *Alleviates and prevents back pain*
- *Builds inner strength and self-awareness*

Ten bodies are better than one

We relate to our physical body, because we can see it, touch it and experience life through it. Others relate to us through our physical body as well. In Yogic Science, we actually have ten bodies, which are just as real, if not more so. They include:

1 The soul body, which is our inner light and stays with us forever;

2 The negative mind, which gives warnings in life;

3 The positive mind, which sees the possibilities;

4 The neutral mind, which balances positive and negative with unbiased intuitive knowledge;

5 The physical body, which is our shell, our sacred temple;

6 The arcline or arc body, which is our life force, going from earlobe to earlobe,

What is Kundalini actually? It is your creative potential. You experience it when the energy of the glandular system combines with the energy of the nervous system to create such a sensitivity that the totality of the brain receives signals and integrates them. Then you become totally and wholly aware; and your creative potential becomes available to you.
Yogi Bhajan

protecting us and projecting who we are;

7 The auric body is the protective electromagnetic energy surrounding up to nine feet around our entire body that can uplift ourselves and others;

8 The pranic body, carries the breath, giving us energy, determination and healing power;

9 The subtle body, gives us mastery of the subtleties of life. It also houses the soul and carries it at death;

10 The radiant body, gives us radiance, courage, and the power of presence. Kundalini Yoga balances and strengthens these ten bodies, so that they can serve us in life. At the time of death, their functions change but are just as important. (To be discussed in Chapter Nine – *The Journey of Death*). The yoga set beginning on page 60, **Awaken Yourself To Your Ten Bodies,** balances the ten bodies.

Kundalini Yoga creates *Balance* in all systems and levels of our being. And of all the wonderful benefits of Kundalini Yoga, the most important is *Awareness*. Practicing it, we can train ourselves to become acutely sensitive to ourselves and the environment around us. We are able to detect illness before it hits us and then know what the body needs to heal. We are more sensitive in relationships, knowing the dynamics and what's required for an effective and harmonious interaction. We can feel situations and what's needed for success. Awareness empowers us to have choices, so we can respond (not just react) with consciousness – and therefore, bring balance once again.

Balance and awareness also give us an experience of union – our finite self with the Infinite self. That union is like nectar, and once experienced, we're addicted to its intoxicatingly blissful sweetness. We experience that merger at the deepest point of our existence, where it is not just belief or desire – we "know" it as a reality. This knowing in life gives us a knowing about death. Instead of death being the greatest unknown – and therefore something we fear – it becomes our friend. It becomes our friend because – just as we have experienced in life – in death our individual infinite self will merge with the Supreme Infinity – the ultimate union and ecstasy.

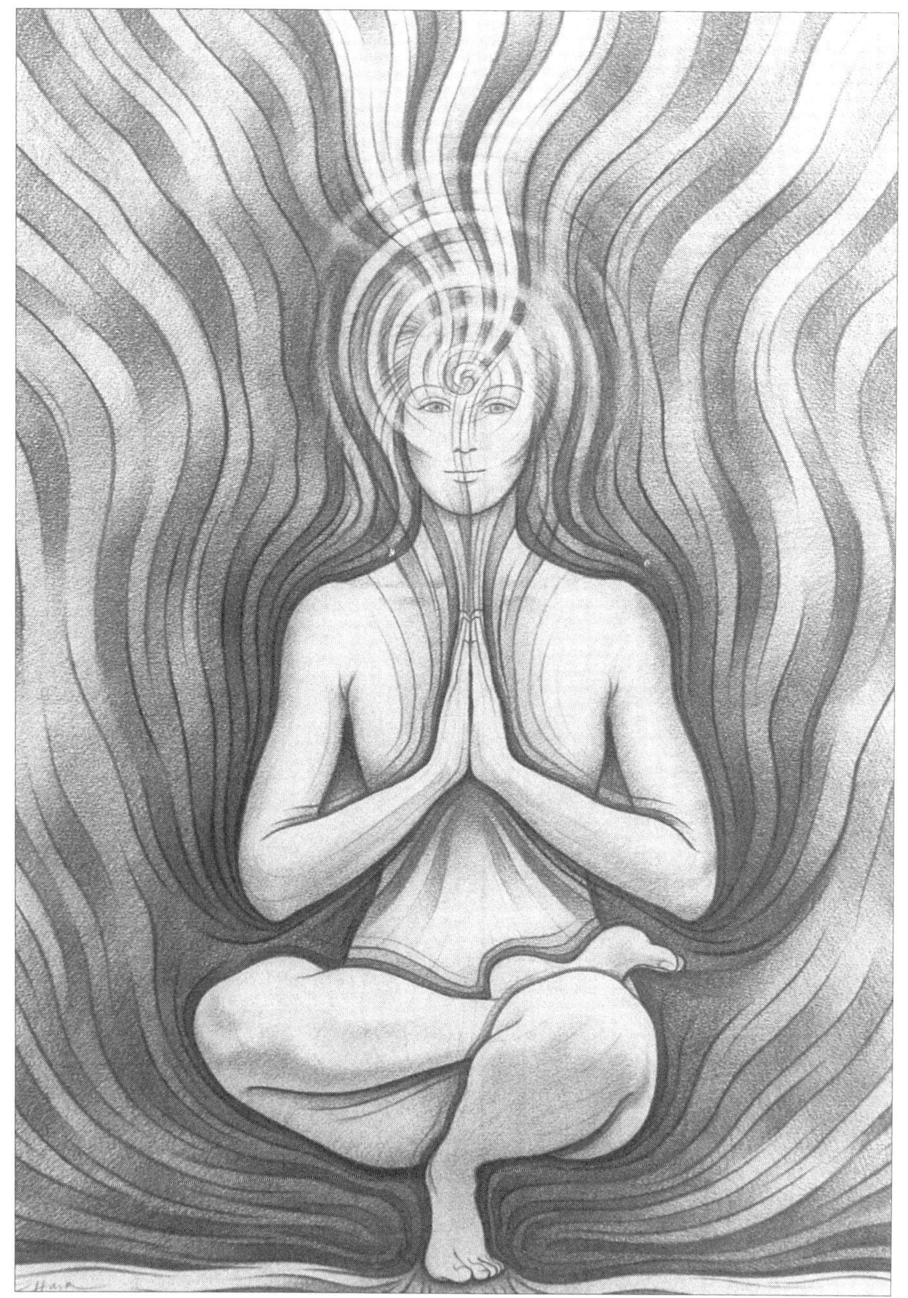

ILLUSTRATION BY HECTOR JARA

PROCESS EXERCISES

1. Reflect on what was said about the benefits of practicing Kundalini Yoga. How do you think KY could help you in your life?
2. Re-read the part about awareness. What was your reaction?
3. How did you relate to the part about – "Our experience of union in life will prepare us for the ultimate union at death."
4. Besides Kundalini Yoga, what other practices help you nurture your relationship with your soul? Dancing
5. Do one of the following practices. Be sure to review the "basics" in Chapter Five. Always begin by Tuning In. How did you feel afterwards?

SAT KRIYA

One of the most powerful and effective kriyas of Kundalini Yoga is Sat Kriya. It can be done at the end of any other kriya or it can be done alone. If you don't have time for anything else, do Sat Kriya. Your whole being will thank you.

Benefits of Sat Kriya

- *This exercise works directly on stimulating and channeling the kundalini energy, so it must always be practiced with the mantra Sat Nam.*
- *People who are suffering from depression, anger, guilt, resentment and other emotions of the grieving process can benefit from this Kriya since these emotions are always connected with an imbalance in the energies of the lower three chakras.*
- *General physical health is improved since all the internal organs receive a gentle rhythmic massage from this exercise.*
- *The heart gets stronger from the rhythmic up-and-down of blood pressure you generate from the pumping motion of the Navel Point.*

How to do Sat Kriya

Sit with a straight spine with the arms overhead and palms together. Interlace the fingers except for the index fingers, which point straight up. Men cross the right thumb over the left thumb; women cross the left thumb over the right. Chant ***Sat*** and pull the Navel Point in; chant ***Naam*** and relax it.

Continue at least 3 minutes.

Then inhale, apply Root Lock *(mulbandh)* and squeeze the muscles tightly from the buttocks all the way up the back, past the shoulders. Mentally allow the energy to flow through the top of the skull. Exhale, hold the breath out and apply all the locks *(mahabandh).* Inhale and relax. (Listen to the accompanying CD for a demonstration.) Root Lock is explained in Chapter Five – starting on page 71.

Notice that you emphasize pulling the Navel Point in. Don't try to apply *Mulbandh. Mulbandh* happens automatically if the navel is pulled. Consequently, the hips and lumbar spine do not rotate or flex. Your spine stays straight and the only motion your arms make is a slight up-and-down stretch with each ***Sat Naam*** as your chest lifts.

SEVEN-WAVE "SAT NAM" MEDITATION

This meditation is a good introduction to Kundalini Yoga. It will open the mind to new experiences. If you can build this meditation to at least 31 minutes per day, the mind will be cleansed just as the ocean waves wash the sandy beach. This is a *bij* (seed) mantra meditation. *Bij* mantras such as Sat *Nam* are sounds, which can totally rearrange habit patterns. We all have habit patterns – we could not function without them. But sometimes the patterns we have created are not wanted. You have changed, so you want the patterns to change. By vibrating the sound current Sat Nam in this manner, you activate the energy of the mind that erases and establishes habits. After chanting this mantra, you will feel calm, relaxed and mellow. This meditation is also good training to pull the energy up the chakras at the time of death. If practiced ahead of time, the person will only need to use their thought to direct the energy up.

How to do it
Sit in *Easy Pose* on the floor or in a chair with the feet flat on the floor. Be sure the spine is straight, with a light Neck Lock (*Jalandhar Bandh* – Review Body Locks in Chapter 5 – *Yoga For Health and Healing*).

Eye position: The eyes are closed, looking up, focusing at the Brow Point.

Mudra: Place the palms flat together at the center of the chest in Prayer Pose, with thumbs touching the center of the sternum.

Mantra: *SAT NAAM*

Breath & Mantra pattern: Inhale deeply, concentrating on the breath. With the exhale, chant the mantra in the law of seven (the law of the tides). Vibrate **SAT** in six waves, and let **NAAM** be the seventh. On each wave, thread the sound through the chakras beginning at the base of the spine at the First Chakra. On **NAAM**, let the energy and sound radiate from the Seventh Chakra at the top of the head through the aura, unto

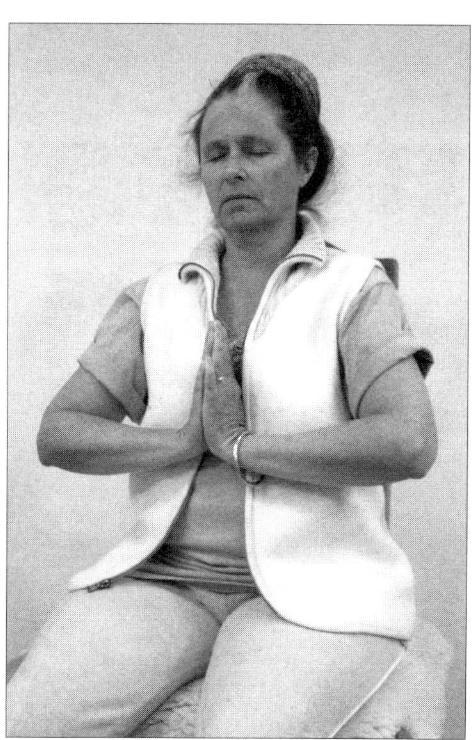

Infinity. As the sound penetrates each chakra. Gently contract the muscles it corresponds to. The first center is the rectum; the second is the sex organs; the third is the Navel Point; the fourth is the heart; the fifth is the throat; the sixth is the Brow Point; and the seventh is the top of the head.

Time: Continue for 11–31 minutes.

AWAKENING YOURSELF TO YOUR TEN BODIES

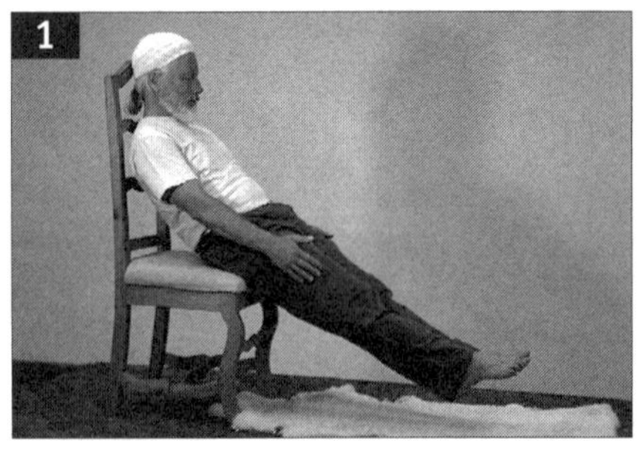

1. Stretch Pose. When practiced sitting in a chair, be sitting away from the back of your chair, (about the center of the chair). Raise the legs six inches and lean back until you feel a pull in your abdomen. Bring your arms straight up at your sides, with the palms facing each other next to the hips to build energy across the navel point. (If this is too difficult for you, hold on to the sides of your chair for stability.) Point the toes, forward. Keep your eyes focused on the tips of the toes and do Breath of Fire. Continue 1–3 minutes.

2. Nose to Knee. Bring one bent knee up with the arms wrapped around it. Keep the other leg down, foot flat on the floor. Tuck the head down toward the knee and begin Breath of Fire for 1 minute. Switch sides for 1 minute.

3. Ego Eradicator. Sitting straight in your chair. Raise the arms to a 60-degree angle, with the fingers tucked into the mounds of the hands. Keep the thumbs pointing up. Eyes closed, concentrate at the Third-Eye point and do Breath of Fire. 1–3 minutes.

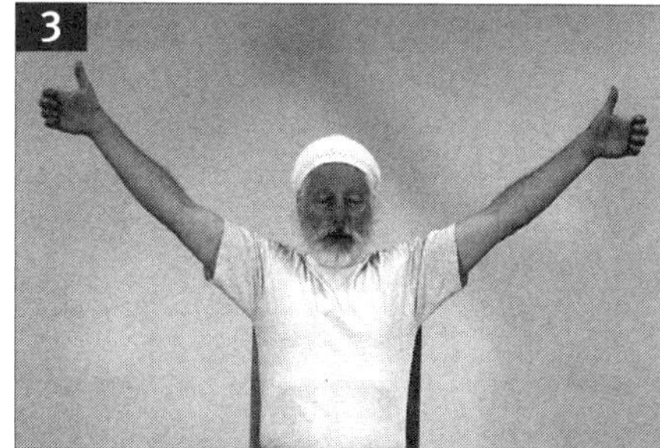

4. Life Nerve Stretch. Sit with the legs stretched wide apart, separated feet are on the ground. (If you have access to chairs, you can put each leg up on a chair) Arms overhead, inhale, then exhale, stretch down and reach toward the left leg. Inhale and come up, and then exhale and stretch down over the right leg. It is most important to bring the torso down, not the head or forehead, which just comes along at the end. This keeps the spinal alignment correct. Continue 1–3 minutes.

5. Life Nerve Stretch. Continue to sit with the legs stretched wide apart. Hold onto the toes (or whatever you can, keeping the knees as flat as possible), exhale and stretch down bringing the forehead down, then inhale and come sitting up. Continue 1–3 minutes.

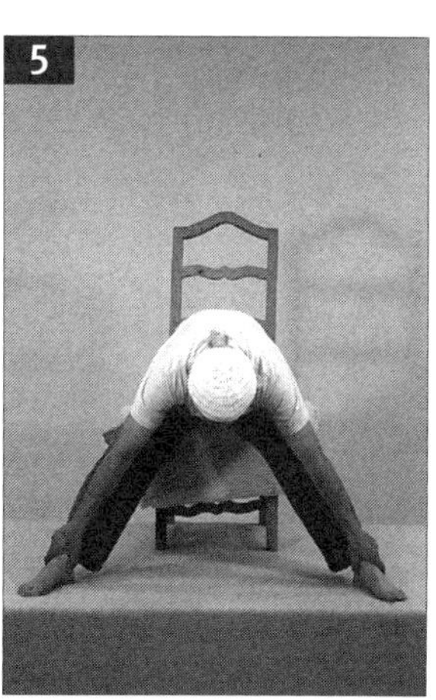

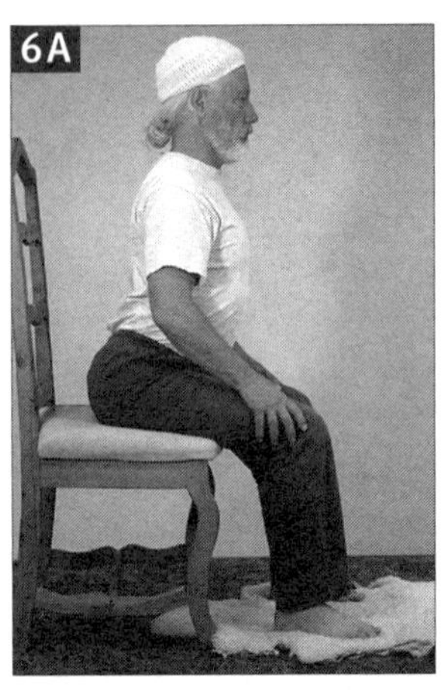

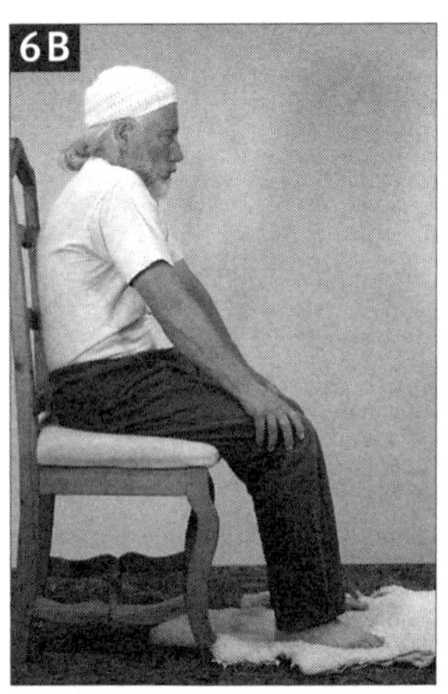

6. Spinal Flex. Sitting straight, grab the middle of the thighs (close to the knee) with both hands. Inhale. Flex the spine forward and rock forward on the buttocks **(6A)**. Then exhale, flex the spine backwards and roll back on the buttocks **(6B)**. Keep the head level and the arms fairly straight and relaxed. Continue 1–3 minutes.

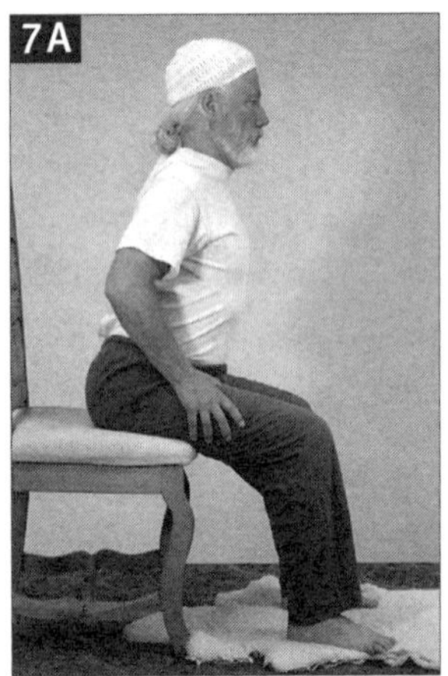

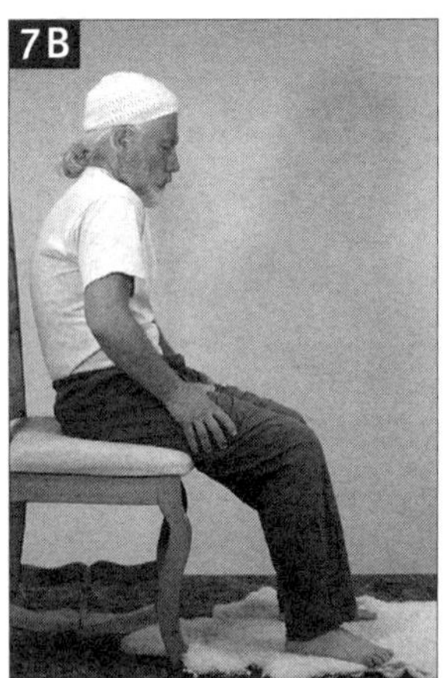

7. Spinal Flex. Place the hands flat on the thighs close to the hips. Flex the spine forward on the inhale **(7A)**, backward on the exhale **(7B)**. Focus at the Third-Eye point. Continue 1–3 minutes.

8. Spinal Twist. Grasp the shoulders with the fingers in front, thumbs in back. Inhale and twist to the left, exhale, twist to the right. Keep the arms parallel to the floor. The action is from the torso, and the head moves along. Continue 1–3 minutes.

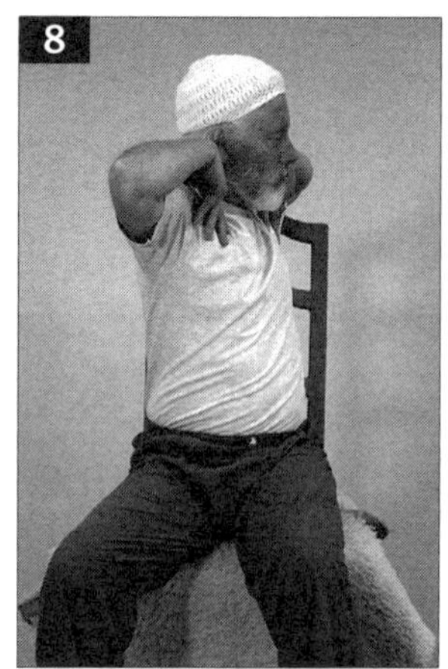

9. Grasp the shoulders as in the previous exercise. Inhale and raise the elbows up so that the backs of the wrists touch behind the neck **(9A, B)**. Exhale and lower the elbows to the original position. Continue 1–3 minutes.

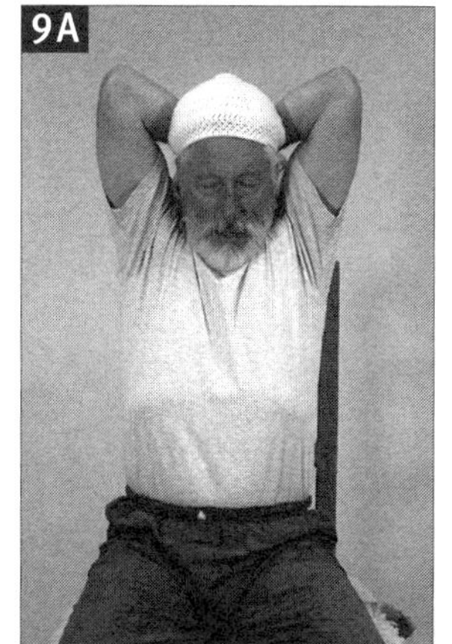
9A

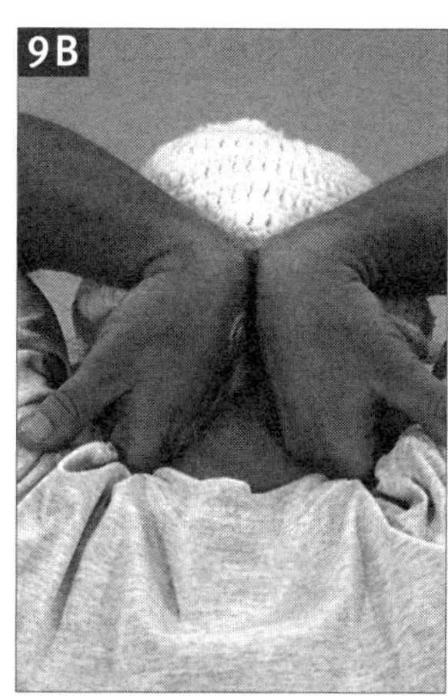
9B

10. Arm pumps. Interlace the fingers in Venus Lock (See page 49 for the hand position/mudra). Inhale and stretch the arms up over the head, then exhale and bring the arms down keeping the arm straight, no bend in the elbows. Continue 1–3 minutes.

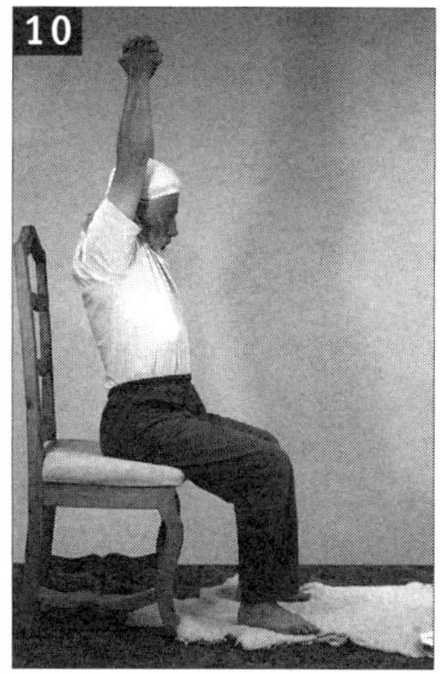
10

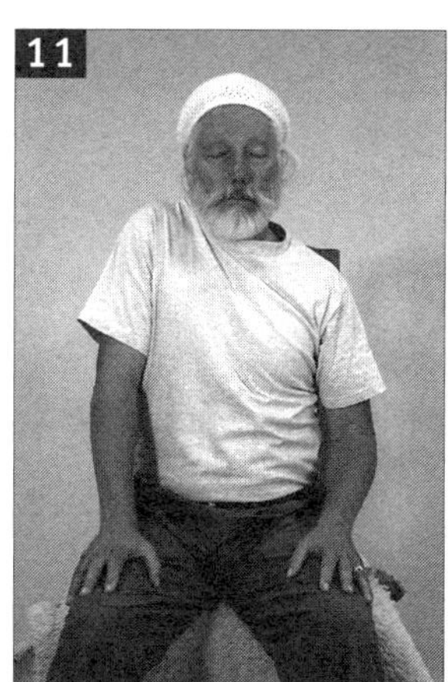
11

11. Alternate shoulder shrugs. Sit straight with the hands resting on the thighs. Inhale and shrug the left shoulder up, while the right shoulder goes down, then exhale and raise the right shoulder up as you lower the left shoulder. Continue for 1 minute. Then, reverse the breath so that you inhale as you shrug the right shoulder up; exhale as you shrug the left shoulder. Continue for 1 minute.

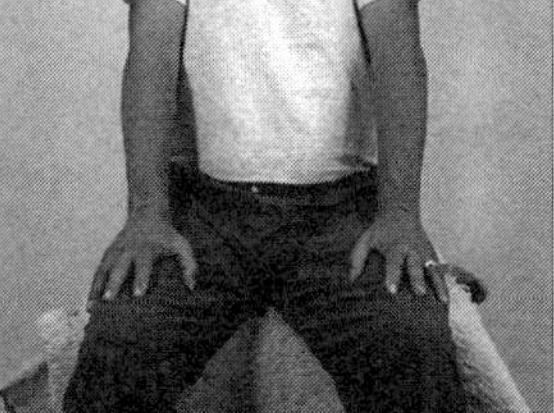
12

12. Shoulder shrugs. Inhale and shrug both shoulders up, exhale down. Continue 1 minute.

13. Neck Rotations. Have the palms on the thighs close to the knees. Be sure the shoulders are relaxed down. Inhale, and rotate your head to the left, and exhale, rotate it to the right, like shaking your head "no." Continue for 1 minute. Then reverse your breath, so that you inhale and rotate to the right, and exhale, rotate to the left. Continue for 1 minute. Inhale deeply, concentrate at the third eye, and slowly exhale.

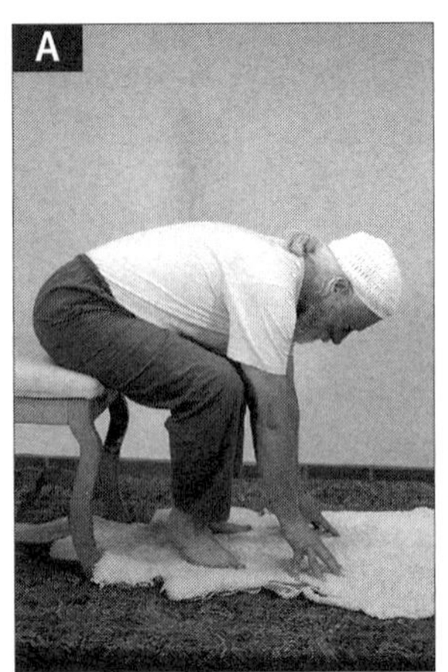

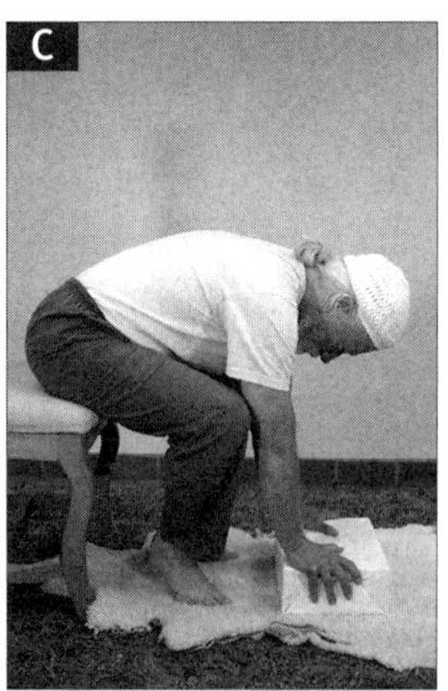

14. Frog Pose. Place the heels together with the toes and knees angled out. Unless too difficult, keep the heals lifted throughout the whole exercise. Bend down so the hands are between the knees on the floor, a little above the feet. Keep the head up. **(14A)**. (If this is too hard for you, put a stool on the floor between your legs. Inhale, keeping the fingers on the ground or stool, bring the buttocks up off the chair with straighten legs and the head down **(14B)**. Exhale, come down into the original position, with the buttocks on the chair and the hands remain on the floor or stool **(14C)**. The inhale and exhale should be strong. Continue this cycle 10–26 times. Do the best you can. If you cannot do the exercise at all, omit it and sit doing Long Deep Breathing.

15. Relaxation. Lean back in your chair and deeply relax.

Laya Yoga Meditation – (included in this yoga set) Sit with a straight spine with the hands on the knees in Gyan Mudra (thumb tips and fingertips together.)

Mantra: Chant ***Ek Ong Kar(ah) Saa-Taa-Naa-Maa(h) Siree Wha(ah) Hay Guroo.*** On each "***ah***" sound in the mantra, pull up on the Mulbandh (simultaneously pull up on the rectum and sex organs and pull in on the navel.) The "***a***" sound is really created by the power of the Mulbandh. This is a 3 ½ cycle meditation. With the breath, visualize the sound spiraling up from the base of the spine to the top of the head in 3 ½ circles. Continue for 11–31 minutes. (Refer to the CD for correct pronunciation and rhythm – 3.)

CHAPTER 5

Yoga For Health and Healing

Kundalini Yoga is uncoiling yourself to find your potential and your vitality and to reach for your virtues. There is nothing from outside. Try to understand that. All is in you. You are the storehouse of your totality.
Yogi Bhajan

I AM A HUGE ADVOCATE OF KUNDALINI YOGA, because I know it works. Again and again, I have seen the technology bring positive changes to people's lives. One of my most rewarding Kundalini Yoga teaching experiences was training caregivers for people living with HIV and AIDS in South Africa. AIDS has infected 50% of the population and is a death sentence. Along with the high unemployment (50%) and crime rate, many feel overwhelmed with sorrow and hopelessness. While many are burying their desperation in crime, drugs or alcohol, a few, like these caregivers, are channeling it in positive ways.

None of them had done yoga, breathing or meditation before, yet they were incredibly enthusiastic and willing to try. Desperation has a way of breaking down myths and misconceptions about the unfamiliar. When they returned the next week, many said that the simple techniques were changing their lives for the better and helping the people they serve. One HIV caregiver said that after practicing meditation all week, he was feeling hopeful for the first time in months. I was touched beyond words by the love and caring, the tenacity and spirit of these people, trying to make a difference in the overwhelming suffering all around them. Today Kundalini Yoga is being practiced in many AIDS clinics throughout South Africa.

When you think of people practicing yoga, what image pops into your head? Does a slender, fit, supple, young man or woman dressed in a stylish leotard come into your mine? Is his or her body in an impossible pretzel-like position on a floor mat? Think again. Imagine a wide age-range of adults, dressed in comfortable loose-fitting clothes, sitting in chairs. Chairs? Yes, yoga can quite effectively be done in a chair…even on a bed. The benefits of yoga do not have to be restricted to a few flexible people who can sit on the floor. Most of the yogic techniques in this book have been adapted to be done in a chair or on a bed, as well as the floor.

There are certain basics before we start.

- Remember that Yoga is not a competition. Do your best and relax.
- Dress comfortably, preferably in 100% cotton clothing.
- It is best not to wear tight or confining clothing, especially jeans or waistlines with belts.
- Keep your feet bare, so the electromagnetic energy can be conducted throughout all 72,000 nerve endings in the bottom of the feet. If you are teaching to an elderly group, it may be too hard and cold to remove their shoes.
- Don't eat 1–2 hours before doing yoga to prevent stomachaches.
- If you have medical restrictions, discuss with a physician your intended practice of yoga. You may want to bring him or her a copy of this book to show the exercises.
- It is best to do your practice in a quiet, out of the way room with lots of fresh air.
- Drink plenty of water during and after your practice. You may sweat and detoxify your body. Water will help to keep you well flushed and hydrated. A recommended amount is one quart.
- Read the instructions thoroughly before starting a Kriya (a group of exercises with a specific purpose) or meditation.
- Pace yourself. Begin slowly, building up your practice consistently. Begin an exercise for the suggested minimum time, building up to the maximum. If you are unable to do the minimum, start where you can and build from there.
- Listen to your body. Be aware of any changes. If you feel nauseous or faint during any of the exercises, stop and wait a few minutes before continuing. You may not be used to the increased oxygen; your body needs time to adjust to its added source of vitality. You may also feel strange from the body detoxifying.
- With every exercise you will be coordinating a breath technique specific to that exercise. It is helpful to have a mental focus. On the inhale, mentally chant "Sat" (meaning truth); on the exhale, mentally chant "Naam" (meaning identity).
- Unless otherwise stated, relax 1–3 minutes between each exercise. This relaxation is crucial, as it allows the body to adjust to the effects of the exercise.
- When you conclude a set, relax lying down on the floor, bed or leaning back in the chair for 5–10 minutes. Breathing deeply and slowly, relax all parts of the body. Listening to soothing music can promote relaxation.
- When you are ready to "wake up," take some deep breaths. Roll the hands in circles at the wrists and the feet in circles at the ankles. Twist and stretch the spine in both directions, left and right. Rub the palms together and the bottoms of the feet together.
- End by chanting the "Sunshine Song." *(sung on the accompanying CD – 4). This song is sung at the end of each Kundalini Yoga class. It blesses everyone and brings peace and mental clarity to all who chant it:*

  May the long time sun shine upon you
  All love surround you
  And the pure light within you
  Guide your way on

  Repeat two times. At the end of the second time, repeat the last line (Guide your way on) three times. At the very end, chant Sat (Truth) Nam (identity) – truth is my identity. The Sat is chanted to eight beats, Nam is chanted to two, approximately.

THE BODY LOCKS (BANDHAS)

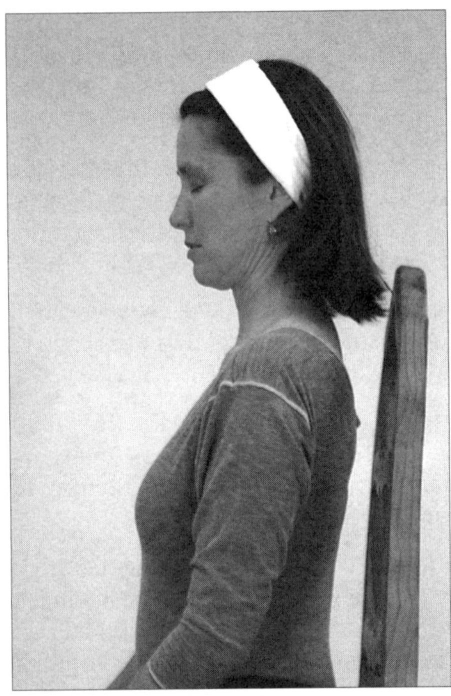

There are certain combinations of muscle contractions called Locks or *Bandhas*. Each lock has a function of changing blood circulation, nerve pressure and the flow of cerebral spinal fluid. They also direct the flow of physical and psychic energy (prana) into the main energy channels that relate to raising the Kundalini energy. Applying the locks during Kundalini Yoga creates balance, self-awareness and self-healing. Practicing the locks during life also prepares us to direct the energy up the chakras and out the Tenth Gate at the time of death, which we will discuss in more detail in Chapter Ten – *Rehearsing Death.*

There are three main bandhas: **Neck Lock (*Jalandhar Bandh*)**, **Diaphragm Lock (*Uddiyana Bandh*)**, **Root Lock (*Mulbandh*)**. When all three locks are applied together, it is called **Great Lock (*Mahabandh*)**.

Neck Lock (Jalandhar Bandh)

This is the most basic and widely used of the locks. One can apply it in all chanting meditations, during most *pranayama* (breath) exercises and while holding the breath in or out. If the Kundalini Energy is stimulated, *Jalandhar Bandh* can allow a clear channel through which the energy can flow up the neck into the top chakras.

How to apply Neck Lock (Jalandhar Bandh)

- Sit in an easy cross-legged position (Easy Pose), be sitting in a chair with the feet flat or lie comfortably – all are with a straight spine.
- Lift the chest and sternum upward.
- Gently stretch the back of the neck straight by pulling the chin toward the back of the neck.
- The head stays level and centered and does not tilt forward or to either side.
- The muscles of the neck and throat remain loose. Keep the muscles of the face and brow relaxed.
- Do not force the head forward or down. That will result in a sore neck. You can imagine a turtle pulling its head back.

Diaphragm Lock (Uddiyana Bandh)

Uddiyana Bandha is a powerful lock, because it allows the pranic force to transform through the Central Nerve Channel of the spine up into the neck region. It gives a sense of compassion and youthfulness to the entire body.

How to apply Diaphragm Lock (Uddiyana Bandh)

- Be sure your stomach is not full before doing this bandh.
- Be sitting in Easy Pose on the floor, in a chair with the feet flat on the floor or lying on a bed with a straight spine. The very best position to do this bandh is standing, so there are no restrictions for the stomach to pull in.
- Inhale deeply, exhale until all of your air is out. The lock is pulled on the exhalation.
- Lift the diaphragm up high into the thorax and pull the upper abdominal muscles back toward the spine. This creates a cavity that gently massages the heart muscles.
- Hold the lock as long as you can (no more than 60 seconds). Then, inhale and relax.

Root Lock (Mulbandh)

This is the most complex of the three body locks. It is like a hydraulic lock at the base of the spine. It coordinates, stimulates and balances the energies involved with the rectum, sex organs and Navel Point. This bandh is frequently applied at the end of an exercise or kriya to consolidate its benefits. It is usually applied in conjunction with the Neck Lock. Root Lock is a smooth motion that consists of three parts.

Mulbandh unites the two major energy flows of the body: *prana* and *apana*. *Prana* is the generative energy of the upper Chakras (the 4th and 5th). *Apana* is the eliminating energy of the 1st, 2nd and 3rd Chakras.

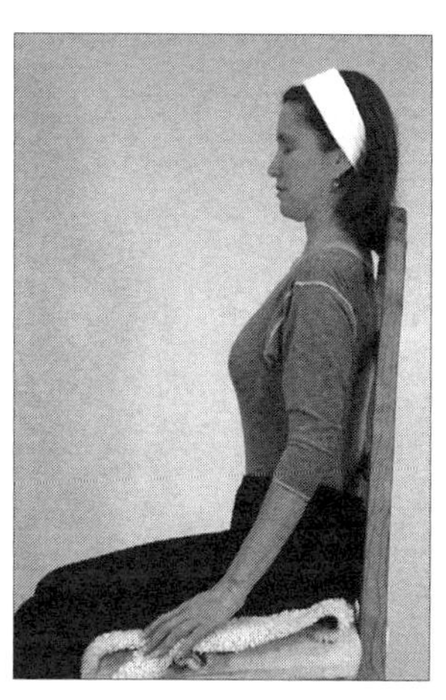

How to apply Root Lock (Mulbandh)

- Sit or lie with a straight spine.
- With the breath held in or out, contract the rectum, lifting the muscles upward and inward, as if trying to hold back a bowel movement..
- Next contract the area around the sex organ. It is like trying to stop the flow of urine.
- Then contract the lower abdominal muscles and the Navel Point toward the spine.
- The rectum and sex organs are drawn up toward the navel point.

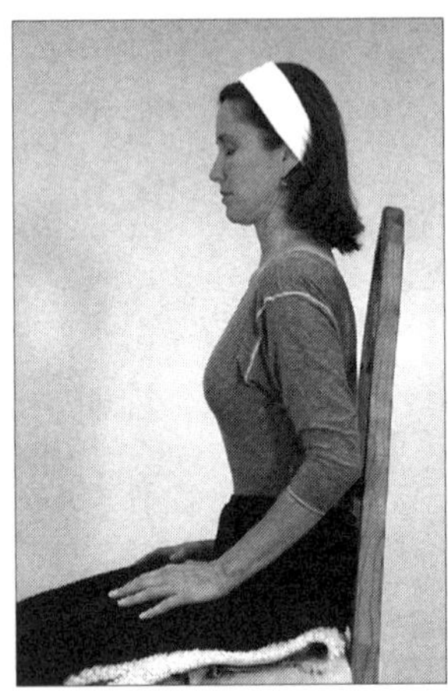

The Great Lock (Mahabandh)

The Great Lock is the application of all three locks simultaneously, with the breath held out. Mulbandh is pulled first and held while you pull Uddiyana Bandh and held while you pull Jalandhar Bandh. It can be done with various postures and mudras. This bandh relieves sexual tension, regulates blood pressure, reduces menstrual cramps, alleviates wet dreams and increases the circulation to the lower glands of the testes and ovaries.

Rock Pose

Doing your practice on the floor

It is nice to have something to sit on when you do yoga. Rubber yoga mats prevent you from slipping, especially if you are doing your practice on a non-carpeted floor. Rubber mats don't give much cushion, so it is also nice to have a small rug, sheepskin or blanket to put on top of the mat. Sheepskins are a good thickness and provide an electromagnetic insulation from the ground. Wool, cotton and silk are the next best materials to sit on. The worst surface to sit on is concrete or stone.

You have probably seen people meditating in a cross-legged position (*Easy Pose*). In the easiest Easy Pose, one foot is under the opposite knee, and the other foot is under the other knee. The spine is straight with the lower spine slightly forward. Placing a meditation pillow under the buttocks helps to relieve lower back pain. Sit on the edge of the pillow, allowing the knees to angle downward to the ground. I have used a meditation pillow for years and it enables me to meditate more comfortably for longer periods of time.

If *Easy Pose* is not "easy," some people find *Rock Pose* to be more comfortable. Start by kneeling on both knees with the top of the feet on the ground, then sit with the heels under the sitting bones. If this position is uncomfortable, place a small pillow between the buttocks and the heels. The spine is straight. This position is known for its digestive benefits. When mastered, it is said that one can "digest rocks." It also makes one solid and balanced like a rock.

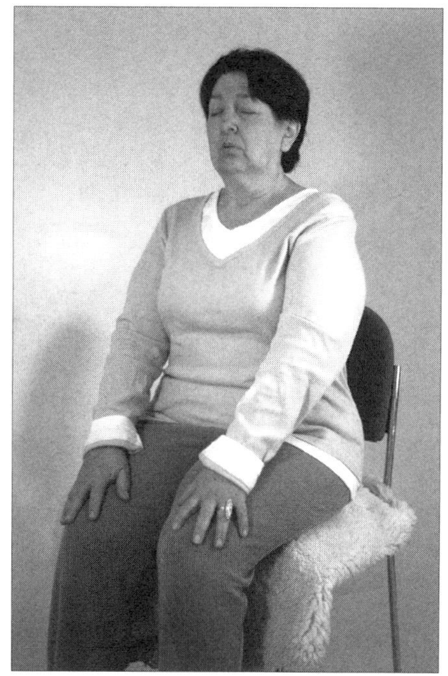

Doing your practice in a chair

Choose a sturdy, straight-backed chair without arms. If a wheelchair is needed, work with the arms the best you can. Only if needed, arms of the chair can give support and stability by holding on to them. Holding onto the sides of the base of the chair can also supply support.

Sit straight, a little away from the back on the chair. The feet are flat on the floor. The hands can be palms down on the tops of the legs or on top of the base of the chair next to the thighs to help straighten and lengthen the spine. For a class setting, put the chairs in a half circle, so everyone can see the instructor's demonstration. Leave space between the chairs for arm movement. If you can't do the exercise, it is fine to either do it the best you can or to leave out the exercise altogether. Sit and visualize yourself doing the exercise with the intention of the benefit.

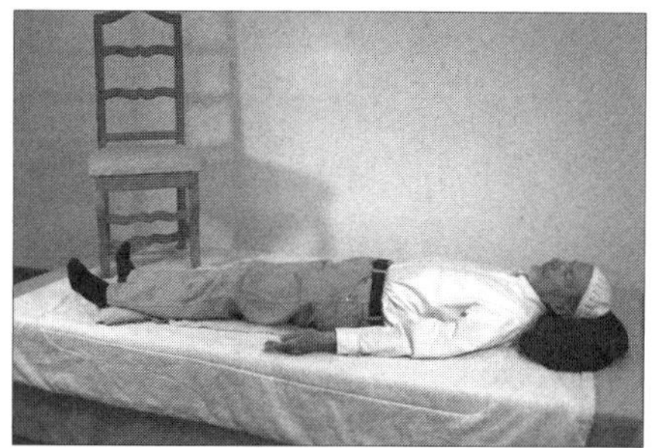

Doing yoga on a bed

Bed yoga would have to be done on an individual basis. If you are instructing someone in a one-on-one situation, you may need to touch the person to help him or her get in and out of the postures. In some states it is illegal to touch the person, unless you are a licensed Chiropractor, Massage Therapist or Minister. Check with your state for its regulations.

Whenever possible use a firm mattress. If a wheelchair is used, keep it near the bed in case it is needed. You may want to do some of the postures on the bed – for example, postures that would normally be done on the floor. For the sitting up postures, you can transfer to the chair.

PROCESS EXERCISES

1. Practice each of the Body Locks or Bandhas separately. Could you feel them stimulating the energy up the Chakras? Begin to practice applying the locks while you are doing yoga or at least at the end of an exercise.

2. Choose one of the following yoga sets and do it. Be sure to first review the basics and remember to Tune In before you begin. When completed, be aware of how you feel.

WAKE UP, WARM UP AND GET UP

Appendix IV has more yoga sets for your health and enjoyment.

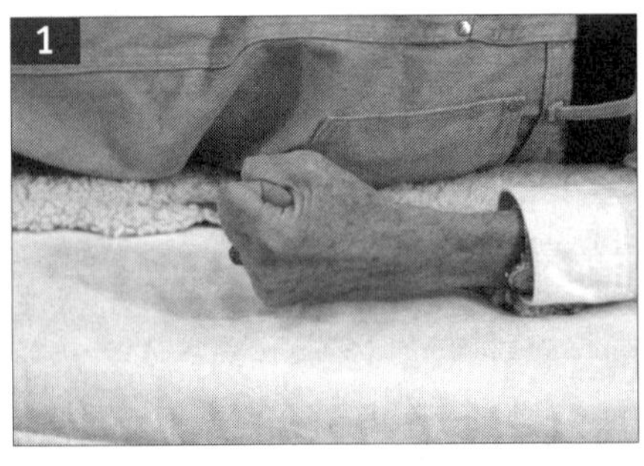

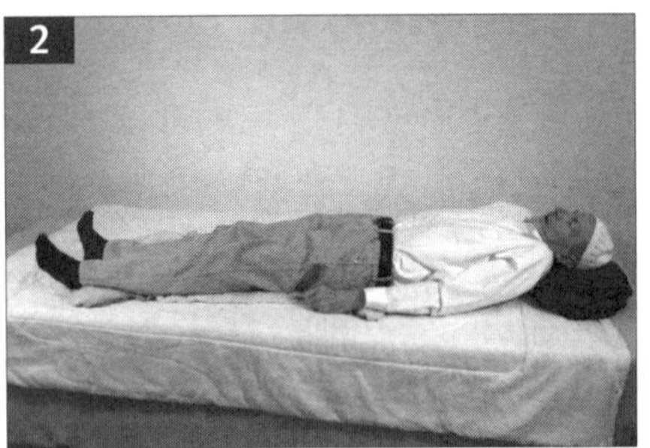

Simple things to do before you get up in the morning. This routine is very helpful on those days when you have to get up and don't want to. If, before getting up and before opening your eyes, you spend one minute doing the following things, you will preserve your health and prevent disease.

1. Make a fist of your hands.

2. Move your shoulders in a circular motion in both directions.

Age is measured by the flexibility of the spine. To stay young, stay flexible. This series works systematically from the base of the spine to the top. All 26 vertebrae receive stimulation and all the chakras receive a burst of energy. This makes it a good series to do as a warm up before another kriya or before meditation. This kriya also increases the circulation of the spinal fluid, a crucial link to good memory. Many people report greater mental clarity after regular practice of this kriya. Note: Root Lock can be pulled when you inhale at the end of any exercise.

3. **Tense and release your lower back.**

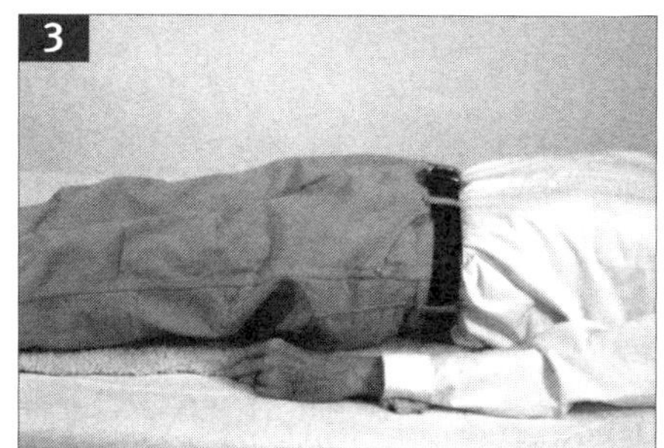

4. **Point your toes forward (4A). Point the toes back (4B).**

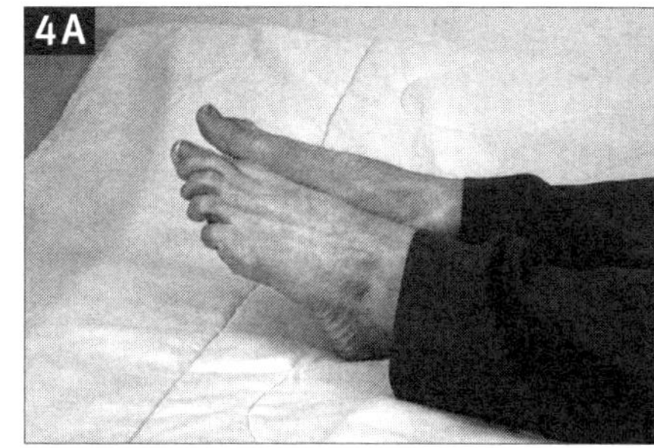

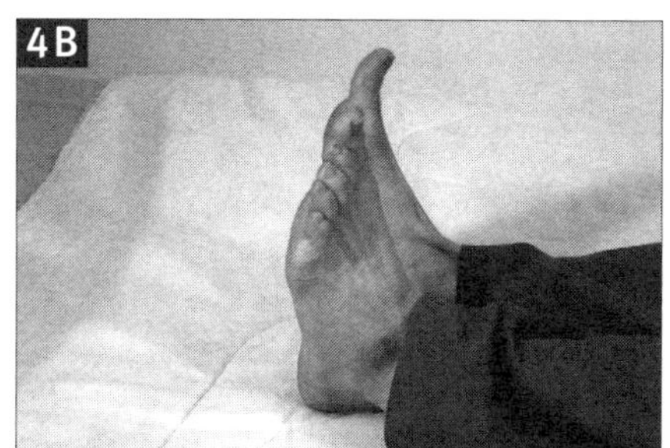

5. **With your hands flat at your sides,** stretch your whole body.
6. **Curl around sinuously like a snake,** 3" left and right.

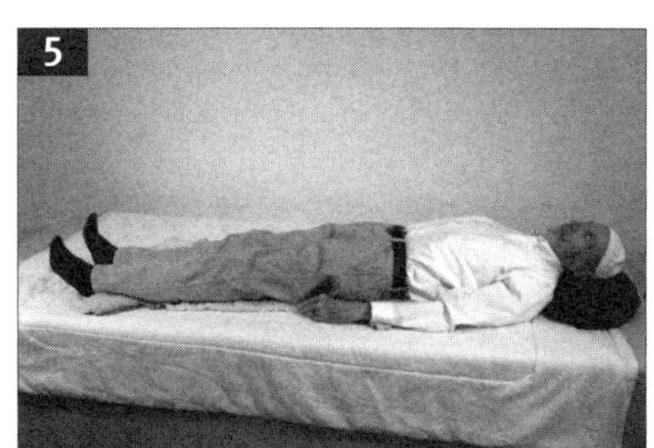

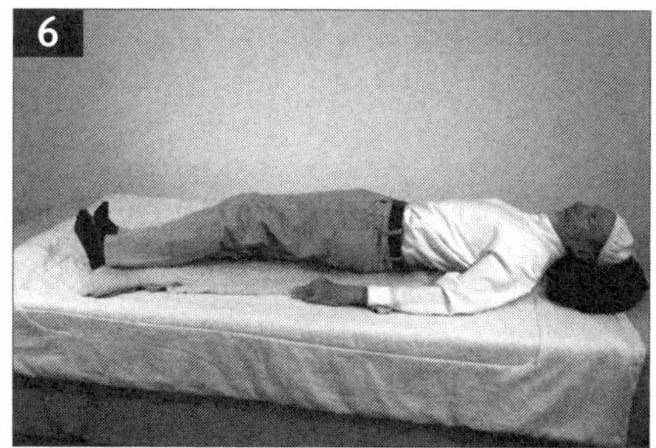

7. **Put the palms of your hands over your eyes,** open your eyes while your hands are covering them, and then slowly move your hands forward and away from your eyes. In this way your eyes become gently introduced to the first light of day.
8. **Massage your mouth and face** with the palms of both hands.

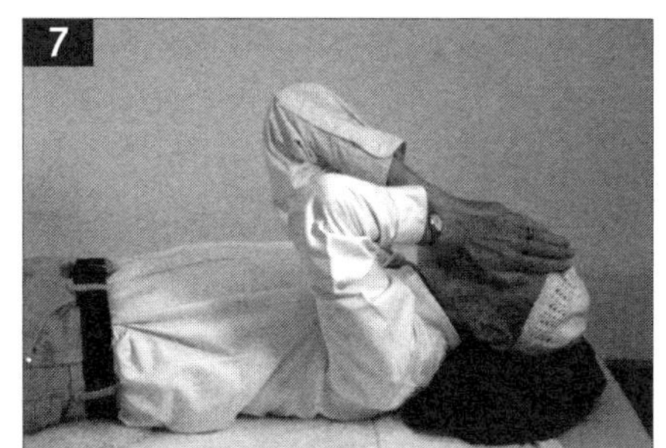

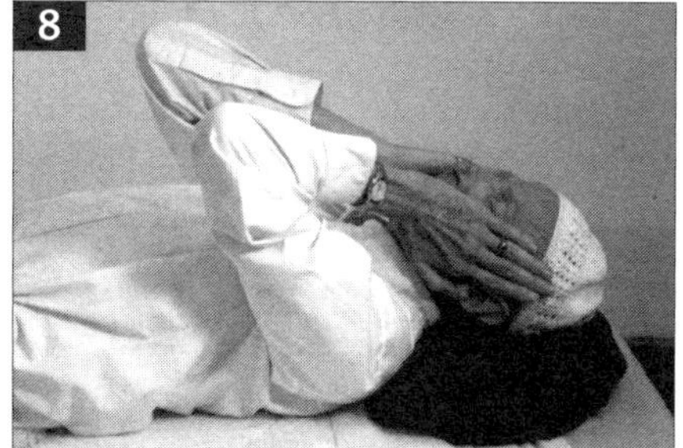

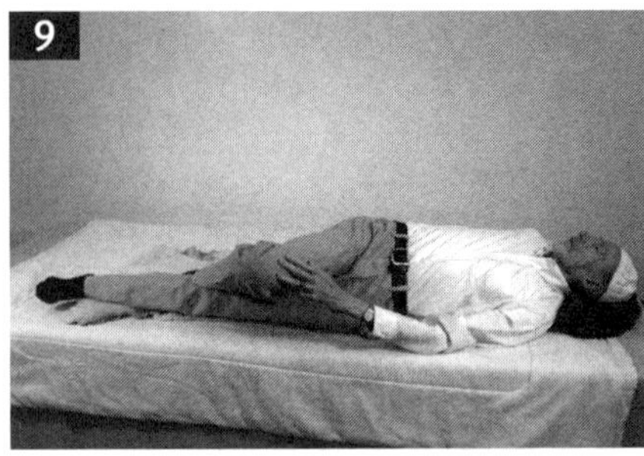

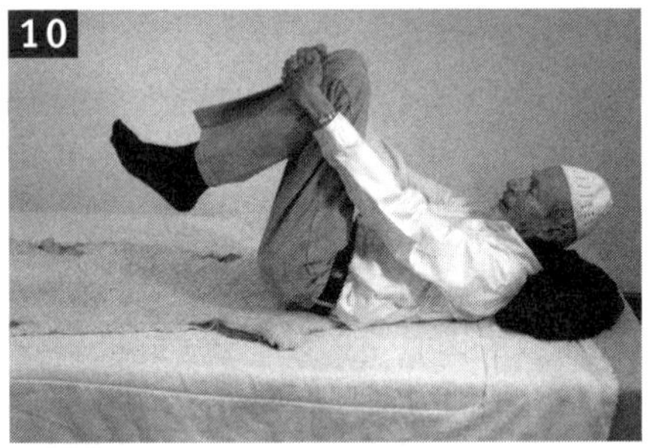

9. **Cat Stretch.** Lying on the back, stretch the right arm over the head and the left arm is to the side perpendicular to the body. Keeping the shoulders on the ground, pull the right knee up and bend it over to the left side of the body on the ground. Do the same with the other leg.

10. **Raise your head up slowly** and pull your knees up to your chest.

Now get up and enjoy your day. If you are doing "bed yoga," this little routine can start you off, followed by one of the other bed yoga sets given.

BASIC SPINAL SERIES *Done in a chair*

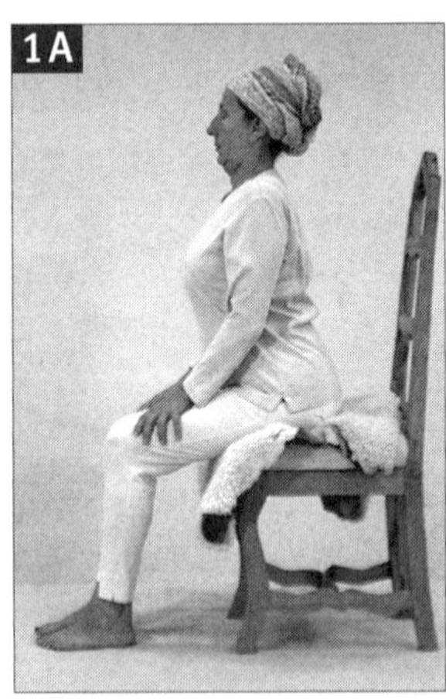

How to do it

1. **Be sitting in a chair with a straight spine.** Place the palms on the tops of the legs toward the knees. As you inhale, flex the spine forward and lift the chest up **(1A)**. On the exhale, flex the spine backwards **(1B)**, emphasize flexing the lower spine. Keep the head level, in a slight neck lock, so it does not "flip-flop." Repeat 1–3 minutes. To finish, inhale, (pull Root Lock – optional) exhale. Rest 1 minute.

2. Place the hands flat on the thighs closer to the hips, fingers facing center. Flex the spine forward on the inhale **(2A)**, backward on the exhale **(2B)**, emphasize the middle back. Think "*Sat*" on the inhale, ***"Naam"*** on the exhale. Repeat 1–3 minutes. Inhale, hold (pull Root Lock – optional), exhale. Rest 2 minutes.

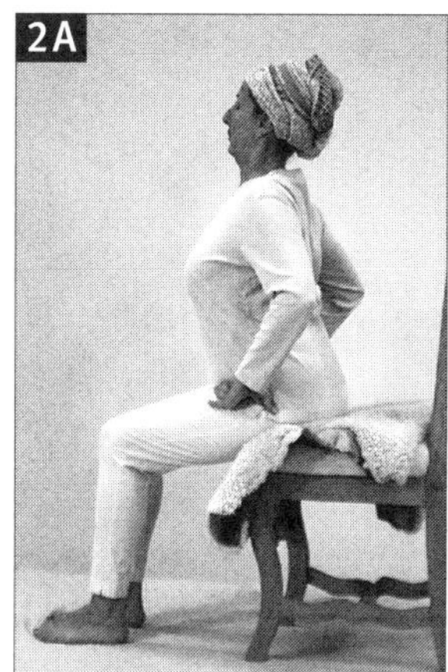

2A

2B

3. Grasp the shoulders with fingers in front, thumbs in back, keep the elbows up parallel to the ground. Inhale and twist to the left, exhale and twist to the right from the waist. Breathing is long and deep. Continue 1–2 minute. To end, inhale, facing forward, exhale. Rest 1 minute.

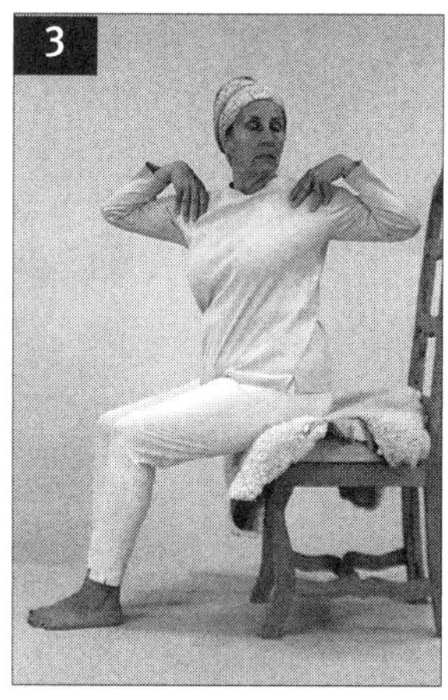

3

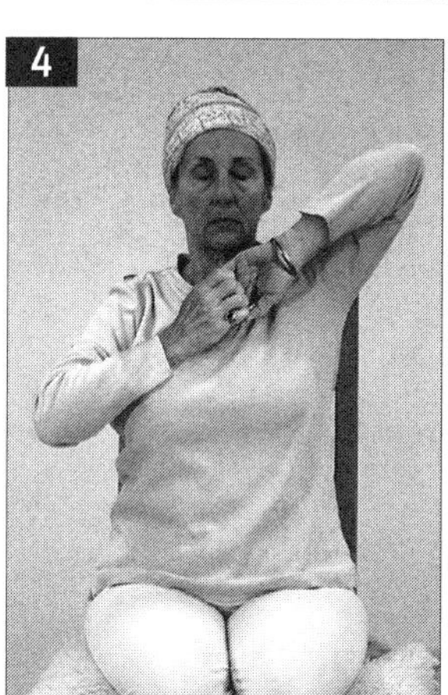

4

4. Lock the fingers in bear grip (Refer to Hand Mudras in Chapter Three page 49) at the heart center. Move the elbows in a seesaw motion, inhaling raise the left elbow goes up, and the right elbow goes down. Then, exhaling, the right elbow goes up and the left down. Continue 1–2 minutes. Inhale, exhale. Relax 30 seconds.

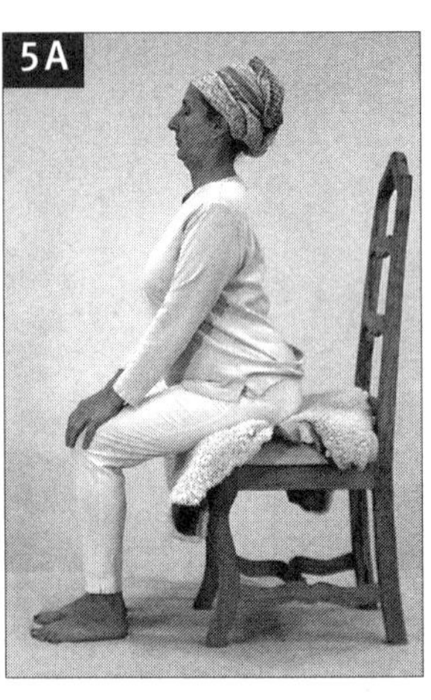

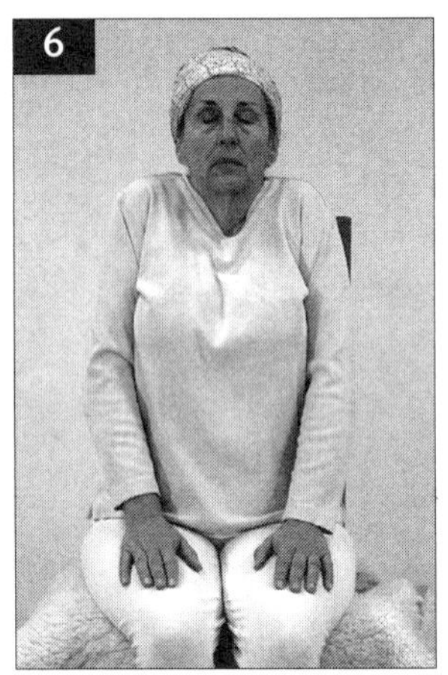

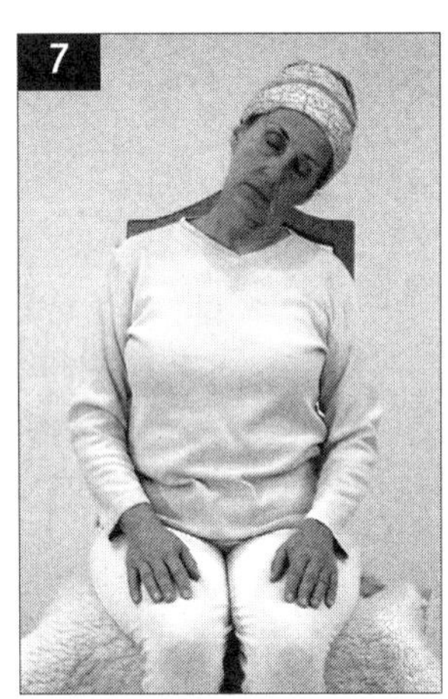

5. Grasp the knees firmly and, keeping the elbows straight, begin to flex the upper spine, exaggerating the motion. Inhale forward **(5A)**, exhale back **(5B)**. Continue for 1–3 minutes. Inhale hold, exhale and relax 1 minute.

6. Shrug both shoulders up on the inhale, down on the exhale. Do this for 1 minute. Inhale and hold 15 seconds with shoulders pressed up. Exhale, relax the shoulders.

7. Roll the neck slowly to the right in a complete circle 5 times, then to the left 5 times. Inhale, pull the neck straight, exhale. Relax.

8. Lock the fingers in Bear Grip at the throat level **(8A)**. Inhale apply Mulbandh (Root Lock). Exhale apply Mulbandh. Then raise the hands above the top of the bead **(8B)**. Inhale apply Mulbandh. Exhale —apply Mulbandh. Repeat two more times.

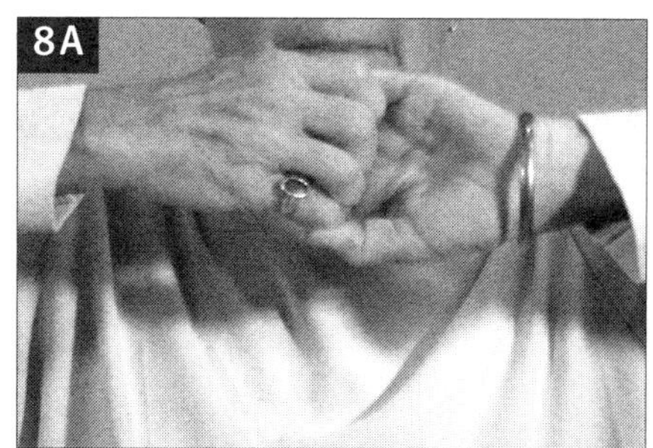
8A

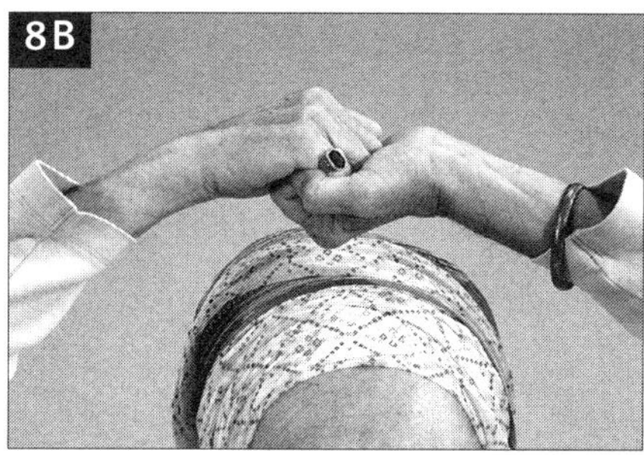
8B

9. Sat Kriya: Sitting in a chair, arms stretched the arms over the head **(9A)**. Interlock the fingers except for the two index fingers, which point straight up **(9B)**. The elbows are kept straight. Say *"Sat"* and pull the navel point In; say *"Naam"* and relax. Continue 1–3 minutes. Then inhale and pull Mulbandh, squeezing the energy from the base of the spine to the top of the skull.

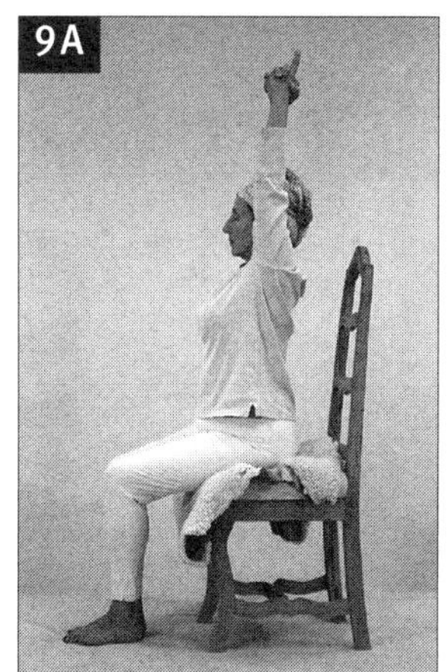
9A

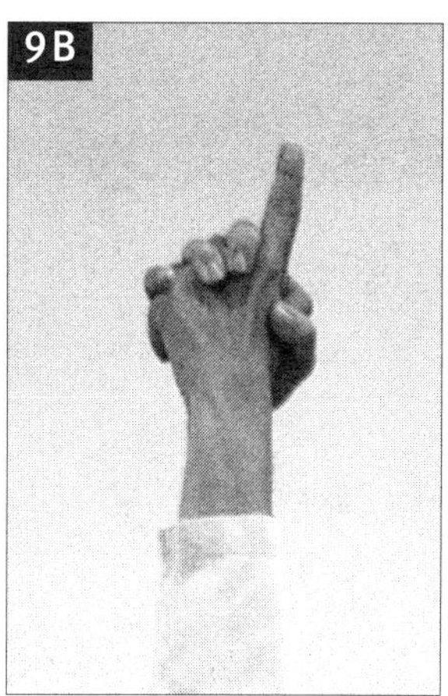
9B

Relax completely leaning back in your chair for 10 – 15 minutes.

GET UP AND GET GOING

This exercise set can be done in your bed and will set you for the whole day. (It can also be done on the floor.)

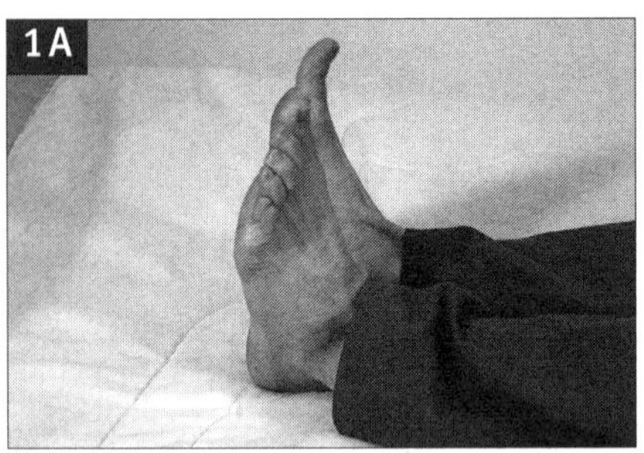
1A

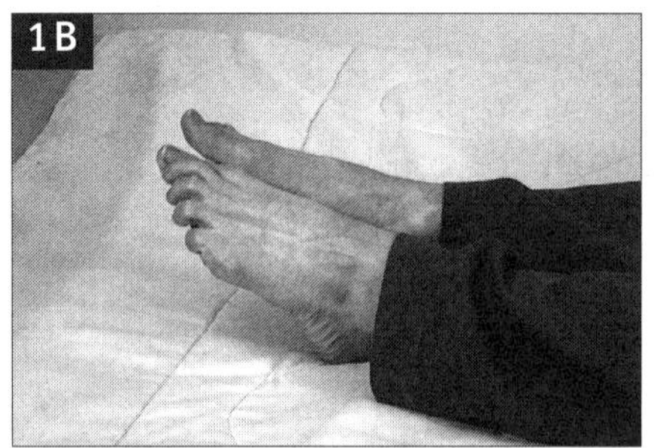
1B

2

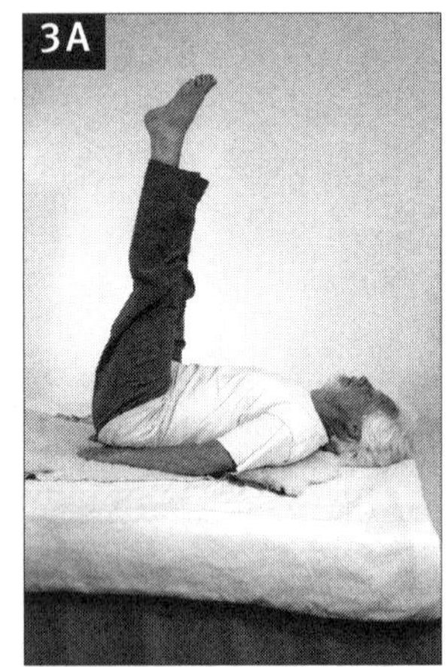
3A

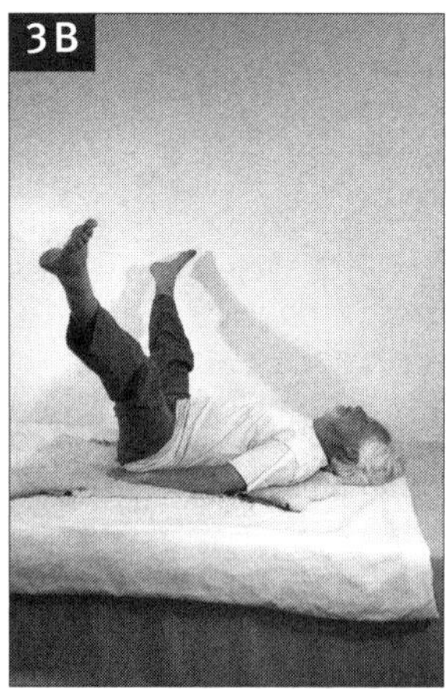
3B

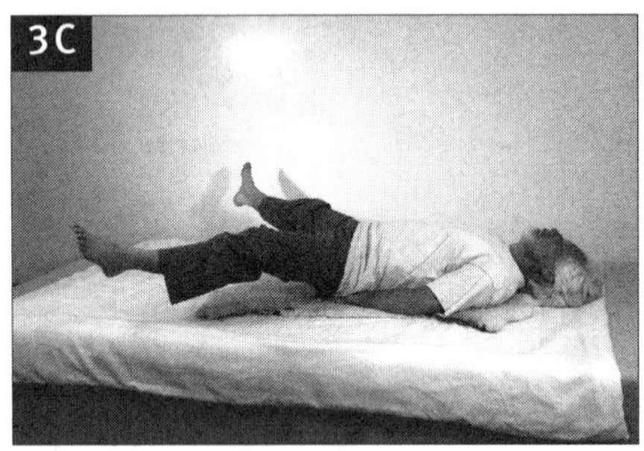
3C

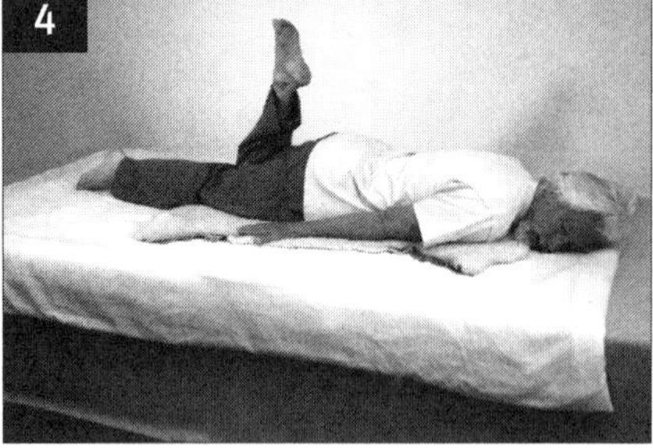
4

1. Lying on your back in bed, with the palms under the hips (to keep the lower spine pressed to the bed and thus protect the lower back), begin moving your feet in unison, flexing and pointing up **(1A)** and down **(1B)**.
Continue 3 minutes.

2. Keeping the palms under the hips, lift both legs to a 90-degree angle. Continue raising and lowering both legs for 3 minutes. If strain is excessive or if there is sharp pain on the lower back, keep one leg bent as you raise and lower the other leg, then switch.

3. Bring both legs up to 90 degrees, **(3A)** spread them as wide apart as you can **(3B)**. Keeping them spread apart, lower them to the bed **(3C)**. When they touch the bed, bring them together again. Continue for 3 minutes.

4. Turn over and lie on the stomach with arms by your sides and head turned to one side. Begin kicking the buttocks with alternate heels.
Continue for 3 minutes.

5. Still on the stomach, the head is facing down with the chin on the bed, begin raising and lowering the pelvic area leaving the knees and shoulders touching the bed. This movement is done rapidly for 3 minutes.

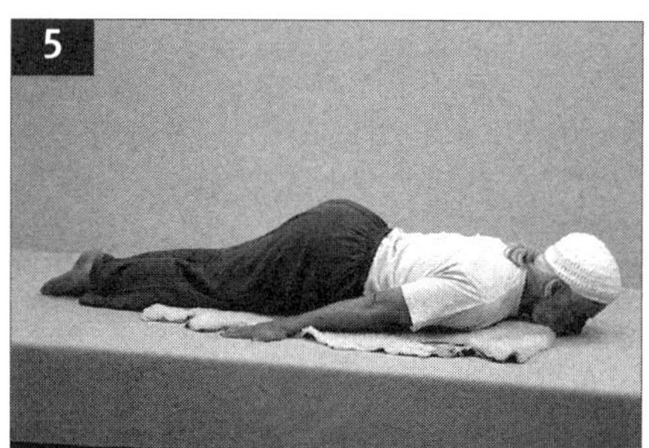

6. Cobra Pose. Still lying on the stomach, the hands are under the shoulders, palms are flat on the bed. Lift the chest and heart up first, and let the head follow as you lean back. Straighten the arms. Do push-ups into a relaxed Cobra Pose, the hips remain on the bed, **(6A)** for 3 minutes. If this puts a strain on the lower back, bend your elbows or put your forearms on the bed and do Half Cobra **(6B)**. Come up on the forearms and press up into Cobra. The head is back in both of these variations.

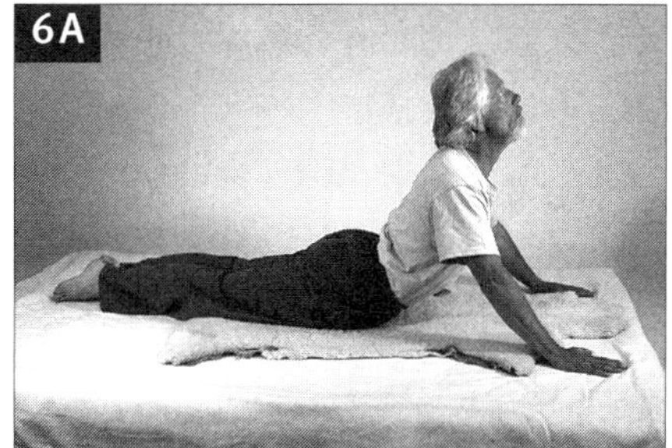

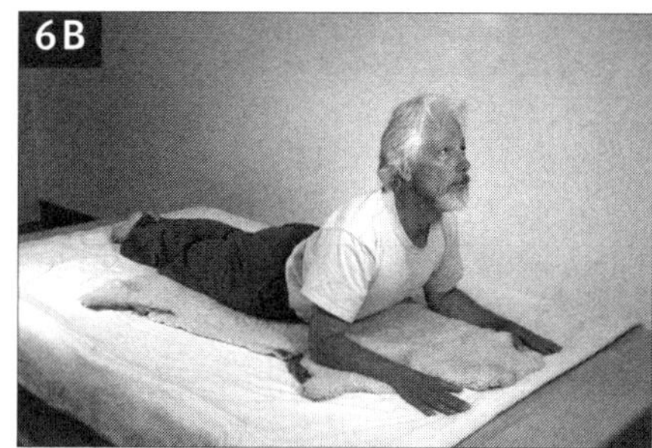

7. Now either you can sit up in your bed in an easy cross-legged pose, or you can sit in a chair with your hands on your thighs **(7A)**. From the sitting position, move the torso down until the forehead is on the bed, keeping the spine as straight as possible, **(7B)** then return to the upright position. Repeat 20 times. If you are in a chair, bend forward, then sit up again. If you are concerned about falling out of the chair as you lean forward, you may want to have the chair facing the bed and to lean toward the bed, holding onto the sides of the chair.

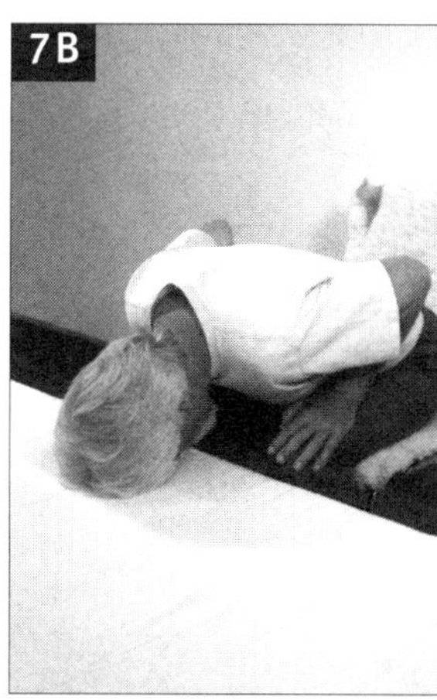

Rise up early in the early hours of the morning and meditate on God.
GURU NANAK

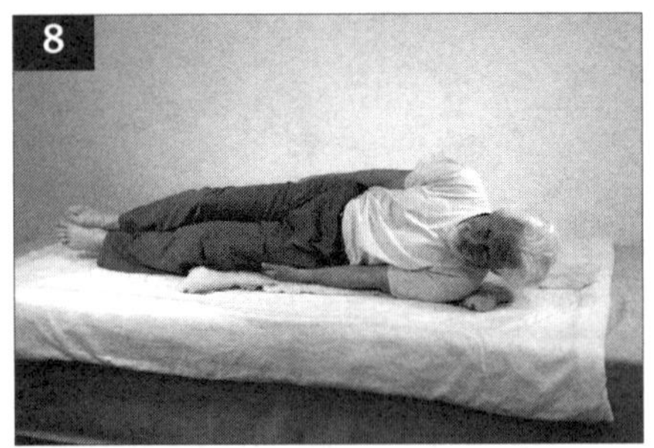

8. Do Bundle Roll. Lie on your back on your bed with legs together and arms at the sides like a bundle of logs tied together. Flip yourself over from back to stomach and from stomach to back without bending the body, arms or legs. Do not bend anywhere. Do the best you can. 3 minutes. If this exercise is too difficult, breathe long and deep during this time, lying on your back with a straight spine.

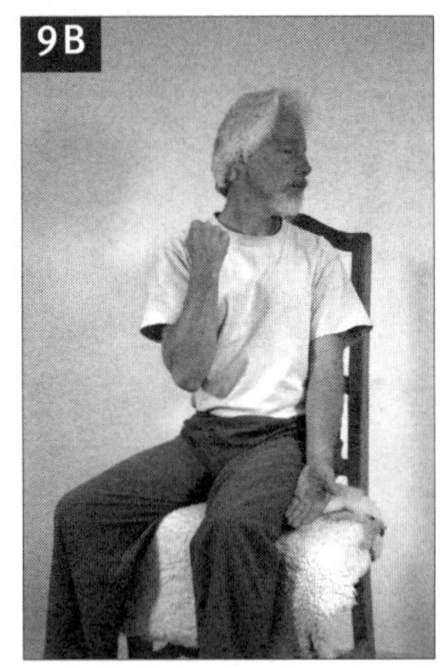

9. Sit straight in a chair. Have your arms at your sides with the palms of your hands facing forward. Make a fist of your right hand and bend your elbow, bringing your fist to your shoulder **(9A)**. Lower your right hand and relax the fist while you make a fist of your left hand and bring it to your shoulder **(9B)**. Continuing this movement, twist your torso from the waist: twisting to the left when your right fist comes up and twisting to the right when your left fist comes up **(9C)**. Once those two movements are coordinated, begin lifting the left knee up as you twist to the left and bring the right fist up. As you twist to the right, bring the right knee up as the left fist comes up **(9D)**. This is like an aerobic movement, so move quickly. Continue for 3 minutes.

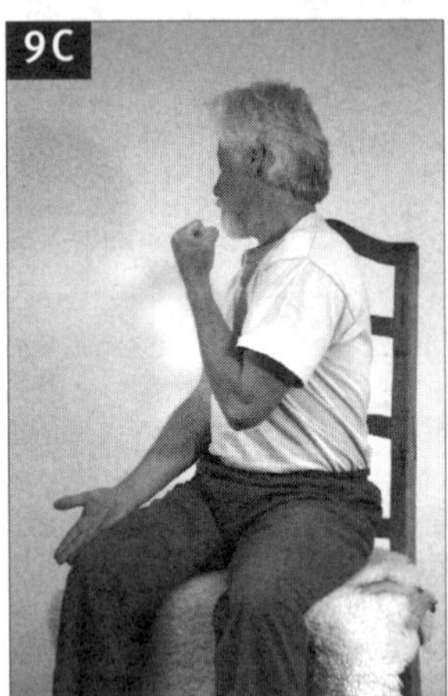

10. Take your shower and begin your day.

IMMUNE FITNESS

This is a Breath and Movement Series to assist the biomechanical and biochemical processes of the immune system.

You may practice these movements individually or in the sequence shown. Pace your movements to your own fitness level. You may practice these while sitting in a chair or comfortably on a pad or exercise mat on the floor.

1. Place your hands on your knees. Moving from the navel point, inhale and flex your spine forward, allowing the rest of the spine to follow **(1A)**. Exhale as you flex your spine back from center, keeping the head straight and the shoulders relaxed **(1B)**. Continue rhythmically for up to 3 minutes. *This exercise balances chakras 1–4, releases grief and builds vitality in the body.*

2. Lion Lick. Continue the spinal flex as in exercise 1, but when your spine is flexed back, draw your chin down to your chest and stick out your whole tongue as you make the sound, "**Hunh**." Inhale though your nose as you flex your spine forward, drawing your tongue back into your mouth. Continue up to 3 minutes. *This exercise detoxifies the body and releases frustration, anger and fear.*

3. As in #1 and 2, place the hands on the knees. Place the tongue directly at the top of the mouth. Inhale through the nose, suspend the breath and flex the spine while the breath is held in. When you can't hold the breath any longer, exhale and repeat. Continue 3 minutes. *This exercise gives a sense of satisfaction and fulfillment.*

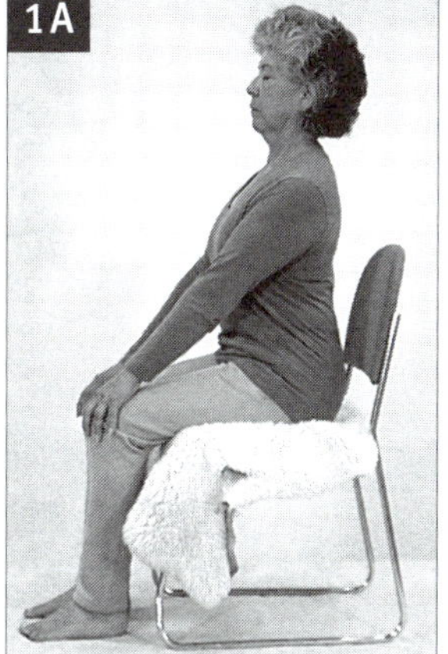
1A

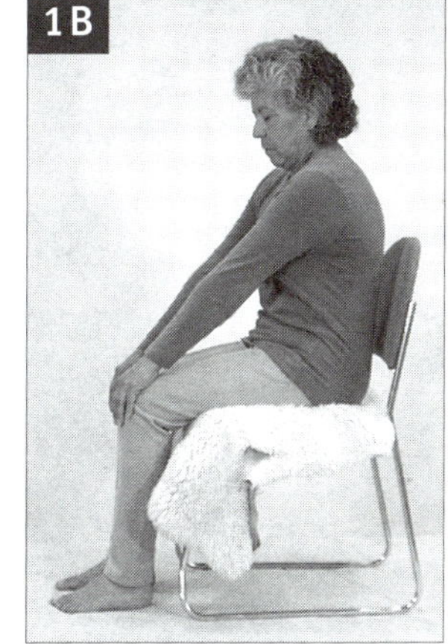
1B

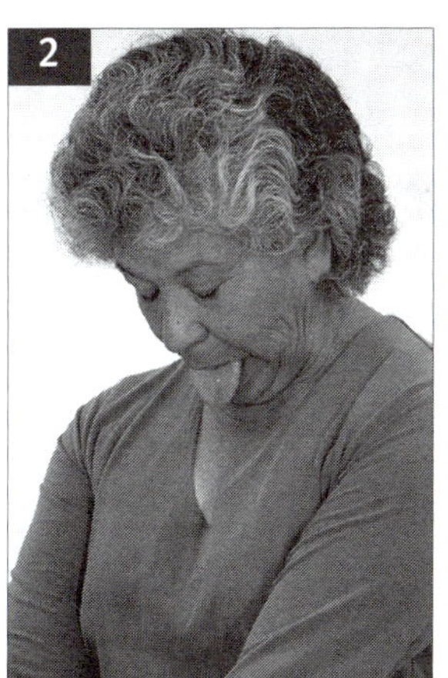
2

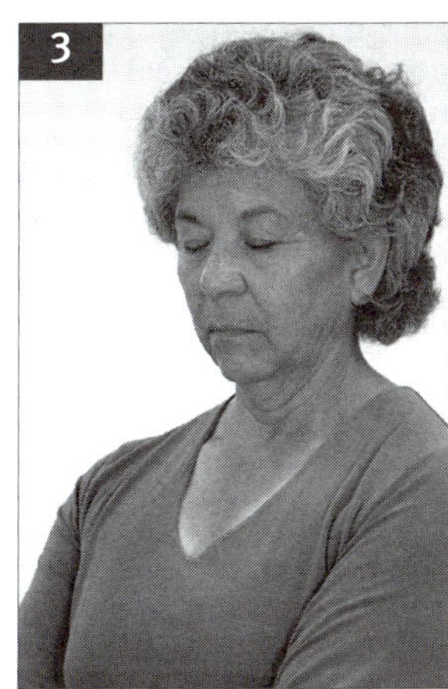
3

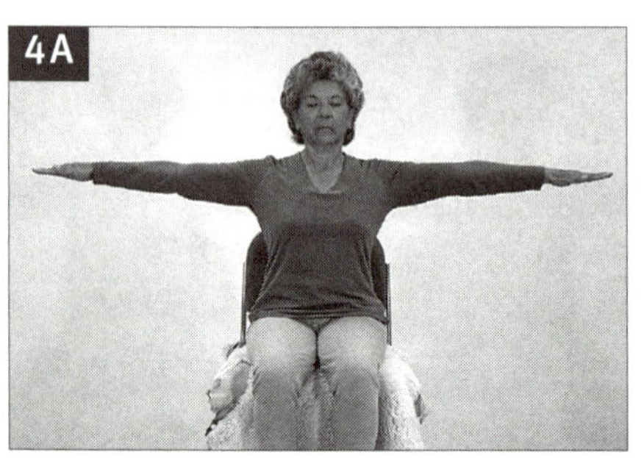
4A

4B

4. Extend your arms straight out to the sides, parallel to the floor, palms facing down **(4A)**. Keeping the elbows straight, begin flapping the arms up and down for 3 counts. On the count of 4, clap your hands over your head **(4B)**. Adjust your breath with the movement and continue for up to 7 minutes. *This exercise combats the long-term fatigue from a chronic illness. It builds vitality in the Pranic Body and strengthens the Magnetic Field or Aura.*

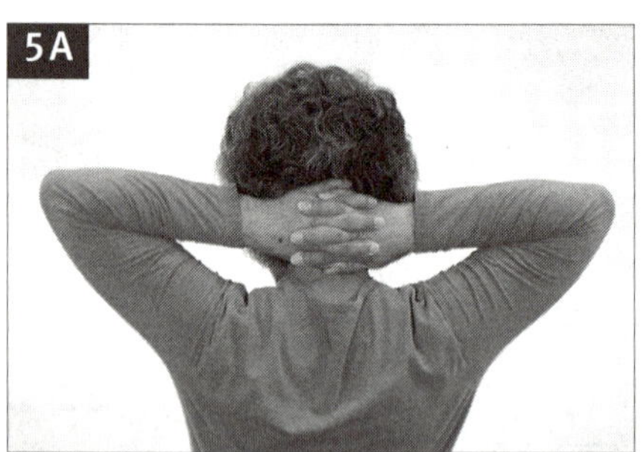
5A

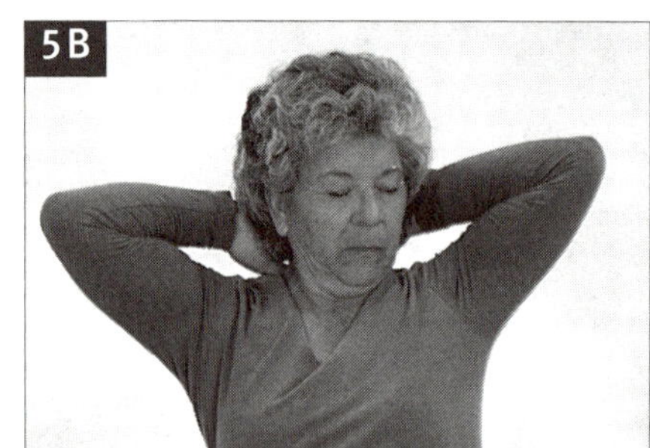
5B

5. Interlace your fingers and place your hands behind your head where the neck and the scalp meet **(5A)**. Extend the elbows straight out to the sides, parallel to the floor. Begin turning from left to right, stopping for 1 count in the center **(5B)**. Inhale to each side, exhale in the center. Continue for up to 7 minutes. *This exercise releases resistance and works on the spleen, releasing anger.*

6

6. Extend the arms straight in front of you at a slight angle outwards, parallel to the floor, the palms facing up. Alternately make fists of the hands and pull them into the armpit area. Inhale as the arm extends out and exhale as you bring it back to the armpit. Continue up to 3 minutes. *This exercise works on emotional balance, the spleen (anger), the lymphatic system (fear), the kidneys (grief).*

7. Extend the arms out to the sides parallel to the floor with the palms up. Make fists out of the hands with the thumbs tucked inside and touching the fleshy mound under the little finger **(7A, 7B)**. Inhale through your mouth and flex the elbows, bringing the fists to the shoulders **(7C)**. As you exhale through the mouth, straighten the arms out to the sides. Move rapidly and breathe powerfully. Continue up to 6 minutes. *This exercise helps to enrich the blood, transform fear, and build the magnetic field.*

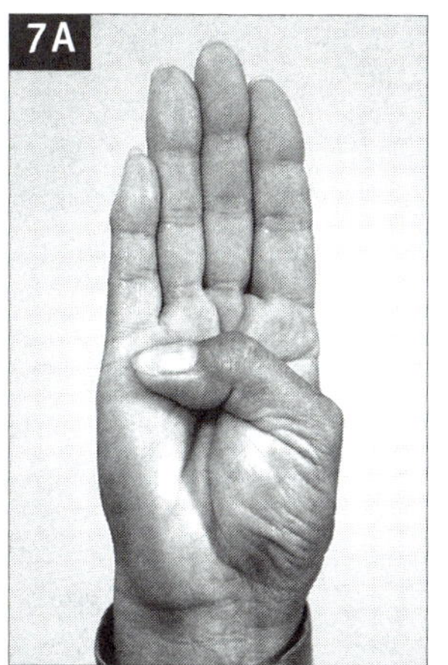
7A

7B

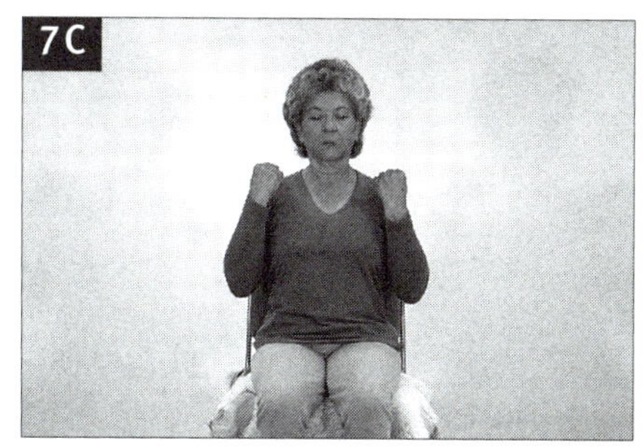
7C

8. Make fists of your hands with the thumbs out **(8A)** and bring your arms up to chest level. Begin tapping your chest, alternating the fists **(8B)**. Create a rhythmic thumping motion. Continue up to 5 minutes. *This exercise works on the thymus, lymph and transforms anger.*

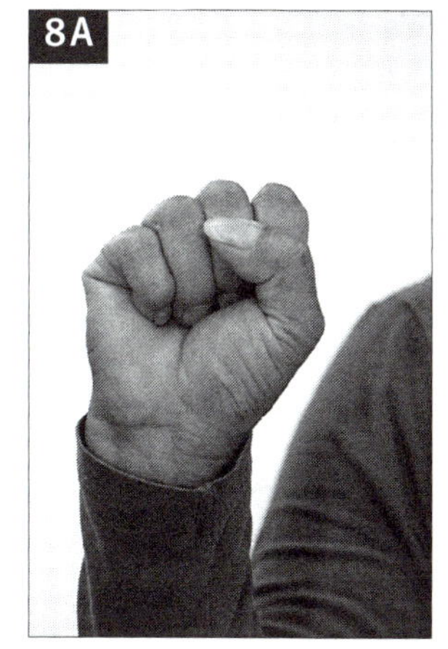
8A

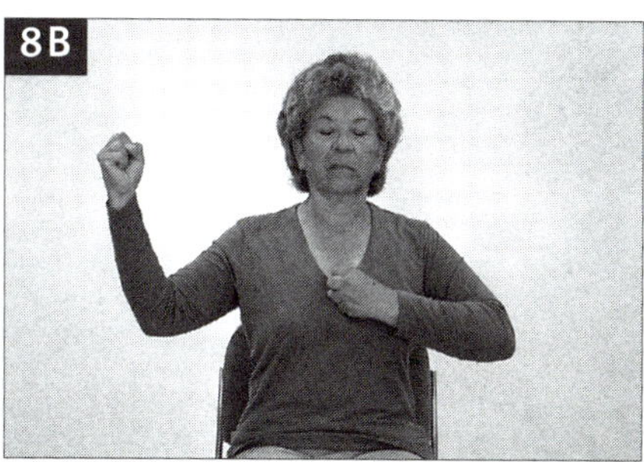
8B

Deeply relax on your back or in your chair for 11 to 22 minutes.

PART II Journey To Consciousness

PERHAPS YOU ARE NOTICING A PATTERN developing in our mandala. With God as the center, supported on all sides by Breath, the Word/Mantra and Yogic Science. In Part Two, we will add another layer – Karma, Dharma, Living Liberation, Reincarnation and Meditation – all are so fluidly interrelated, it is impossible to separate them. For example, in Part One, three of the topics discussed were Breath, the Chakras, and Identity. In Part Two, we will add another dimension to these topics by examining among other things, how the energy of the Chakras creates our heaven or hell on earth…and how identity determines karma…the relationship between breath and suicide. The interconnections are fascinating. Enjoy!

When Yogi Bhajan first introduced these concepts, my mind went on like a light bulb, because they were simple, straightforward and they made sense. They represented Truth. I felt hopeful that I have some say in the determination of my destiny.

Remembering the figure eight train track, I may not be able to always control the track, but I can choose to respond to what happens on the journey with consciousness. The most important aspect of all – I don't have to make the journey alone. The Infinite and like-minded people *(sangat)* are always with me as my touchstone and guides.

I hope you are finding the Process Exercises helpful, and I encourage you to continue with them. Feel free to return to Part One as a reference and to repeat your favorite process exercises. If you are writing down your reactions, you may want to periodically re-read them to give yourself a perspective of then and now. Your views and feelings will probably change during your evolving process.

CHAPTER 6

Karma, Dharma and Reincarnation

Wake up!
Now is the time!
Wake up!
Time is running out!
Wake up!
Sing God's praises and realize your destiny.
Karma makes you sleepy
Dharma wakes you up.
Wake up!
Leave your errors behind you.
Practice Raj Yoga.
Now is the time!
Wake up!
Yogi Bhajan
From Furmaan Khalsa

THE TIMES ARE SHAKING US TO WAKE UP. They are challenging us to drop our past karmas and live in dharma. The key point in the law of karma is self-responsibility in all we say, think and do. At every moment we have the choice to create our future.

In order to fully understand the Yogic philosophy of life and death, it is necessary to explore the concepts of karma (fate), dharma (destiny) and reincarnation. All Eastern paths acknowledge the theory of karma and the transmigration of souls from one form of life to another, until all karmas have been completed, and they are ready to be re-united with their Creator.

Karma

Every action or thought we have in life has a reaction or consequence. If I put my finger over a flame, my finger will be burned. If I drink alcohol and drive, I may get a ticket or even have an accident. If I steal or cheat, that energy will come back to me in some form. If I think negative thoughts about someone, that negativity will come back to haunt me. If I selflessly love someone, love will embrace me. If I work hard and project success, I will be successful. If I feel good about myself, I will attract others to me. Every action and thought is reflected back, negatively or positively. Instead of a judging God after death, punishing or rewarding us, our thoughts and actions have a built-in response during our lives. This is called the Law of Karma and is central to the whole Eastern philosophy. In Physics, it is known as Newton's Third Law – "for every action, there is an equal and opposite reaction."

The hook of karma is *Maya*. Remember back to Chapter One – *God Exists Within Us* – when we discussed basing our identity on the inner undying soul, instead of the external attachments of the world, including possessions, relationships and roles. Lets take that thought, now, to the next level. All of those external identities are Maya. Maya is an illusion, like a veil or a mist, which prevents us from experiencing our Higher Truth. The most obvious face of Maya is possessions, like cars, houses, clothes and money.

"The Zeitgeist Movie."

These things are not "bad" in themselves. They are actually a neutral medium; it is, rather, the consciousness of the person using them. If they have become one's identity, and he or she is using them purely as a means to gratify insecurity and greed at the expense of others, then they are Maya creating undesirable karma. If, on the other hand, one is using these things to also benefit others, the karma will come in the form of blessings. An example of the former might be an employer who exploits his workers for his personal economic benefit. In the latter, the employer might reinvest the profits into improved employee benefits.

Maya includes relationships, of which children and spouses can be the most luring. The roles we identify with, like father, doctor, executive, alcoholic or daughter, may keep us from realizing our True Identities. We may get trapped in the layers of these created karmas and have to face their consequences. Maya can be so clever, deceptive and addictive that it is difficult to break away from its grip. On the other hand, these relationships can be viewed as blessings or tests to maintaining our True Identity. The goal is to consciously, with compassion, courage and inner values, live the life of a warrior for truth.

My husband is the attorney for the New Mexico Medical Board. Doctors, who have been reported for questionable behavior, are brought before the Board for review. In one case, a senior doctor, very well-known and accomplished in his field, made a terrible medication error with a patient. Instead of reporting it to the other doctors involved and to the patient – and thus correcting the error – he tried to cover up his mistake. The doctor's son, also a doctor, found out and did not report the incident. The patient died. The only reason the error was revealed was due to the sensitivity and values of another treating doctor, a radiologist, who then investigated the case. His high ethical standards cost him his job. He was slandered by the two doctors in error and had to seek work out of town.

This is an excellent example of what we have been discussing. The senior doctor's behavior was based on his desire to protect his image as

You come, live, grow and process. It is called a life of karma. In the fluctuating wavelength of your life, you can be stuck on nothing or on people, or on God. Those who are stuck on nothing are in isolation. Those who are stuck on people are processing. Those who are stuck on God reach infinity.

YOGI BHAJAN

Your existence is truth, and that is God; but when you don't realize it, that is maya.

YOGI BHAJAN

Karma
Wherever she goes,
The fish is the queen of the ocean.
But when she bites the bait,
She struggles wildly.
Concentrate on the Naam,
You've already got enough Karma!
Many have been broken,
And many have been mended...
Keep an eye on yourself!
I am the friend of those Great Souls
Who have come under my protection in the end.
In their company...
Karma is ended.
YOGI BHAJAN
From Furmaan Khalsa

an accomplished doctor, more than his duty to serve the patient. The son, trapped in his identities of both doctor and son, could not put them aside and do what was right for the situation. "Captain Karma" bit both father and son; the consequences were severe. The radiologist based his identity on a higher truth. Even though he lost his job, he was a victorious spiritual warrior. This event may have changed the karmas of these individuals for lifetimes.

Whether we add more karmic cars to our train of life or release them is up to us. Life keeps presenting us with tests until the karmas are completed. Just when we think we are finished with an issue, it returns in a more subtle form to check our consciousness. I had a client who based her value on her relationships with men. The tendency was first seen in high school, when she always had to have a boyfriend to feel good about herself. As an adult, she went on to be sexually promiscuous. She felt poorly about herself and exhibited low vitality. Gradually she started to change. She noticed that the same issue would cycle back in more and more refined ways, like she would flirt at parties or seek the approval of men at work. Next she noticed she could contain the pattern in her thoughts and prevent any subsequent actions. Finally the thoughts were gone. She was free at last. How did she win her battle? I bet you can guess the answer. Yes, Kundalini Yoga and Meditation increased her awareness and cleared her subconscious mind of her self-destructive patterns. She was able to base her value and identity on her relationship with her Higher Self.

Besides our personal lives, we can see karma working on a national and global level. Global warming is a result of our excessive lifestyles. In the US, whales are no longer on the endangered list, because we now have laws to protect them. Most wars don't just happen but are the result of greed, power and misunderstandings. Everything has its cause and effect. In these cases, the good of the whole and the good of the future must be considered, instead of the immediate and limited gain.

Dharma

Our cause and effect will sow the seeds that will bear fruit in our next reincarnations (to be discussed next). The only thing that will break this continual cycle is to live dharma. How do we know the difference between karma and dharma? Karma will put us through the cycle of life; dharma will take us to the freedom of life. A path of karma or fate is filled with duality, relating to time and space. Karma is when our mind is our master, throwing us into the cycle of action/reaction. Dharma is our spiritual path or lifestyle. In a yogic lifestyle we call it our Sadhana, which includes practices that elevate our consciousness to live in a healthy, happy and holy way…basically to live our destiny and highest potential above time and space. When your mind is ruled by your Higher Consciousness, that is dharma. Dharma burns karma and can express itself in many forms, cultures and practices. It doesn't matter which path we choose. If we listen to our soul, we will know. All Dharmic Paths lead to dignity, which will lead to divinity, and divinity will lead to Infinity – union with the Creator. Just choose and live every breath with the prayer, *"May I live in 'pana,' the will of God."*

We can also have Dharmic Relationships, bonds with people who are also on a spiritual path – we call them sangat (or congregation). They may not be perfect in their behavior, but they are sincere and active in their spiritual practice. It can be said that when five sangat member are present, God is present. Sometimes that Supreme Force can act more efficiently through the physical form of a group of devotees, consciously working together for the higher good. Individual egos may be present, but in the group consciousness, they are more likely to be neutralized. True sangat gives us support but also lovingly challenges us when we start to go astray from our Truth. Sangat is there to share with us all life brings – the joys of marriage and birth, and the heartfelt agony of illness, hardship and death.

Life is based on karma – on action and reaction. It cannot change. But when you follow dharma, then action and reaction stop. The first rule of dharma is "do not react." Because if you see God in all and you see all action as His, then there is no need for you to react.

Yogi Bhajan

Meditation is not sitting down and closing the eyes. Meditation is seeing and reaching what is beyond the limited self. It gives a moment of beauty and bliss, where all you have is joy. When you direct your mind to that, that is. Your reactivity evaporates and life becomes supremely happy. Everything continues in the same way, but you have contentment, joy and excellence. That is dharma.

Yogi Bhajan

The following poem reflects the strength and comfort Guru Tej Kaur received from the Sadh Sangat, when her daughter (7 years old) died unexpectedly. More about this story in Chapter Eleven – *Children and Death.*

Sadh Sangat

I long for you, oh remover of pain
Oh integrator, oh healer of aloneness
Oh inspirer of the Name.

I sit in your presence
Dive into your midst
Experience your power
Am released from my pain.

I am drawn to your radiance

Where even God longs to abide
Your glory is breathless
I experience an Infinite Pride.

I am enticed by the sweet sound of the Name

The power of the voices becoming one flowing vein,
Merging, transcending time in that upward refrain.

I am in you
I am of you
You are mine to fulfill
You are everyone, no exceptions
All are included by their own free will.

You are God made manifest in the Body of His Saints
With the Power to heal, rebuild and employ.
The Pure Ones merged, amalgamated, an infinite play.

You attract through beauty
The power of the Word
I offer myself and allow myself to merge
All Glory belongs to God
But His Victory lies in His Pure Ones.

S.S. Guru Tej Kaur Khalsa

Living a dharmic life and doing your *sadhana* (daily spiritual practice) will not only bless you, it will extend to your family members as well. Your karmas are linked. As you erase your karmas with dharma, your relatives will benefit as well. In scriptures, it is said that seven generations before and after will be positively affected. You can see this at work in some of the true stories in this book.

When a woman is pregnant, the soul will enter her womb on the 120th day of pregnancy. All souls are pure. It is the subtle body that carries the karma of the previous life. The mother can attract the soul and purify the subtle body with her prayers.

There was once a queen who was told that she had attracted the soul of a demon. The child would be born very disfigured would make hell for her and the kingdom. Only five days after her 120th day, she could tell that something was very wrong inside of her. She went to her spiritual guide and said, "Master, oh my teacher, can you be so kind to bless me? What I have is what I have, what my karma is, my karma is?" He said, "From today onward, meditate on the Name of God. Go and do menial jobs and do them selflessly." She went out into poor places, cooked meals, served, washed dishes and fed the poor. She was a queen and had no lack of funds, but she did those menial jobs. When the child was born he had a serene smile, his hands were in a yogic mudra and there was a mark at this Third-Eye point. He was saintly and very meditative. The queen's dharma had purified the past karmas from the baby's subtle body.

Youth brings enthusiasm and high ideals. Nothing is impossible and one feels invincible. For "Dharma Seekers" aspirations may include living one's destiny, leaving a legacy for the next generations and finishing past karmas. The ultimate target, of course, is liberation, not having to return into another life. When I was 25 years old, these goals seemed reachable. Now that I am over 50, some of my spiritual siblings are experiencing a kind of spiritual pressure. "What if I can't finish my life's mission?" "What if I run out of time before I leave my legacy?" "I haven't overcome

Every person who walks away from his or her destiny is unhappy. Everyone who walks towards his or her destiny is happy.
Yogi Bhajan

The bait looks delicious! But acting from desire, over and over the hook of Karma catches us. A warning not to get stuck in desire motivated action-reaction consciousness, but to chant the Naam, live in Dharma and let our Karmas be ended forever.
Yogi Bhajan.

Life is the baby nursing on the mother's breast. He is nourished and receives what he needs in that lifetime. Death is the momentary detachment when he is between lifetimes, until another one begins again.
Anonymous Source

all of my fears yet." I nod in acknowledgment but also have to chuckle. In our sincere desire to pursue spirituality, our self-imposed expectations of perfection will only stunt our expansion.

It seems we're missing the point. Are we living our destiny according to our will or as God wills? Your mission may be to make AIDS medication available to all who need it. Mine may be to expand through the lessons of Multiple Sclerosis. Someone else's may be to greet Wal-Mart shoppers with a smile. Further, perhaps the mission itself is not as important as the consciousness in which we live. Perhaps our highest mission in life is to be consciously present in every moment of life – no matter how seemingly insignificant or inconsequential the quests.

Reincarnation

An Eastern Master was sitting with his students one day. One of the students asked him to explain the process of life and death. He described it in the following way:

> *Life and death can be compared to a mother nursing her baby. First she nurses him on one breast, which nourishes and satisfies him. When he has received all he can from that side, he is taken off that breast. For a few moments he is unattached. Then, his mother puts him on the other breast.*

Nearly 1 in 5 (18%) Americans believe in reincarnation, reflecting a slow change in views of life after death.

Each one of us has a soul, which has been housed in many forms, lifetime after lifetime. We went from minute forms, to multi-cellular, to sea creatures, to air creatures, to mammals, until after 8.4 million lifetimes, we are granted a human body. We may also reincarnate many times in a human form. As a human, we have a consciousness, and each life is given to us with a certain number of breaths to complete specific karmas or lessons, like doing a job, until we can quit with a clean record and finally merge with God, our Infinite source. Sometimes these lessons take a long time to finish, a long lifetime, into old age. Other times, they may be completed as a young adult or even as a baby. Some souls may mature faster than others, in the Will of the Creator. This concept is comforting, because since life is a continual karmic process, death is never final. It is never a tragedy, no matter the age of the person.

TYPES OF DEATH

Death of a Child

The death of a child is especially difficult to accept. A child evokes our biggest attachment and joy in life. But, if one can truly accept these concepts, the death of a baby or child is not seen as a tragedy or injustice. The child was not cheated out of life, they just finished sooner what they needed to do in this lifetime. The death of a child is never easy for the survivors. The loss and grief is still deeply felt, but according to the yogic philosophy, it is a blessing for the child. We will discuss children and death in more detail in Chapter Eleven.

Death Hits You Five Times

It is a law that no one shall die the first time death attacks. Yogi Bhajan tells us that God is required to give us four warnings. At the fifth time, we will be taken. Before death can hit us, two things must happen – time and space. It is predetermined that we are to be born and die at a specific longitude and latitude of the earth, which shall not change. There is a very powerful mantra to chant before you turn on your car – *Aad Guray Nameh, Jugad Guray Nameh, Sat Guray Nameh, Siri Guru Devay Nameh*. It is a mantra for protection that puts you at a different place in space.

Keeping in mind what we have learned in this chapter, we will see that there are three kinds of death – Accidental Death, Karmic Death and Liberated Death.

Karma decides at what longtitude and latitude you are to be born. Karma decides what physical, mental and earthly facilities you will have. Karma decides what your spiritual faculties will be. You have only one right. You can decide to excel and then all karmas will be dropped and dharma will start. Commitment to dharma is giving yourself the karma to excel?

Yogi Bhajan
(Khalsa Women's Training Cam[p, 1983 p. 182)

Accidental Death

The exception is the unique situation of an accidental death. During an instantaneous accidental death, such as a violent car crash, the soul, in shock and confusion, doesn't have time to prepare for its departure. This usually occurs when the soul for karmic reasons has to be quickly transferred from one body into another. In these cases, the soul does not go through the purification of the ethers (to be discussed in Chapter Nine); it leaves the physical body through the Navel Point (not the Crown Chakra) and reincarnates straight into the fetus of a pregnant woman within 24 hours of death. There can be exceptions in accidental deaths. If the person's consciousness is one with the Infinite, he or she may obtain liberation.

Karmic Death

In a karmic death, the deceased hasn't finished their lessons in the present life and must be reincarnated into the fetus of a pregnant woman to continue that process. It's not a big deal. If we have not completed the job and the lessons this time, we come back again and again until it's done.

Liberated Death

A liberated death is one in which the person has finished. They do not need to take another physical body and remain merged in the Infinite. I can imagine that it is a very blissful experience. We get a slight glimpse of this existence when we meditate. In the next chapter – *Jiwan Mukht*, we will explore how liberation is possible even in life.

It is important to emphasize, though, that there is no pressure here. It doesn't matter how many lives we need. The whole point is to sincerely and humbly develop our consciousness in life…that just as we live each moment of our life, so is the moment of our death.

Suicide

Intertwined in this discussion is the incident of suicide. Since none of us knows when our given number of breaths or our lessons will be completed, suicide poses a real question. The soul has been committed to so many breaths. If the body is gone, where is the soul to go? By committing suicide, the process has been interrupted. After death the soul enters the Subtle Body, which has no connection to the Pranic Body, meaning that the breaths cannot be completed. If the breaths are not used, the soul cannot leave the magnetic field of the earth. Anyone who believes in this yogic philosophy may need to seriously reconsider the consequences of suicide. Could it mean that one would have to start all over again, having to wait another 8.4 million life times just to be granted another human body?

I would like to end this chapter by telling a story about the inevitability of death. None of us knows when we are to die. Since we don't know when our karmas will be completed, we don't know when death will greet us. Wouldn't it seem logical, then, that we would be wise to prepare for death when we are living? This thought will be discussed more thoroughly in Part Three. The following story exemplifies the inevitability of death:

This story comes from the Middle East.

Once a student went into a pub in a town in Persia He was enjoying himself and having a good time with his friends. Later, the Angel of Death entered the pub. Recognizing him, the student became fearful and left. Fearing the Angel of Death, he went to the other side of the country to get away from him.

A few days later, the Angel of Death was again in the same pub. He asked the owner if he knew the student. The owner said that he had, indeed, just seen him a few days before. The Angel of Death remarked that that was very interesting, because he was to meet him in a couple of days on the other side of the country. Taken from *The Tales of the Arabian Knights*.

PROCESS EXERCISES

1 A lot was presented in this chapter. Did anything in particular jump out at you? Reflect upon it. Write about it.

2 Think of a time you created karma. What in you created it? Have you been able to heal that tendency and thus erase that karma? Is there more to do? Do you have a plan?

3 Complete one or all of the following meditations. How did you feel afterwards?

TEN STEPS TO PEACE

To Remove Bad Memories and Painful Experiences

This meditation is also effective in dealing with the daily stress of relationships in the workplace, school, home and community. Clean it out before it becomes a monster.

This meditation takes care of phobias, fears, and neuroses. It can remove unsettling thoughts from the past that surface into the present. It can take difficult situations in the present and release them into the hands of Infinity. All this can be done in just forty-seconds!

YOGI BHAJAN

How To Do It:

1. **Lower the eyelids** until the eyes are only open 1/10th. Concentrate on the tip of the nose. Silently say *Wahe Guru* in the following manner: *Wha* – mentally focus on the right eye. *Hay* – mentally focus on the left eye. *Guroo* – mentally focus on the tip of the nose.
2. **Inhale** and remember the encounter or incident which happened to you.
3. **Exhale** and mentally say *Wahe Guru* in the above manner.
4. **Inhale.** Visualize and re-live the actual feeling of the encounter.
5. **Exhale** and again mentally repeat *Wahe Guru*.
6. **Inhale** and reverse roles in the encounter you are remembering. Become the other person and experience their perspective.
7. **Exhale** and mentally repeat *Wahe Guru*.
8. **Inhale.** Forgive the other person and forgive yourself.
9. **Exhale** and mentally repeat *Wahe Guru*.
10. **Inhale.** Let go of the incident and release it into the Universe.

Repeat if necessary. Relax, breathing long and deep for an additional minute.

STRESS RELIEF AND CLEARING THE EMOTIONS OF THE PAST

This meditation is especially useful for dealing with stressful relationships and with past family issues.

How to do it
Put your hands at the center of your chest with the tips of the thumbs touching each other and each of the fingers touching the corresponding fingers on the opposite hand. There is space between the palms. The fingertips are pointing upward. Look at the tip of your nose and breathe 4 times per minute: inhale 5 seconds, hold 5 seconds, exhale 5 seconds. Continue for 11 minutes or until you feel relief from the stress.

RIP AWAY THE CAUSE AND EFFECT OF KARMA 

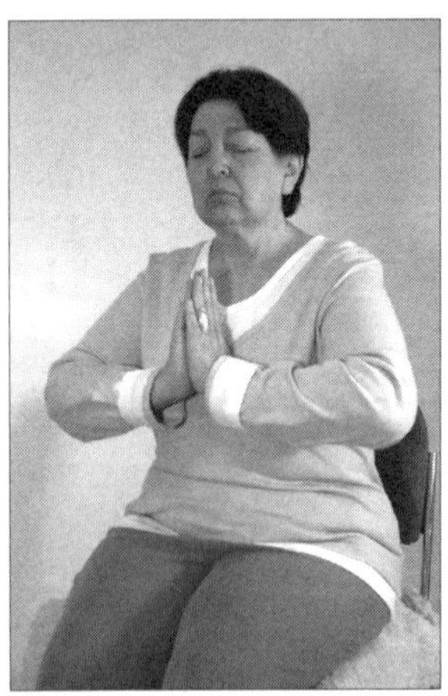

You can do this simple meditation every day. It will rip away the dreadful cause and effect of your karmas by balancing you. In the middle of the meditation, you may freak out, as the rubbing of the hands kicks out your monster energy. At this time, you must steady yourself and stick with it.

How to do it
Be sitting in Easy Pose with the hands in Prayer Mudra in front of your chest.

Eyes: The eyes are closed.

Mantra: Chant rhythmically out loud ***Sat Naam Sat Naam Sat Naam Jee, Wha-hay Guroo, Wha-hay Guroo, Wha-hay Guroo Jee*** (Refer to the accompanying CD for correct pronunciation – 5 or you can buy the instrumental tape *Dhuni,* at Ancient Healing Ways.) Pull the navel as you chant.

Mudra: Slide the hands up and down across the mounds of the hands in rhythm with the mantra. Be constant and consistent.

Time: Continue for 11 minutes.

To End: Inhale deeply, hold, press the hands together in Prayer Mudra as tightly as you can, and stretch the spine upwards. Exhale. Repeat 2 more times. On the last inhale move the energy from the base of the spine to your crown and from the crown to your base 3 times. Relax.

Live Beyond Karma

(Taken from a Yogi Bhajan lecture given in Espanola, NM, USA, February 4th, 2000.)

Every day you want to live. While living, do you produce energy to live, or do you use energy to live? Do emotions and commotions guide your life, or do you guide your own self-esteem, reality and ecstasy? It is that deep inner strength by which a human lives – I am, I am. That is God in us. How you die does not matter. Do you have a legacy behind? If you do not have self-control, self-knowledge and self-awareness, you will be lazy, lousy, complaining, miserable and without manners, sobriety, calmness and depth.

There is a difference between people who talk and people who practice – when there is an avalanche, they stand tall. That human quality is very precious. Even if you can see God, you are useless. So long as you cannot share, you are good for nothing. Actions should be by the call of duty, not of emotions. It is a very difficult way of life. It challenges the very core of human essence. It integrates individual purity and piety with the entire universe. And there is no running away, no hiding, no weakness.

You come, live, grow and process. It is called a life of karma. In the fluctuating wavelength of your life, you can be stuck on nothing or on people or on God. Those who are stuck on nothing are in isolation; those who are stuck on people are processing; those who are stuck on God reach Infinity.

Meditation is not sitting down and closing the eyes. Meditation is seeing and reaching what is beyond the limited self. It gives a moment of beauty and bliss, where all you have is joy. When you direct your mind to that, that is. Your reactivity evaporates and life becomes supremely happy. Everything continues in the same way, but you have contentment, joy and excellence. That is dharma.

Yogi Bhajan

Personal strength is so strong that the Will of God becomes weaker than the man. Make yourself so pure and lofty that, before planning, God should ask you, "What is your opinion?"

The tragedy is that you prostitute yourself. This most precious life God gave you, you lose for nothing. You think you are enjoying – you are putting another brick on your grave! Finally, under the weight of your own karma, you will be destroyed. Prostituting God's gifts, body, mind and spirit, you shall never get reality, even if God grants immunity from this sinful action...because actions have reactions, equal and opposite.

We have the power to create in us the power we need. Screwing around is not what the body was made for. We are part animal, part human and part angel. Our anger is not angelic. That is why we suffer. If you want to drive a car with no brakes, you are sure to have an accident. There are people who talk on a loudspeaker all their lives – no one cares. There are people who say two words – the world listens to them.

SAT KRIYA VARIATION *Angelic Power*

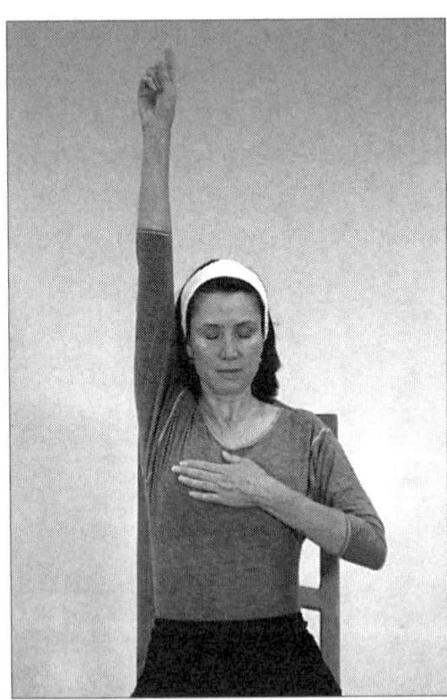

Part I. Sit with a straight spine. Raise the right arm up straight, pointing the index finger. The left hand rests on your heart. Eyes are closed.

Chant "***Sat Naam***" in a constant rhythm, about eight times every ten seconds. Chant the sound "***Sat***" from the navel, and pull the umbilicus all the way in toward the spine. On "***Naam***" relax the belly.

Time: Continue for 11 minutes. During the last minute whistle it – it is difficult but will give you internal relaxation.

To End: inhale deeply, hold, stretch the spine and balance the body. Cannon Fire Exhale (powerfully exhale through the "O" of the mouth). Inhale again, hold and raise both hands straight up pointing the index fingers, stretch the spine, uplift the diaphragm and stretch the navel point. Cannon Fire Exhale. Inhale again, hold and interlock the fingers overhead, lift up your body and stretch the spine. Cannon Fire Exhale.

Relax.

Part II. Sit straight in a chair. Extend the right arm with the index finger pointing forward. The left hand rests on your lap. Rotate the right hand in small clockwise circles as fast as you can.

Time: Continue for 3 minutes.

Relax.

MEDITATION FOR THE ARCLINE AND TO CLEAR THE KARMAS

This meditation is to clear the karma that has been stored up in the arcline. You will experience "***Wahe Guru***." The power of Infinity is not outside of you – it is inside of you. When "I" and Infinity merge we become divine; otherwise, there is duality, which brings misery.

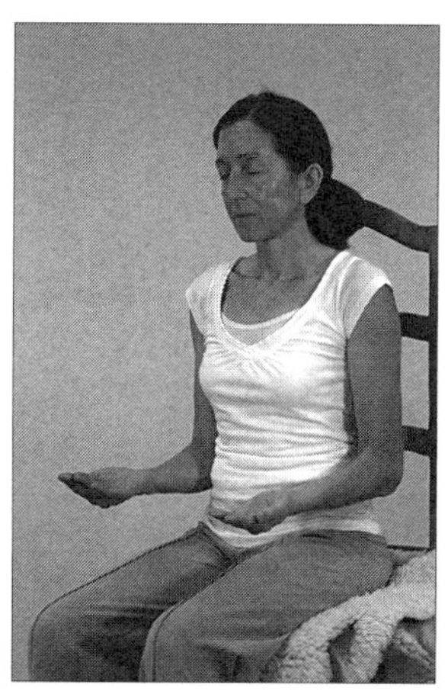

Mudra: Sit with a straight spine. Relax the elbows down by the sides, and bring the forearms straight out in front of your body, palms flat and facing up. Have the palms slightly cupped and place them directly over the thighs.

Movement: Bring the arms up, back behind the head, stretching the hands and arms as far back over the shoulders as you can. Imagine you are scooping water and throwing it through your arcline, over your shoulders,

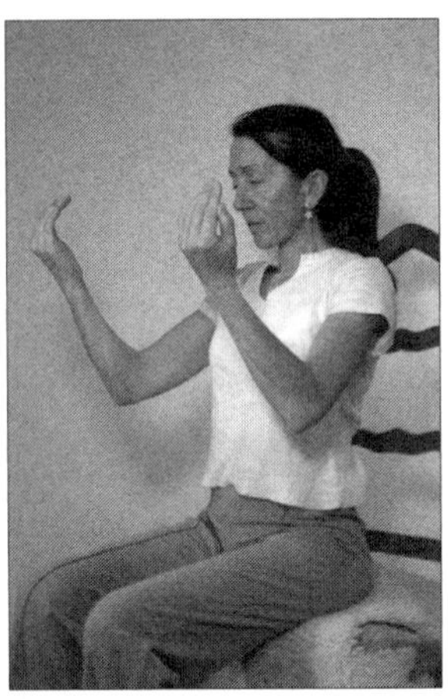

with a flick of the wrists. The movement is smooth and gracefully flows along with the lyrics and rhythm of the music.

Music: "***Wahe Guru, Wahe Guru, Wahe Guru, Wahe Jio***" (Refer to accompanying CD for correct pronunciation – 6 or contact Ancient Healing Ways or Spirit Voyage for Giani Ji's version of this mantra.) On each "***Wha-hay Guroo,***" as well as on the "***Wha-hay Jeeo,***" do one complete round – scooping up, throwing over your shoulders, and come back to the starting position.

Eyes: Closed.

Time: 31 minutes.

To End: Inhale, and stretch your hands back as far as possible, hands right behind your head. Hold 10–15 seconds. Exhale. Repeat 3 times. Relax.

CHAPTER 7

Jiwan Mukht

Liberated While Yet Alive

To die is an art. Everything on this planet, every act is done so that dying may be graceful. There's no dharma, there's no meditation needed. There is nothing. We can go through the karmas all right. All knowledge of spirituality is to mend one thing only – that when we die, we die in grace, without fear, without vengeance, without desire. We should just love to die, that moment, that meditative moment…at that moment, everything is decided. There is no afterwards. Those who seek afterwards get into the cycle of karma.

Yogi Bhajan

INTRICATELY INTERTWINED with what we have just said about karma and dharma, and in fact, everything that has been said up to this point, are concepts about hell and heaven and liberation. Negative karma creates hell on earth (and beyond). As dharma burns bad karma, heaven or liberation can be experienced while alive (and beyond). On the Sikh Path, there is a beautiful concept called **Jiwan Mukht**. **Jiwan** means life, **Mukht** means free or liberated. We can achieve Jiwan-Mukht, liberation while yet alive. Expanding upon that theme, let's look at its various aspects.

The first aspect – freedom, wisdom and the experience of God or the Infinite Self can be realized while we are still alive. It is not the physical body, but the mind that creates a separation from God, that constitutes human bondage and agony (hell on earth). Our imperfection and suffering in this world is due to our ignorance of our own true nature, our Divine nature. When we are in the most anguish, we have forgotten in the core of our being that we are a piece in the mosaic of all Creation. We disengage from what gives us life and sustenance, that loving, ever present energy which will never abandon us. Realizing our relationship to our Infinite consciousness or God and experiencing the true nature of the self alleviates this suffering, bringing heaven on earth.

Remembering or not remembering our connection to the Source will have a profound impact on our consciousness. This brings us to the second aspect of "Jiwan-Mukht." The consciousness in which we live will follow us to death and beyond. In other words, if we are living a honorable, fearless, joyous, God-conscious life on earth, we will carry that state with us when we die. If we are fearful, guilt-ridden or angry, we will bring that state with us to death. The consciousness in which we live is the same in which we die.

Fear binds us to our senses, passions and ego – finite shackles, which unfortunately are all too familiar to us, because we can feel them. They somehow remind us that we are alive. The down side is that as they are ego based, propelled by our smallness, they thus create pain…instead of spirit based, propelled by our greatness, and creating expansion.

Some of our greatest failures in life are the result of our expectations or illusions of what we desire, perhaps originating from a childhood fantasy or our parent's unfulfilled dreams. These attachments thwart our opportunities – like being confined in a box with no openings – we can't see beyond our self-imposed prison. Conversely, living fearlessly means surrendering to what is. It allows us to flow with the creativity of the Master Planner, expanding us to limitless possibilities (heaven).

I am reminded of a member of my spiritual community who, unhappy in his marriage, went to Yogi Bhajan for counsel. Yogi Bhajan told him that he was consumed with his fantasy about what he thought marriage should be. He gave the man a special meditation to do for forty days, telling him that happiness would come if he could drop his illusions of the past, accept what is and build on the positives. Today, this man's marriage is thriving. His personal motto in all areas of his life has become – "Accept what is and build on the positives."

Living fearlessly does not mean that there is a negation of the mind, our will and the senses; in fact, we can develop them to be functioning in an acute state of awareness, while maintaining equilibrium and harmony – thus aiding fearlessness. Through a daily spiritual practice, our negative ego and passions can be transcended into our true nature, orchestrated by a finely tuned intuition, ending our seemingly endless karma of pain and suffering. We will be living fearlessly…and thus joyously – we will become deathless. (One of the meditations at the end of this chapter is for deathlessness – **Pran Bandha Mantra Meditation**.)

When living from our ego consciousness, instead of our God consciousness, most of the time our energy is constantly fluctuating, rising and falling between heaven and hell. Satisfying our desires, we think we are in heaven. Blocked from gratification, we drop into hell. We don't realize that hell is resistance…struggle, while heaven is acceptance… surrender. Hell is the tense jaw of "Me-ness." Heaven

A state of fearlessness is the highest state. That is why Guru Nanak referred to God as NIRBHAO – without fear. Folks, there is no death. Death is what? Going home. …A fearless mind is the highest state of consciousness, because when the mind is fearless then you can go home. Otherwise, you are homeless. If you can develop your mind through the creativity of your experience – that you can experience fearlessness – death will not mean a thing to you. When death doesn't mean anything, you become deathless.

Yogi Bhajan

Death is a process where your consciousness does not exist within the control of your ego.
Yogi Bhajan

is the expanded "We-ness" of the heart, when we dare to reach out and unconditionally love. Our mood and energy swings often reflect an imbalance in the Chakras. For example, a block in the lower three Chakras may result in emotions of fear, guilt and revenge – living hell. The greatest harmony, balance and benefit come when the energy moves in a rhythmic flow up and down the Chakras. Kundalini Yoga is our tool to manage our own Chakra balance and therefore forklift our own energy and consciousness – living in heaven. Refer back to Chapter Four, where you can review the science of the Chakras and will find **The Seven-Wave Meditation** and **Sat Kriya**. Both balance the Chakras.

There is a story of a great Samurai who comes to visit the Zen master, Hakuin. The Samurai approaches the Zen master and bows dutifully, asking, "Sir, I wish to understand the differences between heaven and hell." The Zen master looks at the Samurai and, eying him from head to toe, says, "I would tell you, but I doubt that you have the keenness of wit to understand." The Samurai pulls back in astonishment. "Do you know to whom you are speaking?" He huffs. "Not much," says the Zen master, "I really think you are probably too dull to understand." "What?" says the Samurai. "How can you talk to me like this?" "Oh, don't be silly," says the Zen master. "Who do you think you are? And that thing hanging by your waist, you call that a sword? It's more like a butter knife." The Samurai, becoming enraged, draws his sword and raises it over his head to strike the Zen master. "Ah," says the Zen master. "That is hell." The Samurai's eyes shine with recognition as his heart opens and he bows low, sheathing his sword. "Now that," says the Zen master, "is heaven."

Forgiveness is a key to happiness (heaven on earth). Without it we will be in an unending spiral of pain and living hell. Remembering back to Chapter One – *God Exists Within Us* – we first talked about the "divine trinity" – your Creator, the Guru within you (your own intrinsic inner wisdom) and you. All of us are this trinity. There is no difference, no separation between us. If we can live in this trinity, seeing the God in all – seeing God in each other and ourselves – forgiveness will prevail. We will be able to forgive others and ourselves. We will live as God's children. A good meditation for forgiveness can be found at the end of this chapter – *Meditation to Conquer Self-Animosity*.

A dear friend of mine, Sat Jiwan Singh Khalsa, the Director of the Manhattan Yoga Center, poignantly describes his experience participating in a prayer service at "Ground Zero," the site of the September 11, 2001 World Trade Center disaster, and in so doing gives us a graphic example of God's love and Union between his children amongst intolerable suffering.

> *For an extremely brief moment the thought passed through my mind that maybe an enchanted fog had descended over the towers rendering them invisible, but I caught myself. I felt my chest tighten. This was not a fairy tale; there was nothing enchanted here– no sorcerers, no spells, and definitely no invisible towers, just mind-numbing, heart-wrenching reality.*
>
> *I finished praying and stepped off the stage. An extremely large fireman in full gear was looking at me. He approached to within a foot or two of me, looked at me, and sweetly said, 'Can I have a hug?' And then he gave me a fantastic hug. It was wonderful. He was a chaplain from the Chicago Fire Department…And then he asked, 'Can I have another hug?' What an amazing man of God, of love, and of peace in the midst of hell. A real hero!*
>
> *He inspired me. And God inspired me. I believe this experience to be a metaphor for what we need to be doing now – healing each other with heart-to-heart contact. Prayer is a great healer. But now, more than ever, I think we also really need heartfelt, loving contact. Just as the fireman did for me, we should all be ready to rescue those in need. We*

God has given you everything. If you want to give something, give forgiveness. First forgive yourself. Then forgive your environments, and then forgive all those whom you cannot forgive. That is the beginning of greatness of character.
Yogi Bhajan

can all be heroes if we can overcome our shyness and our fear and step out and touch someone. Let the hand of God work for you like it worked for me. And let the love flow – we can all use it.

(Aquarian Times Magazine, Volume 1, Number 4, Winter 2001, P.10.)

Butterflies count not in months but in moments and have time enough.
RABINDRANATH TAGORE

3. This leads us right into the third aspect of Jiwan-Mukht. Life is not today and death tomorrow. Both exist right now. We can either say "yes" or "no" to life. Each of us must ask the question, am I living or am I dying?

What does this all mean, saying "yes" or "no" to life? Take a moment to think about it. When have you felt really open and alive? Imagine a particular incident and consider how it affected you. What did your body look like? How did you move? Did your voice have a certain quality to it? How was your breathing? What were your thoughts? What were you feeling inside? Consider all of your sensations and ponder over them. Were you feeling good about yourself? Did it affect your behavior? Then, do the same process when you were feeling constricted or dead. Which state felt better? Which took more or less energy? It's all our choice. We can say "no" to life, allowing a part of us to wither away and die. Or we can say "yes," allowing life to expand us.

Saying yes to life means taking risks. It means daring to try something new, to be different. Have you ever heard someone say, "I'm too old to try that" or "That's a bad idea, it will never work." Isn't it really their minds that have shriveled into atrophy? They constrict, not allowing the impossible to become possible. Have you ever seen a parent tell a child their idea was impossible, and then the child made it happen? Who is dead in that case? I know an eighty-five year old woman who refuses to allow death to catch her. She volunteers with "Meals On Wheels," teaches tap dancing at the community college, plays golf with lady friends and takes long walks on the beach with her dog. Her attitude is positive, enjoying every moment of life. She jokes that she wants to die with her tap shoes on. Her friend sits home, watching TV all day, worrying that she is going to die soon. On some level, she has already died.

Starting right this moment say, "yes" to something in your life you've said "no" to before. Take some deep breaths, letting that life force fill you. As you exhale, let go of your fear and hesitation. Start small, saying, "yes" to little things. Gradually build up to bigger and more significant things. When my husband was 49 years old, he learned how to white water kayak. With his long white beard, his much younger kayak buddies call him "River Daddy." When he's on the river, he's in heaven.

Saying "yes" to life also means allowing parts of us to die. It means letting go of old or negative habits, ideas and thoughts, which may not serve us any longer. They may have served a previous purpose, which is no longer, a part of our reality. Let them go, let them die. When we are able to do this, a vacuum is created, making room for the birth of new ideas and habits, which may be more appropriate to our present situation. Each day is a new beginning, a rebirth and each night is a closing or release. In this way, life can be an exciting journey, taking in and letting go, living it to the fullest, until our very last breath. All of life becomes a natural flow of life and death. (The three meditations included at the end of Chapter Six – **Ten Steps To Peace**, **Stress Relief and Clearing The Emotions Of The Past**, and **Rip Away The Cause And Effect Of Karma** will help you clear the past, allowing for the new to emerge.)

The fourth aspect of Jiwan-Mukht relates to serving. As God Conscious beings, we are in the world. Historically, yogis and holy men spent their lives meditating in caves, isolating themselves from the rest of society. In this era, we can be ascetic within and secular without. We are like the lotus flower, with its roots in the mud and its flower floating on the water, untouched by the dirt. Whether we are a street sweeper or a brain surgeon, we can do everything with a consciousness of service. An ingredient of our lifetime pursuit can include sharing our spiritual

This isn't what I expected it to be. This is all new, because my expectations about me being old didn't have this stroke in it. The suffering comes when you try to hold on to continuity – like things I can't do. I can't shift my car. I got a new car before I stroked. And now I get into that car in the seat next to the driver. My attendant drives the car. And, I can either be a driver, which is going to make me suffer on that trip, or I can be somebody who is chauffeured.

Ram Das *speaks in the movie Fierce Grace.*

knowledge for the good of all. The light is too vast to keep contained; the Aquarian Age is requesting that we share it with everyone.

Yogi Bhajan often challenged us to think about what legacy we want to leave to the world. "What do you want to be remembered for?" he'd ask us. This legacy not only involves our accomplishments that will live beyond us but our acts of kindness and service.

My Grandmother, Nana to me, lived during World War I and II and the Great Depression. Through it all, she single-handedly raised my mother and owned and operated a custom drapery shop in Beverly Hills. She made all the draperies, pillow covers and bedspreads herself and gave advise on interior design; many Hollywood movie stars were her customers. This is only the minor part of my Nana's legacy. For in my family, what she is known for is her sweetness. I never heard her say a mean word to or about anyone. She accepted and loved us all for who we were without hesitation or conditions. She was not a particularly "religious" person, but what is more saintly than kindness. That was her legacy.

May we improve ourselves each day. This is the time on Earth where we have to leave behind an impact, a legacy, so that people can find tranquility, peace and grace. Sat Nam.
Yogi Bhajan

What legacy do you want to leave to the world?

The fifth and last aspect of Jiwan-Mukht has to do with our preparation for death. We prepare for death by how we live. The quality of our life will depend upon our understanding and preparation for death. There is a story of a Zen master who asked a student, "Are you prepared to die?" If you are not willing to die, you are not ready to "surrender to life."

Where there is kindness there is God.
Yogi Bhajan

In India a long time ago, there was a tribe called the Shivites that worshipped Shiva, the Lord of death and liberation. They realized that there has to be a respect for death so that there may be a good life. If a person does not understand death, he does not understand life. If a human fears death, he fears life.

The American Indians developed an extraordinary technique to prepare for death by using a death chant. It was used to maintain contact with the Great Spirit in time of threat or stress, such as when riding a runaway horse, confronted by a dangerous animal or when injured or ill. Immediately, the death chant came into their mind. It became a part of them, always available in a time of need. It created a familiarity with the unfamiliar – death.

In the Hindu tradition, there is another instance of this kind of presence of life/death. It is taught and practiced that to die with God's name on your lips is a way of consciously returning to the Source. In an instant, one can drop the mind's projection of the world and just be one with God. When Mahatma Gandhi was assassinated he said, "Ram," as he fell. Ram is one of the names of God in the Hindu tradition. Gandhi lived and died with Ram on his lips and in his heart.

In Kundalini Yoga, we use special mantras, called *Pran Sutras*, or "master keys" for this purpose. They are to be used in life and become such a habit that at the time of death, one automatically chants it. Chapter Ten – *Rehearsing Death* – includes a complete explanation and list of these mantras.

When a car cuts in front of us, almost causing an accident, are we cursing the other driver or can we automatically begin our pran sutra? When we are lying in bed in pain, can we focus on our Long Deep Breathing with the mantra Sat Nam, or are we fearful and angry? When one of our children is asserting his or her identity apart from us, are we angry and threatened or can we see it as a natural sequence of growth and expansion? It is an attitude about life, which becomes such a habit, that we automatically switch to at the time of death. We have to find our Jiwan-Mukht, spiritual connection, now. Waiting until death will be too late. It has to be cultivated and practiced during life, to improve the quality of our life and the quality of our death.

Try to live innocent, straight, calm, quiet and peaceful.
Yogi Bhajan

PROCESS EXERCISES

There is a lot to think about in this chapter. Take your time. You may want to read all or parts of it more than one time. Reflect on all of the interconnections between the concepts we have discussed so far.

1 Did any of the aspects of Jiwan-Mukht especially speak to you in your life right now? Which ones? Why?

2 How did you relate to the Yogi Bhajan quote about fearlessness and deathlessness? Did any light bulbs go on?

3 Choose something to say "yes" to or "no" to in your life. Make a plan about it.

4 What do you want your legacy to be? Write an obituary for a newspaper.

5 Reread The Five Sutras for the Aquarian Age presented at the end of Chapter One on page 23. How do these sutras help us live the concepts of Jiwan-Mukht?

6 Choose a Pran Sutra from Chapter Ten and begin to practice it. Try using it in stressful situations. How does it feel?

7 Practice one or all of the meditations below. How did you feel afterwards?

PRAN BANDHA MANTRA MEDITATION

Pran Bandha Mantra means that mantra, or sound combination, that collects, binds, and commands the life force or prana. In our usual non-liberated state, we are controlled by our attachments. We become attached to our finite identity, to time, space and intensity of emotion. This mantra takes you beyond those finite attachments. It opens the door to another dimension of the Self. It merges you into the unlimited sea of *prana* and life.

This mantra forges a link between you as a finite unit magnetic field and the universal, creative magnetic field of energy that we call consciousness. The mantra is from Guru Nanak's *Japji (*Various stanzas or Paurees of Japji will be presented in Appendix II*)*. One who practices this to perfection experiences deathlessness. You can merge into the greater pranic body (universal energy) at the time of death and therefore become deathless. Prayers and mental desires become much more effective. This meditation can give you the capacity to embody a divine personality, and to become creative and fearless.

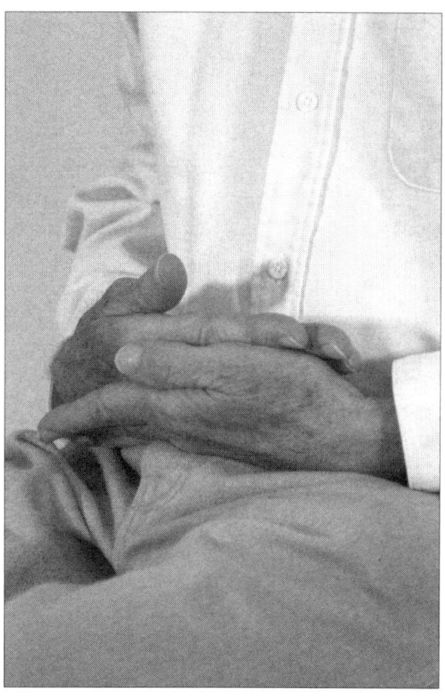

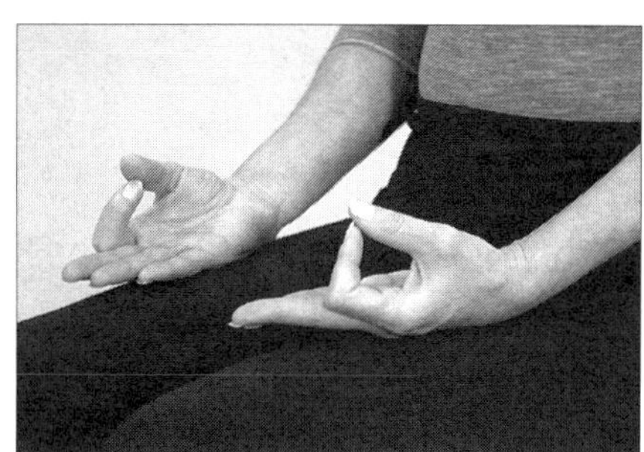

How to do it

Sit with a straight spine, with a light Neck Lock *(Jalandhar Bandh).*

Eye Position: With the eyes closed, focus at the Brow Point, rolling the eyes up slightly.

Mudra: Let the hands rest in the lap, right hand into the left palm. Or just sit with both hands in *Gyan Mudra*. Become completely still, physically and mentally, like a calm ocean. Listen to the chant for a minute. Feel its rhythm in every cell. Then join in the mantra. (The pronunciation of this mantra is on the accompanying CD – 7. Musical versions of this mantra are available from Ancient Healing Ways or Spirit Voyage on Resource Page) "Pavaan Pavaan"

Mantra: *Pavan Pavan Pavan Pavan*
Para Paraa, Pavan Guroo
Pavan Guru, Wha-Hay Guroo
Wha-Hay Guroo, Pavan Guroo

Time: Continue for 11–31 minutes.

MEDITATION TO CONQUER SELF-ANIMOSITY

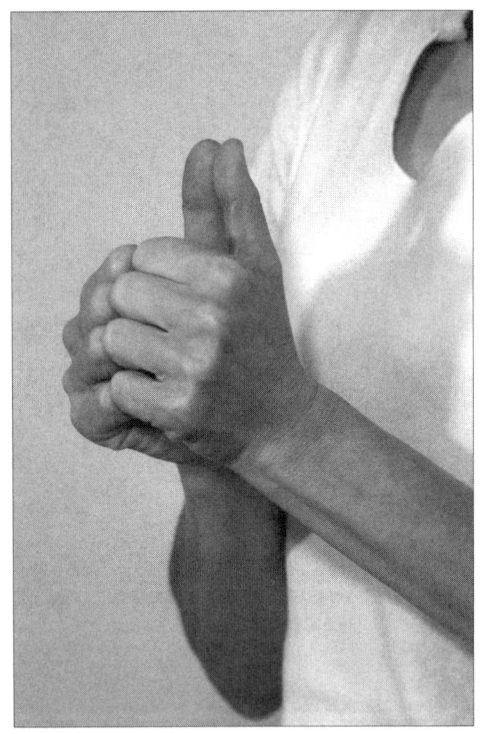

Our greatest enemy is our self. Self-defeating behaviors and attitudes occur when we do not accept ourselves. Our self-animosity distracts us from the real gift of life: the capacity to confront and experience the self in relationship to the Unknown Infinity of our self. This meditation conquers the state of self-animosity and gives us the ability to maintain a consciousness in support of the core self. The result is forgiveness.

How to do it

Sit with a straight spine, with a light *Jalandhar Bandh* (Neck Lock, as in previous meditation)

Mudra: Relax the arms at the sides and raise forearms up and in so that hands are in front of chest at the level of the heart. Draw the hands into fists and point the thumbs straight up toward the sky. Press the fists together in such a manner that the thumbs and fists are touching. The palms are toward each other. This meditation requires the upper torso to be held straight, without rocking back and forth.

Eyes: Fix the eyes at the tip of the nose.

There is no required mantra other than the subtle sound of the breath.

Breath: **Inhale** through the nose.
Exhale completely through the mouth.
Inhale deeply and smoothly through the mouth.
Exhale through the nose.

To End: Inhale and stretch the arms up over the head. Keep the stretched position as you take 3 more deep breaths. Relax.

RELATE TO YOUR DEATHLESSNESS

This meditation can help us get rid of our id, the ego. In this mantra, we are singing to our own deathlessness. This will help us leave a legacy of excellence.

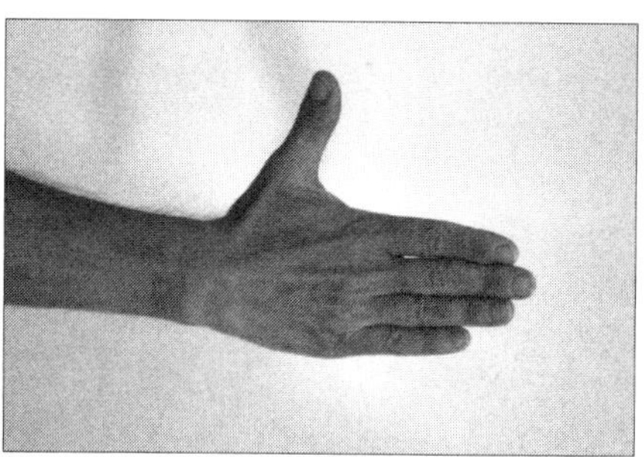

Mudra: Sit with a straight spine. Extend the arms straight out to the sides, parallel to the ground, with no bend in the elbows. The right palm is flat and faces down. The left palm is flat and faces up. The palms and fingers should be very stiff and tough, like iron. Keep the thumbs separated and stretched as far as possible from the fingers.

Eyes: Stare at the tip of the nose.

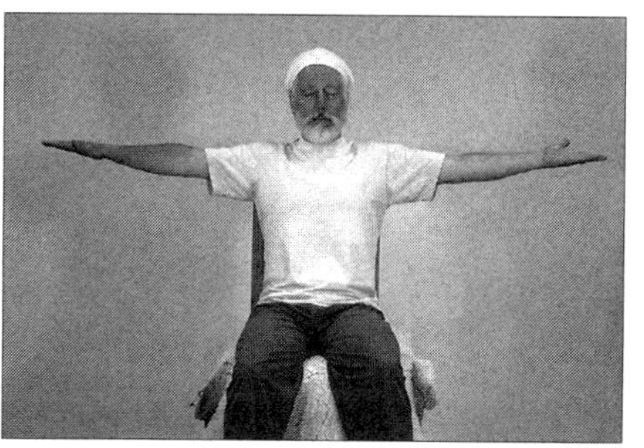

Mantra: ***Sat Siree Siree Akal Siree Akal Maha Akal, Maha Akal Sat Naam Akal Moorat Wha-hay Guroo*** (Refer to accompanying CD for correct pronunciation – 8.)

This is the Aquarian March sung by Nirinjan Kaur. Sing along with the tape. Ancient Healing Ways or Spirit Voyage (Resource Page) has copies of this tape.

Time: 11 minutes.

To End: Inhale deeply; raise the hands over the head, no bend in the elbows and strike the two palms together, forcefully, one time only. Exactly when you clap the hands together, let the breath go. Then bring your hands back into the posture. Inhale and repeat the sequence, seven times total.

Relax.

CHAPTER 8

MEDITATION FOR TRANSFORMATION AND BLISS

By conquering your mind, you can conquer the world.
GURU NANAK
Japji, 28th Pauree

THE MIND IS LIKE A SWING. It will sway in this direction, then in that direction. It will go forwards, backwards and all around. The mind will go wherever we allow it. The interesting point, though, is that we can control the direction of its course. It can either be our best friend or our worst enemy. Our mind gives us thoughts, which ignite emotions, which lead to desires, which manifest actions, which create karma. Lets say you hear that your friend is having a party and you haven't been invited. You think, "She doesn't like me any more. What kind of a friend is she anyway? Did I do something wrong? I didn't really like her anyway." The mind can really spin out of control. Then come the feelings of anger, rejection, betrayal, insecurity and sadness. You call up some of your mutual friends and make up a hurtful story about her. Later you find out that your answering machine was off all day and your friend was trying to leave you an invitation but couldn't. The whole thing was a horrible misunderstanding, but the damage has already been done. If the thought is caught before it becomes emotions – or at least before it becomes the action – the cycle will be broken, thus halting the unending destructive consequences of karma. This skill is developed through meditation.

The mind becomes a monster when it becomes your master.
The mind is an angel when it is your servant.
YOGI BHAJAN

The mind is made up of three minds – The Negative, Positive and Neutral Minds. They are all there to serve us in life. **The Negative (or Protective Mind)** is given for survival. It gives us warnings and protects us from potential danger. "Don't put your hand on the hot stove. It's cold outside, wear your coat. Watch out for the ice on the road; that person is lying to you. That business opportunity looks risky." Literally, if we didn't have the Negative Mind, we'd be dead. But, if we only listen to it, we'd never move forward, either. **The Positive Mind** gives us the possibilities in all situations. It is constructive, risk taking and active. "Oh, yes, you can do it. You can trust that person with your money. That's a good deal. Just think of what we could do with that business opportunity." If we only listen to the Positive Mind, we would be naïve, open to abuse and negative forces affecting us. The Positive and Negative Minds are both necessary and must work together as a team. **The Neutral Mind,** being centered, wise, silent, patient, calm, non-reactive, and fair, observes the Negative and Positive Minds and assesses both in relationship to our Higher Self. Every thought filters through these three minds. If a thought is stuck in either the Negative or Positive Mind, the process is disrupted and will not make it to the Neutral Mind. Meditation balances the interaction between these three minds. Meditation develops the Neutral Mind, which cannot happen on a rational/intellectual level.

What is a mantra? It is mental purification. What is meditation? It is house cleaning.
YOGI BHAJAN

Before my morning Sadhana (spiritual practice) became a habit, my minds would dispute while lying in bed, debating if I was going to get up or not. My Negative Mind would start the debate, "You are just too tired…it's not healthy you know to be so tired…you have a busy day and need your sleep." The Positive Mind would then counter with, "You know Sadhana gives you energy…it centers you for the day…you'll feel better if you get up." The Negative Mind tried more strategies, "It's just too cold. You don't want to get out of this cozy, warm bed to go into the cold bathroom. Most people in the world are sleeping. Why do you have to be so different?" The Positive Mind was tenacious with, "Just turn on the heater in the bathroom. You know you will be glad you got up. Remember how good you felt yesterday morning and every morning? Remember that big business deal you secured last week, and your Sadhana helped you have the intuition to know what to say and do?" All the while, the Neutral Mind was accessing the drama between the Negative and Positive Minds. As the Neutral Mind's mission was to uphold my Higher Self, it supported my Sadhana. It also listened to the Negative Mind's concern about fatigue. The Neutral Mind solved the conflict by saying, "Get up, but take a nap at lunch time. Be sure to go to bed early tonight." Working together the three minds are a wonderful trio. Each needs to be respected and acknowledged for its contribution to the team.

Most people do not understand what real meditation involves. Meditation is a process of cleaning the mind, preventing the dumping of 

toxic thoughts and feelings into the subconscious mind. Yogi Bhajan calls meditation, "cleaning house." We daily wash our bodies, brush our teeth and put on clean clothes. Our subconscious mind also needs to be cleaned daily. If the mind is cluttered with old feelings of anger and fear – our inner demons – how can one hear the higher self or neutral mind speaking? A good meditation is one in which subconscious feelings are stirred up and released. If we can physically not move and allow the process, the mind will become still. We will feel cozy and comfortable with our Infinity. The feeling is beyond words – how to describe bliss?

The following story illustrates this point:

A well-known holy man came to town. A college professor read about the sage's visit in the local newspaper. Curious about his wisdom, the professor decided to pay him a call.

The sage welcomed the professor and offered him a comfortable chair.

"Do you like tea?" the sage asked, passing the professor a cup. The professor nodded, holding the cup as the sage poured from an ornate teapot. The liquid quickly rose to the top of the cup. In anticipation, the professor glanced at the sage, who continued to pour. The tea flowed over the top edge, but the sage persisted.

Quite distressed now, the professor jolted out of his chair, dropping the cup.

"What are you doing?"

The sage picked up the cup, filled it again and offered it to the professor. "This teacup is like your mind. You can't hear anything new because it's already full."

The subconscious mind is like the cup of tea. It is so full of old negative agendas, there isn't room for anything new. We must dare to let our old ideas and perception, which don't serve us any longer, die. Our cups will then be free to be filled with new and positive thoughts.

Meditation is my personal therapy. Like everyone, I've been challenged with a healthy share of insecurities and neurosis. Before I started meditating, they spilled out into my daily life, dominating my thoughts and actions. They interfered with the person I knew I could be – blocking the path to my destiny. Meditation gave me a tool to drop this karmic baggage on a daily basis.

Here's how it works. During meditation issues surface, reflecting what's happening in my life. Let's say that my husband says something that triggers old insecurities within me. Unless I am feeling very centered, neutral and clear, I do not discuss it with him then. I recognize that something feels off and commit to myself that I will deal with it in my morning meditation. This gives me space, I've committed to my process and I haven't made things worse by reacting out of emotion and commotion. The next time I meditate, usually in the early morning, I process the event. I acknowledge what is my stuff, what could be his stuff (although that is not for me to judge or process) and what is our stuff. It's like self-talk. My three minds go into battle mode, I may cry, be angry, fearful, but by the end, the battle is over. The result is peace of mind, because I feel clean – the subconscious mind has been scrubbed. In relation to my husband, there may be issues that need attention, but as I have sorted out and released my issues, they won't cloud what we need to do together. This gives me clarity of how to respond to him with consciousness and not react from emotion. I am spared from creating karma I may regret later.

If you master your mind, you master the whole universe, because once you have mastered your mind and brought it to neutrality, then the Universal mind will serve you.
Yogi Bhajan

Meditation is a lifestyle – like bathing everyday, it needs to be consistent. Even though one can feel the benefits of meditation right away, it takes time to heal from past hurts. You may be able to drop something for good quickly, but usually the issues keep repeating in more subtle forms until they are truly gone. Many times our issues may even be from past life karmas. Things come up that don't make sense in this present life. All of this can be very confusing. You may even get discouraged "Who needs this pain?" and want to stop. Don't!

We usually associate pain with punishment. This pain is healing. Like a benevolent parent holding the child in his lap crying over a broken toy, God holds us in His loving embrace, as we weep and heal something broken in our psyche, and thus we are stronger and better prepared to face life's challenges. Isn't a parent's ultimate wish for his or her child's happiness? Two of Yogi Bhajan's favorite expressions were "Keep Up!!" and "Happiness is your birthright." Meditation will help you get there.

Try not to resist. Allowing the process will ease the struggle. Once meditation gives you the experience of your infinite vastness, you realize that your neurosis is an illusion. Now, when one of my insecurities surface I greet it – "Ah, there you are again. I know you are not my Truth." I stop the thought, not allowing the process to progress into emotions and then destructive actions. Sometimes that's all I need to do; other times I need to process it in my meditation. I am finding that the mental and emotional battles are fewer and shorter. I am able to access my consciousness and then choose how to shift it. The periods of silence are longer and more blissful. In that silence, my intuition speaks…and I listen. I'm happier, and my life is better.

Something like a stroke is so captivating to the consciousness. Like I want to see how this captivates my mind – this stroke, and then I want to pull my consciousness out and be free in the middle of the stroke. That's like an experiment of consciousness.
RAM DAS
Fierce Grace

Meditation is also a time to do strategic planning from the intuition. Instead of "thinking" about it, we can offer a thought to the universe like, "How can I create more prosperity in my life?" – then let it go. Continue with the meditation. As we approach that place of inner silence or nothingness (*shuniya*), the wisdom will start to flow. It's awesome how it works. We are not restricted to the limited intellect. Through meditation, we can tune into the limitless wisdom of the universe. The creative ideas and options are vaster than what we can come up with. It's important to be open, resisting attachment to an outcome, which will only stifle the creative process. Sometimes, there won't be ideas at all. Through our clear intention and strong projection, we can attract positive opportunities to ourselves. All we have to do is get our limited ego out of the way and allow the universe to serve us. Before you know it, an opportunity is knocking at your door, and it's much better than you could have imagined.

Meditation is hard work. It takes commitment and constancy. But, it's worth the effort. It's the best investment I've ever made.

We have discussed how meditation can enhance the quality of one's life. In relation to death, loss and transition, meditation is an invaluable instrument and training. First, it gives us a tool to heal our past karmas, and unfinished business; we can approach death free from "baggage." It also gives us an experience of our individual infinity merging with the Cosmic Infinity while we are still alive. The experience of this merger may differ from person to person. If you are a visual person, you may see lights, images and colors. If you are kinetic, you may feel sensations, like warmth, pulsations and energy circulating in your body. If you are auditory, you may hear music, vibrations, celestial sounds and messages. The experience may be overwhelmingly beautiful, as if every cell of your being is dancing with the Beloved. You may have all of the above experiences; you may have different ones or none of them. The point is that there is no right or wrong experience. We will all end up at the same place – ready to surrender our individual infinity to the Universal Infinity. No matter what your "style," there are some similarities between the experience of meditation and death.

Meditation prepares us for death by giving us the experience of shuniya or nothingness, where everything is nothing and nothing is everything. It's a very Zen concept – like looking at a blade of grass, in which one can experience the totality of the whole universe in that blade of grass. In this altered state of consciousness, not encumbered by our usual earthly boundaries, we feel timeless, spaceless, ageless, limitless, fearless – blissful. Our relationship to Self expands beyond the usual sensations of the physical body. The tattvas of earth, water, fire and air dissolve into pure consciousness of ether. Our identity – no longer father, instructor, woman, swimmer, diabetic or sad person – is vastness. Energy flows, higher consciousness, soul and inner light become familiar friends and guides. We are not just a part of creation, but one with all of it. We are it. We realize that physical matter, as we have known it is limited by our perceptions and viewpoint. In actuality, reality is infinite and boundless. We experience the unknown and instead of fearing it, embrace it with open arms. Surrender becomes a natural habit, because we experience letting go to the God within and feel one with All. When death beckons us, we will be ready

Sit, meditate, consolidate. Let things come to you.
Yogi Bhajan

for the ultimate surrender. (More death meditations are in Chapter 10 – *Rehearsing Death*)

I once wrote the following poem about Sadhana.

Dew Pearled Petals

Jeweled dew envelops me, dark, cool, misty.
I am still...like a flower waiting for dawn.
Within my damp cave, spiraling from the depths,
Currents swirl upward reaching toward the light.
Atomic...molecules are exploding, separating,
Rejoining, remolding into a new consciousness.
Manifesting at my Third-Eye, like a star, glistening,
In the night of today's gloom of disharmony.
And with the aloneness, comes an overwhelming calmness,
Surrounded by warmth, a coziness of my inner glow,
Engulfed in a blanket of peace, totally one with All.
And as the sun peeks over the hill,
My arms reach out to this age-old friend.
Like a flower, awakening from the night's still,
Stretching its dew pearled petals upward.
Bursting forth with songs of praise and gratitude...
for a new day.

Guru Terath Kaur Khalsa

Best Time to Meditate

Any time is good. But the very best time to meditate is before the dawn, between 3 am and 7:00 a.m., when the sun is at a 60-degree angle at your location on the earth. This time is so powerful that Yogi Bhajan says many souls cross the magnetic barrier of the earth during these ambrosial hours. During this time, it is also possible to experience the first three ethers of death, where great purification and guidance is granted, (this will be discussed more thoroughly in the next chapter). This is the optimal time to develop a personal yogic practice, called Sadhana. Sadhana can consist of breathing techniques, yoga, meditation and any special prayers or inspirational readings of your choice. It helps you clean out the old and make way for the new day. Another powerful time to meditate is between 4–7 p.m. in the evening. We call it evening Sadhana. The energy of the universe is low, affecting our energy as well. Relating to the Infinite at that time elevates our energy and spirits.

One of our yoga/Sikh communities recently went through the death process with one of their members. It was a very inspiring and touching experience for everyone. Someone asked the spouse how he was remaining so positive and centered throughout this transitional time. This man has a most consistent Sadhana, having faithfully gone every morning for years. He said that Sadhana prepared him for this time. A friend asked him if he was grieving the imminent loss of his wife. He said that during Sadhana he was able to release his pain. Many mornings he cried throughout his Sadhana, but by the time it was over, he was ready to face the day…clean, calm and steady. Sadhana works.

> *Sadhana (daily spiritual discipline) is not a miracle. It is just imprinting your molecules in an elevated form.*
> **Yogi Bhajan**

Before you start any of the meditations in this chapter, go back to Chapter Three and Four to review the basics. It is very important to mention that we need to be doing yoga at the same time that we have a meditation practice. They compliment each other. Yoga calms the body and enables you to sit. Yoga also strengthens the nervous system to handle the energy generated by meditation. If we were not doing yoga, it would be like sending 220 volts through a 110 volt system. For those people who would like to try a "walking meditation," I recommend getting the book, *Breathwalk*, by Gurucharan Singh Khalsa, PhD (which can be ordered through Ancient Healing Ways or Spirit Voyage on the Resource Page).

To master a meditation, practice on a daily basis is required. Habits control us so much that yogic science tells us that we can change our destiny by changing our habits.

Meditation Minutes and Days

Yogic science tells us that there are specific time lengths required for certain desired benefits during meditation. Most meditations are done for 11 or 31 minutes.

3 minutes affects the electromagnetic field, the circulation and the stability of the blood.

11 minutes begins to change the nerves and the glandular system.

22 minutes balances the three minds, and they begin to work together.

31 minutes allows the glands, breath and concentration to affect all the cells and rhythms of the body. It lets the psyche of the meditation affect the tattvas and all layers of the mind's projections.

62 minutes changes the gray matter in the brain. The subconscious and the outer projection are integrated.

2 ½ hours changes the psyche in its co-relation with the surrounding magnetic field so that the subconscious mind is held firmly in the new pattern by the surrounding universal mind.

It takes 40 days to change a habit.

It takes 90 days to confirm the new habit.

In 120 days, the new habit is who you are.

In 1,000 days, you have mastered the new habit.

PROCESS EXERCISES

Perhaps you have practiced some of the meditations offered in the previous chapters. Now is the time to look more deeply into the practice of meditation.

1 Have you noticed that your mind is like a swing? Examine the patterns of your own insecurities. When are self-destructive thoughts most likely to surface? What do you do now when this happens? How could meditation help you?

2 Try applying all three minds to a situation. How does it work for you?

3 How do you think meditation could help prepare you for death? Reflect on it.

4 Try out different meditations in this chapter. How are they helpful?

5 Choose one of the meditations in this book and do it for at least 11 minutes for 40 days. During that time, you will probably go through many changes. Keep a journal of your process. At the end of the 40 days, re-read your journal. What has changed in you?

LEARNING TO MEDITATE

This is a good meditation for someone who doesn't know how to meditate, or wants to develop the ability of concentration in action. It allows you to control your reactions in any situation and can bring sweetness and one-pointedness to the most outrageous and scattered mind.

How to do it
Have your spine straight and the neck in a light *Jalandhar Bandh. (Neck Lock)*

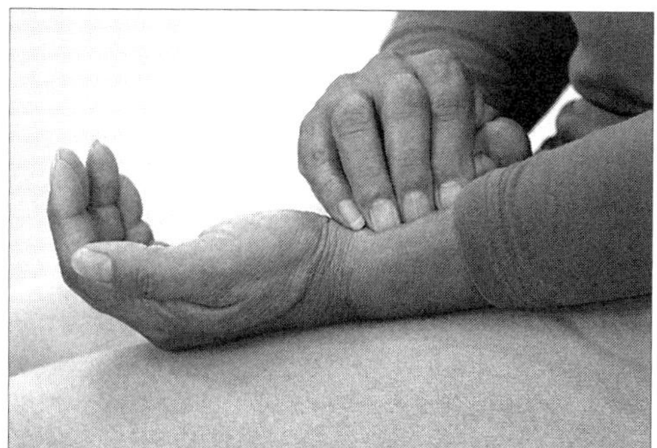

Eye Position: Focus the lightly closed eyes at the Third-Eye Point (between the eyebrows).

Mantra: *Sat Naam*

Mudra: With the four fingers of the right hand, feel the pulse on the left wrist. Place the fingers in a straight line, lightly, so that you can feel the pulse in each fingertip. On each beat of the heart, mentally hear the sound *Sat Naam*

Time: Continue for 5–11 minutes. Build to 31 minutes.

MEDITATION FOR COLD DEPRESSION

Cold depression is desperation, when life doesn't matter, society doesn't matter and relatives don't matter. Nothing matters. One feels limited, small, undercut, neglected and rejected. There is a constant pain. Only strong meditation can burn it out. By very good fortune, we have moments in meditation where we can come together to purify ourselves and be free. This meditation allows you to give your pain to the Infinite.

How to do it
Be in a position with a straight spine.

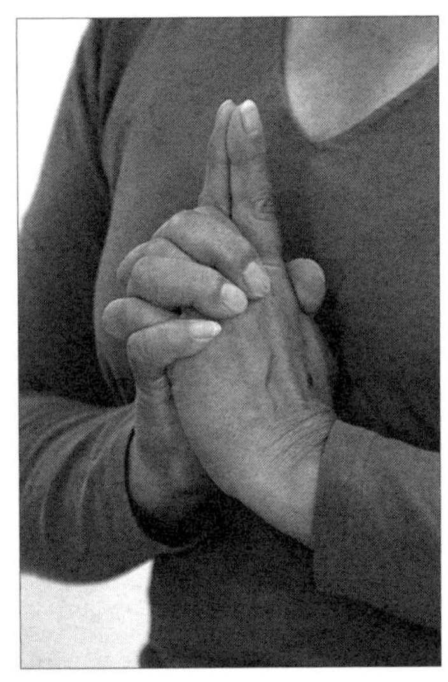

Female Demonstrating.

Mudra: Interlace your hands in Venus Lock in front of the heart, with the index fingers extended upwards.

Eyes: Close your eyes.

Mantra: Sing the mantra "***Wha-hay Guroo***" (refer to CD for melody – 9), chanting "***Wha***" from the navel, "***Hay***" from the heart, and "***Guroo***" from the lips.

Time: Continue for 11 minutes.

To End: Inhale deeply, hold and concentrate on the sound you created from your navel, heart and lips. Exhale. Inhale deeply, hold and give that cold depression to **Wahe Guru**. Exhale. Inhale deeply, hold. God has given you life; give it back to Him, so that in the end it becomes easy. Exhale. Be sure to relax for a few minutes after the meditation is completed.

MEDITATION FOR STRONG NERVES

What It Will Do for You

Practice this meditation to gain a calm balanced mind and strong nerves. It. will help protect you from irrationality.

How To Do It

Be in any position with a straight spine. Hold the right hand at ear level with the thumb tip and the tip of ring finger touching **(1A)** (fingernails don't touch). Place the left hand in the lap with the thumb tip and the tip of the little finger touching **(1B)**. Females should reverse the position so that the left hand has thumb and ring finger touching with hand at ear level, and the right hand is in the lap with the thumb and little finger touching.

The eyes are 1/10 open. Make the breath long and deep but not powerful.

You can practice this meditation anywhere, starting with 11 minutes and working up to 31 minutes. To end the meditation, inhale deeply, open the fingers, raise the hands and shake them rapidly for a few minutes.

Then relax.

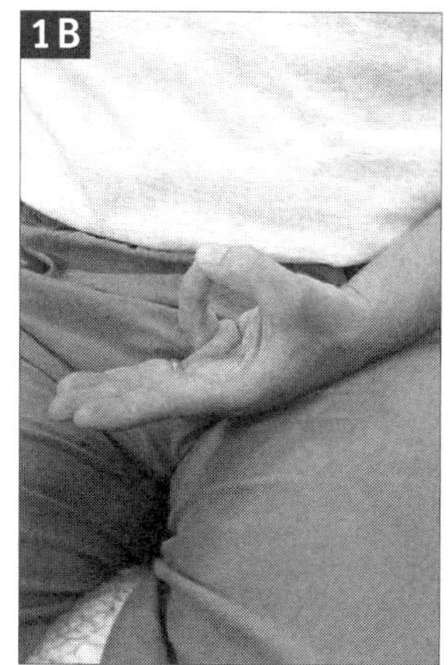

Male Demonstrating.

WAHE GURU KRIYA FOR NERVOUS BALANCE

This kriya builds the nervous system so nothing bothers you. It stimulates the pituitary to secrete and gives you an expanded intuitive sense. It makes the mind clear and decisive. This kriya helps you to direct yourself.

How To Do It

Put the hands on the knees in Gyan Mudra **(1A)**. Let the eyes be nearly closed. Break the inhale into 10 equal parts or "sniffs." With each part of the inhale move the hands mechanically (in small jerks) one-tenth of the way toward the forehead. The palms face up and all the fingers are straight during the inhale **(1B)**. At the tenth inhale the palms are on the forehead with the fingers pointing up **(1C)**. As you exhale join the fingertips of the two hands and let the hands down slowly **(1D)**. Separate the hands at the level of the navel point and return them to Gyan Mudra in the original position. On each

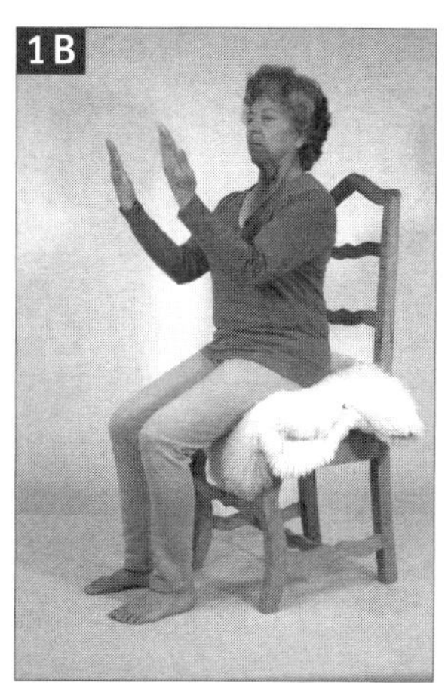

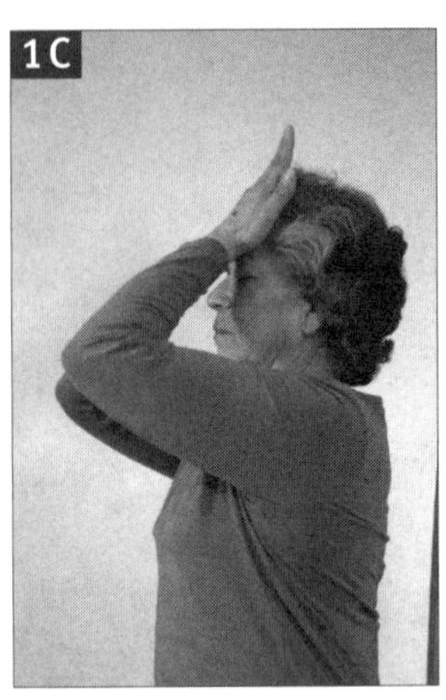

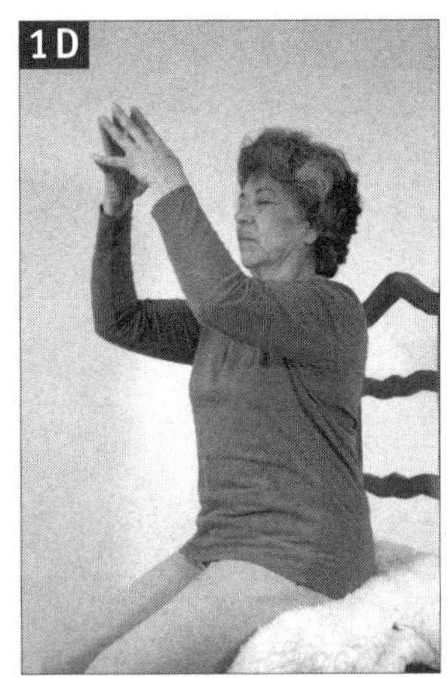

sniff of the inhale mentally vibrate the mantra ***"Wha-hay."*** On the exhale vibrate "***Guroo.***" Continue for 3 to 11 minutes.

Begin the practice for only a few minutes. Then build slowly up to 11 minutes.

GURU RAM DAS: RHYTHMIC HARMONY FOR HAPPINESS

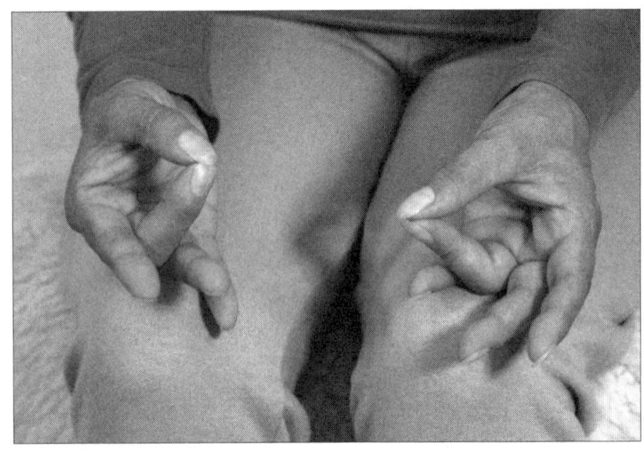

Female demonstrating mudra

How To Do It

Sit in a peaceful meditative pose. Keep the eyes one-tenth open. Men take the left hand and form *Shuni mudra* with the thumb and middle finger. With the right hand, join the thumb to the tip of the ring finger (for women, the mudras are reversed, see photo). Rest the hands on the knees.

Chant in a soft monotone:

Guroo Guroo Wha-hay Guroo Guroo Ram Das Guroo

Each repetition takes about 8 to 10 seconds.
Continue for 11 to 31 minutes.

Guru Ram Das was the fourth Sikh Guru. Born an orphan boy, his unconditional devotion and service earned him a place in the court of the Third Guru, Guru Amar Das, who eventually bestowed upon him the Guruship. He is known for his compassion and healing abilities. He is called the "Guru of Miracles." We chant his name when we want to ease our pain and make the impossible possible.

This meditation brings to the self a meditative peace. It's so vibratory that your lips, your upper palate, your tongue, even your entire surroundings feel a vibratory effect. This meditation is done for protection. It also makes the impossible possible, because you have the given values and you have given yourself, soul and spirit, to those given values righteously. It is then that God manifests everything. And that's why we chant this simple mantra in this mudra.

Yogi Bhajan

MEDITATION TO HANDLE A GRAVE SITUATION

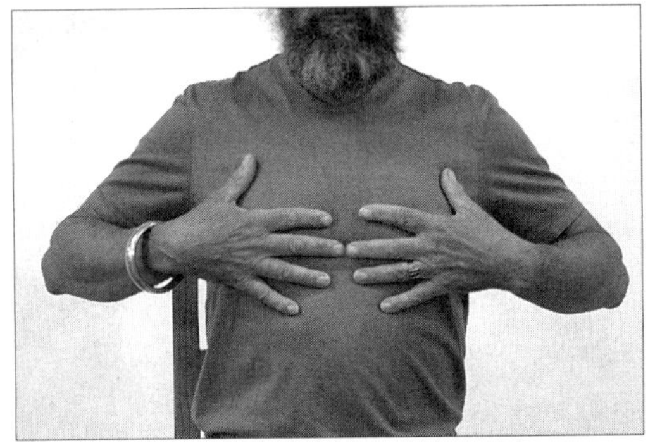

This is a very simple and ancient meditation to resolve conflict in us. It is like psychotherapy. The moment the body knows the breath is out it starts adjusting at the highest rate of efficiency. The theory is that when the breath is out and the prana is not there, the pranic body starts penetrating through the other bodies (See the explanation of the 10 bodies in Chapter Four) to create the combination. The computer must figure out how to allow you and your cells, which need x amount of oxygen, to survive.

If you have a most grave situation to handle, 11 minutes of this can take care of it.

How to Do It
Sit with a straight spine . Press the hands on the breasts, palms in, fingers pointing toward each other The hands are relaxed with the fingers extended and joined. This is a comfortable position with very little pressure and there is no tension in arms, hands and shoulders.

Eyes: The eyes are 1/10 open.

Breath: Deeply inhale for 5 seconds. Completely exhale for 5 seconds, and hold the breath out for 15 seconds.

Time: Begin with 11 minutes and slowly build to 31 minutes.

REJUVENATION MEDITATION

This is a meditation for the glandular system. It is a "medical meditation." Its effects are strong enough to help the system fight disease. It does not replace allopathic forms of medicine, but it does open the healing and preventative capacity of your body. The meditation focuses its effects on the glandular system, the guardians of your health. Be careful to start slowly with this *pranayam* (breathing exercise). It can make you very spacey and dreamy. It is best to practice this before going to bed. If you master it, you will know why the yogis and sages always call breath "the energy of life."

How To Do It

Sitting or lying with a straight spine, with a light *Jalandhar Bandh.*

Eye Position: Focus the eyes past the tip of the nose toward the distant ground and beyond into the depths of the earth.

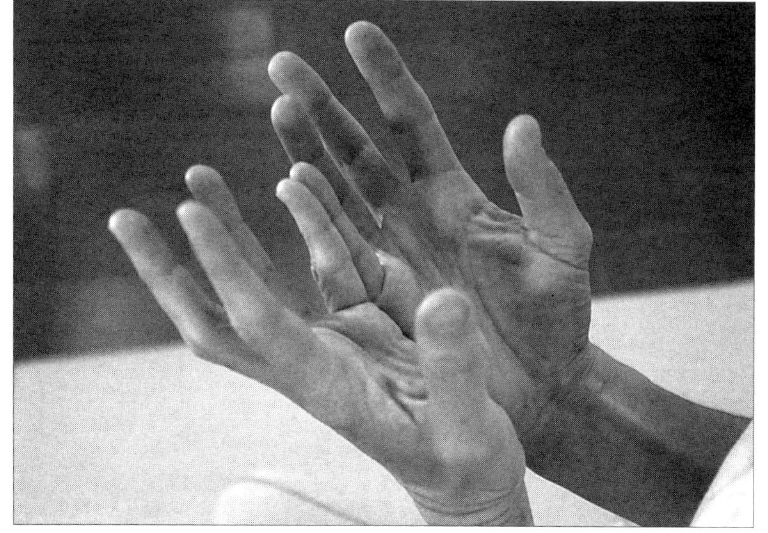

Mudra: Relax the arms down along the sides. Bring the hands in front of the chest with the palms toward the torso. Keep the elbows snug against the side of the ribs. Join the hands along the sides of the palms and the sides of the little fingers. Spread the fingers and thumbs apart.

Breath and Mantra: The breath must be precise. Inhale deeply and slowly through semi-puckered lips. Hold the breath in for 4 seconds (or the length of one mental cycle of the mantra).

Saa Taa Naa Maa

Then exhale powerfully in 4 equal strokes through the nose. As you exhale mentally recite the mantra.

Saa Taa Naa Maa

Then hold the breath out for 2 seconds or the length of one mental ***Whahay Guroo.***

Time: Continue for 11 minutes. With practice, increase to 31 minutes.

ANG SUNG WAHE GURU MEDITATION

It is a creative and self cleansing process of the subconscious. You see the Tibetans? They do it. You don't like their sound. It's not musical, it's not rock and roll, but you do not know the joy of it. It's a different sound than I normally speak and talk or anything. It's boring all right, but for a few minutes it will be boring. Once you create it and it starts effecting you creating a direct vibration, you will start enjoying. It is all beyond the (back) half of the tongue. If you cut my head this way, it will all be in the back. That you have to understand.

This is such a powerful mantra, that when you start chanting it, you will have vaak siddhi – what you say will come true. And any problem, habit, negative thought you have, direct, you can wipe it out. All you have to do is speak once, and listen with your own ear. Once the beat of the drum and the beat of the palate you combine, you combine your God. There are no two opinions about it.

These words we cannot manufacture. These words, if we start to manufacture like this we can't. Someone who has the God's knowledge and who has this perfect Kriya uttered this for us. This means 'God is with me in every molecule.'

YOGI BHAJAN

How To Do It
Sit with a straight spine.

Eye Focus: The eyes are focused on the tip of the nose.

Mantra: ***Ang Sang Wha-hay Guroo***

Time: 31 minutes.

The sound is created in the back of the throat without projecting the breath outwards. Take one breath per repetition. Refer to the CD for proper pronunciation – 10.

It is important to do this meditation when it is possible to relax for at least several hours afterwards (such as at night), and not to drive, etc.

SODARSHAN CHAKRA KRIYA

How To Do It
Sit with a straight spine.

Eyes: At the tip of the nose.

Mudra:
A. Block off the right nostril with the right thumb. Inhale slowly and deeply through the left nostril. Hold the breath. Mentally chant "**Wha Hay Guroo**" 16 times, * pumping the navel point 3 times with each repetition, once on "**Wha**," once on "**Hay**,"

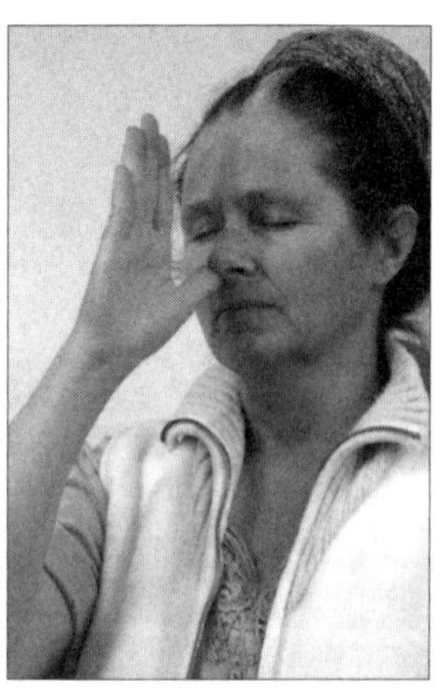

and once on "**Guroo**" – for a total of 48 pumps.
B. Unblock the right nostril. Place the right index finger (pinkie finger can also be used) to block off the left nostril, and exhale slowly and deeply through the right nostril. Continue.

To end: Inhale, hold 5–10 seconds, exhale. Then stretch and shake every part of your body for about 1 minute, so that the energy may spread.

Time Constraints: *There is no time, no place, no space and no condition attached to this mantra. Each garbage pit has its own time to clear. If you are going to clean your own garbage, you must estimate and clean it as fast as you can, or as slow as you want. You have to decide how much time you have to clean up your garbage pit. Suggested length for this Kriya is 31 or 62 minutes a day.*
Yogi Bhajan

Comments: Start doing this meditation for 31 minutes, then after a while do it for 40 minutes, then for 62 minutes. Take time to build up your time, until you can do 2 ½ hours. When practiced 2 ½ hours every day, it makes you a perfect superman or superwoman. It purifies, it takes care of the human life and brings together all 27 facets of life and makes a human perfect, saintly, successful and qualified. This meditation also gives one the pranic power. This kriya never fails. It can give one all the inner happiness a state of ecstasy in life.

---

*Note: This is how Yogi Bhajan keeps track of the counting: Inhale – blocking the right nostril with the right thumb, other fingers held straight up in the air. While holding, count one, two, three –with the pinkie finger moving slightly three times. Four, five six – move the ring finger three times. Seven, eight, nine – move the middle finger three times. Ten, eleven, twelve – move the index finger three times. Thirteen, fourteen, fifteen – move the thumb slightly for three beats. Sixteen – bring the index finger over to block off the left nostril, as you release the right thumb from the right nostril. Then, exhale through the right nostril. And continue.

Of all the twenty types of yoga, including Kundalini Yoga, this is the highest kriya. This meditation cuts through all darkness. It will give you a new start. It is the simplest kriya, but at the same time the hardest. It cuts through all barriers of the neurotic or psychotic inside-nature. When a person is in a very bad state, techniques imposed from the outside will not work. The pressure has to be stimulated from within. Tragedy of life is when the subconscious releases garbage into the conscious mind. This kriya invokes the Kundalini to give you the necessary vitality and intuition to combat the negative effects of the subconscious mind.
Yogi Bhajan

PART THREE Transition

Love is the union of the beautiful memory of thoughts where two become one.
Yogi Bhajan

THINK BACK NOW to the figure eight of our train track. Up until this time, we have been journeying along the left loop labeled LIFE. In this section, we will spend time at the midpoint, then venture into the right loop labeled DEATH. It might be considered the most intriguing section of the book, because we will be taking a much closer look at the process of death itself – the unknown.

We will be adding more complexities to our mandala now, starting with Chapter Nine – *The Journey of Death* – in which we will learn about the death process from a yogic point of view. We will look at what happens to the tattvas, the Ten Bodies, the Chakras and the journey of the soul. This information will prepare us for the next chapter – *Rehearsing Death* – where we will actually practice dying. Included in this chapter are many meditations and visualizations Yogi Bhajan gave to us to rehearse the big event. We will also look at how one can serve as a coach for another person preparing to die. The last chapter – *Children and Death* – is also included in Part Three. The stories in this chapter will touch your heart, (have a Kleenex handy), and you will find their perspective of death intriguing and uplifting. They have much to teach us.

Create a story when you want to guide a child. Children love the tales of the unknown. They enjoy it, so add to their joy. The child will love it.
Yogi Bhajan

CHAPTER 9

The Journey of Death

The experience of death can be described as either a wall or a door. As a wall, death is the disorganization of the material matter and the end of all possibility of life. As a door, what is real need not be equated with what is material; thus the dissolution of the physical body need not be the end of the process. Death is the door through which the soul enters into a time of transition.

If we imagine that we are merely physical, death will be a wall. If we recognize that we are more than the body, death will be a door. We see that we have a physical body, but it is not who we really are. Just as one may have an overcoat, that is not you. One honors and cares for the overcoat because it protects us on our winter's journey. When it is spring, one doesn't need the overcoat any more and puts it aside. Our physical body houses our real self. It has been given to us to wear and use in this life.

Just think how consciously a consciousness will look at the death. It will look like this: One has come, one has adapted the technology, one has purified oneself, one has done his karma, and one has quit this life of cause and effect and has escaped into the dignity of the destiny unto infinity. Just look how peaceful it is.
Yogi Bhajan

Before you read on, you may want to refer back to Chapter Four – *Understanding Yogic Science*, because we will now discuss many things explained there – like the Kundalini Energy, the Ida and Pingala, the Eight Chakras, and the Ten Bodies – in relation to the death process.

The Moment of Death

The medical field has given us the concept of the "moment of death." As the life functions shut down, one moment they are measurable, at another they are not. This measurability of life has led to the concept of the "moment of death." Actually, death can be described as a gradual process of melting or dissolving, which can take minutes or hours to complete, long after the instruments have stopped measuring life.

If we believe that our body is the temple for our soul, it should be treated with sacredness. Just as we would clean, maintain and revere a shrine of spiritual significance, we should clean, maintain and revere our body that is the shrine of our spirit. With this consciousness, each moment of life will let go into death with grace, understanding and serenity.

Our physical body is made up of five elements – earth, water, fire, air and ether. At the time of death, these elements dissolve one into another.

It is very common for some one nearing death to stop eating and drinking, signs that the body has started the process of shutting down.

As death approaches, the earth element is the first to dissolve. The body loses its feeling of solidity, hardness and boundaries. The body feels heavy, and its edges seem less defined. One feels "out" of the body, to the point of not being able to move the limbs at will. Peristalsis slows, the bowels no longer move without aid. As the organs shut down, the person stops eating and drinking. The person will go in and out of consciousness, having one foot in life and the other in death. As the earth element dissolves into the water element, the person's identity is less attached to the solid, and there is a feeling of fluidity.

> As it came closer and closer, his physical body energetically shrunk. I could see his body disintegrating...his elements disappearing. I could see it. Then, he lost control of his bodily functions. It was the smell of death. As the time went on, his face was absolutely radiant and his eyes were powerful. There was like a glow about his whole head. And everything else was just nothing...like a curtain, not even there. I would sit with him and joke with him or sit and hold his hand and meditate with him. I would talk to him, not verbally...it was really amazing. I could sense where he was and we talked soul to soul.
>
> *Siri Amrit Singh talks about the death of his Grandfather*

As the water element begins to melt into the fire element, the feeling of fluidity becomes more like a warm mist. Bodily fluids have slowed, the mouth and eyes are dry, circulation is sluggish and blood pressure drops. Blood settles in the extremities, resulting in a feeling of lightness. The fire element then melts into the air element, when feelings of warmth, cold or any physical sensations cease. The body temperature drops and the skin becomes cool and pale. There is a feeling of weightlessness and boundrylessness, as one dissolves into more subtle realms. Finally, as the air element dissolves, the out breath is longer than the in breath, with long pauses between breaths. The sound of the breath may take on a rattle quality. One experiences a sense of expanding into pure consciousness, which is the ether element.

Guru Singh is one of our most loved Los Angeles-based Kundalini Yoga Teachers. He graciously agreed to an interview about the passing of his mother. After his Mom broke her hip, she moved in with Guru Singh and his wife. They had six wonderful years together, just having fun. Then one summer day Guru Singh's Mother fell and suffered a slight stroke. From that day on, things were different. She became less and less responsive. She died exactly forty days after her fall. There are many excerpts sprinkled throughout the rest of this book about Guru Singh's experience. This first one describes his mother's shutting down process – the dissolving of her elements.

> *The last week, she was really starting to shut down. She stopped eating. We watched the process of God disassembling her contact with the world. The first ten days after the fall, she was saying, 'Guru Singh, I feel vacant in the middle. I can't figure out what's going on.' She was losing her cognitive powers. She was very proud of her mental capabilities. She was a brilliant woman. This was challenging for her. Then, my father started visiting her on a nightly basis. She would wake up and tell the caregiver that she had been out dancing with my Dad. Her exact words were, 'Damned if we didn't have to walk home. Boy, am I tired.' This is how she was explaining why she was so exhausted.*

And what is it to cease breathing, but to free the breath from its restless tides, that it may rise and expand and seek God unencumbered?
Kahlil Gibran

Each stage is accompanied by less solidity, the edges are less defined and less external input is received. The process of dying seems to be accompanied by a sense of expanding beyond oneself or dissolving out of form. This could be a very frightening experience if one resists the sensations of melting. Again, we are reminded of the importance of consciously preparing for death. It is not uncommon for one to have similar experiences during meditation or while relaxing after a yoga set. In the excerpt below, Guru Singh further describes the dissolving process of his mother. It is also evident how comforting he was for his mother, lovingly coaching her through the progression of letting go.

About 72 hours leading up to her passing, we cancelled everything else that was happening. It was getting close. Shabds (spiritual music) had been playing and candles were lit round the clock. We hung out with her all the time. She went into a semi-coma, but she would periodically come back into consciousness. I would climb in bed with her to hang out with her. She'd wake up and say, 'Don't leave me.' 'Don't worry, Mom, we're together forever. We've been together. We're going to be together.' So she'd feel really good. I was absolutely determined to witness her final breath. We were getting really tired. Her breath became erratic, breathing and then not breathing. I kept following her breath and taking her pulse. All of sudden it became what they call the 'death rattle.' I got in her ear and said, 'Mom, when everything else disappears, just go for the light.' She was reaching for a breath, but there was nothing in her lungs.

She started looking more and more like the totems the North-West Indians carve or the head of an eagle. It was like she was pushing forward, through time and space. Everything was stretching; reaching for the breath, jaw jutting forward. She was reaching for every breath. Not that she was stuck here or afraid to go, but she was going to breath until she didn't. There was this look of total awareness. Her eyes closed and her mouth opened, she looked like there was nothing she didn't understand in the universe. The facial expression was pressed out against the threshold of time.

Everything stopped. We immediately checked the clock and started chanting Akal (the chant to free the soul) at the top of our lungs. The hospice nurse was Catholic from the Philippines and was reading the Bible. We were chanting Akal. The day nurse was praying. We also did Kirtan Sohila – The Sikh prayer done at the time of death. (See Appendix I)

As the ethers dissolve at the time of death, so do the Chakras. It is a very subtle process, but a trained Yogi can use these energies at the time of death to raise his or her soul up the chakras and out the Crown Chakra. If the soul leaves through the Tenth Gate, it is more likely to go straight to the Fourth Ether. During yoga and meditation, the Yogi has learned how to raise his energy up the chakras to experience higher states of consciousness and ecstasy. At death, it is the same process. Instead of directing the

Kundalini or energy up through the chakras, the yogi is guiding the soul toward the Tenth Gate. In the next chapter, *Rehearsing Death*, we will practice how to do this.

In Chapter Four we discussed the Ten Bodies and their functions during life. At the time of death, they do not all leave together for they serve different purposes.

In the first ten seconds — one minute, the positive, negative and neutral minds will review and judge the panorama of our life. During this time, we will be challenged with three questions:

1. *In this incarnation, why did you come to earth in this particular body?*
2. *What did you do here? You watch and feel all of your actions and reactions of your whole life.*
3. *Did you fulfill your purpose and destiny in this lifetime?*

In the coma of death, we will go through a thirty second to three minute process called "divine grinding." Yogi Bhajan referred to this process as taking thirty seconds in some lectures and three minutes in others. The point is that it is a very short period of time in earthly time. In our experience, it will not seem short. In the first ten seconds to one minute, we will review our life. In the second ten seconds to one minute, we must meditate on Infinity. In the last ten seconds to one minute, the pranic body leaves the physical body.

This is a very revealing, and for some a painful process, because we will be confronted with the naked truth about ourselves; all of our actions and interactions, feelings, neurosis and relationships…how these actions impacted on others and their feelings and reactions. All of this will be reflected to us, as though looking at a movie about our life, except that we are not detached watchers. We feel everything deeply.

Our mind truthfully reviews our movie and makes the judgment. For this reason, it is critical during the next ten seconds to one minute, that we connect to our Divine Infinity. We can accomplish this by repeating a *pran sutra,* a mantra, which will give us the experience of uniting with the One. Chanting them in life will prepare us to automatically chant them in death and thus assist us in an easier death passage. (Many pran sutras are presented at the end of this chapter after the Process Exercises.)

If we assess from our consciousness that there is more to be done, learned and cleared, we will be sent to the next reincarnation. In Chapter Seven – *Jiwan-Mukht*, we discussed the importance of forgiveness in life, and a "*Meditation To Conquer Self-Animosity*" was also given for this purpose. If we can develop a consciousness of blamelessness and forgiveness in life, then at the time of death, we will automatically merge our consciousness with God and be freed. It is important to restate that rebirth is not a punishment…it is all just a process. When this evaluation process is completed, the job of the mental bodies is over.

In the last ten seconds to one minute, our breath leaves the physical body. Normally in life, we breathe predominately through one nostril or the other at any given time. At the time of death, we must breathe through both nostrils equally at the same time. Breath needs to be neutral; ida and pingala both have to work equally together. Refer back to Chapter Two – *The Breath of Life*, where we discussed left and right nostril breathing, and where you will find a "*Meditation To Prevent Freaking Out*" – a pranayama exercise that will help you develop the skill of controlling nostril breathing. At the end of this chapter is a more advanced meditation, "*Meditation To Know the Unknown.*" It will help you develop the ability to use the breath to prevent death.

During class a student asked Yogi Bhajan about a person who dies in their sleep. Would there be a problem guiding the consciousness? He said that nobody dies in his or her sleep. The person may look like they are asleep but he or she is actually fully aware and will go through the panorama show. Even people in a coma go through it.

So, you take your subtle body, which has to go with your soul and decorate it with the flowers of consciousness, the God's grace – the Guru Mantra (pran sutras). Decorating your consciousness with these flowers, you will go into the realm of infinity. Just keep on singing and chanting and walk towards God's home, which is your home.
Yogi Bhajan

The soul is the finite aspect of Infinity. When it leaves, the auric and arc bodies leave; and once these bodies are neutralized the prana cannot reenter the body. The physical body then begins to disintegrate. In the first four days after death, the subtle body is still hanging around with relatives and with the physical body itself. After the four day period, the subtle body and the soul leave as a unit and go through a cylindrical movement to the center of the earth, where it is very calm and quiet. On both sides we will find our beloved relatives and friends beckoning us. At the end of the corridor, there is a light, The Chamber of Light. It is important to remember to keep going toward the light, and not let the attachments on either side distract us. At the end, we will find two doors or openings. One side is dark, cozy, warm, like a restaurant and is very welcoming. The other side is like a bright, snowy mountain path. We may find ourself attracted to the cozy and warm side. But, if our Dharma (spiritual practice) and Pran Sutra is holding us, we will choose the white, snowy path. If we choose the cozy warm door, we will reincarnate into another physical body. Once a door is picked, going back is impossible. That is the path the soul has to travel.

Five-Seed Prashad

There is a special ***Prashad*** (blessed food) that can be served during the first four days after a death. It is made of whole-wheat flour, honey, ghee, water and five seeds, which represent the five elements – pumpkin, earth; cardamom, water; sesame, fire; poppy, air; and sunflower, ether. The proportions of seeds are more subjective and intuitive. Yogi Bhajan's wife Bibiji thought that it was about ¼ – ½ cup of the combined seeds to every cup of flour This blessed food can be served after a birth or a death and signifies completion. Thoroughly read the recipe and process before beginning.

Recipe for Five-Seed Prashad

For approximately 25 people, use 1 ½+ cups ghee (2 cups butter – 1 lb), a scant 2 cups whole-wheat flour, 1 ½ cups honey, 3 ½ cups water and ½ cup of seeds. For approximately 50 people, use 3 cups ghee (4 cups butter – 2 lbs.), a scant 4 cups whole-wheat flour, 3 cups honey, 7 cups water and 1 cup seeds. For approximately 200 people, use 12 cups ghee (16 cups butter – 8 lbs.), 16 cups flour, 12 cups honey, 28 cups water and 4 cups seeds. Keep in mind that butters may differ in the amount of ghee they produce.

Sikhs do a prayer called Ardas before they make prashad, with the intention and prayer for whatever the Ardas is blessing. Otherwise, just do your own prayer. The whole time you are making the prashad, chant either *"Wahe Guru,"* Mul Mantra *"Ek Ong Kar Sat Nam Karta Purarkh Nirbho Nirvair Akal Moorit Ajoonee Saibhang Gurprasad Jap Ad Sach Jugod Sach Haibee Sach Nanak Hosee Bhee Sach."* Or, you can recite the whole *Japji*, doing it by heart, holding a Nitnem to read the words in one hand, while you stir with the other or chant with a CD.

1. Begin by measuring out ahead of time all the ingredients you will need. Once you do your prayer or Ardas, the process needs to be done in the spirit of reverence, like a meditation.
2. Make ghee by simmering butter at a low heat (a crock pot can also be used). Allow all of the impurities to fall to the bottom of the pot. What is left is the clarified ghee on the top. Stir frequently to prevent burning. Having the ghee ready ahead of time makes the process a little easier.
3. Boil the water; add the honey. Allow any impurities to form and skim off the top.
4. When the ghee is finished, pour the ghee into a wok, (which is best but other stainless steel pots can be used as well.) Gradually add the flour, stirring constantly to prevent it from burning or lumping. It is important to thoroughly cook the flour. It will have a toasty smell when it is done.
5. Next, add to the flour the boiling water and honey mixture. There will be a lot of steam and hissing. Stir briskly and continuously until the ingredients are thoroughly blended. The mixture should be the consistency of a thick pudding. If it is too watery, continue to cook and stir until the right consistency is obtained.
6. When the prashad is done, stir in the seeds.
7. Immediately turn off the flame and slide the mixture into a stainless steel bowl and cover with tinfoil until served.
8. The prashad should look like a thick pudding that sticks together and when cooled can easily be scooped with one hand. Prashad is only served with the bare hand; no utensils are used. A single serving can range from just a taste to about a fourth of a cup, or a small handful. One who is receiving prashad places their hands with the outer edges together making a cup; the arms are stretched up with the head slightly bowed in reverence. The attitude is one of gratitude in receiving God's blessing.

Yogi Bhajan's Death Experience

Yogi Bhajan had just finished a steep climb up to Vaishnoo Devee's cave, a sacred shrine in India. After taking ice-cold water, he lost consciousness. In his own words he recounts his experience.

You have two paths to go, in the first five seconds when you die. When the soul is going from the pranic body into the subtle body its total weight is reduced to less than ¼ oz. and the size is reduced to the size of the first thumb joint, like a gas flame. That's how it leaves. Afterwards, it goes through a cylindrical movement, just like a cylinder, and it is very peaceful.

Death is very peaceful. It is the most peaceful experience in the world. I went through it personally. And after going through the cylindrical experience you reach a point where you feel very calm, very peaceful and very together. Before that, in that time you are shown the entire action of your life in a panorama, showing from the first breath to that second. There is nothing in life you don't know you have done, bad, good – it's your karma. You condemn yourself or you accept yourself that is your problem. And when you go in the cylindrical thing and you reach a point of calmness, quiet and peacefulness, there comes a big circle of light, very bright. On one side you will see a kind of a beautiful old, grayish door. You always see it. None of you can go without this process. And inside you see warm, and you can smell food. If you turn that way, that is the path to reincarnation. On the other side you find a straight path going through icy snow mountains. Choose! On both sides are your relatives whom you love and like. At that moment I stood still and I thought, 'No, I am not going to either side, because this is a holy place where I have fallen unconscious and to die here will mean that all people who go to such holy places of pilgrimage will lose the faith.' I bent down in prayer and I said: 'Oh Divine Mother, I mean no harm to the faith of the people.' She replied: 'Then go back and spread the faith.' When I woke up there were about 30 or 40 blankets around me. The doctor had already declared me dead and it was all over. When I got up, they all ran away. The doctor privately told me, 'It was 45 minutes ago that you died.' I just decided not to go. It was a holy place and I thought none of my family would go there if I died there.

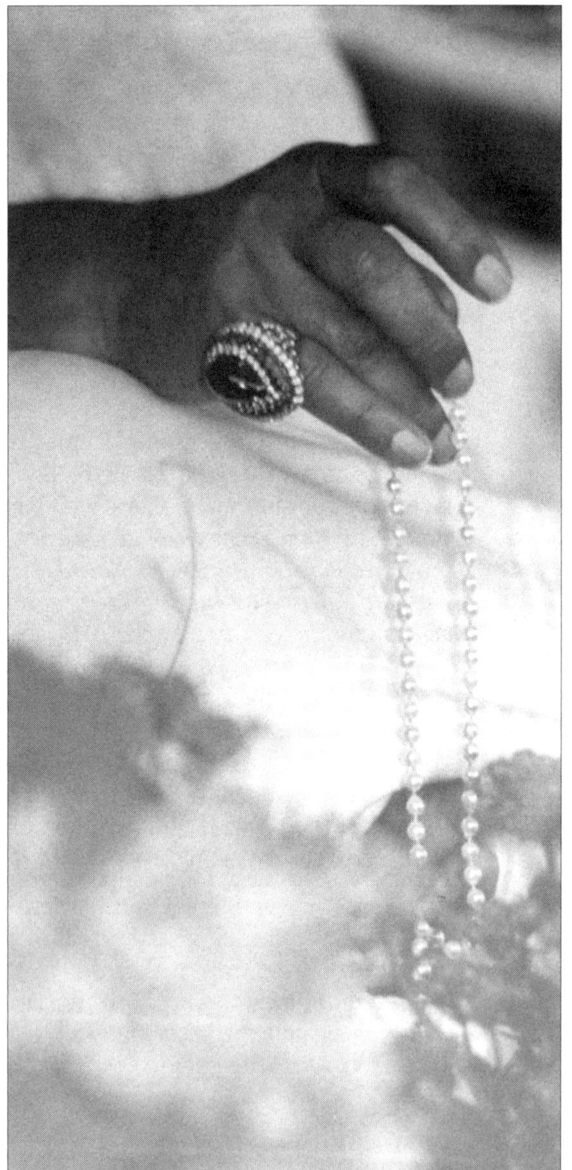

Some people who have experienced the death of a friend or loved one have observed the person's spirit (encased in the subtle body) leaving the dead body. Some have seen it lifting out of the body through the solar plexus, the heart or the crown chakra. Placing their hand at these places, they report feeling an energy leaving, and the hand feeling tingly and odd. Years ago, I was at an Elizabeth Kubler-Ross workshop, where one of the participants had photos of her husband's death process. In one photo taken just a few minutes after he was pronounced dead, her husband's life force could be seen leaving out the crown chakra. It looked like a brilliant swirl of light spiraling up from the crown chakra to the opposite corner of the photo. It was awesome. In subsequent photos the light got dimmer until it was no longer visible in the photo.

On the third or fourth day after death, the soul leaves the tattvas altogether. Leaving the spiral, no matter which side we join, we all must cross the electro-magnetic field of the earth during the next 13–17 days. Many souls are not able to cross, because they are either afraid to leave or are attached to the earth. These souls become ghosts, which will be discussed on the next page. This is the time to use the pran sutra. It will give you the force and velocity to cross the electro-magnetic field of the earth. It is like a toll road. You pay the toll (the pran sutra) and you go free. Choose a personal pran sutra and learn it so well that any time crisis hits you automatically begin chanting it.

Chanting Akal for the soul for 3–17 days after the death can help it cross the electro-magnetic field. *Akal* means, "that which never dies." With this mantra, we encourage the soul to go on to its True Home, releasing any attachment to the earth. Yogi Bhajan has suggested that we chant *Akal* several times, preferably for 11 minutes. For the best results, he recommends that at least 5 people chant *Akal* for 31 minutes a day for 17 days, starting the day of the death. When this is not possible or appropriate, it is also effective to chant "***Akal***" one time. Any number of people can do the chant, including one. (Refer to accompanying CD for correct pronunciation – 11.)

When my son died suddenly of a heart attack in 1998, at the age of 49, I discovered the incredible blessing of being part of this 3HO family. Members of the community rallied around and virtually cushioned me through all the preparations. Knowing death to be a journey home, I had ordered "Bon Voyage" balloons for the funeral. I knew it had to be a celebration. James was finally free of the heavy karma of this incarnation. As the casket was about to be consigned to the flames of the crematorium, about 50 of us chanted Akal, Akal, Akal, over and over, led by Yogi Bhajan whose voice resonated with such power and passion, it was as if there were thousands and thousands of beings chanting with us, joining in and echoing the call to deathlessness.

Shakti Parwha Kaur, author of *Kundalini Yoga: The Flow of Eternal Power*

Ghosts

A ghost is the soul in the subtle body that cannot cross the electro-magnetic field of the earth. Each soul has 13–17 days to cross it, and until it does, the soul is earth-bound. All souls are given the opportunity to have a spiritual teacher in life but some are not receptive to this guidance. In such cases, these souls do not have a spiritual teacher or guides to help them cross over. They have not trained their mind to go for Infinity and instead desire earth. Some souls don't leave the physical body at all and hover over the body, which is what can be found in graveyards; but such souls will hover around any place where they were not able to break their attachments. It can be a terrible curse, because the ghost has all the feelings of the human but has no physical form to express it. There is no satisfaction. Some times these souls can be released through the prayers of earthly beings.

Such was the case one summer, at the Solstice Sadhana Yoga Intensive in New Mexico. Yogi Bhajan was leading about a thousand of us in blissful and powerful chanting. After chanting for at least 31 minutes, the weather turned into a dramatic show of nature, with roaring winds, thunderous lightening and hail the size of chickpeas. Yogi Bhajan said that he wished we had his eyes to see what was going on above us. Our ancestors, who had been trapped in the earth-bound circuit for thousands, millions and zillions of years, were all seeking liberation.

It was an amazing sight to see. It was a wonder of God. That is why, this time, when we prayed: 'Let God speak to us!' we heard a huge thunder. God poured us mercy, not because we were very wonderful human beings, but because those thousands and hundred of thousands of souls got relieved and released. That's called yaagnaa...

Yogi Bhajan

The Five Blue Ethers

Once we successfully cross the electro-magnetic field of the earth, we are ready to begin our passage through the five blue ethers. Depending upon our spiritual orientation, we usually have at least one guide to direct us through these realms of consciousness. For example, a Christian may have Christ, Mother Mary or St. Francis; a Jew may have Abraham or Moses; a Sikh may have Guru Nanak. When I die, my spiritual teacher, Yogi Bhajan will be there, along with the Sikh Gurus to usher me on my way.

The First Blue Ether, called *Karta Purakh*, contains the Akashic Records, also referred to as the Cosmic Library or Storehouse, where all the information of the universe is kept, including the life histories of all beings. The Subtle Body is the capsule of the Soul and it contains our "cosmic file" as well. When we pass through the first blue ether our individual file becomes a part of the cosmic library or storehouse. When we are reincarnated, we retain the same subtle body, imprinted with our old unfinished karmas. In the first blue ether, we access ourselves and are accounted for, according to our karmas. It is like an audit, a factual viewing so to speak. The soul intuitively knows that there is the next step – lessons to learn, debts to pay – a period of purification.

The Soul in the Subtle Body goes on to the second and third blue ethers, by passing through a kind of shield, or doorway, which separates one realm from the next. It is only when we undergo our internal process and reach a certain level of purification that we are granted passage into the next realm. The result of the thirty-second to three minute test of the mind, along with instruction from our enlightened guides, will determine specifically which lessons we will receive in these first and second blue ethers. The goal of this purification is to be able to perceive harmony of the Self.

The Second Blue Ether is called *Sopurakh* and is where we assess where we are in the cosmic play and what lessons we have yet to learn to further our consciousness. We not only acknowledge the need for these lessons, but we must next learn how to consistently maintain them throughout the test of Time and Space. This means that our efforts are able to demonstrate our consciousness through constancy of actions in all situations. For example, lets say that one of our lessons in life was detachment from personal success. In the second ether we are not only presented with that lesson and must acknowledge it, we are also tested with situations in which we are forced to prove our neutrality. If our efforts are not able to pass this test, we will have to return to another life. In order to pay off that karma, we are assigned a way to complete it. Whether we are a beggar or a king, a man or a woman; whether we live in Iran or France, have a violent parent or are born without sight. We may even have to teach our lessons to others in our next life to complete the karmic cycle.

It is important to note here that during meditation, it is possible to have similar experiences as in the first three blue ethers. It's like having a trial run. You can imagine how advantageous this can be for our purification and growth while alive and in preparation for death. Through meditation, we can come into contact with our Akashic Records and purify and release that which is blocking our highest potential in this life. In the second and third blue ethers, we can utilize the wisdom and guidance of Divine beings – depending upon our spiritual orientation, like Christ, Buddha, Guru Ram Das, St. Claire, Moses – to face our challenges in Time and Space. By doing this work in life, through meditation, our time in this incarnation will be less painful, we will be able to fulfill our true destiny and our passage at the time of death into the fourth and fifth ethers will be swift and blissful. It is comforting to know, though, that we are given a chance at death to complete our karmas. It is up to us to prepare our minds to be ready and fearless when this opportunity presents itself to us.

The Third Blue Ether, called *Purakh*, is the etheric realm of Khalsa. Up to this point, we have faced our karmas and received the tools we need to pay them off. Now in the third ether, free of the lessons of Time and Space, we move into a more refined realm, that of Khalsa, or pure one. There is a grace and dignity, which relates to spiritual consciousness. Instead of focusing on oneself, we turn our awareness to serving and blessing others. We have moved from individual identity to infinite identity. Free of the confines of an individual identity, there is no shield between the third and fourth ether, allowing us to easily slip into the next realm.

Between the third and Fourth Blue Ether, there is a huge shift. The fourth blue ether, called *Brahm Prakash,* is the realm of radiance or the lighted self. Once we reach this ether, we cannot reincarnate into another life without the will of God. From this layer, we can penetrate into all realms of existence and bliss is experienced. At the time of death, if we have a spiritual teacher, he or she can use their meditative powers during the ambrosial hours to penetrate through the magnetic field and help our soul slip into the fourth ether, freeing us. If the soul leaves through the *Tenth Gate*, it will be more likely to reach the fourth ether. The Soul Body is still present in the Fourth Ether. It has a kind of skin – both a connection and a separation between the finite and Infinite soul. It does not exist in the fifth layer, where there is a total merger and one becomes formless.

The Fifth Blue Ether, called *Brahm or God*, is the ultimate flow and merger into God, where out of the formless, limitlessness exists and all of creation comes into being. In ancient scriptures, it is said that in this realm, one experiences the divine gaze of the Creator.

If one meditates during life and at the time of death, it is possible to reach all five ethers. It is by becoming very subtle (conscious and aware) that we can be so light that we rise to the highest sphere. Guru Ram Das's soul has merged with the Infinite in the Fifth Ether, but His Subtle Body is available to us in the fourth ether. He is the source of creative unity and abundance, spiritually as well as materially. One who meditates on Guru Ram Das can manifest the essence of this reality. (Look in Chapter Nine at Meditation for Transformation and Bliss for a more complete explanation of Guru Ram Das and a specific meditation to do.) There is no time limit on how long one can stay in the fourth ether. This is where the souls of lovers and devotees of God dwell. Those who find God are endless. They are still alive guiding us – more so than when they were alive in their physical body. When we don't live in a physical body, we live in the Subtle and Radiant Bodies. The Radiant Body has no end. As long as the sun shall shine, the radiant body will live. The purpose of these radiant beings is to fulfill the positive desires of all. They are as the candle is to darkness.

There is no exact set time it takes the soul to progress through the ethers. It may be easier for the soul to progress on its journey during the ambrosial hours, between 3–6 a.m., when the rays of the sun are hitting and projecting at 60 degrees to the earth. It is a law of the sun energy. If we meditate during the ambrosial hours of the morning, this practice during life, this divine habit, will carry us through the ethers like a lightening bolt at the time of death. The soul has one other choice. If the soul has completed its journey to the fourth ether, it can choose to reincarnate into a human form, with God's will. It can return as a spiritual teacher, or someone who has an enormous mission on earth, requiring an enlightened consciousness to carry it out. Examples of this phenomenon might include such exalted personalities as Christ, Guru Nanak, Guru Gobind Singh, Mohammed, Buddha, and Moses. Of course it may also be the case that their karma was to do "the job" in order to be liberated. Once the soul merges with God in the fifth ether, this option is gone.

While I was researching information for this book, I interviewed many people. One of them, Gurucharan Singh Khalsa, Ph.D., was the first Kundalini Yoga teacher to set up an official and credited Kundalini Yoga Teacher Training Program in the United States. He is one of our most knowledgeable teachers and trainers. I asked him how we experience liberated beings that are merged in the fourth layer. He said that we would experience them differently. Some will experience them through subconscious dreams – the Mental Bodies; some will experience them through the intuition – the Neutral Mind; some will feel it through the constant flow of life through the Radiant Body; some will feel it almost like a merger of hearts – the Subtle Body. Since Yogi Bhajan's death, there is a personal and an impersonal reality. Personally, Guru Ram Das acted like a door to help Yogi Bhajan's soul slip into the fifth ether; impersonally, Yogi Bhajan's identity and role as a teacher projects into all realms, enabling him to guide us in life. Everyone will experience him differently; no way is better than any other. And, at the time of our death, he will guide our soul from ether to ether. (The last chapter, *The Master Goes Home*, has quotes from students' experiences of Yogi Bhajan since his death.)

The Five Blue Ethers are beautifully described in Japji Sahib – Paurees 34–37 – the first ether in Pauree 34, the second ether in Pauree 35, the third ether in Pauree 36 and ethers forth and fifth in Pauree 37. I have included them in Appendix II – Guru Nanak's Japji – for your further exploration.

Angels

Women angels are called devis, men are devas and exist in the third ether. They can't have a physical body (but long for one), and they have no will of their own. Their job or purpose, which is their blessing, is to serve the will of God. We all have angels guiding us, but we must be careful not to depend upon them. In this age of the awakened self, we must develop our relationship with our own intuition – our infinite self. As we have discussed numerous times in this book, the way to develop our intuition is by maintaining a consistent spiritual practice.

> *The only other time I have experienced that kind of thickness in a room was when our children were born in our home. It was so obvious that angels surrounded her. She had gotten carried from earth. It felt like a crowded room. Just like when we go to the Golden Temple and are shoulder-to-shoulder, arm-to-arm and leg-to-leg. There is no space. There were legions of angels carrying or guiding this soul. And after my father's death eighteen years ago, I felt he was my guardian angel.*
>
> Interview with Guru Singh

In the eyes of the Lord, may you be like angels uplifting humanity. In His Grace we pray that this humble wish may come true. Sat Nam.

Yogi Bhajan

> *At dawn I awoke and saw many angels around his bed. Tremendous love seemed to bathe the room in a soft glow as the first light streamed through the sheer curtains...I felt a deep and profoundly peaceful energy inside and around me. The deepest pain can bear fruit and become the highest bliss. I felt my dad was taking me there; it was exquisite, this special time with him.*
>
> Sat Kirin Kaur shares the death of her father

Rehearsing Death

Some may find it helpful to "rehearse" dying. The next chapter, *Rehearsing Death*, contains numerous meditations and visualizations for this purpose. Those who are caring for the dying may want to utilize some of these techniques. It is important to keep an attitude of nonattachment. We never really know what our death experience will be like. We can practice dying and then let go of the expectation of that experience. The key is to live consciously and then the journey at the time of death will be natural and easy. One's consciousness will already be one with the Creator

Guruka Singh's Near Death Experience

As a child, living in New York City, I remember lying in bed at night, in that twilight between waking and sleeping, and being able to leave my physical body and travel to other places through my subtle body. I flew out over the fire escape of our 13th floor apartment, over the city and the Hudson River. Each time, I would come back to my body through a thread, a silver cord. At first these flying experiences were fun, but a little scary. Once I realized that the cord was my safety, I welcomed and enjoyed these excursions. I believe that all children have this ability. But society tells them these occurrences are imaginary, ("No dear, you just dreamed that you were flying") so they eventually fade from their experience.

Once I started meditating, these experiences recurred. My subtle body could fly free from my physical body, I and could hear and see the same as with the physical ears and eyes. Sometimes I could visit with someone else's subtle body and experience what they did.

When I was 18 or 19 years old, I had a near death experience. I left my physical body as I had done before. I traveled vertically up through the silver cord, just like before. It was very beautiful. The Universe was so magnificent. There was no distance. We can travel anywhere and experience everything. I experienced the Divinity of everything. We are all connected – God is in everything. There are no words to describe the vastness, the universality, and the sacredness of the experience.

There was no physical body. I was pure consciousness, in which I experienced my whole life laid out before me. During this time, I felt everything I did and said in my life very deeply. I saw how everything I said and did affected every person with whom I interacted. I actually felt their feelings. I see how this can be a very heavy process if one hasn't looked in the mirror during life. There are two sides. One is warm and cozy. The other is unlimited, vast and full of light. After feeling all this so deeply, if one is in a state of guilt or fear, he will be pulled to the warm side...back into another life. If one is in a state of joy and ecstasy, he will let go. It's not so much a process of choosing the Infinite side, as it is letting go of the other side. It helps to know what to expect ahead of time, like knowing what you are going to see on a trip. There was nothing to fear.

I didn't want to come back. I was shown in pictures that my karma wasn't done. If I chose to break the silver cord, I would have to be reincarnated. As I knew I would have to come back anyway, I decided to come back into my present body. It was not a big deal, one body or another. There was still work to be done.

This experience affected me very deeply. Knowing what death is removes all fear of it. Death is as simple and natural as changing your clothes. Fear of death is God's greatest joke. Living without any fear of death let me be fearless in my life. After all, what's the worst thing that can happen to you? Certainly not dying. Actually the worst thing that can happen is estrangement from our awareness of our own, and everyone else's infinite nature at each moment – in life or death.

and will long to join with that Infinite Light.

PROCESS EXERCISES

Whether the information is familiar or totally new, there is a lot to assimilate in this chapter. Take some time.

1 How do you relate to what was said? Keeping in mind the previous chapters, does it make sense to you?

2 How does this way of viewing death resonate with what you already believe? Is it possible to incorporate some of it, all of it or none of it with your current beliefs?

3 Refer back to the "three questions" which will be presented to us in the first ten seconds of "Divine Grinding." How would you answer these questions now?

4 Practice the Kriya on the next page to "Correct The Five Tattvas." How did it feel?

5 Try some of the Pran Sutras given on the next five pages. Do any resonate with you? Start using them in your daily life. Choose one or two to use in the following chapter during the Practice Dying meditations and visualizations.

6 A more advanced meditation, "Meditation To Know the Unknown," is on page 160. By this time in the book, you are ready for it. You'll enjoy it. Notice what it does for you.

You die to your flesh and are born into your spirit. You identify yourself with the consciousness and life of which your body is but the vehicle. You die to the vehicle and become identified in your consciousness with that of which the vehicle is the carrier. That is the God.

Joseph Campbell
The Power of Myth

This kriya is grounding and can be used when there is shock, trauma or overwhelm. It is effective for caregivers or terminally ill patients to release

CORRECT THE FIVE TATTVAS

built up anger and frustration, by unlocking their diaphragm and returning them to the innocent state of childhood.

Posture: Sit straight in a chair with your elbows bent, palms facing each other about shoulder height.

Hand Mudra: Touch the tip of the Mercury (pinkie) finger to the tip of the thumb. Keep the other three fingers straight so that your Sun, Saturn and Jupiter antennae are lined up.

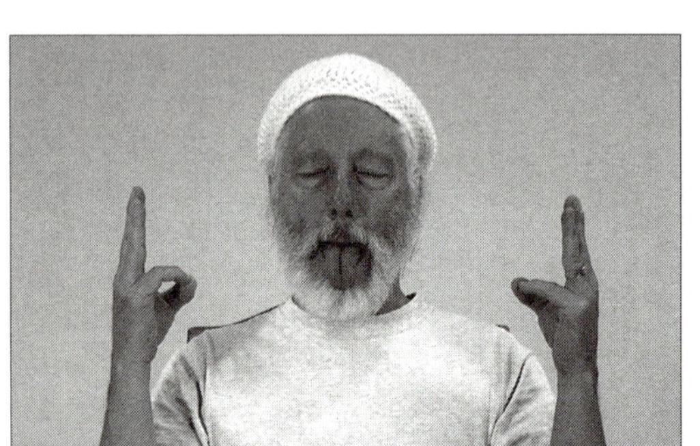

Breath: Stick your tongue all the way out and breathe in and out through your mouth as fast as you can, called Dog Breath. Close your eyes and listen to the breath. The sound of this breath is "Har."

Time: 11 minutes

To finish: Inhale deeply, roll your tongue inward, and hold your breath for 15 seconds. Exhale. Repeat this sequence two more times.

Yogi Bhajan gave a very powerful Pran Sutra at a conference in Chicago, September 4, 1993. The mantra is "**Ek Ong Kaar**," and was given by Guru Nanak. "**Ek**" meaning *One*, is a sharp sound chanted at the back of the throat as you pull in the navel center. In relation to this mantra, its sound is the opening key to "**Ong**," which means *Creator* and is chanted by blocking off the back of the throat with the tongue. It is a nasal sound, producing a humming vibration at the Third-Eye Point. (You will know you are doing it correctly if the sound will not come out while holding the nose.) The vibration created from the sound "**Ong**" stimulates the "Cavity of the Conch," where the nasal passages, the breath of life and the throat meet. When you do this sound, the entire brain is exercised and energized, making you excellent. According to Yogi Bhajan, excellent means that you can serve others in such a way that pain and suffering

is relieved. "**Kaar**," means *Creation* and is chanted with an open throat. Its vibratory sound will open the heart and adjust the energy throughout the body. Chanting "**Ek Ong Kaar**" opens our *Agia Chakra*, the seventh chakra, the optimum exit route of the soul from the body. This mantra will enable us to live in excellence and prepare us to meet our Creator.

*If you refer to the accompanying CD, all of the pran sutras are recited for your clarification and convenience – 12. A printed copy of Kirtan Sohila is included in Appendix I. If you contact Ancient Healing Ways or Spirit Voyage on the Resource Page, you can find out how to get a beautifully bound copy, and there are many wonderful spoken versions available on cassette or CD. Ancient Healing Ways also has videos available of the above conference.

You must practice to change the breath of the nostrils anytime at your control,

Pran Sutras

There are many pran sutras. All religions have their own special prayers, (like a rosary for Catholics) a form of a pran sutra. Each of us may relate to a different one. The following pran sutras or mantras are like *"master keys,"* and can be said by anyone of any religion or spiritual path. One such mantra is:

Naanak too(n) lehnaa too(n) hai, gur amar too(n) veechaariaa. Dhan dhan Ram Das gur, jin siriaa tinai savaariaa.

(from the Sawayas in praise of Guru Ram Das, Siri Guru Granth Sahib, p.968)
You are Nanak, Guru Angad, and Guru Amar Das. Honored and praised is Ram Das the Guru. The One who created you, has embellished and adorned you!

A complementary sutra to the previous one would be:

Pooree hoee karaamaat, Aap sirajanahaarai dhaari-aa

Perfect is your Miracle: The Creator Himself has installed you on the throne.

Other Pran Sutras include:

"Wha-hay Guroo," *you do not have to go through the panorama of death – pronounced in four syllables –* ***"Wa"*** *(rhyming with ma),* ***"He"*** *(rhyming with hey),* ***"Gu"*** *(rhyming with you), and* ***"Ru"*** *(the R is a hard sound like a D, the tongue hitting on the hard palate behind the front teeth and rhymes with moo)*

"Saat Nam," *you merge with the angels – pronounced in two syllables –* ***"Saat"*** *is long in four to six beats and rhymes with ma.* ***"Nam"*** *is short in one or two beats and rhymes with mom.*

"Hari" *all karmas go – pronounced in two syllables –* ***"Ha"****, rhyming with ma and* ***"Ri"*** *with the same hard* ***"D"*** *sound, rhyming with me.*

"Ram," *universality of God pleads for you – pronounced in one syllable, the* ***"R"*** *is soft as in red and it rhymes with mom.*

"Kirtan Sohila," *if this prayer is recited by memory, you will not have to go into the coma of death, where you go through the panorama of death. If the dying individual doesn't know it, recite it for them.* (Appendix)

It is important to note that these teachings give us the "potential" of these mantras. Whether we achieve the exact goal stated or not, they will help us face life and death in a more conscious way. Note that many of the Pran Sutras are the mantras that are used in the meditations in this manual.

MEDITATION TO KNOW THE UNKNOWN

Taken from Aquarian Times, Vol.3 #3, Fall 2003

otherwise when the breath starts going through both the nostrils (at the same time), within three minutes you die. It doesn't mater how great and healthy you are. They call it the central breath of death. But if you don't want to go, you can survive. If you are a yogi, if you have the conscious power to change the unconscious nostril, you can change the nostril. You don't conquer death by taking a medicine; you only heal the body. Death is beyond the body. Having a good car and a tuned car doesn't mean that you have gasoline in it. Your ida and pingala determine your breath, and your life and death. There are advanced Kriyas which require you to consciously regulate the breath through the nostrils, to bring the unconscious breathing to conscious breathing. If you press on the side of the rib cage, the nostril will change.

Yogi Bhajan

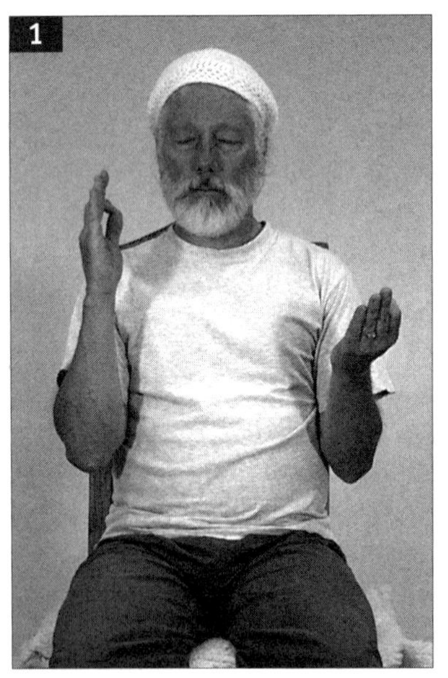

Part I

Sitting with a straight spine, place the hands in Gyan Mudra at the sides with the elbows bent. Consciously try to inhale through the right nostril as you raise the right hand up to the level of your nose (figure 1). Exhale through the right nostril as you lower the right arm pressing the upper arm against the side of your ribs. Then inhale through the left nostril as you raise the left arm and exhale through the left nostril as you lower the arm pressing it against the ribs. Breathe and move at the rate of one breath (inhale/exhale) per second. Continue this breath and movement for 5 minutes.

Part 2

Interlace your fingers and place them about 2–4 inches above your head.

Extend the thumbs out behind you and begin to rotate them around in circles together, without touching each other or your head. You can rotate them in a clockwise or counterclockwise direction **(2A)**. Use the same breath as in Part 1, (inhale and exhale through the right nostril, then inhale and exhale through the left nostril, taking one complete breath on each rotation of the thumbs, about 1–2 breaths per second). Breathe powerfully, opening up the rib cage.

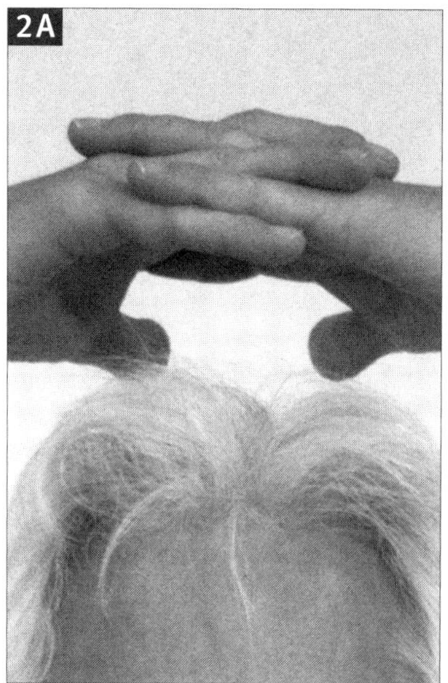
2A

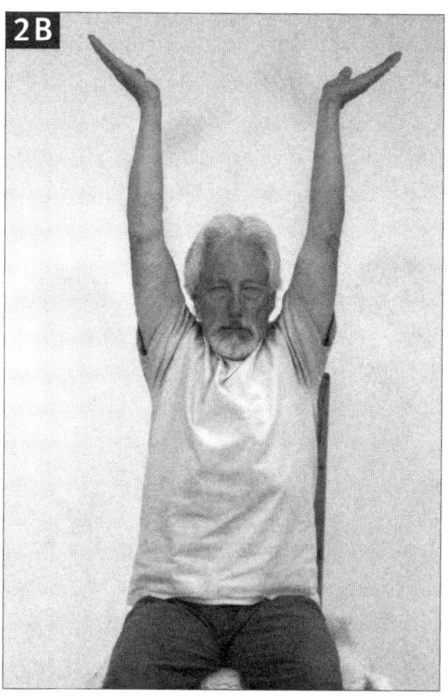
2B

Continue for 7 minutes, then inhale deeply and stretch your arms up straight, and strong like steel, keeping the elbows straight and bend the hands back so the palms face up **(2B)**. Create a strong pressure on the inside of the wrists. Inhale and pull the rib cage up. Hold for 30 seconds and exhale. Repeat the inhale, hold and exhale 2 more times.

According to ancient yogic teachings, this exercise will make you healthy, and your arcline will be like a halo.

CHAPTER 10

Rehearsing Death

What's extraordinary is that I didn't have a spiritual thought, 'I'm dying.' All I remember is looking at the pipes on the ceiling. Here I am Mr. Spiritual and in my death, I didn't orient towards the spirit. It shows me I have some work to do, because that's the test. So I flunked the test.

Ram Das
Speaking about his encounter with death when he had a stroke from the movie 'Fierce Grace'

All goes onward and outward, nothing collapses. And to die is different from what any one supposed, and luckier. Has any one supposed it lucky to be born? I hasten to inform him or her it is just as lucky to die, and I know it.

Walt Whitman
Leaves of Grass, 1855

WE ALL EXPERIENCE TWO PARAMOUNT ADVENTURES – birth and death. These two portals bring us into life with a scream and usher us out with a sigh. Couples prepare for birth by going to birthing classes, reading books, exercising and remodeling their home. We also need to train for the other great adventure – death.

The techniques we have learned in this book can be such a training. We have learned how to let go of old ideas and habits in meditation. We have learned how to surrender to a Higher Power and deeper universal truths. We have had the experience of altered states of consciousness, melting out of our denseness into the ocean of pure being. All of these things will prepare us for that supreme journey of death.

In this chapter, we are going to put it all together, so to speak. Keeping in mind what we have learned in the previous chapters and using Yogi Bhajan's death visualizations and meditations in this chapter, we will have a Death Rehearsal.

Some may find it comforting and helpful to have a gentle guide or "coach," to help them on their passage. Some, who have not been able to prepare with the tools in this book, may need a more direct guide. The coach may find it helpful to "rehearse" dying with the person. The process of the body shutting down can be frightening and confusing. Educating the person to the process and then taking them through a guided meditation may be reassuring. Such trial runs, though, must be taken lightly with an attitude of "maybe." For, if we cling to expectations, they could hinder our swift transition when it is our time. Helping someone else prepare for death will prepare us for our own grand exit as well.

A coach could be a family member, friend, caregiver or spiritual guide. Many times family members are too attached and heavily grieving to be neutral coaches. It is best if the person in transition can choose the death coach ahead of time, and have them be accepted by the family (if possible). If none of this is possible, the coaching can still happen. One in transition with one foot in life and one in death isn't totally present in either state. As the physical body begins to shut down, the spirit journeys into more etheric realms, making it possible to communicate on a soul level. If verbally talking to the dying person is not possible, the coach can still communicate non-verbally through the heart center and Third-Eye. The person will gratefully hear the direction. Always be sensitive to the dying person. They will let you know in subtle ways what they need. Investigate what are their beliefs; never ever try to sway the person with your viewpoints. Enrich the significance of their experience by incorporating their beliefs into the meditations and guided visualization.

If Death Won't Come

If for some reason the dying person seems to be stuck and can't leave, here are some things to consider. Are relatives hanging on to their loved one? They may need some counseling about the importance of letting go. The dying person may need to hear them say, "It's OK for you to go. You lived a good life. Your job was done well. We'll be fine. Accept everything. Let go to God." Is there any unfinished business, which is bothering the dying person or disputes going on between family members? The dying person may be stuck in one element, unable to allow the death

---

Guruka Singh's Mother's Death – A story about subtle communication, as told by Guruka Singh

My Mom had a stroke and lost the power to speak. She was in the hospital in New York City. I flew from New Mexico to New York to see her. I sat by the side of the bed and I held her hand. She couldn't talk. She was very radiant and beautiful. She was angry about something. I couldn't figure out what it was. She reached up and grabbed my beard and began yanking on it. I realized that she was really frustrated and trying to tell me something. After spending 3 days by her bedside, massaging her and caressing her and being present with her, I came back to New Mexico. I got a call from the hospital saying that it was only the NG tube (feeding tube) that was keeping her alive. I said that she didn't want to be on the NG Tube. The person on the other end said that I would have to talk to someone on the Ethics Committee of the hospital. I said 'why do I have to talk to the Ethics Committee if those were her wishes?' She said I was the closest relative, so I would have to talk to the head of the Ethics Committee.

The next morning, I was out walking and all of a sudden my mother came into my head and said, 'GET ME OUT OF HERE.' I heard it absolutely clearly in her voice. And, I said, 'OK, I'll take care of it.' When I got home, the phone rang and it is the doctor on the Ethics Committee. It was a woman. I said that I didn't know how to express this, so I just blurted it out...I said, 'Look my mom came into my head this morning and said, 'Get me out of here.' She doesn't want to be kept alive by this tube. She told me quite clearly. Luckily this woman was intuitive enough to say, 'I understand,' and she went to the Ethics Committee and made it happen. Thank God.

It was about two weeks later that my mom died. I was meditating at my altar, and I knew she had left her body. I chanted Akal, even though I hadn't been told she left her body. I knew in my consciousness. It was the weekend. The phone rang later that morning, someone calling from the hospital saying that she had passed that morning.

My mother had been an atheist. She was very adamant about it. She used to say, 'When you die, you die, that's it. When it's over, you're just gone.' I remember chuckling and laughing while I rubbed her feet. You know, she was actually a very spiritual woman. She was an artist and loved all beautiful things. She had exquisite Italian clay angels hanging all over the house. I used to tell her, 'Mom, when you die, you are going to be so surprised. Remember this moment of my talking to you, because you are going to be free...you aren't going to just disappear and have it all over. It's going to be wonderful and I will be right there with you.' She scoffed and lit another cigarette.

That day she died, we took our family to a water park in Albuquerque. As I was driving, all of a sudden my mom's voice clearly came into my head again and said, 'You were right. I'm as light as a feather, I can fly.' She was spiraling up – completely, in ecstasy. It was the sweetest moment.

What this story meant to me is that she was better communicating with me when she had lost the power of speech than when she could talk. When someone has had a stroke, it doesn't mean that you can't communicate with him or her absolutely clearly...even enough to take action."

---

process. For example, as the earth element is dissolving, he or she may be anxious about the sensation of gravity – the body feeling heavy – and not relax with the experience. Or, as the air element is dissolving, there may be a resistance to changes in their breath pattern. All of these things can slow down the process of letting go. Also reading *Kirtan Sohila* can help. It only needs to be read one time and will help to release any resistances. (*Kirtan Sohila* can be found in Appendix I.)

Coaching The Relatives

Coaching the relatives can be a delicate task. The person coaching the dying can also coach the family and relatives, although a different person may be needed to coach this latter group. Watching a loved one go through the dying process is a heart wrenching experience. No two people will respond in the same way. The best thing a coach can do is be present, trying to be sensitive to family members' needs and styles of processing. It is not the time to counsel in the usual way of bringing about change in the person's behaviors or attitudes. This is the time to flow with the needs of the individual. Maintaining an attitude of sacredness and subtly communicating through your Third-Eye and heart center can have a profound effect on the harmony of the whole family scene. Some members may even need permission and encouragement to grieve. Above all, judgment has no place or benefit in this setting.

Har Nal Kaur Khalsa, who working many years as a homecare and hospice nurse, frequently found herself in the role of a subtle coach to family members, tells the following heartfelt, poetic story.

Today I am sharing with you from my heart, my own personal experiences of death and dying.

You are alive and then you are dead. The finality of it! One second you are here on the earth and the next you are not. When the soul leaves the body it becomes a useless mass. Its purpose as the temple of the soul is completed.

'We received the news that your time has come. Will it be months, days, maybe years? Funny, I have passed that tree coming home so many times before, but now it will never look the same. Nothing will be the same again.'

The death process – the breath slows and the body relaxes. Another breath and it's gone. A golden glow of love permeates the air, uniting all present – a blissful feeling of peace. I am in awe for the blessing of sharing this sacred time.

How do you be with someone who is dying? Everyone deals with it the best they can.

Best there be no judgments.

One sister is there every day: 'I work so hard. They don't help, but they tell me what to do. The others don't come. Don't they love our mother?'

One brother is out with his friends. Can you see the pain – the anger from the love he never had, the times they never share, the betrayal, unforgiven?

One daughter wants to touch him. She sees his fear, but her resentment stops her from reaching out to calm him.

A son cannot bear to see his mother fade away. He cannot come. He cannot cry. Maybe he cries alone. Maybe he cries inside. So deep into eternity are the tears.

'O, do not tell father he is dying.' Whispers announce what he already knows, unshared...or spoken through silence.

Best there be no judgments.

It is a time to be real...to share...to laugh...to love. Bring all the skeletons out of the closet. Dare to reconcile – a chance to heal. It is a tender time...so sweet ...too intense.

What is the pain? Between 1–10...it is a 10+. All the morphine won't touch...the emotional pain. Confusion and questions flood the mind. 'How did I live my life? What has been my purpose? What have I done? What have I been? Do I have regrets? Who will be left behind? Priorities shift. Where am I going?'

One dies in fear. One dies in peace. One dies in pain. One dies alone, while another dies surrounded by family. One tries to fend off death. Another can't wait, but death will not come. She waits to say one last goodbye.

Best there be no judgments.

'Such a tender touch! Thank you for being so kind. You are an angel. Sing to me.'

Sitting in the early golden glow of sunlight, she looks at him – so simple. A lifetime shared, deeply. It is a precious time. An intruder, transfixed, I cannot return to the din outside the room.

'Thru truth man merges in his real Self in his home and deaths' myrmidon can devour him not.' (Siri Guru Granth Sahib, Pp. 228–229).

...And there is bliss.

'I see Infinity in his eyes. He has one foot on earth and one in the ethers.'

...And there is awe.

Holding hands around you we pray, 'Mother Mary full of grace, blessed art Thou amongst women.' (Catholic Rosary).

...and there is love.

We have some holy dirt from Chimayo. ' Here is some for you to sprinkle on him when it's your turn to tell him goodbye.'

...And we join hands.

'You are Christian...I am Sikh. Our souls merge in our depth of devotion and love...sharing this precious moment.'

...And we are one.

Useful Legal Documents

With all of Har Nal Kaur's years of nursing experience, she emphasized the benefit of arranging medical wishes and needs ahead of time. Every state has laws that are a little different. In New Mexico, where Nar Nal practices, she is familiar with some very useful documents. One is called a "Living Will," in which a person declares what life-saving measures he or she wants taken in the event of an emergency, like CPR, oxygen, an IV, or a feeding tube. Another is a "Durable Medical Power of Attorney," where one person and an alternate (can be family members) are chosen to make medical decisions if the patient is not capable. Patients and relatives need to check with their hospital or doctor to make sure they can sign such documents.

It is advisable that you sign these documents while you are able to make decisions for yourself. Don't wait until you are ill or unable to make reasonable decisions. Do it now while you are able. Be sure to copy these documents in duplicate and give them to family members, the doctors and appropriate caregivers. Display a copy in a prominent place in the home for easy viewing by paramedics or other health care professionals.

When an emergency happens, the family has to make difficult decisions. If we have thought about and documented ahead of time what we want, it makes the decision process much easier for our loved ones, and we will get the care we prefer. No matter what the professionals, family members and friends advise, we have the right to make the final decisions about what is best for our body. Coaches can give a great gift to patients by helping them through this process. We all have the right to choose our life and death.

Coaching The Soul of a Sudden Death

Many near death experiences have been lived by people who were in an accident and out of confusion, as if in a dream, hovered over their physical body, not realizing that they were dead until they reentered their body again.

It may be possible for the soul to be so trained in life that it will automatically know what to do. There was a very divine young man, Bhai

Sahib Dyal Singh, who through his meditation and righteous living was ready for death. He was sleeping in the back seat of a car when it crashed. According to Yogi Bhajan, his subtle body was already out of its physical body. His consciousness was already one with the sound current at the Golden Temple (the Sikhs' "mother temple" in India) when the accident occurred. His soul was not confused; it was already there.

In accidental deaths, as it may not be absolutely definitive whether the person's soul has the opportunity to go through the ethers or not, survivors may need to assist the soul on its journey by saying something like, "My friend, you have died. Your body is no longer a suitable dwelling for your spirit or your consciousness." The deceased may need coaching to know where to direct its soul and consciousness. The coach can talk the person through the process with words, mantras, visualization and meditation. This would be a good time to apply a Pran Sutra. If other people surround the deceased and you are not able to talk directly to the person, silently speak through your heart center and Third-Eye. As they are in a spirit realm, they will hear you and welcome the guidance. Chanting Akal will assist the soul as well.

It is also possible to coach someone who is thousands of miles away. You do not have to be physically present with the person. You can prepare them for death and after death, you can guide their soul home. As they are in a spirit realm, there will not be the resistance that comes with the physical body. The communication can be absolutely clear and intimate. The following story poignantly demonstrates this point.

Guruka Kaur's Father's Death – A story about coaching at a distance, as told by Guruka Singh

This story is about my wife's father, Martin. He was a very hard worker. He had a wonderful sense of justice and righteousness, equality and kindness. He always took care of the people who worked for him. He was the foreman of a sheet metal shop in New York. They used to cut and bend it to make the heating ducts for houses. When he retired, he was honored with a huge retirement dinner. Everyone loved him. He retired and moved from New York to Florida.

Every morning, he woke up at 4:00 am. He could never figure out why he got up at that hour. He'd walk around the house, get a cup of coffee and wait for the newspaper to come. I'd say to him, 'You wake up early, because in other lifetimes it was a part of your natural rhythm – it was your time for meditation.' He didn't really understand what I was talking about.

When he was dying, he had a lot of fear. I was here in New Mexico, and he was in Florida. He came to me in my meditation and said, 'What will happen to me? I haven't even been a good Jew.' I showed him in images how he had been so kind to people and stood up for the rights of others. I took him through this and said, 'That is who you are and that is what it is to be a good Jew.' He laughed and understood.

He was still processing his fear of letting go of the physical plane and came to me again a few days later and said, 'I'm scared. What is actually going to happen to me when I die?' Again, I showed him pictures. I showed him an image of what it feels like for the subtle body to leave and for the soul to leave...and what it felt like to come out through the tenth gate when the body isn't working any more and is being left behind. I said, 'All of you and your radiance and all of your infinity is there, see? It was a very technical question and I showed him in pictures exactly what happens. Then, he relaxed and said, 'I understand.'

He came back to me a third time. I knew he was afraid of letting go of his body. He identified with his physical body, and it was hard for him to imagine letting go of it. I remembered that he had told me a story years ago about moving the sheet metal shop from its old location to a new building, and so what I showed him in pictures this time was, 'Dad, you remember in the shop when you have to move a piece of equipment from one location to the other? You have to pull the plugs out and disconnect the pipes? Then, you prepared it to be moved, put it in the truck and then it goes to the new location. I used the image he could easily understand – disconnecting and moving a piece of equipment. He got it right away and said, 'Oh, I'm just being moved from one place to another.' He completely relaxed. I felt it. Then he was able to leave.

He processed his fear and doubt remotely with me over two thousand miles of distance in an absolutely clear communication through pictures and images. It is something he never would have discussed with me in the same room. He couldn't talk about those things. Even though his intellectual mind scoffed about my being a Sikh, when it came right down to it, he needed to understand spiritually what was going on and he knew to come to me.

So, I think the message about all of this is that if you open yourself and create a space for the person who is dying to communicate with you...in other words if you make yourself available in your meditation and open yourself up to them and say that you are there for them, they will feel that. If you haven't opened the space to them, they may just yell at you to get your attention. You can be with someone in the most intimate way, even when you are not able to physically be there with him or her. Many times more can be done in the spiritual realms than you could do in the physical.

DEATH MEDITATIONS

Now we will begin the numerous meditations and visualizations on death. You may find it helpful to familiarize yourself with all of them before you choose a couple to try. If you are going to use them to coach others, it would be advisable to practice all of them yourself. With a wider range of experiences, you will be better equipped to meet individual needs. Whether you are using the visualization for yourself or someone else, it is advisable to tape your voice saying the visualization, allowing the participant to fully engage in the experience.

MEDITATION ON DEATH

Yogi Bhajan gave this meditation November 2, 1986 in Los Angeles.

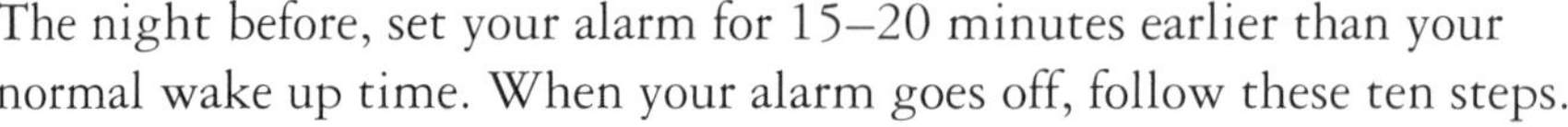

The night before, set your alarm for 15–20 minutes earlier than your normal wake up time. When your alarm goes off, follow these ten steps.

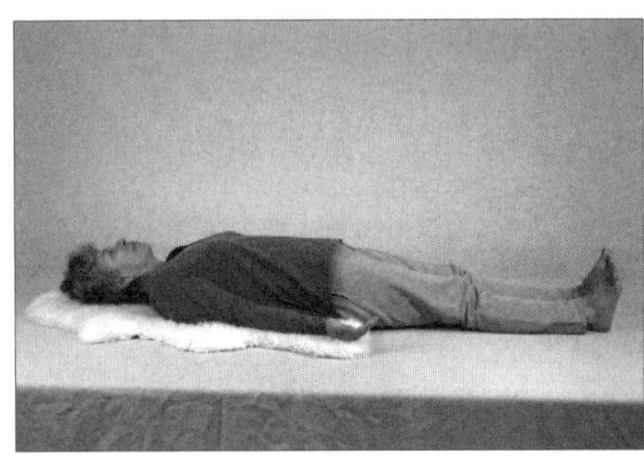

1 **Don't get up.** Say *"Wha-hay Guroo."*

2 **Lie in Corpse Pose** (flat on your back with the arms next to your sides and the palms up). Consciously die.

3 **Relate to your soul.**

4 **Decorate your subtle body** with the mantra *"Wha-hay Guroo,"* as you would decorate the Palki Sahib with flowers (a covered sacred carriage or altar for the Sikh scriptures or Guru, which has four poles, one on each end, to allow the sangat or congregation to carry it).

5 **Make a Palki of it** – walk and chant.

6 **Carry it yourself** to the Infinity of God.

7 **Settle there,** purify yourself and enjoy the ecstasy.

8 Then with the speed of one utterance of the word, *""Wha-hay Guroo,"* come back into your body. This will give you mastery over space.

9 Next, come into Dhandwaat Pranaam: lie flat on your stomach with the heels together. The arms are outstretched in front of you with the palms in Prayer Pose. Thank God. This will give you mastery over space.

10 Start your day.

Practice this for at least forty days. You can also extend it up to three to six months, so you may never forget it at the time of death.

...a day will come when you will drop your body. You will know that day. You call it 'death.' We call it 'going home'...It is a conscious action. Unconscious death will give the rebirth right here. Subconscious death will take you through 8.4 million cycles of death and breath and then you come out to whatever you thought of subconsciously. What you call 'Nirvana', 'Jiwan-Mukht', etc., it's all a very simple process.

Yogi Bhajan

YOGI BHAJAN'S VISUALIZATION ON DEATH

Yogi Bhajan gave this visualization on death at a conference in Chicago, September 4, 1993. Before you begin this meditation, refer to the accompanying CD, where his voice is recorded leading this visualization. The mantra is chanted in a very specific way.

Be sitting in a chair with a straight spine and both feet flat on the floor, or lying down with the arms crossed over the chest with hands on opposite shoulders. Close your eyes.

Just start sinking. I am happy. I am dying. My earth job is done. I am going to a beautiful new home, bright, light, divine, perfect, projected. Wow! There shall be no sweat. There shall be no pain. All will be nothing but happy, happy union. In this communion, I am going. I am going to my Creator. I am meeting the One who made me. I am meeting the One who gave my body. I am meeting the One who made my mind. I am meeting the One who gave me my soul. I am meeting the One who made me to meet yogis, swamis, Jews, Catholics, Muslims, idiots, wise. It was all that great duality. I am free!

It is that freedom, that sovereignty that ecstasy I am enjoying. I am going slowly, gradually. I am aware. I am aware, absolute aware. I know the Perfect has a perfect happiness...all waiting for me. I'll be loved, hugged, merged in that ecstasy. I am going very slowly, very relaxed. I am relaxed. I am relaxed. I am relaxed. I am absolutely passing that phase where there is no sweat, no pain, no departure, no anxiety and no difficulty. I am free. I have done my job. My journey is complete. I have reached the destination and the destiny. I have reached my end. Now it is not my end. It is the end of my difficulties, my sweat, my fear, my scene. After meeting my Almighty Creator, who gave me the soul, mind and body, I shall live in His will, all the will that will decide me and my next step.

I am, I am, I am, I am, I am, I am, I am, I am, I am, I am, I am, I am, I am, I am, I am. Concentrate. Let me concentrate through the difficult passage of my life through death...through the sound of vibratory mega sense, so no fear can catch me when I am dying. I am, I am, I am, I am, I am, I am, I am, I am, I am, I am, I am, I am, I am, I am, I am, I am, I am, I am.

Please tap your shoulders, strongly. Don't be very gentle. Hard! Beat them up. Beat! Beat! Beat! Beat! Beat! All right. You may live, but that is the sound. It is three-mega seven-watt alpha sound, which will come through and carries you, because your cells have to vibrate to create that energy.

If you would like a copy of the original video, contact Ancient Healing Ways (Resource Page)

Separating the mind from the spirit bodies

In Chapter Eight, we discussed the mind and its commanding influence in our life – especially its relationship to our thoughts, emotions, desires and actions – and how we can use meditation to manage the mind to serve us. As experienced in our daily lives, this powerful mind is interrelated to our physical and spirit bodies as well. In relation to illness, it is often the stress on the mind that lodges in the physical body, creating disease. It is our mind that sets boundaries to our potential and abilities. We often identify with the physical, forgetting that in truth we are spirit. It can be most advantageous to be able to split the mind from the physical and spirit bodies – to experience them as separate entities. By separating them, we are able to experience our vastness, and thus our true reality. Wouldn't it be wonderful if we could separate the mind from the body in times of illness and pain? Of course we need our mind, but think about how grand it would be if we had the skill to choose when to separate them or not?

Developing this ability in life will also give us a tremendous advantage at the time of death. By separating our mental body from the physical, it won't risk getting trapped with the physical. The physical body can proceed with its shutting down process without the mind's resistance. Also, by putting the mind aside, the spirit can expedite its journey without the judgments of the mind.

COORDINATION OF BODY/MIND AND SPIRIT

Taught by Yogi Bhajan, October 20, 2001 – Espanola, New Mexico

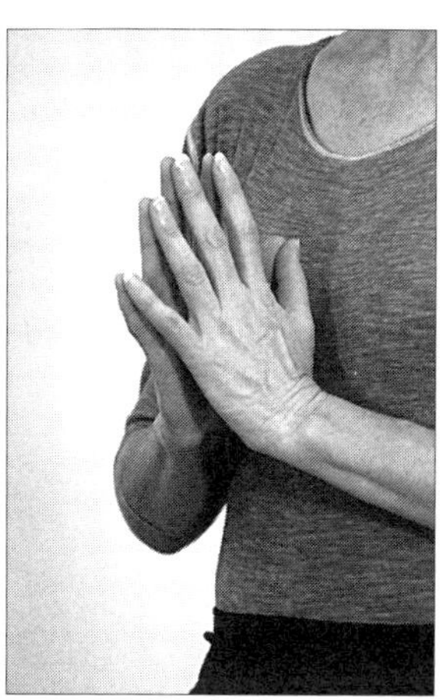

You may want to purchase the video or audio of this class from Ancient Healing Ways (resource page), so you can listen to Yogi Bhajan's voice as you do this meditation, or you may want to record your own voice.

Sit or lie with a straight spine. Bring your hands in front of your heart center, with the fingertips touching and the palms spread. The breath is very long and down to the navel point, hold and then exhale completely out. Continue.

The Guided Meditation by Yogi Bhajan

Try to see how the energy moves. You will feel the reality of the body. Inhale deep and ride on the breath, in and out, long and deep, as honestly as you can. Take your body – the inner being in this body, simply by meditative force. Do not try to understand that you cannot do it. It is not difficult, but it is a great experience. Pull your mental body out of your physical body. Just take it out. Just simply coordinate between you, your environments, your activities and your own preciousness.

Your mental body, when you command it, is very pure, very clear. And it is yours. It is not related to the physical activities, although the mental body is with you. Things are corrupt only when you are in your physical body and your mental body is not combined. So, do coordinate. (But for now use your power) and take it out, out of your being.

The power we have is our virtue…value, we give; virtues we experience. The majority of the time we forget that we have values…and once a person follows one's own values, that is all divinity is all about. So keep the breath long, deep and evaluate yourself. Give yourself values. The first value you can give yourself is: I am virtuous. I am beautiful. God created me in the best form. Thank God has given me health, happiness and wealth. You are a wonder of the world. Recognize the fact. Concentrate on these things.

Now comes the secret of the Shintoism, the Japanese faith. See that you are just a blade of grass, beautiful, green and you are covering your values. Start covering your values as a blade of grass, with an extreme sense of self-cooperation. …I asked a Japanese master, 'What is Shinto?' He replied, 'It is a personal religion. 'Can I know about it?' He picked a blade of grass and said, "What do you see?' …I said, 'God.' He asked, 'Where is it?' I said 'In this blade.' He said, 'You know Shinto. That's it.'"

The tips of the fingers must meet so that circulation can coordinate the two parts of the body, and your valuable and virtuous and wonderful body is right, at this time, under manual control and your mental body is taken out.

The mental body is looking at your physical body as you are sitting. Practice this split. Once you can separate your mental body and practice to separate it, as you keep on doing, there will be no problems – at the time of death you can split your mental body and be free of karma. You will never have a rebirth again. That is guaranteed.

Your breath has to be very long and deep because your spiritual body, your physical body, your mental body and your being are separate. You have never been taught this. You have never been told. You think you are one bundle.

Feel the super and extreme contentment. That will bring you prosperity. Ride on your breath and just feel supremely contented. That will give you the prosperity that you are looking for. It's no use living rich, it's no use living poor, it's no use being great if you cannot demonstrate to yourself that you can separate your bodies as you can separate that strength. And you can not only visualize, but also experience it. In this experience, you are the Supreme.

Your mental body and your radiant body – have you ever put them together? They are yours. Nobody will know it, but you will be charged and recharged with the energy. What is more beautiful on this earth than you? What is more pure and shining than you? What is more cool and calm and quiet than you? In the eyes of God you are everything.

Take a long deep breath and ride on it. Fortune and misfortune are two wavelengths. By yourself it pulses – you can put your body on any wavelength you need. In common man's language we call it repetition.

The body's membranes, the body's readjustment and the body's main nervous system are going to adjust now. You are within that time. Please breathe long and deep and cure yourself forever. Heal! Take long deep breaths and ride on it, and keep your mental body away. Only look at where the tips of the fingers meet.

Circulate your breath. Keep the mental body separate. Concentrate on the physical body, in the realm of personal consciousness. You are beautiful, you are bountiful, you are blissful, you are virtuous and you have vigor, self-control. Apply all of that.

A deep breath can touch the central nerve in the navel point. A split mental body can give you a vast area of coexistence. Your all five channels and tattvas are totally balanced at the moment. Your arc line is clear. Can you believe the little bit that we have done? We suffer here, there, everywhere. What for? America needs peace and it needs love. It needs tons of smiles. It needs us – we the people.

Now is the time. Breathe long and deep. Get it when it is available. Bring in you the coziness. Colorful coziness. Split the light inside. Bring in the special Breath of Life. If you know how to concentrate, meditate and breathe. This is the time.

To end

Breathe in deep and hold it tight. Breathe out. Breathe in deep and hold it tight. Breathe out. Breathe in all the virtues of God and breathe out peace for the world. Breathe in long and deep, hold it, love it, feel it, and then let it go. Now put all the pressure on the fingertips. Inhale deep. Put a tight grip on the fingers. Let it go. Inhale deep. Make the fingers very tight. Feel the purpose of life and prosperity. Let it go. Inhale deeply, exhale and relax.

Using The Chakras

In Chapter Four, we discussed the science of the Kundalini Energy moving up the Chakras. We experimented with raising this energy by using the meditations in that chapter, Sat Kriya and The Seven-Wave Meditation and the Body Locks or Bandhs presented in Chapter Five. We have also used eye position to direct the energy up. Not only can that technology be used to manage our energy levels and consciousness in life, we can adapt it to the time of our death. We can also coach someone else preparing for his or her passage.

Basically, as the elements are dissolving at the time of death, we use our pure intent to consciously move the energy up the chakras until the soul exits out through the Crown Chakra. For the following visualization, experiment pulling a slight to moderate Mulbandh combined with a slight Neck Lock, which will give you an experience of the energy moving up the chakras. It's important to remain relaxed, so only pull the Bandhas as tight as you can while maintaining relaxation. Keep the eyes "softly" (no need to strain) focused up at the Third-Eye and higher. As you have used these techniques during your yoga practice, you will be familiar with how they feel. During death, we will not need to physically apply a lock. Our energy will be more subtle but powerful as well. Merely focusing our attention up should be sufficient to pull the soul up and out the Crown Chakra.

GUIDED VISUALIZATION ON DEATH

This is an example visualization created by the author using the teachings. You can embellish it and make it personal for yourself or the person you are working with. You may even want to tape your voice saying the visualization. Be lying down in a comfortable position, preferably with the arms to the sides, palms facing up. The eyes are closed. Begin mentally chanting your pran sutra, which you chose in the last chapter. Keep it constantly playing in your head and vibrating through your whole being. Your eyes are softly focused at the Third-Eye Point and above. Start taking long, deep breaths. Imagine that there is a very small opening in your nostrils, allowing your breath to be very slow and deep, inflating the lower lobes of the lungs first, the stomach and lower rib cage expands. Keep inhaling, until the upper lobes are full as well, feeling the chest and collarbone rise. Then, begin exhaling, first from the throat, then the chest, and finally allowing the abdominal area to lower. Continue breathing, watching the journey of the breath, feeling all of your sensations. The sensations associated with the air entering your nostrils, traveling into your lungs…and the sensations which they produce…perhaps calmness and relaxation. Combine your pran sutra with your breath.

Be aware of any other sensations…like sounds in the room, sounds outside, (mention ones you hear, like water from the fountain, birds singing, dogs barking, music, cars, your voice). Be aware of all of these sounds at the same time, none is more or less important than the other. Notice what sensations are produced by these sounds, without judging them, without labeling them. Just allow them and be with them. Notice other sensations like the wind on your skin, being aware of how that sensation resonates. Keep including other sensations, internal sensations, like your heart beating, the flow of your energy in your body, the movement of blood and your pran sutra beating in every pore of your being. Be aware of all of these sensations at the same time.

Feeling very relaxed now. Begin to spread that relaxation into all parts of your body. Notice that your body is starting to feel heavy. Your feet…legs…buttocks…spine…hands…and arms…are all sinking into the softness of the bed (floor). The shoulders, neck, muscles of the face and head are so dense you can't move them. Your physical form is sinking so deep, your earth element is dissolving now. Feel your energy in the First Chakra at the rectum. Pull a slight or moderate Mulbandh and hold the lock. Surrender to the process, allow, allow, allow the earth element to dissolve into the water element, moving your awareness into your Second Chakra, the sex organs. Now, the fluids of the body are sluggish, moving ever so slowly. Your mouth and eyes may feel dry. Let go of any resistance. You may see a light. Go toward it. There is nothing to worry about now. Everything is perfect. Surrender the water element to fire, moving your awareness into the Third Chakra at the navel center, merging with pure energy…beyond time…space…and form. Keep going toward the light. Not aware now of any heat or cold, allow the fire element to merge with the air element. Maintain the Bandh.

Your consciousness is at your Heart Center, the Fourth Chakra. The breath is slowing. The pause between the exhale and the inhale is lengthening. Go with it. Don't be afraid. As the element air dissolves into ether, the lightest

of the elements, the energy flows into the Fifth Chakra, the Throat Center. From here, the purest of energies flows up into the Sixth Chakra, the Third-Eye Point. Feel suspended between this world and the next. Surrender, yield to your merger with the One. You might hear music or other celestial sounds. You might see images. Enjoy them, but don't get distracted. The light is waiting for you. Keep going toward it. Don't allow things and people to lure you. Keep focused on the light. Feel its brightness. You're almost there. Bringing your awareness to your Seventh Chakra, the Crown Chakra at the top of your head, allow your energy/soul to fly free. Relax the Bandh.

Your life's panorama will come before you. Bless yourself with acceptance, forgiveness, compassion and love. Purify and expand your consciousness with your pran sutra. Two paths may be approaching. One is warm, cozy and luring. The other is a snowy path…cold, crisp, pure. Go toward the snowy path. Remain focused and don't delay. Allow your pran sutra to guide you. You're almost Home. Surrender to God's loving arms…and be free.

Be creative with this. If you are assisting someone who does not know about the energy flows of the Chakras, use your visualization and intention to assist them to raise their energy up.

ILLUSTRATION BY KIRN JOT KAUR

When assisting someone else, you may also sense that the person is stuck in a particular chakra or is having a hard time releasing from one element to another. You can tell this by observing their emotional states. For example, if someone is especially grieving or sad, there may be a block in the Heart Center (which includes the lungs) and the air element. If the person is overly attached to personal possessions or that their loved ones are not going to be taken care of, there could be a block in the earth element and the First Chakra. If you sense that the person needs to express something and can't, there may be an imbalance in the Throat Chakra and the element ether. If the person is angry, bitter or trying to control everything around him or her, this may be an indication that the Navel Center and the fire element need balancing. These blocks may be released by guiding the person in the above visualization.

Another way one can balance their chakras is by being at their Third-Eye Point. By focusing at the Third-Eye Point, one is able to see that all of their attachments are just illusions, thus enabling them to surrender to Infinity. This is the consciousness we want to help the dying person reach. Have him or her close their eyes and focus up at their Third-Eye Point, while taking very long and deep breaths. Chant with them ***God and Me, Me and God are One*** or ***Ang Sang Wahe Guru*** (in every limb of me I am One with God). You can also use any of the ***Pran Sutras*** or any of the other mantras that help the person experience a state of bliss and union with the One.

Quotes from a lecture by Yogi Bhajan, *The Strength of a Teacher Part I*, the first annual teachers conference, June 6, 1994.

The moment you know your time has come, you'll start seeing the panorama show, (Yogi Bhajan points to his Third-Eye point). Immediately look at the chin to clarify your mind, right in a second. Sometimes you will know about three minutes earlier and sometimes only 30 seconds before. But you must get thirty seconds. There's no way that that chance will not be with you, however helpless you may look. Concentrate on the chin for a second or two or three. You'll still have 27 seconds. Really. And secondly concentrate at the tip of the nose, to pull yourself up. Then concentrate at the Third Eye Point, and clearly know how rotten you are and how right you are, it doesn't matter. And then ask in prayer, that you gotta go straight. Then you concentrate at the top of the head, The Crown Center, (The Tenth Gate), and you'll be gone. That soft point when you are a baby. That's the exit gate. You should practice meditating at these points in this order. You have to practice. You have to practice.

CROSSING THE HOUR

Yogi Bhajan's class on death – April 16, 1986, Los Angeles
Starting at 11pm and ending just after midnight

There comes a moment between life and death, when you shall be alone. How you are going to cross that hour, normally, that is the purpose of life. It is how you determine yourself. Everything else is paraphernalia. It doesn't mean a thing. If a person cannot determine his crossing hour, he or she cannot cross. And that's a fact. If religion has done you any favor, it has done you one favor that it has talked about it. And if it has done you this favor it has not told you what to do. So, I thought it would be better.

This is a very powerful meditation, during which Yogi Bhajan played the gong. For anyone who is preparing for his or her own death, or helping someone else to do so, I highly recommend this video or audio tape. You can purchase a copy by contacting Ancient Healing Ways (Resource Page).

Meditation: Take your hands and cross them at the throat level. The right hand is crossed over the left; palms are facing toward the body. There is no space between the fingers and the thumbs. Start looking at the palms. Go into a natural posture, with the elbows down next to the lower rib cage. Have an extremely relaxed body. Start closing your eyes. Breathe long and deep…a hard breath. (Eyes are 1/10 open only.)

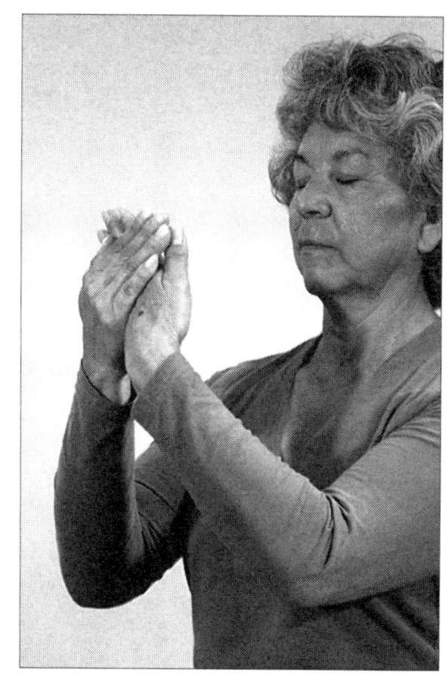

Start looking in the hands. Relate to the breath – hard. Feel the hard breath. Make the breath harder and harder. Breathe from the lower ribs. It is called crossing the hour. When you are hit by that moment, systematically the breath becomes hard. It is called "solid breath," and you start breathing by the lower ribs. It means the lower lungs start becoming inflated. 5 minutes.

Now, transfer the breath to the mouth. Breathe with an effort. Totally close the eyes. Concentrate that you are letting the soul go, from the top of the skull. Make the breath harder and harder. Practice while you are alive and well. 3 minutes.

Start losing your body and fall back, slowly. It is called dying in consciousness. Enjoy dying. What is the big deal? That is how it happens.

Just lie down anywhere. Hands are crossed at the Heart Center.

Start going deeper and deeper, napping and going deeper…losing physical control and awareness. Consciously pass out. Start sinking and dying. Practically prepare yourself for death. Go deeper as you are going to touch the center of the earth in a cylindrical form. Lose conscious control of your physical body. Sink into the barrel of death, as you are being sucked by a power beyond you. Elevating out, like you are going down in a lift.

Leave mental control and conscious control of the physical existence. Let it go, down deep in your heart, let it go. And let the thought go. You are going home.

Thoughts are the quality of the earth. Relate to no thought except you are going through the lift in a cylindrical form…reaching a vast area of very bright light. Light is brighter and death is deeper. Visualize. Give yourself a deep place, where you see nothing but deathly bright light.

Now visualize two sides. One is warm and cozy. The other is very shining, dazzlingly ice and cold. There is a pathway. Start walking that pathway. A winding pathway, going through the hills…absolutely dazzlingly light…and snowy atmosphere.

Dazzlingly, snowy pathway is the valley to the heavens. Start moving through it. Passing through the windy dazzling path, freezing, snowy windy path. Stop not. Feel no physical contact. Move as a transparent body. Feel no physical senses, contact. Move as a transparent body. You are a transparent body in the beginning. Transform yourself into a transparent body now.

Go through the penetrating body and walk through this valley of dazzling light, leaving behind the coziness of senses. Leaving behind the coziness of senses. Let it go. Let it go. Let the opaqueness go. 16 minutes.

At this point Yogi Bhajan started playing the gong, with the tape, (Sat Nam Wahe Guru #1), for approximately 11 minutes. As he continued to play the gong…

Evaluate your senses and resurrect yourself. Lift up your physical form. Be here and now – active and valid, (sitting up).

Within you resound. Merge into the chanting sound. Now penetrate your sound with the sound of the gong, and listening to that sound is the power of your prayer. Elevate yourself as best as you can. Power of the shabd and power of divine sound are going to contrast. Penetrate with your strength. 30 minutes.

To finish: Inhale, hold. Exhale. Repeat 6 times.

We have tried to practice. Crossing the hour, or crossing into the solitary valley – the entrance into the depth of the death. Determining and dying consciously is a very factual thing. And, if you can practice it, you can make it. Something that is horrible, horrifying, which is drying your prosperity out of life, living, happiness, once practiced and conquered, becomes a play. It becomes a matter of joy. We will get together again and practice. It is 2 minutes past midnight. You have crossed the hour.

Prayer is when the mind is one-pointed and man talks to Infinity. Meditation is when the mind becomes totally clean and receptive, and Infinity talks to the man.
YOGI BHAJAN

Prayer and Meditation

Some times we don't know what to do in situations where a loved one is dying. Prayer and meditation are lovely ways to express our love at this time.

During your meditation, come into relation with your loved one. Use your visualization, intention and purity of heart to lovingly reduce pain or any resistance to letting go. They may want to be touched or not. Holding the person's hand can be soothing. He or she may also respond to a light hand or foot massage. If touch is not desired, use the healing power of your presence. The following meditation will give you the gift of healing.

RAA MAA DAA SAA SAA SAY SO HUNG

Healing Meditation

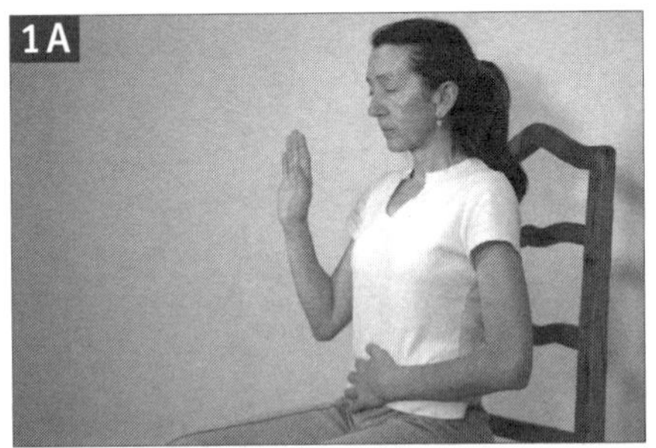
1A

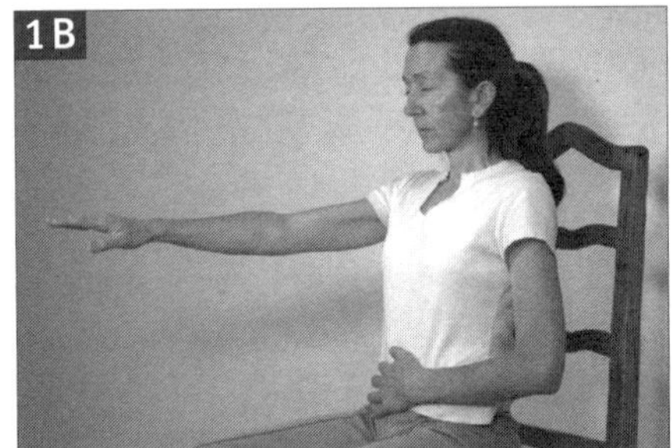
1B

Yogi Bhajan said that this is a meditation to practice for the rest of your life. It is a simple exercise that can give you the power to heal.

How To Do It

Sit with a straight spine. Put your left hand on your navel point. Your right arm is at your right shoulder level, elbow bent, with the palm facing forward. You are holding your right hand up as if you are taking an oath **(1A)**. This meditation can be done with one of the Ra Ma Da Sa Sa Say So Hung tapes or CD's (contact Ancient Healing Ways or Spirit Voyage on Resource Page). You may either chant out loud or meditate silently. The movement of the kriya is timed with the chanting of "***Raa Maa Daa Saa Saa Say So Hung.***" (Refer to accompanying CD for correct pronunciation – 13.) At "***Raa***" slowly begin moving your right arm forward from the starting position and continue slowly moving so that your arm is straight out in front of you (parallel to the ground) with the palm facing downward at "***Hung***." The movement begins with "***Raa***" and is completed at "**Hung**" **(1B)**. Then the right arm moves back to the starting position by your side and the movement begins again at "***Raa***." The right arm moves as if giving a blessing. Start with 11 minutes and work up to 31 minutes. Gradually, over time, very serious meditators can increase the time to a maximum practice time of 2 1/2 hours.

2

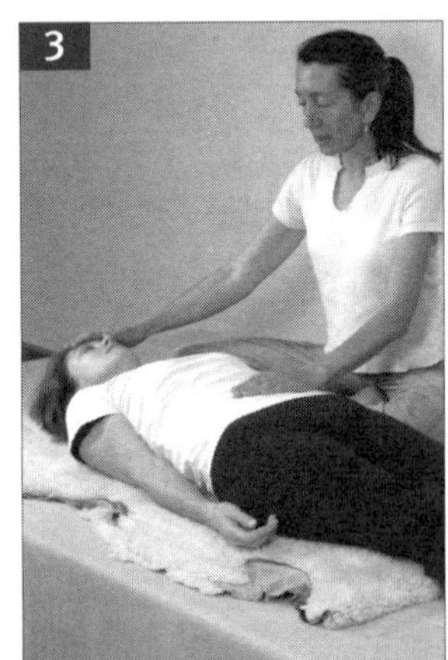
3

Variations for healing others:

2 You may do this kriya using your left hand to hold the hand of the person you want to heal. The right hand moves as described above. You may chant the mantra out loud or mentally and silently. OR –

3 If the person needing healing is very ill, shaking and shivering, you can place your left hand on their navel point and place your right hand on their pituitary. You may chant the mantra out loud or mentally and silently.

Prayer is a projection of heart and mind... when the head is bowed, the heart penetrates through the mind and reaches God direct. For the yogi, prayer is a humble "intunement," which means that we are consciously "in tune" with the unknown within us. Prayer is the power of God in us. As a part of the Infinite, there is no lower or higher, we pray from the inside to the inside. There is an appreciation from the known (us) for the unknown (God), which exists in all. Prayer is not an intellectual exercise and is best carried with an open heart and projection. An example might be something like, "Lord God, give me the courage to face Your will with grace and serenity. May Mom's light shine in me forever, and may that light spread into eternity."

A student asked Yogi Bhajan, "Can a person be liberated by someone praying for him or her?" He responded, *"The power of prayer can carry across anything. Prayer is the ultimate power."*

While in South Africa, I was working with a young woman, Anna, who had AIDS. She was the daughter-in-law of our friend, Tandi, at the Johannesburg Ashram. Since going into Soweto, the largest township in South Africa can be a dangerous place for a white woman, Tandi escorted me and another healer. Anna was staying with her parents and many of her other relatives in a modest one-bedroom brick house. Her parents were so grateful that they freshly painted their front cement porch before our first visit. As simple as the house was, it was immaculate. Many of her relatives greeted us and expressed their immense gratitude. Somehow I got the impression that they thought we were going to create a miraculous healing.

Anna was very weak the last time we visited her. She was sleeping a lot and eating only small amounts of food, but she was also up part of the time, enjoying her children. Anna loved the healing sessions. They relaxed her and eased the pain. After we finished the last session,

As long as you are itchy, as long as you cannot sit still, you cannot get your prayer answered, because you cannot send the signal out. You have to be absolutely still physically, mentally and spiritually. Then you can penetrate through anything. This is your power.

Yogi Bhajan

When prayer becomes the vibration of the soul, mind and self, we can create a miracle.

Yogi Bhajan

we took photos in the front yard. It was a joyous occasion. Three days later Anna died. Friends teased me that our treatment must have killed Anna. Actually, a miracle did occur. Anna was able to let go of any resistance, surrendering to Infinity.

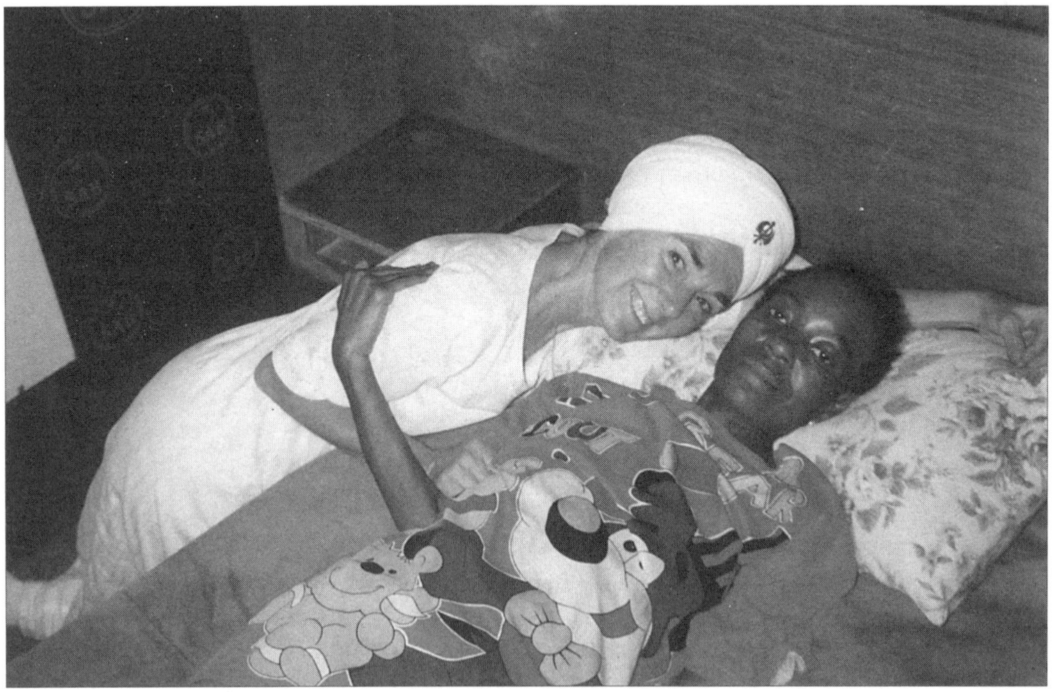

Guru Terath Kaur and Anna

PROCESS EXERCISES

I guess we could say that this whole chapter was one big practice exercise. Let's process your experience.

1 Which of the meditations or visualizations were helpful for you? Pick one to do for 40 days, even longer if you wish. Keep a log of how you feel and note how your experience changes over time. How does the practice change your life?

2 If you are using these techniques to help someone else, keep a log noting which ones were especially helpful. Keep in mind that no two people will have exactly the same experience and may vary in their preferences. If the person is open to it, help them process their experience by listening to them. They might want to log their experience or do the next exercise.

3 Some times it is hard to find words to express your experience. Find another medium, like dancing, painting, pottery, flower arranging – anything that unlocks your creative expression.

When you were born,
you cried and the world rejoiced.
Live your life in such a manner that when you die the world cries and you rejoice.

ANONYMOUS AMERICAN INDIAN SAYING

CHAPTER 11

Children And Death

A child is just God passing through your hand. That's what a child is, a living god. And one who raised the child is very divine.
Yogi Bhajan

CHILDREN ARE OUR BIGGEST JOY AND ATTACHMENT. For anyone who has gone through pregnancy and birth, a baby doesn't just seem like a miracle – it is one. We see their innocence and honesty and are reminded of our own. They can open the most closed heart and freely give unconditional love and trust, accepting us all for who we are. Their reality includes magic and the spirit world, so close are they to God and the marvels of His Creation. They invite our inner child (who for whatever reason got pushed aside along the way to adulthood) to come out to play. They are our hope for a better tomorrow and give us a purpose for life itself. When we hold them in our arms, we know we are holding a piece of God.

When a child is taken prematurely in death, no matter what one's culture, religion or beliefs, it is always the most heartbreaking of losses. In the natural course of life cycles we experience smaller losses as our little ones go off to school, camp and visits to grandparents. We feel the emptiness in our gut when they leave home for college and when they set up their own households. And as hard as these "pullings away" are, they are gradual and natural according to the accepted cycles of change.

The death of a child hits us the hardest because it seems so unnatural and in some way unjust to the scheme of what "should be." Every pore and cell of us screams out –"No, no, no, this is not what's suppose to happen." We feel short-changed and denied of our expected entitlement – perhaps even somehow betrayed.

It was a time of great rejoicing, because there was to be a wedding. The groom's parents went to the village Zen Master asking for a wedding gift or blessing. The Zen Master said that he did, in fact, have a very appropriate gift to give the couple. He said, "Grandfather dies, Father dies, son dies." Visibly upset, the couple asked the Master why he had given such a sad blessing. He replied that it was the greatest gift because it would be tragic if the deaths were in any other order.

The information and technology in this book has probably put you through some changes. You may have been challenged to look at death differently than before; you may have been confronted about your own mortality; and maybe old feelings of grief have surfaced. Maybe you feel more confident and empowered now that you have tools to prepare for and face death in a more uplifting way. This chapter will put all of this to the ultimate test.

I may be able to surrender to my death with more consciousness and even help someone else do so, but could I apply all of this to the death of my child? Take some deep breaths. We'll take this step-by-step together.

Steve and Anita Isser's daughter was murdered.

Anita relates, "I felt like my heart had just been ripped open and I didn't see how I could go on."

Steve – "I think I felt that I'd never get past the pain. The pain would always be there and there'd be no future."

The following is a letter written to them from their spiritual teacher, Ram Das. It was a catalyst to begin their road to healing.

Dear Steve and Anita,

Rachel finished her brief work on earth and left the stage in a manner that leaves those of us left behind with a cry of agony in our hearts, as the fragile threads of faith are dealt with so violently. Is anyone strong enough to stay conscious through such teachings as you are receiving? Probably very few! And even they would only have a whisper of equanimity in the spacious peace, which the screaming trumpets of their rage, grief, horror and desolation.

I cannot assuage your pain with my words nor should I, for your pain is Rachel's legacy to you. Not that she or I would inflict such pain by choice, but there it is – and it must burn its purifying way to completion. You may emerge from this ordeal more dead than alive, for some thing with you dies when you bear the unbearable. And it is only in that dark night of the soul that you are prepared to see as God sees and to love as God loves.

Now is the time to let your grief find expression, no false strength. Now is the time to sit quietly and speak to Rachel and thank her for being with you for these few years and encourage her to go on with her work, knowing that you will grow with compassion and wisdom from this experience.

In my heart I know that you and she will meet again and again and recognize the many ways in which you have known each other. And when you meet you will in a flash know what now it is not given to you to know – why this had to be the way it was. Your rational minds could never understand what has happened, but your hearts, if you can keep them open to God, will find their own intuitive way.

Rachel came through you to do her work on earth, which included her manner of death. Now her soul is free and the love you can share with her is invulnerable to the winds of the changing time and space. In that deep love include me too.

So Much Love, Ram Das

Anita – "I heard the truth in the letter. It was the light at the end of the tunnel."

The loss of a child is so devastating, because as parents, it is our job to protect them from injury and pain. It is unthinkable to imagine one of them suffering from a debilitating illness or a violent death. It doesn't fit into our perception of a parents' role. Aren't we supposed to keep them safe from harm's way? When disaster hits, our faith is challenged to the point of extinction. The question, "Can I accept the will of God?" seems like a test too insurmountable to pass.

What we must never forget is that our children also have their own karmas and destinies. They too were given a specific number of breaths in which to complete their job on earth. Sometimes the number is large, other times it is small. As much as we want to carry them into adulthood, that is not for us to decide. What we can decide, though, is how we live each day – to the very fullest, acknowledging how sacred and precious it is.

I worked with a family where a 2-year-old son was diagnosed with cancer. The parents thought they had life figured out. Their son's illness threw them into feelings of powerlessness, blame and guilt. All of their expectations and dreams were shattered. This young couple had done yoga before as a fitness regime. Now, they found this training to be helpful, a strenuous Kundalini Yoga helped them to sweat and release their emotions on a cellular level. They also found meditating for longer periods of time to be helpful. They were able to get to a place of accepting what was instead of what was supposed to be. They were able to bringing meaning to their son's illness and death.

Suffering is such a subjective thing. This little boy was in pain, but he was still joyous. He had everything he needed – parents who loved and cherished him. Being so young, he could remember the spirit world between lives. He had no fear; therefore, he did not suffer.

The really amazing thing is that the parents got it. Whereas they had previously done yoga for fitness, now they realized that the real purpose of Kundalini Yoga was to have an experience of Union with the One. They were able to transform their feelings of anger into a knowing that the soul of their son only needed a short time on earth to complete its job.

Shanti Shanti Kaur Khalsa,
Director of the Guru Ram Das Center for Medicine and Humanology 

The really interesting thing is that children, especially young children, seem less attached to the physical world than adults. Perhaps it is because they have just returned from the spirit world and know it is nothing to fear. To them, letting go to the light is going home. By the time we get to adulthood, we have been programmed into replacing our memories of the spirit world with our attachments to the physical one. The best thing we

Let our children be, and give them the basic spiritual values. Deal with their spirit – uplift and keep it up, and give them faith. That is the most positive thing they need.
YOGI BHAJAN

can do for our children and ourselves is to develop the relationship with the Infinite – individually and together as a family. Honor, embrace and encourage that special connection they instinctively have with God.

It seems like God plucks the most precious young flowers from us. Have you ever known a young child or youth, who was loved by everyone, who was always happy and kind – only to have them taken by an accident or illness? What's further intriguing is that many times these young ones "know" that they are not going to be around very long on earth. This may have been their agreement before they decided to come back into another reincarnation. They only have a short time to "finish up," and even give signs of their departure. One such case was, Nav Jiwan Kaur, a seven year old girl.

> *She chanted all the time. I've never known anyone who did that. One time she pointed out the break in the lifeline of her hand and asked what it meant. Four days before her death, Nav Jiwan asked me questions about reincarnation. I told her that I would not choose to be reincarnated but would want to go home to God. Looking back on it now, I feel she was preparing herself for what she would have to do. Sometimes when I looked at her, subconsciously I knew she would never be an adult. Something in me just knew, but of course I shut out those thoughts, as would any parent.*
>
> *The night before her death, there was a Gurdwara (religious service). Nav Jiwan Kaur came up behind me and put her little arms around me and felt so big, as though we switched places – Nav Jiwan was the mother and I was the daughter. It felt like I was sitting in her lap, much like she had frequently sat in my lap. The energy between us was so special that night that I felt she said goodbye to me in that way.*
>
> Guru Tej Kaur, Mother of Nav Jiwan, talks about her experience.

Also striking were other things Nav Jiwan did. A few nights before her death, Nav Jiwan made a tape for her Papaji in which she said over and over, 'Goodbye Papaji, goodbye Papaji, goodbye.' Nav Jiwan also drew a picture three times, exactly identical a few days before her death. The picture is of a little girl on a horse waving good-bye. There is a bird flying into the sun and the sun has a happy face with glasses on, (Nav Jiwan Kaur wore glasses.) A copy of that picture is on the following page.

One of her classmates recalls that the morning of her death, Nav Jiwan was especially happy. Giving all of her friends hugs and a flower, she said goodbye. But, then, she remembers that Nav Jiwan was always happy and kind, no matter what the circumstance, even when other kids were mean to her. Her classmate found that to be remarkable.

It seems as though the degree of agony and the level of possible personal growth are correlated. It is at these times that the heart is the most open, the ego the most shattered, the psyche the most vulnerable – and therefore, the consciousness the most open to transformation. These are the opportunities to either shrivel up and harden or expand beyond the unbearable into the arms of the One. This is when our spiritual practice and spiritual community will cradle us and carry us to the light beyond the darkness of the bottomless abyss. In my interview with Guru Tej Kaur, she said that it was her morning Sadhana (yoga, meditation and prayers) that pulled her out of her depression. Her practice strengthened her aura, nervous and glandular systems and general well-being, enabling her to climb out and join the land of the living once again. Nav Jiwan's father had a similar experience.

In my own experience perhaps the most pivotal episode of my life was the death of my daughter, Nav Jiwan Kaur, who died in 1981 at the age of seven and a half. As a young parent I could imagine no greater dread than the loss of a child, especially a child so bright and beauti-

The picture Nav Jiwan drew three times, exactly identical a few days before her death. Note the sun has a happy face with glasses on, (Nav Jiwan Kaur wore glasses.)

ful as she. Still that day came for us. It is not possible to describe the impact of that experience, yet in the solitary shock of that moment, I saw clearly that I had two options. I could either accept it as the will of God and make a quantum leap in my own consciousness, or I could fight, resent it, and end up old, miserable and dysfunctional.

Two things made that transition possible for me. They were the guidance of my spiritual teacher, Yogi Bhajan, and the support of the community. These helped me in every way: inspired and uplifted me, gave me comfort and hope, and gave me the opportunity to pull my best out of myself. In fact, through that whole process I found many opportunities to comfort and elevate others who also mourned her loss and were stuck in that pain. It started, though, with my Teacher who would not let me get depressed. He pushed me to chant for her soul, to help her on her path home to God. In that way I was able to transcend my own grief, and my life changed.

Quotes from Guru Tej Singh on the death of his daughter, taken from Aquarian Times, Vol. 1, Number 4, Winter 2001

Guru Nam Kaur, the teacher who was with Nav Jiwan when she died, shares her intense and amazing experience.

I was teaching at the Preschool Program in Espanola. Siri Darshan Singh, was in my class but his sister Nav Jiwan Kaur was not. We were planning a trip to Nambe Falls. For some reason Nav Jiwan really, really wanted to come and came to me 4–5 times asking if she could come. I said yes, after checking with her parents and her teacher. It was very important to her to come. While we were walking to the falls, she climbed up on some rocks and fell down, landing on some rocks, splitting open her skull. I could feel her spirit leaving her body. As I was picking her up, I was pleading with this big spirit that was gathering her into his lap. It felt like Guru Ram Das to me. I remember pleading with him, 'Please, please, don't take her. Let me get her to the hospital in time.' I could feel she was going and went quickly. I had to leave the other children there and carried Nav Jiwan out to the parking lot and called for help. That was obviously very heavy.

I was dreading meeting her parents at the hospital. As I walked in, Guru Tej Kaur opened her arms and hugged me and said, 'I'm so glad you were there with her when she left.' That was so amazing to me. It was an amazing experience, because obviously it was so painful for me. Part of my pain was – 'Was I guilty, did I do something wrong?' I couldn't imagine how a mother could deal with this situation.

There were three days between the death and the cremation. I had a dream over and over again during those three days where Nav Jiwan was asking me to make three garlands with the roses, which grew next to my house. She wanted them to be red and white – one to be put on the Guru (Sikh Scriptures) here in Espanola, one on the Guru in Albuquerque and one on her body. It was such a strange dream, but such a strong communication. I asked Bibiji (Yogi Bhajan's wife) about it and she said, 'Yes, you should do it. She's asking you for it.' I helped prepare her body, which was an amazing, graceful experience. I had such a strong sense that she was happy to go. There was no sense that she was stuck somewhere. She was so gone and so free.

The next summer Yogi Bhajan sent me to India to work with our children going to school there. While in India, I had the experience time and time again of being pushed from behind beyond my capacity. I had the sense that the same being that took Nav Jiwan Kaur (Guru Ram

Das) was there…so strong that I would look over my shoulder. This being was pushing me and yet behind me. Over and over the sensation was, 'you can't do this but I can.'

When Children Lose Someone They Love

It has become clear to me that children's views of death depend upon their past karmas and the environment in which they are raised. If a child is an old soul, they have been reincarnated many times and know what to expect – going home is a joyous occasion. If raised by people who give them a spiritual perspective, death becomes a natural occurrence. Sat Hari Kaur was one of Nav Jiwan's friends. She remembers not feeling particularly sad, because death had been explained to her as an opportunity to "move on." Yogi Bhajan told the community that Nav Jiwan had progressed into the Fourth Blue Ether and was therefore liberated. Sat Hari remembers feeling a little jealous, because Nav Jiwan had gone to such an exalted place and she herself was still stuck here on the earth.

In this next case, a young boy instinctive knew that death was going to come to his family years before it actually did. He wasn't afraid of this knowledge, but he also knew that as a young boy he was not ready and so requested that God wait until he was older and more mature. No person told him any of this. He just intuitively knew.

As a young boy of four or five, I remember beginning to think about death. I thought about the death of my parents and knew that I wasn't ready yet to face such a monumental loss. I still remember my prayer. It was very clear and powerful – 'Please let my parents live several more years, until I am strong enough.' Around the age of 15, I started meditating on death as a process, which gave me a deeper perspective of life. In 2000–01, Mom was diagnosed with breast cancer. It wasn't a big shock. It's difficult to explain, but somehow I intuitively saw it coming and felt it was right for her. It was hard for me to see her in pain and sick from the chemotherapy. On the other hand, it was OK. It was all part of her process.

Children need to be included in the whole process of dying. They are very sensitive creatures. They know, see, hear and feel things that most adults cannot. Explain to them what's happening. Allow them to ask questions. They instinctively know that something is occurring. It is far better to talk about it. Otherwise the combination of their sensitivity with lack of knowledge of how to deal with it produces misconceptions and fear. I interviewed a young woman in our spiritual community, who at the age of eight had a very traumatic experience with the death of her Grandfather.

My Grandfather lived next door. He had had three open-heart surgeries. He was very skinny, tall and gaunt – like Frankenstein. He was so frail that I couldn't play with him. We got the call that something was wrong with Grandpa. I instinctively knew that he was dead. It scared me. No one talked to my brother or me about what had happened then or later. I started having nightmares, where I would be home alone and Grandma called saying, 'Get one of your Father's guns and come over. Grandpa has come back and he's chasing me around the house with a gun.' For years I'd expect Grandpa to look through my window at night, and for this reason, it took me a long time to fall asleep. Years later, I learned that Grandpa abused Grandma. Energetically I think I was picking up his energy and maybe my Mother and Grandmother's fear. After his death, Grandpa used to visit me...I could feel him there when I was sitting in the kitchen doing my homework. I'd tell him that he'd have to leave...he was scaring me. Now I realize that he came to me because I was sensitive. No one else in my family would have felt him.

If children are included in the whole process, their experiences will be natural and uplifting.

At the crematorium, as the baby's body was slid into the furnace, her older sister, three years old at the time, looked up and saw a male spirit hovering over her mother's shoulder. She told her mother what she saw. Mother nodded and smiled, thinking that her daughter was grieving for her baby sister and fabricating a baby brother to comfort herself. Ten months later her baby brother was born.

And from a male youth

Death is a reality of life. It's just a completion of a cycle. A spiritual person plans and lives his life to the fullest, and plans and prepares for his death to the fullest…and goes just as happy as he came. I'm not sure where I learned this, perhaps from my mother or just living this lifestyle. As a seeker of the Guru, we are trained to give our head and be willing to give our head and bow to His will.

When I was going to school in India, I found out that my mother almost died. It was a harsh reality of how close to death we all are.

Then, my Grandfather got really sick. I went to visit him. He had always been closed off. When he realized that it was almost his time to go, he totally changed. He told my father things he was never able to say. All of us grandchildren and cousins and everyone would go talk to him and come out crying. He would just talk to us about love. I decided that I don't want to wait…I want to love now.

Siri Amrit Singh

Invite children to spend quality time with the dying loved one, even participating in simple care giving chores. They need to feel useful and it's a way for them to channel some of their grieving into constructive actions. There may be a meaningful project they can do together in bed, like making a photo album of shared memories. There may be heart talk they need to say to the dying before they go. Sometimes the dying need their loved ones to give them permission to go.

I cried a lot, especially when I realized that the end was coming. It was OK to cry in front of Mom. We cried together. Crying is good. I always felt better afterward.

...Mom prepared me before she left. There was nothing left to do. She took care of the big things that mothers are supposed to do. The day before she died, I told her, 'Mom, you have given me everything. It's OK for you to go.' We talked about it. She said, 'It looks like I'm going ahead with this dying thing.' We joked about it. It was hard for my big sister. She was close to Mom and could always rely on her. She helped prepare the body. It was hard."

A son talks about his mother's death.

When death comes, encourage them to say goodbye to the body, which will help them accept the death. They may need to talk about their loss and express their many conflicting feelings, like anger to their parent for leaving them, or confusion over the future of their family, or sadness, because their sibling and playmate is gone. These feelings need to come out in words, tears, pictures, movement, poems, sculpture, drumming or whatever is meaningful to the child. It is natural for parents to want to shield their children from the pain, and it is important to try to keep up with some sort of normalcy, but it is also important to share the grief together as a family. Hugs and tears are healing… as well as lots and lots of reminiscing.

> *I use to play a game with the kids, where we would say everything was God and would then name all the things that have God in it. When Siri Darshan Singh (five years old) was told about his sister's death, he remembered that game. He said, 'God is in everything. Nav Jiwan Kaur is with God. Now we will see her in the sky, the flowers, the birds, the light, our food – everything.'*
>
> Guru Tej Kaur

When A Child Has A Terminal Illness

The tendency is to deny the illness and want to will it away. It is essential that the ill child be informed and aware of their illness, according to what is age appropriate. Younger children may need it explained in symbolic language, "Once upon a time, Snowflake the cat was very sick, and her mother and father and brother took care of her." Older children may want to read all they can about their illness and the latest medications and research on the Internet. These little people are very intuitive and already know that they are seriously ill. It is far better to be open and honest with them and the rest of the siblings. Tender moments will sprout from these truths that will become unforgettably precious memories.

> *Born with a cleft palate, our baby had a gaping hole in her upper lip. Her three year old sister didn't see this abnormality as strange. One day while holding her baby sister, she looked up at me and said, 'Oh Mama, isn't she beautiful.'*

This proud sister saw the soul, not the physical of her baby sister. This memory will be treasured forever.

It is important to allow siblings to contribute to the care and entertainment of their ill brother or sister in whatever way they can – bringing them water, reading to them, feeding them, watching videos together in bed or doing a project. You may want to even have a second bed set up in the middle of the family activities, so the sick child continues to feel a part of the daily events. Yes, continue "living" together as a family, but also prepare for death as a family, including every member no matter how young. You will be amazed at the wisdom of these siblings. Tragedy stretches their little consciousnesses as well. Allow this growth. They will be much more sensitive, aware and mature for their experience with death.

Coach the dying child about what to expect in death, of course, according to what is age appropriate. It is very important for him or her to understand that the members of the family are going to be OK. There is no need to hesitate or lag behind. Encourage him or her to go toward the light. You can use the visualizations from the previous Chapter – *Rehearsing Death* – modifying them as is appropriate to the age and circumstance.

When death does come, invite siblings to participate in whatever way they feel comfortable. They may want to draw a picture for their brother or sister to go with them on their journey or decorate the coffin or make cookies for visiting relatives. An older child may want to honor their sibling by writing a poem that is read at the service. As Mom and Dad are busy with funeral arrangements and grieving, it can be helpful to have a favorite Aunt, Uncle or older friend available for the sibling(s) to talk to and do things with.

No matter what the relationship of the loss, younger children may need to draw pictures, write letters or play-act the death with friends. This is their therapy and should not be discouraged. It is wise to alert the other parents of such play and to monitor it from a distance. If it gets too morbid (you'll have to use your intuition) you may need to redirect and uplift the energy... like doing a meditation with them and then discussing their feelings.

A man in our community, Raghu Rai Singh was dying of leukemia. The children in our preschool frequently visited him and watched the process of his physical body wither away as his soul got ready to take flight. After his death, the children wrote notes and drew pictures for him, which were placed on the altar at his memorial service. Here is one of those letters.

The following is a true story. The names have been changed.

Baby Ravi was born with many complications. She lived for six months, during which time her older sister, Prem (three years old), experienced the whole play of the traumatic birth – the trips to the hospital, the community chanting for her sister, the tears of her parents, Ravi's condition getting worse and worse – and the eventual death. At the time, Prem was going to a very supportive little preschool, at which I was a teacher.

All of the children and their parents were members of the same spiritual community.

Every recess and lunch break would find Prem and her friends acting out her sister's story. One time Prem would act the part of her sister, while her friends took the parts of the other members of the family. They switched roles and play-acted the scenarios over and over until gradually this play got less frequent and eventually stopped completely.

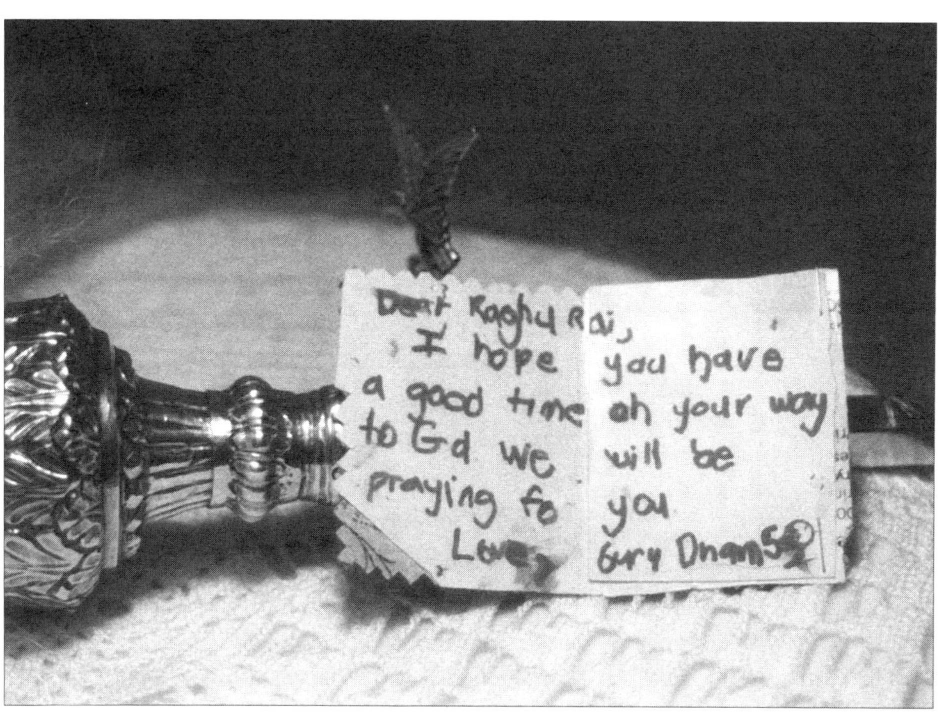

A child's note to Raghu Rai Singh after his death. "Dear Raghu Rai, I hope you have a good time on your way to God. We will be praying for you. Love Guru Dham Singh."

I always felt this was extremely therapeutic for Prem and all the children. As I tearfully stood at the door watching them, I marveled at their wisdom and compassion.

Lessons Learned From Death

While interviewing these young people, I was infinitely touched by their wisdom and lessons learned from the loss of their loved one. Whether their karma was to die or experience the death, it seems like the soul agreements are made long before this reincarnation began – so interconnected are their karmas and soul relationships. Who can say? Perhaps losing someone we love pressurizes us into becoming the diamond. Out of that pain, our crystallized light will transform darkness. You be the judge of the following comments. I myself was encouraged. With this kind of consciousness, our future will be in good hands.

I am no different than anyone else, but I've been given this huge loss at a young age. I don't know how it will affect my life. I'll see as I go. My friends had different reactions. I was a bit overwhelmed with the love shown to my family and me. One friend called me crying hysterically. I was shocked. He expressed so much love to me. 'I'm just so sorry,' he sobbed, coming from a place of deep empathy and strength. When someone is going through a tough time, those little things really mean the world. Send flowers or a card, make food, give a hug and listen to them. Above all, don't try to fix anything or judge them. I was really lucky. So many people were there for me.

And –

I advise everyone to prepare for death early. Resolve what you can. Don't leave unfinished stuff. It gives you a good edge on life. Mom had some unresolved issues, not big ones, but there were some. At one point, she accepted that she couldn't resolve everything. Perhaps that's the biggest surrender of all – we may not be able to resolve everything, and that's OK.

And from another youth –

This experience was very awakening. It took my consciousness to the next level of reality...that this is really just another life of our souls. I will be more appreciative of what I have...the people...the experiences. It lightens the load. Don't take things so seriously. It's just another life and it could end soon or not. Just live in the moment as much as possible...stop trying to think and control and guide your life with your mind...but just listen to what you are suppose to do...surrender. It's not up to us. Its God's will that we are all here and its His will when we go...so serve and give the best we can. If I don't make it this time, I'll come back again. I'm OK with that. When I die, I want to be surrounded by family and friends, all chanting and celebrating life.

Siri Amrit Singh

Other Perspectives of Death

There is a Sikh school (Grades 1–12) in Northern India in the Sikh center called Amritsar, where the students are raised in a spiritual, vegetarian and yogic lifestyle. When asked about their views of death, their comments were very revealing.

When I was born my heart stopped. I'm glad I didn't die. My Mom would have been very sad. I also hope I can do something good in my life... like stopping people from polluting or saving the entire human race. If I had died, though, I think I would have gone to heaven. It's not polluted in heaven, and I'd see my cat, Cosmo.

Guru Prakash Singh, Grade 3

If you do good deeds and serve others, you won't have to fear death.

Guru Karam Singh, Grade 3

When my bird, Bagie died, I missed the sound of his chirping. He'll always be in my heart.

Siri Radha Kaur, Grade 3

Death is just change, nothing more.

Sat Prakash Kaur, Grade 8

God gives the gift of life to all, and He must take this gift back to give to others. Though you may elude death once or twice, it shall come for you. The only dignified way to meet death is to greet it with a smile and be on your way to meet the True Lord.

Simranjit Kaur, Grade 8

When my grandpa died, I was sad. It felt like a part of me had disappeared. It hurt a lot. But, Yogi Bhajan gave my grandpa an image of me in his mind; and he gave me an image of my grandpa in my mind. It was a cool feeling. I keep it with me even today.

Guru Shabd Singh, Grade 8

The only way to prepare for death is by accepting it.

Sat Santokh Singh, Grade 8.

I believe that life is a test and if we pass it, we will merge with God. If we don't pass the test, we will go back into the cycle of births and deaths.

Fateh Singh, Grade 8

When I was small, I thought a lot about death. It is not a bad thing.

What does death mean? To me it means freedom. And actually, death answers all of our questions about life. God made death to create balance in life.

Amrit Singh, Grade 9

Karam Kaur,* Age 13 – ***What I Think About Death***

What is death? Hmm, that's a tough question. To me, death can be many things. I think that a person can die in many different ways…be it spiritually, mentally or physically. When people are constantly getting drunk or they work at strip clubs – that is like a death. When a person goes through a difficult time and closes up to the world – that is a kind of death.

When my parents got divorced, there were times when I felt dead. It felt like things were never going to get better. My parents argued about most things, but the worst was when they argued about my sister and me. In those times, I sensed the presence of death. It was almost like part of me was missing and if I went to look for it, I wouldn't be able to find it. Luckily, my mother came to the rescue. She would sit with me for hours and just listen to what I had to say. Sometimes, she would offer advice, but mostly she would just sit and listen. Slowly that missing part of me returned and things got better.

People say that they fear death. What do they fear? Do they fear the actual dying part or is it the process of moving on? When people die, where do they go? What do they do? How does it happen? Does it hurt? These are all questions that we all ask. The fact that any one of these questions can get a million and one answers is what's scary. It's like when you are about to ride a roller coaster for the first time. You are standing in line with your friend, who has been on the ride many times. They spend the whole time in line telling you everything about the ride down to the last turn. Then, when you are finally waiting in your seat for the ride to start, you may feel a little anxious, but you are no longer scared, because you know what to expect. That's the problem with death. A person cannot know what to expect, because there is no one there to explain it to you.

What is death? I can't exactly say what death is. I don't see death as an ending. I see it as a new beginning…a way to see life from a different perspective. A person once said, 'Death is always smiling up at you. All you can do is smile back.' I may not know yet what death is. I do know that I will know when I need to know. Until then I will live my life happy.

(*The name of this girl was changed to protect the integrity and privacy of her family.)

Yoga and Meditation For Children

Children can benefit from yoga and meditation too. I highly recommend that you get Shakta Kaur's book, *Fly Like A Butterfly.* Ancient Healing Ways or Spirit Voyage has it (See the Resource Page). Yoga for younger children is more like playing animals while you tell a story. Elementary and older can begin to do modified adult yoga – for a shorter period of time. Children under twelve should not pump their navel, as in Breath of Fire or exercises like Sat Kriya. They should not do any Body Locks. Teens up to 18 should be treated like sensitive adults. Over 18, they can do anything adults would. The most important thing is to make it fun and challenging, encouraging them to feel their inner strength and power.

Children like to meditate. The meditation below can be done by any age child, adapting the length of time done according to the age of the child. For example, children under five could start with 3 minutes. Elementary age children can build up to 11 minutes. This meditation is a good choice, because it combines, mantra with arm movements, something children enjoy. You can experiment with the other meditations included in this book and see how they respond. Go over the basics with them and teach them how to **Tune In.** Meditate with them at first. It's a beautiful activity to share. Talk to them about the benefits of meditation. You can teach them what you have learned in this book, making it age appropriate. You will become better in your practice by teaching your children.

SURROUND YOURSELF WITH PROTECTION

*Chii-a Kriya**

How To Do It

Sit with a straight spine. The hands are in Gyan Mudra. Touch the tip of the thumb and the tip of the Jupiter finger together (index finger). The other fingers are relaxed. With your hands in this mudra, close your eyes, and move your arms in the following sequence. Chant using the tip of your tongue. (Refer to CD for pronunciation –14.)

1. **Stretch your arms out to the sides** with the palms facing forward. Keep your elbows straight. Chant "***Har.***"
2. **Without bringing your hands near your shoulders,** move your hands directly in front of you with your palms down, elbows by your sides, and your forearms pointing straight out in front of your body. Chant "***Haray.***"
3. **Bring your hands up by your shoulders,** palms facing forward. Chant "***Haree.***"
4. **Stretch your arms out to the sides again.** Chant "***Wha.***"
5. **Bring your arms directly to the front,** palms down. Chant "***Hay.***"
6. **Bring your hands up near your shoulders.** Chant "***Guroo.***"

Continue for 11 Minutes.

To finish: Inhale, hold the breath 15–20 seconds, keep your arms in position #3 and squeeze your rib cage as you stretch your spine upward. Exhale. Repeat this sequence two more times.

*Chii-a is the Gurmukhi word for "six". In this Kriya there are six unchangeable sounds, which affect the six directions.

**Vaak Siddhi is a spiritual power that whatever you say, happens.

There comes a moment in your life when nothing works. If all shelter and hope is gone. When the enemies overcome and friends have left. Do this meditation: "Har, Haray, Haree, Wha-hay Guroo." It has six sounds, don't take it as a mantra, these are six unchangeable sounds. What surrounds you is six: the four directions and up and down. Meditate on these six in this way and they will cover you.

*The sound current has an Infinite power on God. It can bind God. It has the power. It is the only power, which is given to the human. Vaak Siddhi** is the perfection of the sound projection. Guru Nanak explained it, 'Through the mouth you utter a sound current, to which God listens with love.' What you talk is not a sound current. The sound current is that which you create with the organic matter of your body where you use your pranas and that has a projective power.*

Yogi Bhajan

PROCESS EXERCISES

Many of the Process Exercises in other chapters can be adapted to children, as long as they are made age appropriate. Keep in mind that children love to move their bodies and express themselves through artistic articulation. Above all, listen to them without judgment. Some of their feelings may be very intense. Help them express their feelings of anger, sadness, abandonment...whatever... in a constructive way...so it won't surface in negative ways like illness, drugs or sexual promiscuity later.

1 Puppets can be very effective with young children. One puppet can be designated as the deceased or dying person; another puppet can be the child. An adult can take the part of the deceased and the child play him or herself, or the child can play both puppets. Another option would be to use dolls or stuffed animals to represent the various players of the family. The child is encouraged to share feelings and whatever needs to be expressed.

2 The child can create a book about their loved one, complete with illustrations and a story...or a photo album.

3 Older children may want to write a poem about their loved one, create a sculpture, a bird house or a memorial garden...drawing upon the talents of the child or youth. Encourage them to choose their own medium of expression.

PART IV Transformation

CURVING AROUND NOW on the right loop of our figure eight labeled DEATH, the final touches are etched on our mandala. And even though we are approaching the end of our journey together in this book, this is where we are faced with the biggest opportunities of transformation and personal growth. When the goodbyes are said, the ceremonies completed and the relatives back home, the intensity of the grieving process takes hold. Everyone grieves differently but everyone must grieve. Processing that pain enables us to reinvest the relationship and move on to growth and expansion. In Chapter Twelve – *Death Rituals and Saying Goodbye* – we will see the importance of our goodbyes and the fact that we have options to how we do so. In Chapter Thirteen –*Healing Through Grief* – we will explore the stages of grief as a natural process. Either we can expand beyond the pain and, in fact, because of it…or we shrivel, becoming it. You may find the section titled, *Spirits Merging*, especially compelling. Chapter Fourteen – *Other Helpful Gems* – is packed with further tools for your personal tool kit, (compatible to Kundalini Yoga), which will help in the progression of recovery. The last and Fifteenth Chapter, *The Master Goes Home,* is a perfect conclusion to the book, because it exemplifies a conscious death. Yogi Bhajan was a master even in his death.

Be sure to check out the Appendixes – Appendix I – *Kirtan Sohila*; Appendix II – *Guru Nanak's Japji*; and Appendix III – *Sikh Procedures Following a Death.*

We have gone through a beautiful internal quest together, and now that we are nearing the end, you may want to evaluate what has changed for you. Have any of your views, attitudes, and feelings shifted? If you kept a journal or did some of the Process Exercises, this would be a good time to reread them or go back and complete others. There is more information and technology in this book than you can possibly digest in one reading. Use this book as a reference, referring back to it as needed. Yogi Bhajan's mission was to create teachers. Now that you have this knowledge, it will be up to you to share it with someone else. We are all teachers. Be the lighthouse… uplift someone in need.

Become the lighthouse for others. Beam out to everybody you touch.
YOGI BHAJAN

CHAPTER 12

Death Rituals and Saying Goodbye

Bury me if you can catch me.
Socrates

Our beliefs and spiritual orientations determine our death rituals and serve important functions for both the departed and the survivors. For the one dying, how their body is disposed of, prayers and other death practices can help free their soul. For survivors, death rituals provide a time and space to say goodbye and to celebrate the life of their loved one. In years past, before the funeral home industry evolved, everything was done by the deceased's family and friends. Usually the person died at home, surrounded by his loved ones and even members of the village. Dying at home, the person had been taken care of by his family, allowing everyone time to prepare for the upcoming death. Everyone was present for the actual death, including the youngest child.

Following the death, everyone participated in some way with the preparations of the death rituals. Members of the family bathed and clothed the body, which was then laid out in the living room in order for relatives and friends to pay their last respects. The house was cleaned and food prepared. Depending upon one's traditions, the body was disposed of in some manner – again, by members of the family and village. Family members carried the body to the grave or funeral pyre, which they had lovingly prepared themselves. Specific prayers and chants were recited during the whole process. When it was time to lower the body into the grave or light the funeral pyre, they did it themselves. Usually a feast followed the service at the family home, where all could come to mourn their loss and gain support from one another. All family members and friends were a part of this process of saying goodbye to the departed loved one. Life followed by death was a natural and inevitable sequence.

A simple analogy for death that appeals to me is the butterfly leaving the cocoon. In a burial and memorial service, consider focusing on the beauty of the living butterfly instead of the cocoon.
Duda, 1987

Consider the vast differences of our procedures today, compared to the times of our ancestors. Most people die in hospitals where strangers take care of them instead of family members. The dead body is whisked off to some funeral home, embalmed and prepared by some artful mortician. The person is dressed in their best clothes, cotton is stuffed in their cheeks, a smile is sewn on their lips and make-up covers up any imperfections.

Can you imagine the confusion for some poor woman whose husband has died a slow death? She watched him deteriorate, his body withering away, his skin color becoming gray, his cheeks sunken in. After death, he looks better than when he was alive. To her, he looks like he could just be sleeping, thus making the acceptance of death even harder.

Sometimes the body is viewed at the mortuary, but many times it is not. The casket is either open or closed and is set on a pedestal, where family and friends don't dare touch, hug or kiss their loved one. Many times the family departs from the funeral, letting the caretakers of the cemetery perform the actual burial. It's as though we have estranged ourselves and our loved ones from death. Is it any wonder then, that we consider death to be a time of great loneliness and fear? Where are our loved ones when we need their support in our time of departure and transition? Instead of being a time of pushing away, it could be a time of tremendous love, cohesiveness and completion.

As we enter the twenty-first century, our attitudes about death rituals are changing. Many more people are requesting to die at home with family and friends nearby. Arrangements for the funeral or memorial services are being made before the death, according to the dying person's wishes. Within the legal codes of each state, individuals are bringing more meaning and creativity into their death rituals. As our attitudes about death evolve, so do our death rituals.

People are recognizing that by being involved, they can more easily accept their loved one's death, say goodbye and let go. By being with the person at the time of death and after, they are better able to accept that the dead body is merely a cocoon which used to house their loved one's spirit. In observing the softness of their loved one's face and the peacefulness of their expression, it is easier to accept that they are "in good hands." They can then rejoice in the release of the butterfly from its cocoon.

 In the Sikh Tradition, it is customary to bath the body with yogurt. 

Yogurt kills bacteria on the body and serves as a ritual of purification. Devi Kaur from Los Angeles recalls her experience of taking part in this ritual with a dear woman friend.

There were eight of us women. We massaged yogurt into every part of the body, including the hair, and then dressed her in beautiful white bana (traditional Sikh attire of tunic and leggings) and the 5 K's (kara, a steel bangle; kesh, uncut hair; kanga, a small wooden comb; kirpan, a small ceremonial dagger; and kachera, Sikh underwear). As we washed the body, we chanted the Mul mantra (Ek Ong Kar Sat Nam Karta Purkh Nirbho Nirvair Akal Murat Ajooni Saibang Gurprasad Jap Aad Such Jugod Such Haibhi Such Nanak Hosibhi Such). The transformation was striking. Before we began, the body felt like an empty shell – cold and stiff. By the end, the body felt soft and peaceful, the skin was smooth, pink and radiant. The room was filled with light. It was a respectful service, of which I was grateful to be a part.

This does not mean that the survivors won't grieve. By being involved, one cannot deny the death and can thus allow the grieving process to occur. Loved ones must grieve before the healing process of "acceptance" can be completed.

Elizabeth Kubler-Ross compares the death experience to the sport of football. One may be either a spectator or a player in the game. That's how it is with the response to death. Some may attempt to keep it an intellectual concept, some are passive spectators, some active spectators, and some are players. Since the grief work depends upon the recognition of the game as being real and the willingness of the participants to be involved, it is likely that those who choose to get bruised by playing the game will have the greatest awareness of the reality of death and will come to understand their response to that death best.

The morning after her death, I had this sensation like a young person in love. I know it was her and my father reconnecting. The heart was all a flutter, just unbelievable. I also felt very euphoric and uplifted. Then around 10 or 11 o'clock, the van from the mortuary arrived. There was just one man. He asked me how I wanted to do it. I told him I wanted to carry her out of the house. She wore her hair in a bun on her head. The caregiver and my wife bathed her and dressed her in her best clothes. We chanted Japji. (There was a long pause. Guru Singh broke down and cried periodically as he told his story...which he did at this point as well.) This isn't sadness. This is gratitude for being able to do this. (Another pause) It dawned on me that she and my Dad had carried me into the house. Now, I was able to return the favor. So I scooped her up. She didn't weigh much by that time. I carried her throughout the whole bottom floor of the house. It felt so profound. I carried her out the front door, into the bright sunlight. I put her on the gurney in the van.

Excerpt from Guru Singh's interview about his mother's passing.

A sudden death is especially shocking and difficult for the survivors to accept. In these cases, the active participation of the survivors is particularly important. Being involved in the preparation of the body and ceremonies allows time to finish old business and say goodbye.

In Western Society, there are two ways of disposing of the dead body – burial and cremation.

Burials

The tradition of burying our dead began in agricultural communities some 10,000 years ago. In those agrarian societies, seeds were revered with great respect, because they were an integral part of their very survival. Seeds were returned to the earth so that they could begin the cycle of life anew. It was with this concept in mind that the custom of burying their dead was begun. From the dead, new life could begin again.

This theme was common in the myths of the planting cultures. One such story comes from Polynesia:

> *There was once a girl who loved to bathe in a certain pool. A great eel was also swimming around in the pool, and day after day he scraped across her thigh as she was bathing. Then one fine day, he turned into a young man and became her lover for a moment. Then he went away and came back again, and went away and came back again. But one time when he came, he said, "Now, next time I come to visit you, you must kill me, cut off my head and bury it." She did so, and there grew from the buried head a coconut tree. Now when you pick a coconut, you can see it is just the size of a head. You can even see eyes and the little nodules that simulate the head."*
>
> Joseph Campbell, 1988

Since those times, that concept has been greatly distorted. Today, our dead are embalmed and placed in bronze, airtight caskets. The casket will probably never disintegrate and the body could take a few hundred years to decompose. This ritual further reinforces our denial of death. We want our loved ones to be preserved forever. These practices may hinder rather than help the soul's journey. According to the Eastern traditions, embalming makes it difficult for the ethers to be released and therefore harder for the soul to be freed as well.

If burial were one's preferred method, then it would seem advantageous to resume the original method, of returning the body to the earth. Special prayers and meditations can be performed to help the soul release itself from the body.

Cremations

There is a tendency for the soul to attach itself to the physical body. In the Eastern/Yogic tradition, the dead are cremated. Fire purifies everything; the tattvas (the elements of earth, water, fire, air and ether in the body) dissolve, making it easier for the soul to be released. This is a good time to recite ***Kirtan Sohila***, which helps the soul release from the body. Family and friends can recite other meaningful prayers, staying as long or short as they feel is necessary for them.

Many more people in the West are using cremation to dispose of the bodies of their loved ones. It is easier, cleaner and much less costly than a typical modern burial. Many are combining cremation with a later memorial service as the preferred death ritual. Cremations make the death very final, which seems to aid the survivors in their process of letting go. Usually more creative and non-traditional rituals can be done at a memorial service. They can be performed at the loved one's home or even in a natural setting. The ashes can be scattered during the ceremony.

> *She passed away on a waxing moon. She was cremated on the full moon. At the funeral home, my wife and I walked down three flights of stairs to the crematorium. They cremate them in cardboard. We lifted the lid, put some things in there and did Ardas, (Sikh Prayer) looking at her. We pushed the two buttons that start the gas and flames. When the sound of the jets came on, that's when we felt like a rocket ship was taking off.*
>
> Excerpts from Guru Singh's interview

Witnessing a cremation, when the body is actually put into the flames, is a very intense experience. Family members are often given the choice to push the switch starting the furnace. The roar of the furnace takes your breath away, and you know 'this is it.' It is a good time to recite

If I should die before I wake,
All my bones and skin you take.

Put me in the compost pile,
To decompose me for a while.

Worms...water...sun will have their way
Returning me to common clay.

All that I am will feed the trees,
And little fishes in the seas.

When radishes and corn you munch,
You may be having me for lunch.

And then excrete me with a grin,
Chuckling, there goes Lee again.

LEE HAYES,
Musician for The Weavers

Kirtan Sohila or another prayer of choice. One cremation I attended was especially powerful. When the children pushed the switch, they started crying uncontrollably. The *sangat* (congregation) started chanting immediately. As our voices rose in strength and focus, the power of the Naad or sacred sound uplifted our spirits. The children stopped their weeping, joined in with the prayer and were swept up in the healing power of the sound.

> *When we all went back outside, a good friend – who frequently played favorite songs on his guitar for the deceased – spontaneously started playing some of those songs. Also spontaneously, the wife started dancing. We all joined in. The dancing was not solemn in the least. Our movements were free flowing and joyous – a celebration of liberation. When I later talked to the wife, she said she felt her husband's soul dancing inside her body. The ecstasy was indescribable. He was free at last.*

When considering death rites, it is optimal that they have meaning for both the departed and for the survivors. Whenever possible, thought and planning should occur before the death, so that at the time of death, irrational decisions will not be made. Make your wishes known ahead of time and write them down in a Last Will and Testament. Include how you want your body to be disposed, burial or cremation. Also include any spiritual rituals you prefer and any other requests you may have. Make sure you state that you want no embalming fluid used. Then, if there is a conflict among family members, at least your wishes will be on record. Without a will, the parents of the deceased can determine what to do, when there is no spouse. Be sure the will is done legally according to the laws of the state where the deceased lived and put it in a safe place. Tell family members where your Last Will and Testament is kept and its contents. This is a legal document and will assure that your wishes are followed.

The ceremony was incredible and helped me in many ways. She went out in style. She had requested ahead of time for certain songs to be sung – Let It Be *and* Dancing In The Street. *All seven of her brothers spoke. A lot of barriers were broken down between family members. For the first time, I saw my mother as someone other than my Mom. All of the speeches gave me a bigger perspective of who she was. We are so quick to put people in little boxes. I had my mother in a "Mom Box." This is so wrong. She was much more expansive. I have more appreciation for ceremonies now. It mattered who was there. I'm going to go to people's ceremonies more, give gifts and cards. It matters so much.*

A son tells of his mother's memorial service.

Conscious Funeral Home

While researching information for this book, I visited a man, Dharma Singh, in Freiburg, Germany, who runs a very unique funeral home, named *Horizonte*, (which means *The Horizon).* Dharma Singh's mission is to facilitate the deceased's transition at the time of death in a loving and dignified way. He believes that taking care of the body in a graceful way helps the soul let go. He also provides a safe place for the family to grieve.

In Germany, a deceased loved one can stay at home for up to three days following the death. This gives time for family members to say goodbye in their familiar environment. Dharma Singh often goes to the home, where he makes the first contact with the deceased and the family. He begins by introducing himself to the deceased and explains what has happened. When the body arrives at *Horizonte*, Dharma Singh begins by giving him or her 10–15 minutes to adjust to the new surroundings. He explains everything to the person – where he or she is and what he is going to do. He is very respectful, treating the body as though it were in a deep coma.

The body is washed, the hair shampooed, any wounds are patched, the hands and face are massaged with a cream that relaxes the skin, and the anus, mouth and pharyngeal cavity are filled with cotton wool so that no fluids can excrete. No make up is used nor is an artificial smile stitched on the mouth. While this is being done, family members can be present and may help, in order to comprehend the death of their loved one – how death feels, how it smells, how the dead body becomes only a shell and changes. Family members have the option to be as involved in the whole process as they choose.

A mother's coffin colorfully decorated by her young children. Photo provided by Dharam SIngh (Horizonte)

There is no embalming in Germany, and as all coffins must disintegrate in seven years, they are usually made of a soft wood; no metal or cement is permitted. At *Horizonte*, family members are given the option of decorating the coffin as they wish.

Dharma Singh also does soul talk, explaining to the soul the journey it must make – telling it not to linger with the physical body but to go on with its passage. He is very careful not to impose any of his beliefs on the deceased or the families. His facility is very eclectic and open to all religions, paths and ceremonial preferences.

Every family is provided with a lovely room, where they can stay day and night with their loved one. They are encouraged to decorate the room with photos, candles, religious articles – whatever they like. They are given a key to the facility and can come and go as much as is needed. Many people choose to sleep in the room with their loved one. Dharma Singh offers grief counseling to help family members in their grieving process. When the time is right, the family members are encouraged to participate in the closing of the coffin before the funeral service. When there is a cremation, the process is much the same, except in the end the body is cremated instead of buried.

I asked Dharma Singh how he deals with so much grief. He said he has seen others in his field get hardened, closed and burned out. To prevent that from happening to him, he doesn't hold his feelings in but allows himself to cry with the families. He does a strong daily practice of Kundalini Yoga and Meditation, which he said is invaluable in maintaining balance and giving up his grief to a Higher Power. He also has a wonderful family life that supplies him a lot of children's laughter and hugs. And, of course, there are the families he serves, who give him plenty of love and positive feedback. They are so grateful for *Horizante*, where their loved one is treated with so much loving consciousness.

Horizonte is also available for concerts, seminars and exhibitions on the subject of death and dying. School children visit the facility. Courses are also provided for doctors, nurses, priests, police officers and other interested parties, so that an alternative way of dealing with death can be demonstrated.

Riding on the train leaving Freiburg, I noticed that I felt uplifted and even joyful. How could this be? Hadn't I just visited a funeral home? Shouldn't I rather be feeling weighted down and melancholy? Here is a man, Dharma Singh, who is living the yogic philosophy about death in his work – no, not just his work – his mission in life. He enables the deceased bodies to be cared for with such grace that the soul can be released to the light. What could be more elevating and exhilarating than assisting souls in going home?

PROCESS EXERCISES

1 Have you attended a funeral or memorial service? What were the things you liked about the service? How did you feel? What are the purposes of services?

2 Think about how you would want your service to be. Consider the location, music, stories, etc. Would you want to be buried or cremated?

3 What ever you decide you want, make your wishes known to your loved ones, preferably in writing and notarized.

CHAPTER 13

Healing Through Grief

Weeping may endure for a night, but joy cometh in the morning.
Psalms 30:5

UP TO THIS POINT, we have been examining the Yogic technology and philosophy of death and loss. These beliefs about death and after life may uplift and comfort us, and our *Dharmic* practices may give us an experience of bliss and prepare us for death. But when death comes to someone we love and cherish, we will feel sorrow. As social creatures, we bond and make attachments to one another. It is natural to grieve when a loved one leaves us. Grief can also be felt for other losses, like a divorce, a child leaving home, a lost job or a home destroyed in a fire. Other losses can include one's health, vitality, hair, body parts, eyesight and short-term memory. What differs is the time it takes one to go through the grief process and the intensity felt during our process.

Bereavement, Grief and Mourning

The word *bereavement* comes from a root word meaning torn up – as if something had been suddenly yanked away or stripped away against our will. It is common for the bereaved to describe their loss as a physical sensation of something being ripped from them, (commonly at the Solar Plexus and the Heart Center), leaving a raw open wound. *Grief* is our emotional response to the event of loss. It is important we consider the full range of emotions that might be present – sadness and sorrow, as well as relief, anger, disgust, guilt, self-pity and fear. *Mourning* is the outward expression of loss, which varies tremendously according to our culture, personal orientation and societal mores. After a death or loss, we must reorient our self in relation to that which was lost, the self and the external world.

The Grief Process

Elizabeth Kubler-Ross, known as the "mother of death and dying," had the courage and great wisdom to bring death into the open, recognizing it for what it was – a universal natural process. In her work with dying patients and their families, she identified six stages of grief – denial/shock, anger, bargaining, depression, acceptance and transformation. Once her revolutionary work was recognized, others in the field of the psychology of grieving added their theories about the grief process. I will try to summarize some of the most important points.

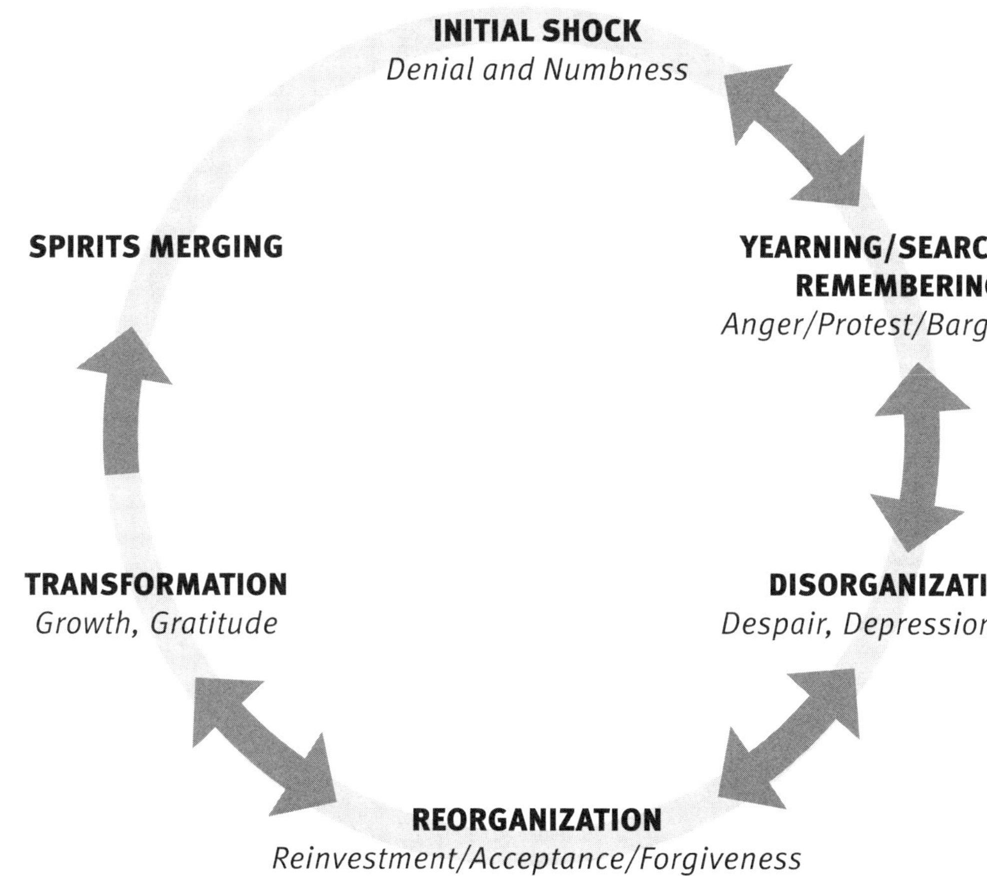

The process of grieving is not linear or static, but wavelike or cyclical, with each cycle initiated by another "trigger" or confrontation with the reality of the death. We may experience all of the stages or some of them. We may go through many stages in a day or remain in one for days or months. As the arrows show on the chart, we can move forward and then back many times before we finally reach Transformation and Growth. Some never reach it.

The first stage or experience of grief is ***Initial Shock***. Shock, disbelief, numbness and avoidance are characteristic of this stage. Phrases like, "There must have been a mistake," "This isn't happening to me," "God wouldn't do this," are common. Denial serves an important function. A compassionate gift, it buffers us from the initial shock of the event. Denial is a cushion until we are ready to deal with the reality of the loss.

Some people remain in this state of denial throughout their whole grieving process and never reach a state of acceptance. They are unable to heal or come to any completion with the loss, paralyzing them from moving forward and reinvesting in their life. In order to cycle out of denial, one must face three realizations: the death has actually occurred, the death is irreversible and final, and awareness of the extent and meaning of what has been lost.

The next stage includes ***Yearning, Searching and Remembering***. Out of our missing and yearning for our loved one, we may experience them in dreams, meditations and visions. They may give us endearing messages of love and farewell, many times using symbolic language. If there was unfinished business, they may come to us to comfort and reassure us. It is common for the bereaved to create memorials, put up pictures of their loved ones and tell endless stories of past memories. This "remembering" is crucial for healing. It gives the survivors a time and place to grieve together and immortalize their loved one's life. These expressions of the heart can bring families together and sometimes are a catalyst for dropping old hurtful familial patterns.

> *My father's hobby was gardening. He had hundreds of cacti in his greenhouse in Seattle. After his passing, I got five of his cacti and brought them to Los Angeles. Only two of them lived. One of them was a flowering cactus, but it never flowered after his passing – not once in nineteen years. Then, one week after Mom fell, this cactus sent out two*

blooms that were so close together, that instead of being round, they shared one flat side. Now, they are two dead buds, joined in the middle. When this happened, I called my sister and she came right down, because we knew it was a sign from Dad. He was going to take her home soon. Before I had the chance to contact Yogi Bhajan about Mom's passing, he had given a lecture in Gurdwara (Temple) about when two people love each other; their love knows no time and space. They meet again on the other side. Their love defies the magnetic field of the earth and lives in God forever. This was my Mom and Dad. His words became part of Mom's memorial service.

Excerpt from Guru Singh's interview

Included in this stage is ***Anger and Protest.*** These feelings are easy to identify, because everyone has experienced them at some time. "Why me?" "Why not the slob down the street?" "What have I done to deserve this?" "Life is so unfair," are characteristic phrases of this stage. If we can accept our anger, recognizing its source and power, we will be more likely to move through it. If allowed to consume us, anger constricts, thwarting our healing process. Anger can destroy us, or we can transform it into determination, courage and profound personal growth.

Some people experience ***Bargaining*** in the Yearning Stage, which includes "trade-offs" "I'll never yell at my kids again," "I'll volunteer at the hospital," "I'll give all my money to charity." We think that if we can just please God, a miracle will happen.

When we realize that the bargaining isn't working, we may go into the Disorganization Stage, with despair, guilt and depression dominating our emotions. Feeling hopelessly out of control, we are powerless, a victim of our circumstances – like we are suffocating in a dark room with no doors or windows. Guilt tenaciously raises its ugly head with "if only." If only I had not smoked for 25 years;" "If only I had spent more

time with my husband;" "If only I had not let my son go to the party that night." mercilessly torments us. It is as if we are drowning in an ocean of loss and longing, we literally feel like we are dying as well. In those moments of greatest despair, we are the most vulnerable to change, and we experience spiritual growth, because our egos, masks and games are shattered, leaving us innocent and pure. If we can let go, surrendering to a Higher Power, there will be an opening, like a ray of light through the darkened sky, when tremendous spiritual realizations and insights can occur. The battle will be over, allowing us to walk on the course toward Reorganization and Acceptance.

Taken from *Time Magazine*, April 17, 2006, p.65

The year was 1968, April 4th. Robert Kennedy was running for the Democratic presidential nomination, and he was in Indianapolis to give a campaign speech. He was just informed of Martin Luther King's assassination. The world had not yet received the grave news. "Ladies and gentlemen," he began, rather formally, respectfully. "I 'm only gong to talk to you just for a minute or so this evening because I have some very sad news..." His voice caught, and he turned it into a slight cough, a throat clearing, "and that is that Martin Luther King was shot and was killed tonight in Memphis, Tennessee."

There were screams, wailing – just the rawest, most visceral sounds of pain that human voices can summon. As the screams died, Kennedy resumed, slowly, pausing frequently, measuring his words: "Martin Luther King... dedicated his life...to love...and to justice between fellow human beings, and he died in the cause of that effort." There was near total silence now. One senses, listening to the tape years later, the audience's trust in the man on the podium, a man who didn't merely feel the crowd's pain but shared it. And Kennedy reciprocated: he laid himself bare for them; speaking of the death of his brother – something he'd never done publicly and rarely privately – and then he said, "My favorite poem, my favorite poet was Aeschylus. He once wrote, 'Even in our sleep, pain which cannot forget falls drop by drop upon the heart.'" He paused, his voice quivering slightly as he caressed every word. The silence had deepened, somehow; the moment was stunning. "'Until...in our own despair, against our will, comes wisdom through the awful grace of God.'"

Grief process. My favorite place to sob is in the shower, surrounded by water. It's an intense readjustment. Mom lived with us for six years. In that time, we were together every day. My tears are tears of deep gratitude. Torrents of sobbing…no holding on, except for those dastardly thoughts, "Did I do right." Shakti Parwha Kaur helped me a lot. She told me you have to grieve…it's human. My greatest concern was having to introduce the speakers at the Memorial Service. Every once and a while, I would start to cry. People in the audience who know me, would clap and cheer me on, 'Go ahead, Guru Singh and let it out.'

Excerpt from Guru Singh's interview

In the ***Reorganization/Acceptance*** Stage the struggle is over. *Reorganize* means that we are accepting our loss and reinvesting energies. *Acceptance* doesn't mean that we have given up. *Acceptance* means that we are "willing," willing to put our situation into perspective, like in the case of a terminal illness, willing to take responsibility for the cause and the cure of our condition.

In the case of a loved one's death, willingness means that we have been able to accept our loss and pain. And we can also accept that our loved one's soul has gone on to the next form of existence. We accept that even though we cannot recapture our previous relationship with our loved one, we can develop a new one in its place. We can move on and *Reorganize* or reinvest in our life. Perhaps we start a new job, go back to school or go on a cruise. A powerful ingredient for a broken heart is ***forgiveness.*** With willingness to forgive our self, our loved one, and other family members, the black cloud lifts, unveiling the serenity of acceptance.

The grieving process can be very confusing and disconcerting. Just when we feel stable and somewhat "normal," a photo or smell or song will trigger the swell of emotions all over again. It is important to remember that we are not going crazy. It is all a part of a natural process. Gradually,

the emotions will fade and have less and less impact. As long as we consciously go through the stages of grieving, time can be a friend and help heal the broken heart.

In the beginning of her work, Elizabeth Kubler-Ross identified only five stages of the Grief Process. After many years of observing these stages in her patients and their families, she recognized another stage after Acceptance – ***Growth* and *Transformation*.** In this stage, we take a step beyond acceptance. We recognize that an ultimate good has occurred because of the death. Perhaps a scholarship fund is created in honor of our loved one, a dramatic positive transformation occurs in one of our family members, a co-worker fights for tougher DWI laws, a family friend decides to become an oncologist, a memorial neighborhood playground is built, or we are able to slow down enough to enjoy the flowers of life. I am adding another dimension to this stage – ***Gratitude*.** We are not grateful that our loved one died, but because of the death, we are grateful for life itself and for the added richness in our lives.

> *How has Mom's death affected my daily life? I go to class, I see clients – I go through the motions. I am many times, many moments in a different place. I can't describe that place. It's beyond description. I'm a huge activist. Now I have a different outlook. I care, but I'm not attached. Yogi Bhajan said, 'no matter how long you live, it seems like nothing at all.' There's no time. It's an illusion. I'm just grateful for love…grateful for children…we have it really good. We have commitment, dedication…in a world that's mad with insanity.*
>
> Guru Singh

At some point in the grieving process, it can be very helpful to reorganize our environments. This may include remodeling our home, clearing out  our loved one's room or giving away his or her possessions that are not keepsakes. Tearing down walls, putting in an additional window, painting, putting up new pictures, all can change the energy of the house and be a piece in the healing mosaic. Of course there will be the meaningful things we want to keep – perhaps things like Mom and Dad's wedding photographs, Josh's tennis awards, Nana's pearl ring, Aunt Maude's antique china, Uncle George's carpentry tools and other special mementos. Members of the family may have requests of what they would like to keep of their loved one. It is generally recommended that one not make a major decision, like selling a house or moving to another town for the first year after the death of a loved one. This may vary, of course, depending upon the circumstances. One friend of mine took care of her ailing parents for nine years. Within a few months after their death, she sold the family home and moved to another state to be near close friends. She had done much of her processing before their deaths and was ready to move on.

An Added Stage – *Spirits Merging*

In my experience as a spiritual person, and in my grief work with spiritual individuals and families, I believe that there is yet another stage – ***Spirits Merging***. Over time, grief becomes an experience of the heart, where the actual physical form looses its importance. Our hearts merge, in love, until they reach the final stage – *Spirits Merging.* This is where our Dharmic practice can serve us. Through Yoga, Meditation and reciting the Shabd Guru, our hearts and souls will merge into Oneness. I have heard people say that they will greet their loved ones in Heaven. We don't have to wait. In the quietness of our meditation, in the whisper of the trees, in the joy of our songs, we can experience that union while alive.

To demonstrate this stage, I am going to tell you an extraordinary story about a husband, Pritam Singh, and his wife, Siri Pritam Kaur, who reached this state of consciousness. Pritam Singh was an exceptional chiropractor and healer. Many people from all over the world came to him for treatments. Even after he suffered a stroke in which he lost the use of the right side of his body, Pritam's treatments became more subtle but also more powerful. He would merely gently touch the patient in a particular spot and healing would occur. Often he would use his wife to touch the patient. The more subtle Pritam became, the more aware and in tune Siri Pritam had to become as well. She often intuitively knew what he was trying to convey to the patient. She now realizes that this subtle communication prepared her for their future relationship after Pritam's death.

> *I think the grief you experience at death is from what you have not been able to express in life – the unspoken love. All the things that happened or didn't happen, things said or not said become insignificant at the time of death. There just has to be forgiveness and gratitude. 'Thank you for all you taught me, did for me, all the experiences you gave me – I love you for all of it – good or bad – it doesn't matter.' It's never too late to express this love, even after death.*
>
> *The most striking adjustment after Pritam's death was not having the physical presence there, but we definitely communicate. I confer with him about the children, the business…as things come up…not all the time. I close my eyes and meditate on him. He is right there in front of me. We talk. Sometimes he will treat one of our children in my meditation. Recently I conferred with him about our daughter, who has been ill. He gave her a treatment by simply touching her upper spine…then said that she was OK. She is now getting better. His communication in relation to me this time was serene, but other times he is very direct and commanding about something I may have to take care of. I usually contact him when something comes up which I can't figure out.*
>
> *Recently I have been reorganizing our chiropractic office. I had a dream where I was walking past the chiropractic building and I walked in. A woman was washing the floor and asked me to not come*

in. I did so anyway. I walked to the back of the building, where I saw a small opening into a room where Pritam was sitting at a table on the left. I asked him why he was sitting on the left. He said he is not to be seen. He is very much still a part of the chiropractic practice but now he is in the background... that is very much my experience. This relationship is not out of the ordinary; it has always been this way, it's just an extension of our relationship in life.

Siri Pritam Kaur talks about the relationship with her husband following his death

You should only consider yourself married when you are on the death bed. If by that time the husband is still there, shake hands with him and declare yourselves married. Otherwise, there is no such thing as marriage, it doesn't exist.

Yogi Bhajan

Another example of "Spirits Merging" comes from a story told by Shanti Shanti Kaur, who uses Kundalini Yoga and meditation with people who have serious illnesses.

I used to teach a Kundalini Yoga class for 25–30 people who were HIV+, most of whom were men. In those early days of AIDS, before medications were saving lives, being diagnosed as HIV+ was a death sentence. Many in the AIDS community faced their death by having an attitude of, 'Well, if I'm going to die anyway, I might as well run up my credit card and have a lot of sex.' The members of the yoga class wanted a different way – a way of consciously dealing with their illness, the remaining of their life and their subsequent death. The class became like a 'tribe.' Their friends didn't support them, so they really looked to each other for encouragement and inspiration. New members joined, some left, many died. Many times friends and family members would come to class to gain an understanding of how their loved one was benefiting from yoga.

Many of the members of the tribe died; you can imagine the grief and fear. They knew their time was not far off. To help deal with

their feelings they had a tradition of sitting in the same spot every class. When one of them died, they held that spot for the person for at least 17 days (the time it takes for the soul to leave the electromagnetic force of the earth). One particular time was especially moving.

I was in the office filing yoga sets. All of a sudden I felt the soul of one of our class members. He had recently died and was visiting me to tell me that he was OK. The really amazing thing is that within the first seventeen days after his death, he visited every single person in that class. His goodbye message to all of them was basically the same – 'I'm OK. It's cool. You can hang here. Don't be afraid.' Such a compassionate act of love…to help his tribe members face their own deaths fearlessly.

Shanti Shanti Kaur Khalsa– Director of the Guru Ram Das Center for Medicine and Humanology

I can't emphasize enough the importance of our Dharmic practice (Sadhana). Our goal is not to avoid the grieving process. Our Sadhana will help us through it and even give us a more elevated experience. Kundalini Yoga, in particular, is invaluable. Our emotions process through our nervous and glandular systems. If they are strong at the time of a loss, they will help us maintain emotional stability. It is also common for the immune system to be compromised during and after a loss. Illness is common among survivors, making the grieving process more difficult. Practice for the worst, enjoy the moment of each day, and you'll be better prepared to skillfully navigate through the tumultuous grieving period.

Can I Be Spiritual and Grieve?

In the beginning years of our Yogic/Spiritual Community, there was some confusion about the appropriateness of grieving. If the soul of the deceased has gone Home, it should be a joyous occasion, and our prayers and chants

Added Points About Grieving

1. Grieving is hard work and takes time. The optimum situation is to be able to take some time off to just allow the grief process to happen.

2. Not everyone grieves in the same way. There is a masculine and feminine style of grieving, which is not gender specific. A masculine style grieving would include isolating oneself and doing something, like building a memorial. It would be more thought oriented, analyzing and wanting to take control. A feminine style would include the need to share feelings with others and be inclusive. It is more accepting and willing to surrender control. It is important to be non-judgmental of one's style. If someone is grieving differently than you, it doesn't mean that they are not grieving or feeling the loss. Be accepting and allowing of all ways of grieving.

   When my husband was eleven years old, his mother died. As the eldest son, he thought he wasn't supposed to cry. His younger brother, who did cry, was angry with his older brother. For years he carried around the misunderstanding that his older brother didn't care. What a relief and healing when finally as adult men, they talked about it.

3. Needs of the Mourner:
   - Validation of the loss
   - Support and permission to grieve, which includes sharing emotions and memories
   - Permission to withdraw from usual activities, if needed
   - Permission to change and grow from the loss
   - Complicated Mourning is when there are extraordinary circumstances, which may require an extended grief period and extra family and societal support for the mourner

4. Such complications might include:

   Before the Death
   - Multiple losses – in a short amount of time
   - Previous psychiatric history
   - Personality variables – if a person has more self-reliance, he will do better
   - Absence of a spiritual/existential frame of reference for loss/tragedy
   - Relationship with the deceased

   At the Time of Death
   - Violence in the death – mutilation of the body, if the deceased suffered, suicide, murder
   - Quality of the death – whether one can say goodbye and finish business
   - Kinship and life-cycle timing – 92-year-old mother vs. 3 year old son
   - Ambiguity of loss – body isn't found or Alzheimer's – i.e. mind dies first
   - Multiple deaths at the same time, as in a car accident or school shooting

   Factors After the Death
   - Social support – friends bring food and keep in touch; boss gives time off
   - Concurrent stressors and secondary losses – lost both child and house in a fire

   Survivors of 9/11 may be suffering from complicated mourning, except for the societal support, rituals and mourning as a country. The dead were immortalized and made into heroes. These are factors which will aid the survivors in their recovery.

will help the soul on its journey. But, if I grieve for the person could I hold the soul to the earth's magnetic field, preventing it from going through the blue ethers? We were in conflict, wanting to rejoice in the soul's completion, but also feeling really horrible about our loss. But now we have realized that it is only human to grieve. There has to be an outlet to release one's pain from separation.

Shakti Parwha Kaur was the very first student of Yogi Bhajan. She tells the story about the death of a young man, with whom she had developed a very strong attachment. Intellectually she knew that she should be rejoicing in his liberation, but she was grief stricken with this loss. Trying to maintain a stoic "yogic" non-attached manner, especially to her spiritual teacher, she relates this story.

> *Yogi Bhajan had just returned from a lecture tour when he was told of Bhai Sahib Dayal Singh's unexpected death. There were several of us sitting in the living room, still in shock from the news. Every few minutes, overcome with emotion, I would go into the bathroom and cry. Then I would splash cold water on my face and return, trying to keep my composure. After a few such exits and entrances, Yogi Bhajan asked me what I was doing. I said, 'I know I shouldn't cry, but …' He wouldn't let me finish the sentence. He simply said, 'You're human aren't you?'*
>
> *Kundalini Yoga: The Flow of Eternal Power*,
> by Shakti Parwha Kaur Khalsa, 1996

You may find it easier to grieve openly with friends and loved ones, or grieve privately with God. You may find that not all of your friends and family members are able to openly grieve, especially those who are uncomfortable with death itself and with their own mortality. You may find some counseling with a grief counselor helpful, or a grief support group to help you put into perspective your many conflicting feelings.

Allow others to be there with you.

Often, good friends are invaluable in cushioning our loss and helping us to get on with life. Many times friends want to do something but don't know what would be helpful or appreciated. You don't have to face your loss alone. Allow those with whom you feel comfortable to share your vulnerability. Being brave includes asking for help. Be specific. Designate one trusted friend to organize your "needs list." Everyone grows and goodness shines.

My husband and I have always lived in Sikh communities. There is a feeling of "village," where members are there for each other – in times of joy and in times of sorrow, in every day occurrences and in times of the extraordinary. The following story demonstrates the power and love of community. The names have been changed, but the facts are absolutely correct as best I remember them. At the time, we were living in an ashram of around 16 adults and 6 children. Shanti had had a difficult pregnancy, but now she was finally in labor. Births were always a joyous occasion in our community, so there was much chanting happening outside Shanti's room to help her bring in this new saint. I was on the third floor, putting my 4 children to bed. A yoga class was happening on the first floor. I was preparing to go down to the second floor to join the chanting when all of a sudden I heard sirens and loud thuds going up the second floor steps, leading to Shanti's room. There was something very wrong. The baby wasn't breathing. Shanti immediately did CPR on her newborn. Within a few minutes the paramedics whisked her away to the hospital. We were numb. How could this have happened? We were young and healthy. We meditated. Nothing bad was supposed to happen to us. We were in shock, but we sprung into action immediately, helping the family cope with this grave situation.

The community did everything. We cooked the meals, did the laundry

and helped with childcare for her 3–½ year old daughter. The baby, Ravi, was in the hospital and so were we: a 24-hour vigil was scheduled, with members of the community and yoga students taking turns to chant to our littlest angel. The nursing staff felt all the babies in the pediatric intensive care ward were benefiting from our loving and spiritual vibrations.
The healing power of Naad (chanting) was ever powerful. In addition, for 40 consecutive evenings, a healing meditation was done for Ravi and her family at the ashram. Shanti and her husband said they felt cradled in love and support. After 6 grueling months, with the community supporting this family in every possible way, Ravi left her earthly body. Here too, the community gave endless support in the death ritual. Shanti said she doesn't know how she would have coped with this most difficult situation without the constant support of the community.

PROCESS EXERCISES

All of us have experienced losses, and probably most of us have faced death as well. Grieving is natural and necessary before the wounds can heal.

1 Try to identify your grief process. Did you go through the stages described in this chapter – all of them, some of them? Did you lean more toward the masculine or feminine style? What helped you go through it? What didn't help? Do you have more work to do?

2 Draw a picture expressing your grief cycle. Don't worry about your artistic proficiency. Using colors and emotions from the heart, allow them to flow onto the paper.

3 From your own experience of the grieving process, what would you tell someone else going through it? Write an actual or imaginary letter expressing yourself.

4 This beautiful exercise is to help resolve unfinished business. This exercise can be done alone or with a trusted friend, counselor or death coach. If you are a death coach or counselor, this is a wonderful exercise to be done with a client. Be in a secure and quiet place.

Imagine that you are with your loved one (who has either already died or is dying). Close your eyes and take some deep breaths. Meditate on the Sutras of the Aquarian Age, which were presented in the First Chapter – God Exists Within Us. *Every sutra can be applied in this exercise, especially the first and last one:*

- Recognize that the other person is you, *and*
- Understand through compassion or you will misunderstand the times.

Keeping these sutras in mind, imagine that you are your loved one. Take on the persona of that person...their personality, feelings and thoughts. Now, talk as if you were your loved one talking to you. What would the person say? How does he or she feel? Is there something he or she needs to say to you or to other members of the family? Is there something you need to say back to him or her? Have a conversation back and forth. Go as long as you need, allowing for silences and emotions to surface.

When you finish journal your experience. You may want to repeat this exercise more than one time, comparing journal entries. Does this exercise help you resolve unfinished issues? Note how you feel.

5 Do one or more of the following meditations. How did you feel afterwards? Do one with a friend in need.

MEDITATION FOR STRESS OR SUDDEN SHOCK

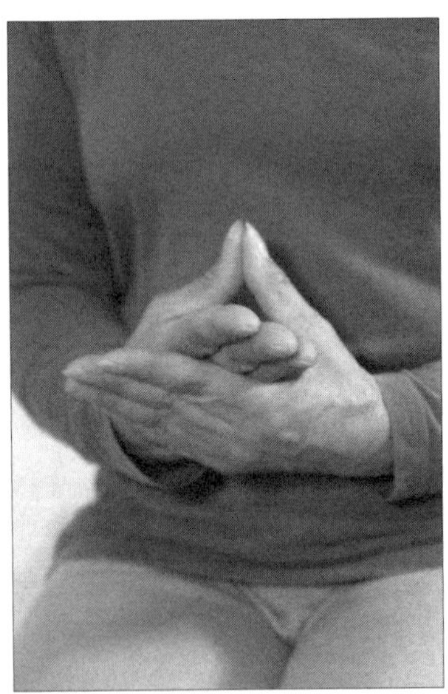

This meditation balances the left hemisphere of the brain with the base of the right hemisphere. This enables the brain to maintain its equilibrium under stress or the weight of a sudden shock. It also keeps the nerves from being shattered under those circumstances.

Sit with a straight spine, with a light *Jalandhar Bandh (Neck Lock).*

Mudra: Relax the arms down with the elbows bent. Draw the forearms in toward each other until the hands meet in front of the body about 1 inch (2.5 cm) above the navel. Point both palms up. and rest the right hand in the palm of the left hand. Pull the thumbs toward the body, and press the thumb tips together.

Eye Position: Look at the tip of the nose, the *Lotus Point*.

Mantra: Deeply inhale and completely exhale as you chant the mantra three times. The entire mantra must be chanted in only one breath. Use the tip of the tongue to pronounce each word exactly, and chant in a monotone. The rhythm must also be exact. (Refer to accompanying CD for correct pronunciation and rhythm – 15.)

> *Sat Naam Sat Naam Sat Naam Sat Naam*
> *Sat Naam Sat Naam Wha-hay Guroo*

Time: Begin with 11 minutes and slowly build up to 31 minutes.

To End: Inhale and completely exhale 5 times. Then deeply inhale, hold the breath and stretch the arms up over the head as high as possible, stretching completely. Repeat twice. Relax down.

33 MINUTES TO ELIMINATE STRESS

Create Vitality Inside To Get Rid of Stress

In times of extreme stress, like the loss of one's home and possessions in a fire, the trauma of a mass murder in one's community or the death of a loved one, all of the systems of the body are under severe duress. Extreme stress can also be felt when it has accumulated – such as the loss of a job, a child leaving home, multiple deadlines at work, placing an elder parent in a nursing home, an ill child or going through a divorce – all occurring in a relatively short period of time, where there is no opportunity to sufficiently process the magnitude of each individual stress. This kriya balances the liver, the glandular system, the chakras, and the three nervous systems, which will enable you to handle the stress with greater equanimity and stability. The times done for these three kriyas must be exact – no more and no less than 11 minutes each.

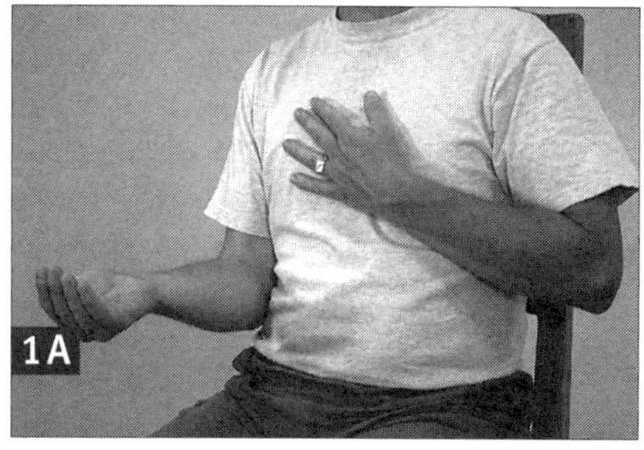

1A

1. Pitta Kriya: Sit in Easy Pose. Put your left palm on the center of your chest. Bend your right elbow. Make a cup of your right hand **(1A)**. Move your cupped hand past your right ear, as if you are throwing water over your shoulder **(1B)**. Keep your right arm moving back and forth, making sure that the right wrist passes the right ear. Continue 11 minutes.

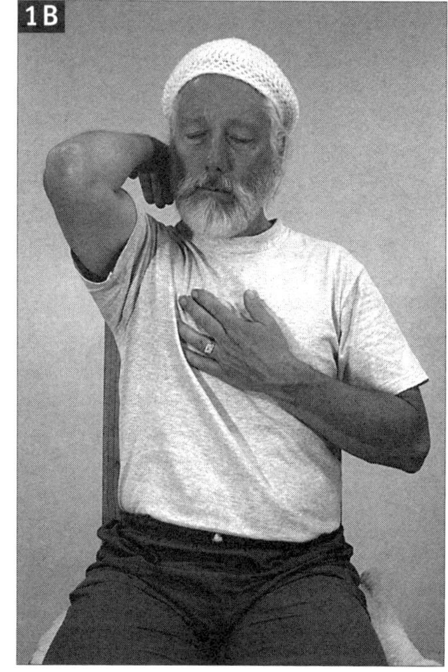

1B

To End: Inhale deeply and hold your breath for 20 seconds as you press your right arm as far back as possible, stretching the armpit. Exhale like a cannon fire through the mouth. Repeat this sequence two more times.

This exercise works on the liver, which cleans the bloodstream of impurities. Since the bloodstream interacts with every cell of your body, when it is polluted, it is very difficult to maintain a healthy balance in the body's chemistry. This exercise also stimulates the glands to secrete and improve the chemistry of the blood.

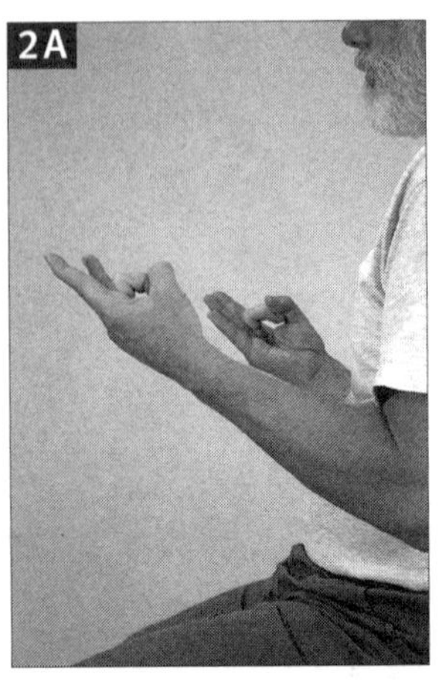

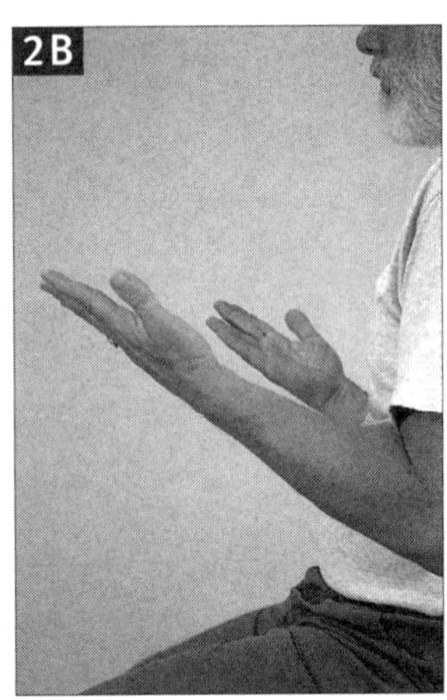

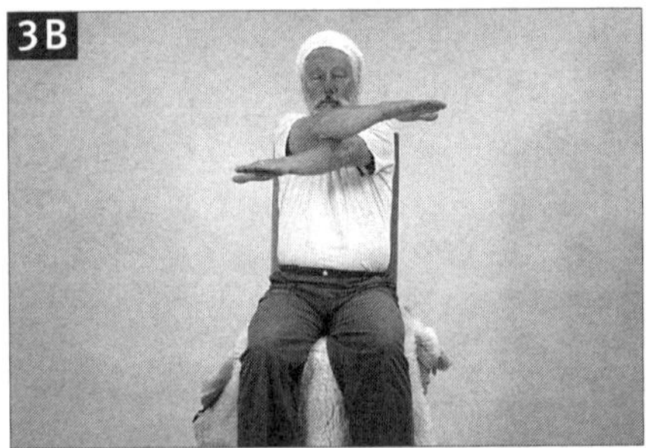

2. Sit with a straight spine. Focus your eyes at the tip of your nose. Bend your elbows and press them against your rib cage so that your forearms angle upward. With your palms facing up, hold down the first joint of each middle (Saturn) finger with the thumb **(2A)**. Flick both Saturn fingers at the same time as you chant "**Har**" **(2B)**. Continue rapidly flicking the fingers and chanting, using the tip of your tongue to chant. Continue 11 minutes.

To End: Inhale deeply, hold the breath 15–20 seconds and continue to flick the Saturn fingers. Exhale and repeat this sequence two more times.

This exercise brings all the chakras into balance and balances the Saturn energy (the energy of purity and discipline) in your psyche.

3. Sit with a straight spine. Focus your eyes at the tip of your nose. Extend both arms out to the sides, parallel to the floor, palms down **(3A)**. Allow no bend in the elbows. Criss-cross your arms in front of you, horizontally, over and under (alternating which arm crosses on top **3B)**. Chant "**Har**" each time your arms cross. Continue 11 minutes.

To End: Inhale deeply, hold the breath for 5–10 seconds and continue to criss-cross your arms. Exhale and repeat this sequence two more times.

This exercise strengthens and balances the parasympathetic and sympathetic nervous systems so the action nervous system may correctly know what to do.

MEDITATION TO KEEP THE BRAIN FROM GOING BACK INTO SHOCK

(Originally, this meditation was given by Yogi Bhajan February 5, 2001 in Espanola, New Mexico and was called *"Self Sensory System III – Oneness."* Later in response to the horrors of 9/11, the threat of terrorist attacks and many natural disasters, Guru Dev Singh, Master of Sat Nam Rasayan, gave this meditation in the context of stabilizing the brain after a traumatic event.)

Shock and denial can cushion us from the intolerable pain following a sudden trauma. We become spaced out and are not grounded on the earth. If we stay in this state or keep flipping back into it, our reality becomes distorted, which can become self-destructive. This meditation will stimulate and balance the frontal lobe, the hypothalamus and the thalamus.

The frontal lobe brings our personality back into unison and is stimulated by the optic nerve. When we focus at the tip of the nose, the forehead begins to feel heavy and our Third-Eye will open, which will break the blocks of the frontal lobe; the intuition will command. The hypothalamus sends information throughout the body in the form of chemical messengers that trigger emotions, metabolic activity and actions in a nonlinear wavelike manner. The thalamus filters sensations and chooses which sensations and thoughts will make it to consciousness. Once these areas are again balanced, we can regain our center and face more effectively and neutrally the reality of the situation.

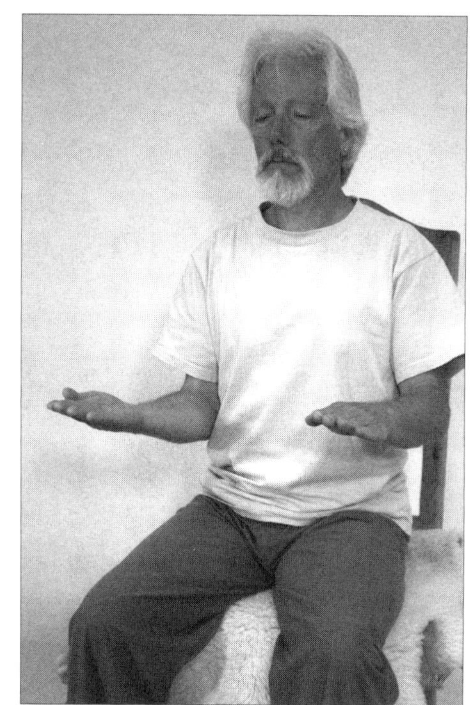

Part One

Sit with a straight spine. The elbows are bent at the sides, with the forearms parallel to the floor straight in front of you. The right palm is up; the left palm is down. The eyes are 1/10 open, focused at the tip of the nose. The breath is long and deep. Do not suspend the breath between the inhale and the exhale. Just breathe as long and deep as you can. Continue for 11 minutes.

Part Two

Remain in the same position and breathe deeper and deeper with self-control. Your body will start balancing itself and that is where the expansion of your mind comes from.

Continue for 11 more minutes.

Part Three

Remaining in the same position, do Breath of Fire, moving the navel powerfully with the strength of your diaphragm. Breathe consciously. Spread and regenerate the energy.

Continue for 3 minutes.

To End: When finished, deeply inhale, hold, exhale. Repeat 2 more times.

MEDITATION FOR GRIEF

This meditation could not be found in any of Yogi Bhajan's lectures, and therefore is not KRI approved in this book. It is included here, though, because Shanti Shanti Kaur and I both remember doing it in class. It can be used to release grief. When Yogi Bhajan gave it, he said that it was a practice he observed in India in villages when there was a death. Loved ones would go into a river or lake up to their navel and do this meditation together. If you don't have a natural body of water to go into, go navel deep into a swimming pool or at least a bathtub.

Mudra: Sit or stand with a straight spine. Relax the elbows down by the sides and bring the forearms straight out in front of your body, palms flat and facing up. Have the palms slightly cupped, and place them a few inches above the knees **(1A)**.

Movement: Bring the arms up **(1B)**, back behind the head, stretching hands and arms as far back over the shoulders as you can **(1C)**. Imagine you are scooping water, and throwing it through your arcline, over your shoulders, with a flick of the wrist. The movement is flowing.

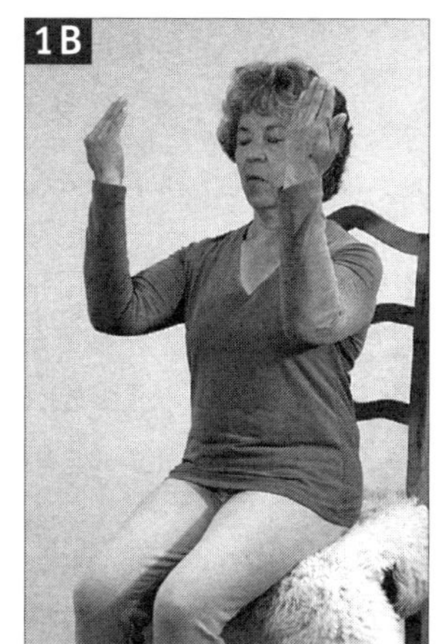

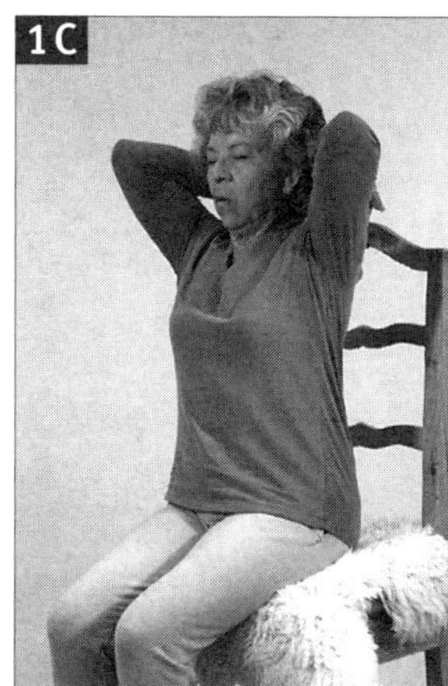

Breath: The breath is powerful through the O of the mouth from the throat. Inhale as the arms are down (parallel to the ground), exhale as the arms toss the water over the shoulders. Make the breath heavy and "throaty."

Be vigorous in throwing the water over your shoulders – "*All my worries, all my negativity, all my anger, all my grief, all my anxiety is being thrown over my shoulders*." Allow yourself to cry; allow yourself to release whatever emotions come up – until you feel clean and calm. Do it alone. Do it as a family. Shanti Shanti Kaur said that she and her family did this when her mother died and it was a very healing and powerful experience.

MEDITATION TO RELEASE SADNESS & EMPTINESS IN THE HEART

This meditation was first given by Yogi Bhajan at Master Touch II in Espanola, New Mexico, July 27, 1999. Yogi Bhajan said in this lecture that as the coldness of the world disappears from within, inner happiness and security develops. This meditation helps to release sadness and emptiness from a grieving heart.

Part One

Eyes: Closed

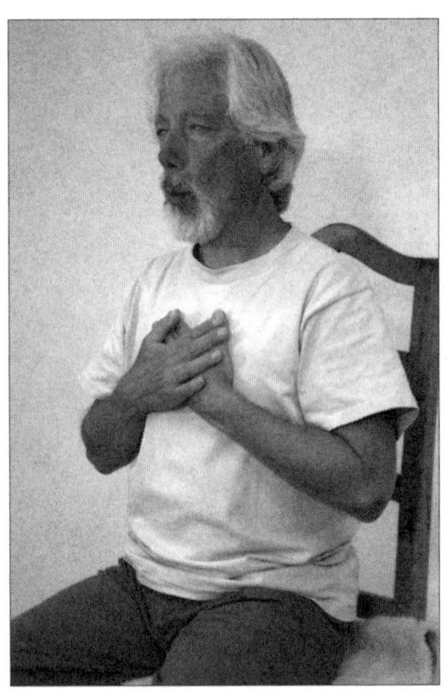

Breath: Make an "O" of the mouth. Breathe in through the "O" of the mouth very powerfully. Exhale through the nose.

Mudra: The left palm is flat against the Heart Center, and the right palm is flat on top of the left.

Time: Continue for 11–31 minutes.

To End: Inhale and press the palms against the chest. Suspend the breath, then exhale. Repeat.

Part Two

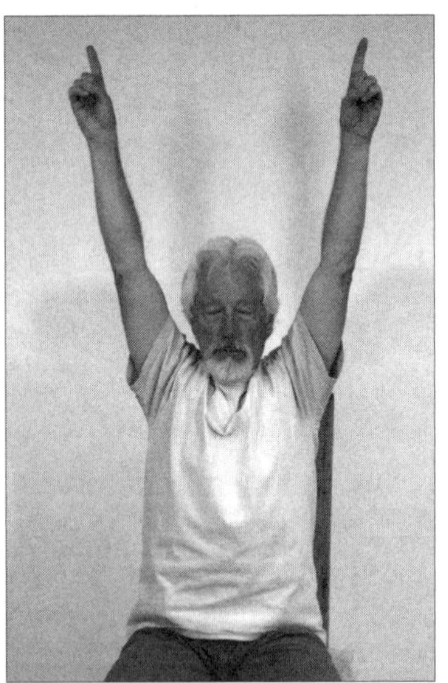

Mudra: Bring the arms straight over the head, with the fists and the index fingers pointing up. Begin making small, fast circles with the arms circling from the outside in – about 3 per second. The spine will move. Chant as you move.

Mantra:

Chattr chakkr vartee Chattr chakkr bhugatay
Suyumbhav subhang sarab daa sarab jugtay
Dukaalang pranaasee dayaalang saroopay
Sadaa ung sungay abhangang bibhootay

Thou art pervading in all the four directions,
The enjoyer in all the four directions.
Thou art self-illumined and united with all.
Destroyer of bad times, embodiment of mercy.
Thou art ever within us.
Thou are the everlasting giver of indestructible power.

Refer to the accompanying CD for a correct pronunciation – 16 or contact Ancient Healing Ways or Spirit Voyage (Resource Page), who has CD's with various versions of this mantra.

Time: Continue for 5 minutes.

To End: Inhale, suspend the breath, exhale and relax.

For more meditations, refer to Chapter 9 – *Meditation For Transformation and Bliss*.

Do not stand at my grave and weep;
I am not there. I do not sleep.
I am a thousand winds that blow.
I am the diamond glints on snow.
I am the sunlight on ripened grain.
I am the gentle autumn's rain.
When you awaken in the morning's hush,
I am the swift uplifting rush
Of quiet birds in circled flight.
I am the soft stars that shine at night.
Do not stand at my grave and cry:
I am not there. I did not die.

ANONYMOUS

CHAPTER 14

Other Helpful Gems

Work does not kill you – food does. God does not kill you – food does. Food is your first and last enemy. If you take in more than you can handle, it takes all of your energy to digest it.
YOGI BHAJAN

IN THE LAST CHAPTER, we explored Yogic techniques that are beneficial during the grieving process. This chapter contains other helpful gems – complimentary to yogic philosophy – which include **Foods For Recovery, Tips For Being Good to Yourself, Remedies For Trauma and Recovery, Changing Your Environment,** and **The Healing Power of Laughter and Play.** I think you will find these suggestions invaluable, uplifting and fun. (The information in this chapter is not intended to diagnose, treat, cure, or prevent any disease.)

This chapter is intended for anyone going through the process of loss. I want to especially emphasize here the importance of caregivers. They also need to take care of themselves. Sometimes it is much harder to take care of yourself than someone else. These "gems" will enable the caregiver to keep giving longer...with more joy and fulfillment.

Foods For Recovery

What you eat is very important. Since it is difficult to eat differently when under stress, start eating a light, healthy diet today. A habit of healthy eating will give you the nutrients, vitamins and energy to support your body in normal conditions and when under duress. When there is a loss, it is common to lose one's appetite. It is important to keep your blood sugar stable, so eat at least small amounts, even if you are not hungry. It is common to feel spaced out; eating will ground you.

1. Eat plenty of high-quality vegetarian protein, found in legumes (beans, lentils and split peas), nuts, dairy and soybean products. Coconuts contain all of the amino acids and are a complete protein. Easily assimilated proteins will give you brainpower and endurance. Conversely, meat, especially red meat, will weigh you down. It is very hard to digest and will acidify your blood. There are many books written on this subject. Being light in body means being light in the mind as well. It only makes sense that lightness in mind and body will aid your ability to meditate and therefore ignite your inner light.

2. If you smoke, stop. You know all the reasons why. In relation to going through crisis and loss, it will only make things much worse and harder to cope. Smokers are generally more irritable, nervous, impatient and absolutely cannot meditate. Smoking destroys your ability to focus and access your Third-Eye. Smoking is the anti-spiritual drug and will not allow a calm mind. Don't wait for a crisis to hit. Stop now. You know my words are truth. Find the support you need and just do it. You deserve this gift to yourself.

3. Avoid saturated fats. Saturated fats can inhibit the synthesis of neurotransmitters in the brain, cause the blood cells to clump together and result in poor circulation to the brain. You need the brain to function at its best capacity.

4. Avoid caffeine and sugar. Caffeine and sugar create an imbalance in the body's metabolism. They weaken the adrenals and nervous system. One may feel great surges of energy, followed by tremendous fatigue and even depression. They acidify the blood, making one irritable and vulnerable to illness.

5. Increase your consumption of tryptophan-rich foods
Tryptophan is the amino acid responsible for the production of serotonin. Serotonin is the neurotransmitter, which regulates our mood and sleep cycles. Amino Acids found in a high meat protein diet may inhabit the absorption of Tryptophan in the brain, while a carbohydrate-rich diet can help the body's ability to absorb it. Milk, bananas, figs and dates are good sources of tryptophan. See date milk recipe below.

6. Consume raw fruits and vegetables and their juices, as well as legumes and whole grains. Rich in complex carbohydrates, they will increase the production of brain serotonin.

7. Drink lots of fresh vegetable juice for the nervous system.

Celery juice (6 oz.) can be combined with dandelion (6 oz.), parsley (3 oz.), asparagus (2 oz.) and carrot (4 oz.) for sweetness.

If you can just keep your food light, you will have these advantages: You will be healthy and you will live a longtime.
YOGI BHAJAN

8. Nutrients can help with depression and emotional swings as well. **Biotin** can be helpful. It is abundant in soybeans, whole-wheat flour and rice bran. Other nutrients include: **Folic Acid**, **Vitamin B6**, **Vitamin B12**, **Riboflavin**, **Thiamin**, **Vitamin C** (bell peppers, apples, coconut milk, grapes, papayas, olives, citrus), **Calcium** (dairy, greens, bananas, cabbage, sesame seeds, watercress, figs, lemons, oranges, papayas, parsley, almonds), **Iron** (artichokes, apricots, bananas, parsley), **Magnesium** (apples, coconut, grapes, lemons, oranges), **Potassium** (apples, bananas, coconut, grapes, lemons, olives, raisins, yogurt, zucchini), and **Omega-6 fatty acids** (primrose oil).

9. Drink large quantities of water – 6–8 glasses a day. Water keeps you regular and hydrated. It cools the nervous system and detoxifies the body.

10. Dates are a concentrated nourishing food. They are easy to digest, are a source of quick energy and bring heat to the body. **Date milk** is very nutritious. Take 8 oz of milk, 6–8 dates sliced in half and pitted. On very low heat or in a double boiler, let the dates and milk simmer about 20 minutes. Strain and serve. Very yummy!

11. Drink a lot of Yogi Tea. Yogi Tea is great for the nerves, gives you steadiness and strength. It is a blood purifier, aids in digestion, builds strong bones and prevents illness.

Recipe for Yog i Tea:

20 cracked cardamom pods
20 whole peppercorns
15 cloves
3 cinnamon sticks
1 inch of grated ginger.

Boil in 2 quarts of water for 30 minutes. Then, turn off the flame and add a pinch of black tea (can be decaffeinated tea). For each cup of Yogi Tea, add ½ cup of milk (any kind – cow, goat, soy, rice, almond). Your favorite sweetener can also be added, such as maple syrup, honey, stevia or barley syrup. Enjoy!!

Yogi Tea is also available in tea bags and freeze-dried bulk in most health food stores.

Remedies For Trauma and Recovery

Homeopathic

1. Aconite – is effective when there is fear involved, such as in a sudden death, accident or murder. If someone witnesses the death, like a heart attack or an auto accident, give this remedy.
2. Antimonium Tartaricum – This remedy relieves the "death rattle", enabling the dying person to breath more easily.
3. Arsenicum Album – This is a wonderful remedy to help the dying person let go of their resistance to the dying process. It relieves anxiety and helps the person die peacefully.
4. Carbo Vegetabilis – If a person or animal looks dead, give this remedy immediately. It will not stop an imminent death, but it can help with situations, which are borderline – as in near death experiences. This is a good remedy to have at births to help with a baby who is having a hard time getting going.
5. Ignatia – This remedy is good for grief. Taking this remedy will help the person not mask or suppress his or her emotions, while at the same time helping them get back into his or her center, so daily life can resume.
6. Natrum Muriaticum – This remedy is good for chronic grief, when the person has not expressed his or her grief. The emotions are buried, affecting other areas of their life. The person may be suffering from compounded grief, where there has been multiple deaths.
7. Kali Phosphoricum – This remedy helps to restore the nervous system. When there is a death, the nervous system goes on overload, many times resulting in illness. In extreme cases there is a nervous breakdown. Use Ignatia first in the acute stage, then switch to Kali Phosphoricum.

Bach Flower Remedies

8. Rescue Remedy – This is a remedy to give someone immediately after the shock of the death. It can be given every few minutes to help the person stay grounded.
9. Star of Bethlehem – This remedy is restorative and calming for people who have suffered a trauma or shock. It is especially helpful for persons who have not adequately addressed a loss from the past.

There are many other flower essences that might help the grieving person. If you contact your local health food store, they may be able to refer you to a practitioner who uses these amazing essences.

When you eat, how you eat, and where you eat all directly and indirectly influence your mind, body and spiritual awareness.
Yogi Bhajan

Tips for Being Good To Yourself

These are just a few tips. Make your own list of what elevates you.

1. **Pamper yourself.** Take a hot mineral bath; get a massage or a pedicure.

2. **Do Hydrotherapy.** Get in the habit now of taking cold showers. They are great for the circulatory, immune and nervous systems. They give you energy and balance your emotions.

   How To Do It – I'm a chicken when it comes to my cold shower. I'll tell you my secrets. In the winter especially, first thing I do is turn on the heater in the bathroom, and while I'm brushing my teeth, etc. the bathroom is getting warm. Next I vigorously rub my body with almond oil and do Breath of Fire (Chapter Two) before I enter the shower. When I enter the shower, I first put my big toes in then my feet, then my legs, then my arms, etc. while I am madly rubbing the whole time, until pretty soon my whole body is in and I'm jumping around like a barefooted kid on a hot sandy beach and chanting "Wahe Guru" and a few other words. I go in and out of the cold water – continuing to rub my body – in and out in and out until the water isn't cold any longer. Yelling "Wahe Guru" really helps. It sure feels good when it's over and my skin looks great, all pink and healthy. Who needs coffee to wake up? And this is much healthier.

When you are depressed, when you feel sadness or shakiness, take a cold shower. Then take a towel and massage your body until it is flushed. Your disturbing thoughts will go.
YOGI BHAJAN

3. **Exercise.** Trick yourself any way you can to get out and move. Get an exercise buddy. There's nothing like getting your heart pumping and enjoying those natural endorphins.

4. **YOGA, YOGA, YOGA.** Go to a yoga class and daily practice at home. Yoga can rebalance all the systems of the body, especially the nervous system, glandular system and immune system, which are commonly imbalanced after a trauma.

5. **Meditate.** Meditation is invaluable in stabilizing the emotions, the mind and connects you to your Infinity.
6. **Engage in a creative activity.** Paint, garden, cook, build something, arrange flowers, dance, create a web site, etc.
7. **Do something for someone else.** Volunteer to help someone else, like the Soup Kitchen, the Salvation Army, Literacy Volunteers, your local school…whatever.
8. **Keep your spiritual connections.** Go to the church or temple of your choice.
9. **Spend time in nature.** All those negative ions heal.
10. **Allow yourself to think about life a year from now.** You may not be ready to actualize anything yet, but its OK to fantasize into the future. Perhaps you want to take a dream trip, go back to college or start your own business.

Now go make your own list of ten tips.

The Healing Power of Laughter and Play

Humor and laughter affect the body in a positive way. Stress has been shown to create unhealthy physiological changes. The connection between stress and high blood pressure, muscle tension, immunosuppression and many other changes has been known for years. Laughter creates the opposite effects. As early as the 1300's, Henri de Mondeville, professor of surgery, wrote *"Let the surgeon take care to regulate the whole regimen of the patient's life for joy and happiness, allowing his relatives and special friends to cheer him and by having someone to tell him jokes."* Now we have scientific proof to support Dr. de Mondeville's beliefs. At Loma Linda University School of Medicine's Department of Clinical Immunology, studies have shown that

the experience of laughter stimulates the immune system and balances the connection between the mind, body and spirit. – Sarah Steen Lauterback, EdD, RN. Holistic Nursing Practice 1996:10(2):57-68

Humor can be an empowerment tool. We may not be able to control events in our external world, but we can control how we view these events and the emotional response we give to them. Humor gives us a different perspective to our problems. They are seen a little detached, which gives us a sense of self-reliance and control over our environment. As comedian Bill Cosby is fond of saying, *"If you can laugh at it, you can survive it."*

How can we improve our humor outlook to nurture our body, mind and spirit?

- Learn how to laugh at yourself. You may need to hang around someone who has this skill to learn its nuances. Some comedians have mastered this art.
- Rekindle the inner child and playfulness. Spend time with children. They are the best teachers.
- Collect jokes and exchange them with others.
- Invite a child to a children's movie.
- Train yourself to see the funny in serious situations.
- Do something different, like eat with the opposite hand.
- Schedule playtime. If you don't, it won't happen.
- It's OK to be silly. When things get too serious, sometimes nonsense makes the most sense.
- Exaggerate the negative and then laugh about it.
- Go see funny movies.

At various places in this book, we have talked about the Chakra Energy and how we can modify our moods by directing the energy from one Chakra to another. Laughing is actually very yogic. It stimulates the Navel Center, the Heart Center and the Throat Center, by breaking up stagnant energy of anxiety and depression in the Navel Center and transforms it into good feelings of the heart and openness of the throat.

We use tears to empty the tragedy from us…why not laughter. Through laughter, we can become one with the gods and thus can endure life. It helps us overcome all the horror, waste and suffering here on earth. Sometimes events seem unfair or cruel, karma from a thousand lifetimes ago, or perhaps even one. By laughing about death we take the mystery out of it and thus tame our anxiety and fears about it. Isn't it through laughter that we stay human?

The much-loved folk singer, Arlo Gutherie, has a way of touching the hearts of his audience by telling stories about himself that have a spiritual or socially conscious twist that make the listener think. Coated with humor and told in his famous folksy drawl, he says things that people might be thinking about but don't normally talk about, and it's all done so casually that you feel that you and everyone else are all somehow related, sitting in Arlo's living room telling stories around a cozy fire. If you've ever been to one of his concerts or heard him on a CD, you're probably like me, catching yourself laughing and crying in the same moment. The following story of Arlo's is just such an example. His topic here is death and dying. See any similarities to the discussion we had in Chapter Seven on Jiwan Mukht – liberated while yet alive?

> *We live in a crazy world some times. I've been losing friends of mine and all kinds of things, you know to AIDS. Some of these people we can't afford to lose in this world...they'd be helping others, even though they're not feeling as well as those they were helping out. Although sometimes...even now, I'm getting the feeling they're still around...you know...even more around than the people still walking around. I'm getting the feeling that death isn't all it's cracked up to be. I even said to myself the other day, you know, I said, 'Arlo, if you was dead, a lot of stuff that pisses you off probably wouldn't bother you so much.' I'm getting a new plan, I guess is what I'm saying it's sorta like, 'die now and go later.'*
>
> Arlo Gutherie – Together Again In Concert, Vol. II.

The following Zen tale provides a model for treating death with both wisdom and humor.

Ikkyu, the Zen master, was very clever as a boy. His teacher had a precious teacup, a rare antique. Ikkyu happened to break this cup and was very worried. Hearing the footsteps of his teacher, he hid the pieces of the cup behind his back. When the master appeared, Ikkyu asked: "Why do people have to die?"

"This is natural," explained the teacher. "Everything has to die and has just so long to live."

Ikkyu producing the shattered cup, added: "It was time for your cup to die."

For a person who is dying, humor can be a way of coping with failing body functions, unfamiliar medical procedures and confused emotions. Here is one example:

A woman very near death, refused to eat any more food. She said she wanted to die. The following day, she announced her intention to die again, and again the day passed without her demise. This went on for several days. Then one day she arose from her bed and joined the rest of her family at the breakfast table. The amazed family members wanted to know why she was joining them for breakfast after so many days of not eating. The frail elderly lady turned and answered, "So who wants to die on an empty stomach?"

Both of the above stories were taken from an article by Allen Klein, *"Humor & Death."*

When someone is terminally ill, it is common for others to forget that they are more than just their disease. Out of our grief, we may unintentionally separate ourselves from them. We become 'the well' and they become 'the sick.' What could be a time of tremendous love, tenderness and completion becomes a time of loneliness. Laughter is one way to break down that separation and remind us that life continues until the very last breath.

For survivors, humor can also be an effective emotional release in the story-telling process. It is common to tell stories about the deceased at funerals and memorial services. These stories do not have to be only solemn. In fact telling funny stories about the loved one can be a wonderful way to keep their memory alive. Laughing and crying at the same moment can open our hearts to expand into healing.

Well, I don't get angry, okay? I mean I have a tendency to internalize. I can't express anger. That's one of the problems I have. I-I grow a tumor instead.

Isaac Davis in *Manhattan* by Woody Allen and Marshall Brickman

When a dear friend, Pritam Singh, died, we spent a good part of the funeral weekend telling stories about him. At the service, many of the family friends were asked to speak. The stories were my favorite part of the service. Not only were some of the stories uplifting, many were funny and revealed the human side of Pritam.

One story was told by a fellow chiropractor. He said that when they were in chiropractic school together the students couldn't believe Pritam's study style. They would all be feverishly taking notes, while Pritam wouldn't take a single note. *"How can you get straight 'A's without taking notes in class,"* one classmate asked. Pritam replied, *"I sleep with the book under my pillow."*

A Punjabi Indian Sikh man told my favorite Pritam story. Pritam Singh had clown red hair and beard, his skin was fair and freckled and he had a strong Oklahoma accent. One day, this Punjabi friend and Pritam were together at an event, where Pritam introduced him to the host. "*I'd like you to meet my brother*," Pritam said. The host looking at Pritam's fair skin and red beard then at his friend's dark skin and black beard, questioned, "*Did you have the same mother?*" Smiling broadly, Pritam put his arm around his friend and said, "*Yep, we sure did.*" Perplexed, the host then quickly retorted, "*And did you have the same father as well?*" Still smiling broadly, Pritam said, "*Yes, of course.*" This story exemplifies Pritam's unconditional love and acceptance. He considered this friend to be his brother. Skin and hair color were insignificant.

CHAPTER 15

The Master Goes Home

HAVE YOU EVER BEEN INVOLVED IN A PROJECT that seemed to be an entity all of its own? Such has been the case of this book. I declared this fact in the very first chapter, and so it seems fitting that I declare it again in the concluding chapter. Throughout the writing of the book, I felt like I was just a channel to put the Siri Singh Sahib Yogi Bhajan's teaching about death on paper. Not only did the content have a life of its own…but the timing of its completion as well. By September of 2004, it seemed like this book was finished. I was wrong. It was only after Yogi Bhajan's death, October 6, 2004, that I realized that there needed to be yet one final chapter. This chapter will use the death of Yogi Bhajan to exemplify what we have been exploring in this book. Many publications have celebrated the life of Yogi Bhajan. This chapter is a tribute to his death. He was a Master, even in death.

The beauty of life is that the beginning, the now, and the end, are all one and the same.
YOGI BHAJAN

Yogi Bhajan's Death was a Process and a Training

Yogi Bhajan started quite early training us for his death. "*I am walking my last mile. Soon it will be time for me to leave my physical body behind.*" He said this in Mendocino, California, at the third Summer Solstice Yoga Celebration, 1972. He never wanted us to attach ourselves to his physical body. He taught us to love him through his teachings.

He wanted us to relate to him through his Subtle Body. To develop that subtle connection to him and the wisdom of the entire Golden Chain of the lineage of Kundalini Yoga, he told us to meditate on his Tratakum picture. Tratakum means beaming with a steady gaze. This photo was taken when he was in a deep state of Turiya consciousness. Turiya is the same as Samadhi, the state of total merger with the Universe.

Don't love me, love my teachings.
YOGI BHAJAN

He said to mount the photo on an orange matte and place it at eye level with low lights, perhaps candles, on either side of it. Sit in front of that picture and stare with fixed open eyes into the eyes of the picture and meditate. Chant long *Sat Nam* and allow the connection to happen. The meditation can be performed for any length of time. End by closing the eyes and internally see the image of the picture at the brow point.

Here is the Tratakum picture. For a better quality one, contact Ancient Healing Ways – Resource Page.

The day you come to see me, and sit here and see the unseen of me, not me; when you come here to listen, and there will be nobody to talk, and still you will listen; that day, between you and God there shall be no difference. Now we are practicing. It is the journey towards reality.
Yogi Bhajan

Over the years, Yogi Bhajan prepared us for his death by slowly removing himself physically from us. For many years, he was readily accessible to us, keeping a grueling travel and teaching schedule. He was up into the wee hours intimately involved in trying to help people resolve conflicts in their lives. Every weekend he would fly to another city, another country, or even another continent to teach and serve. His body paid dearly. He was in a lot of physical pain much of the time.

Gradually over time, instead of being in the middle of the action, there was a shift. Especially in the last three years, his environments needed to be progressively calmer, clearer and more neutral, free of emotionalism, so that his energies could focus on his own healing. He had the best doctors in the world, of all disciplines. Acupuncturists, Homeopaths, Massage Therapists, Chiropractors, General Internists, Heart Specialists and many more gave him the very best care. Even with all of their expert and loving treatments and advise, it was still important to him to make the final decisions for his own body. Here again he was a model to us. It is important to listen and follow the treatment plan of our caregivers. But, at the end of the day, it is up to us to listen to our intuition and do what we feel is best for our body.

One of Yogi Bhajan's personal attendants, Hari Nam Kaur, reflected that during the many years that she served him, he trained her to be a *"sensory human."* She had to be so attuned with him that words were not necessary.

> *Our consciousnesses were linked. We got to the point where a glance or a nod of the head told me what he wanted. Preparing himself for the etheric world, he went in and out of this world and spent much time in meditation or staring at pictures of the Gurus and the Harimandir Sahib* (the Golden Temple in Amritsar, India). *Occasionally, he would look up and remark, 'If you could only see what I see.' Other*

times, usually late at night, he would recollect about his life. It was very enjoyable, like he was savoring with great delight the events of his life. We would laugh and his humanness was palpable. Those were precious times for me.

I knew that even though my personal shock and sorrow would be great, his death would free him of his pain. As one that had watched him suffer for so long, I knew that his death would also be an event of tremendous relief, joy and celebration. His soul would be free of the confines of his physical body. His physical body is not with us any longer, but his teachings are eternal and will guide all who practice them for many, many generations to come.

Guru Dev Singh is the Master of Sat Nam Rasayan, a healing form using only the practitioner's awareness with the intention to heal, given to us by Yogi Bhajan and imparted to Guru Dev Singh to teach. Over the years, he frequently treated Yogi Bhajan for varying ailments. He said that Yogi Bhajan's death was a process. It didn't happen suddenly. It was a gradual process for our benefit.

In the last year of his life, when I treated him, he was in a different aspect of meditation. Even though he went in and out of being consciously present, he was in a very stable state of prabhupati. (Master of the universe. This is a state of neutrality, where the conscious and subconscious minds merge, and there is no conflict in the persona. The person is one with the super-consciousness of the universe and in harmony with All.) *Whereas the individual is controlled by the elements, earth, water, fire, air and ether, which are constantly changing, the presence of the soul and the psyche remain constant. Yogi Bhajan was stable in this Shuniya state, that state of deep*

> *contemplation, emptiness and oneness with the One. His consciousness was able to journey into all realms of the universe. Being in relation to his consciousness, I learned more about yoga, meditation and spirituality during that year than any other time. It was the most humbling experience for me.*

All during the summer of 2004, Yogi Bhajan's health was dramatically declining. As he had been near death before, we all wanted to believe that maybe he would pull through this time as well. Besides training us to relate to his subtle body, he had trained us well in all levels. He was a Virgo. He trained us to be organized, even in the planning of his death. Systems were in place. Preparations were made in the event that his passing was close. Minus the date, press releases were written; an international phone chain was created; the procedures for the body directly after the death were put into place; a grieving CD to be sent to the world-wide yoga community was published; the plans for the various services had began; and legal matters were in order. He recognized, as we earlier discussed that it is much less complicated for loved ones, if things are in order.

I went off on a seven-month teaching tour in September. By the first of October, I was in Amritsar, India, working in the first 3HO run drug rehabilitation program in India, called SuperHealth, based on Yogi Bhajan's teachings on addiction.

When Yogi Bhajan came to the West, India was not ready for his teachings. How odd that the country that had birthed Kundalini Yoga had lost touch with its ancient yogic technology. It was his dream to bring the art and science of Kundalini Yoga back to his homeland. For eleven years, he had been offering a de-addiction program, based on Kundalini Yoga and Meditation to the Indian Government to combat its tremendous drug problem. Even though statistics show that Northern India has one of the highest drug rates in the world, there was no interest. Finally, out of desperation, in the Spring of 2004, the Indian Government requested that 3HO run a 90-day pilot SuperHealth Drug Rehabilitation Program in Amritsar to start October 8, 2004. His dream was finally going to be realized. Kundalini Yoga was coming home.

Out of my immense gratitude to what Yogi Bhajan had done for my life, my prayer was that I would be able to serve him in some significant way. I did not tell him in person about my prayer. One morning as I meditated before his Tratakum picture, I made the commitment. The opportunity soon came. I volunteered to work as a Counselor and Director of Yogic Studies for SuperHealth India. As a pilot program there was no budget. We paid for our own plane tickets and worked without salaries. It was the least I could do for all the Master had done for me. Before I left, my only prayer was, "*Please don't die during SuperHealth.*" I could have postponed the rest of my trip, but I knew that if he left during SuperHealth, there would be no way I could leave the program and come home.

Even in his leaving, Yogi Bhajan was masterful. He said goodbye in various ways.

He had been very sick, going in and out of consciousness for months. Miraculously, just a few days before his passing, he came out of his dome for one last tour of the ashram grounds in his wheelchair. He greeted people who happened to be around. Everyone wanted to believe that he was getting better, but this was actually his last spurt of energy – the last time they saw him alive. He was saying goodbye.

He said goodbye in other ways. Some experienced him in dreams or visions. Kirn Kaur, from Espanola, had a vision.

> *Two days before his death, while lying in bed – it was 4:00 am – I opened my eyes and saw a beautiful swirling blue light. I tried to touch*

it but it was out of reach. At first I thought it might be lights from a car, but there were no windows. Also amazing, it was swirling right in front of a picture of Buddha on the wall. It felt like that same blue Tantric energy – powerful and yet peaceful. (White Tantric is a powerful yoga done in pairs, that uses the diagonal energy to heal.)

Yogi Bhajan's Farewell Message – Sunday, October 3, 2004 Gurdwara – three days before he left his earthly body

"Wahe Guru Ji Ka Khalsa, Wahe Guru Ji Ki Fateh. God and soul are permanent. Everlasting. We are bound to go. Definitely we come and go. One day you will be at that stage. The body will become a permanent soul.

We must know that the way we must go, that's the way we should go. Let us understand we are the infinite ray of God. We should be as God is. That's the way we can connect to God. We can connect ourselves with each breath of life. With every breath we can become cleaner and cleaner. It is the rule of God's kingdom to cleanse ourselves, and then our ray can shine.

Our lives will be happier then. That's how it can be. Our rhythm of life, each atom, can vibrate in that truth. That will give us truth forever. Then when we are real, we can create. In this realm we can make ourselves whatever we want to be.

Life is to live for each other. It is to live for each other. Wahe Guru Ji Ka Khalsa, Wahe Guru Ji Ki Fateh."

Two days before the opening ceremony of SuperHealth India, October 6, 2004, Yogi Bhajan left his earthly body at 9:05 pm, MDT in Espanola, New Mexico.

Yogiji had many doctors. His primary physician, who discontinued his private practice so he could be with him full time, was Dr. Siri Atma Singh. He said that at the very end, he left quickly. "I have seen hundreds of deaths. I have never seen a soul leave the physical body so quickly and easily as the Siri Singh Sahib Yogi Bhajan."

At the same time, twelve thousand miles away, children at our school, Miri Piri Academy, were all chanting (*Guru Guru Wahe Guru Guru Ram Das Guru*). The parents of these children were students of Yogi Bhajan and had raised them according to his teachings. He was their spiritual teacher as well. One such thirteen-year-old girl, Dharma Kaur, from Espanola, New Mexico, remembers chanting in the school's Gurdwara (temple).

We had been told that he was very sick and may die. While I was chanting, I had a vision. I was with a bunch of people. He was rising

up to the sky. We didn't want him to go. We stretched our arms toward him, trying to pull him back. The first time we were successful in pulling him back; then, he rose a second time and again we were able to pull him back. On the third time, he did not come back. He disappeared into the ethers.

Yogi Bhajan's death occurred close to that exact time on the other side of the world.

Saying Goodbye To Our Teacher

Almost immediately following Yogiji's death, everyone in the Espanola Ashram community was invited by Yogi Bhajan's wife, Bibiji to come into his dome. It was a very moving experience for the Sadh Sangat (congregation) to have this intimate time with him to personally express their gratitude and to say goodbye.

When we were all called over to the dome, I was very nervous, because I didn't know how I would feel. But, the moment I walked into the dome, I instantly felt completely comfortable and at peace. I felt him telling me, 'It's so easy. I did it. You can too. And, I'll be there to help you when it's your time.' I felt him in that room. I feel him now. He hasn't left. It's just different. Some times he comes to me in dreams.

Hari Dharm Kaur, Espanola

Not everyone, who went into Yogi Bhajan's dome that night had a long physical relationship with him. It didn't matter. Ardas Kaur expressed that the experience of seeing him at death changed her life.

We did not have a personal relationship. Perhaps you spoke just a dozen words to me. But what we lacked in an earthly connection was made up in our sacred teacher-student relationship. I learned from your presence, your words and your life. You heard my prayers and healed me through my dreams. You showed me the Me in myself; the reality of life.

People tell stories of your greatness – stories of miracles, acts of great compassion – a life so full of nobility, royalty and reality – and examples of your undying faith in God. They say you were as powerful as a king and commanded life like lightening. But a hundred stories of your life could not match the greatest lesson I felt – at your death.

It is strange to say that I learned more from your death than from your life, but its true. The grace with which you died said everything to me. All of your teachings wrapped up in one single moment. The expression of Oneness on your face and the subtle smile on your lips said it all – a life of love and sacrifice – a life's mission completed – all expressed in the serenity on your face. You were a lighthouse to millions while alive, and the glow of your soul shined even brighter through your breathless body. Your radiance aglow was beyond time and space. I shall forever keep that image in my mind's eye to direct my life. Thank you, Sir.

Ardas Kaur, Espanola

Journey of the Privileged Soul

As discussed in Chapter Nine – *The Journey of Death* – during the time directly following death, the soul goes through a purification process and has seventeen days to cross the electro-magnetic field of the earth. The soul then journeys through the blue ethers. This process is not exactly the same for a privileged soul, the soul of a highly respected and saintly person, who devoted their life to serving God. Years before, when such a man died, Yogi Bhajan described the journey of the privileged soul in the following way:

You must understand. The privileged soul has certain privileges. When the journey begins, the soul leaves in the subtle body. The first privilege of the soul is to say goodbye to all friends and foes equally. I'm talking of the privileged soul. Then the soul travels to all places of reverence – those places, which were sacred to it. That's called 'the last journey.'…

The third privilege is to visit all the places of the altar. That means the Guru's places. A privileged soul has very exalted manners and a responsibility to say a graceful goodbye before going home. That is why it became customary that when a person leaves, the relatives do kirtan (spiritual chanting), they do lofty 'bandage,' praising the Lord for all these days. Some do it for seventeen days, …

After visiting all the altars, the soul has the privilege to travel in the company of the angelic world. The privileged soul does not go through the normal path of the human. It doesn't pass through the test and triumph and trials.

After finishing its duties on the earth, it travels to the angelic world. In the angelic world it entertains itself into the entire brightness, lightness, humor and glow, and practices forgiveness for the whole universe through which it has traveled many lifetimes.

You must understand – the soul which is privileged soul has to enter the akal abode, the infinity. The angelic world is defined. It is all good and masterly wonderful and excellently wonderful, but still it is defined.

After enjoying the privilege of the angelic world, the soul travels into the third blue ether. That is its own great abode of prayer. In its purity, in its piety, it settles its own account. Thereafter it crosses to the fourth blue ether. Chauthe par, the fourth step, is to find infinite salvation.

Therefore, if you join at this time in this journey, it will guarantee your journey in the future.

The Seventeen Days Following

To be a part of this special time following the death of a privileged soul, especially during the seventeen days, we were encouraged to spend as much time as possible doing yoga, meditation, prayer, selfless service and other devotional practices. This is the time the soul is released. People came to Espanola from all over the world to be a part of this powerful time. Volunteers worked tirelessly round the clock, shopping, cooking, and serving so that food would be available continuously. Yoga and meditation classes were held every evening, free of charge. Every evening the Sadh Sangat (congregation) gathered outside Yogi Bhajan's dome to chant and meditate, (***Guru Guru Wahe Guru Guru Ram Das Guru***). This chant was not only done in Espanola but in Kundalini Yoga and Sikh communities all over the world. Akand Paths (continuous reading of the Sikh scriptures) were also done worldwide.

Kirn Kaur, from Espanola, was a part of the team of teachers who taught yoga classes every evening.

> *It seemed like all of his wisdom, knowledge and energy was now available to anyone who wanted it. It felt like internal fireworks... you know, like the finale of a huge fireworks display. All of that explosive energy accessible just by tuning into the Golden Chain (Ong Namo Guru Dev Namo).*

There I was in India, twelve thousand miles away. I was devastated. I was experiencing firsthand how important it is to be with family and friends after a significant loss in one's life. I desperately wanted to come home to grieve with those with whom I felt the most support and love. I wanted to be a part of the ceremonies to say goodbye to and celebrate the life of my spiritual teacher, one of the most important people in my life. I owe my identity and mission in life to his teachings and personal guidance.

In my meditation the morning after his passing he came to me. I pleaded with him to come home. "Please Sir, this is too big of a sacrifice. I want to come home to be with my spiritual family to grieve your passing and to attend the ceremonies."

"Didn't you say you wanted to do something really big, really significant for me," he reminded me. I knew he had me. Reluctantly, I admitted, "Yes." "Well, this is it. And as hard as it is, I am asking you to stay and serve me in this way," he added. Of course… I stayed. As grief-stricken and disappointed as I was, I was honored that he came to me and asked for my service.

Others experienced him in dreams, meditations and visions. Being in Espanola was not important. Many all over the world – whether they had ever met him or not – were visited by him. He gave messages, blessings and directions for their lives. Some wrote beautiful stories, songs and poems inspired by their connection to him. Everyone got exactly what he or she needed.

The following song was written by Swami Dev Singh, Dallas Texas – October 11, 2004.

Master of Masters

Master of Masters
Teacher of Teachers
Eternally Humble
Leader of Leaders

Sending us on to fulfill Your quest
Now you have earned Your eternal rest
Leaving us to live your legacy
You've created the teachers for the age to be

Master of Masters
Teacher of Teachers
Gone to your home in the realm of the ethers

A Sage of all Sages
A Healer of Healers
Through all of the Ages
A peerless Believer

Master of Masters
Teacher of Teachers
Gone to Your home in the realm of the ethers

A saint of all Saints
A Soldier's Soldier
The Blessings You've rained fall with love on our shoulders
Like the Sun
You Shine on All
All of the Pure Ones will answer Your call

Jini Naam Dhiaia
Gae Masakat Ghaal
Nanak Te Mukh Ujale
Keti Chuti Naal

You will always go with a radiant face
And may many others be freed by your grace
And may many others be freed by your grace
And may many others be freed by your grace

To Siri Singh Sahib Bhai Sahib Harbhajan Singh Khalsa Yogiji
With Eternal Reverence and Gratitude

One Hundred Ninth Congress
of the
United States of America

AT THE FIRST SESSION

Begun and held at the City of Washington on Tuesday, the fourth day of January, two thousand and five

Concurrent Resolution

Resolved by the House of Representatives (the Senate concurring) that the Congress

Recognizes that the teachings of Yogi Bhajan about Sikhism and yoga, and the businesses formed under his inspiration, improved the personal, political, spiritual, and professional relations between citizens of the United States and the citizens of India;

Recognizes the legendary compassion, wisdom, kindness, and courage of Yogi Bhajan, and his wealth of accomplishments on behalf of the Sikh community;

Extends its condolences to Inderjit Kaur, the wife of Yogi Bhajan, his 3 children and 5 grandchildren, and to the Sikh and "Healthy, Happy, Holy Organization (3HO)" communities around the Nation and the world upon the death on October 6, 2004, of Yogi Bhajan, an individual who was a wise teacher and mentor, an outstanding pioneer, a champion of peace, and a compassionate human being.

H.Con.Res.34 Agreed to April 6, 2005

To view the Resolution in its entirety, log on to www.sikhnet.com/yogibhajan

U.S. Congress honors Yogi Bhajan.

Ceremonies

When a Sikh dies, the body is washed in a yogurt solution. The yogurt kills any bacteria on the body and is a ritual of purification. The body is then dressed in white clothes, including the 5 K's, symbols for Sikhs, including, *kesh* (uncut hair covered by a turban), *kara* (a steel bangle worn on the right wrist of the man), *kanga* (small wooden comb worn in the hair), *kirpan* (small religious dagger). Besides Yogi Bhajan's two sons, Ranbir Singh and Kulbir Singh, other close men were invited for this privilege. One, Narinjan Singh, said that participating in this ceremony was very important for him and a great honor. Meeting the Siri Singh Sahib Yogi Bhajan when he was seventeen years old, and now being fifty-four, Narinjan's relationship with his spiritual teacher had been for his whole adult life.

It made his death more real to me and therefore the transition of my relationship with him easier. I could feel his presence around the room. It was a very uplifting experience.

Cremation Service

Nearly a thousand family members, students and friends as well as religious and political leaders from around the world came together to both mourn the passing and celebrate the life of the man who brought Sikh Dharma to the West. The casket was open, allowing the sangat to pay their last respects. Sikh music and prayers were sung. Many speakers spoke about their moving personal memories of this great spiritual leader and of his enormous contribution to humanity.

One member of our sangat, Amritpal Singh from Mexico, told me that he had a very beautiful experience when he went up to the casket to pay his last respects.

> *Since I didn't have a close physical relationship with Yogi Bhajan, I connected with him in a subtle way. On the day of the cremation, I wanted to see him, but the people next to his body were so sad. Then, when I looked at his face, I got a big surprise. He face was filled with so much bliss and joy, I couldn't help but smile. Feeling a little embarrassed, I quickly left in silence. Later I read that when a holy man dies, he dies in bliss and that energy and vitality stays in the body even after death.*

The following account is from one of Yogi Bhajan's bodyguards, Guru Tej Singh. As many turban-tying yogis were having a challenge finding employment in the early 1970's, Yogi Bhajan told Guru Tej Singh to start Akal Security to provide jobs and offer a viable service to the community. Today Akal Security is a national and international half a billion-dollar business.

> *It was my good fortune to have traveled the world with the Siri Singh Sahib. I had the privilege of sleeping outside his door, of helping him to get dressed, or undressed and of cleaning his feet. I was especially fortunate because his love for me, for reasons only he understood, was so great that he never hesitated to hammer me with the full impact of the Saturn teacher that he was. The bond that he established and sustained with me was the most sacred and precious thing in my life.*
>
> *When he passed, we maintained twenty-four hour coverage at the funeral home from the moment we delivered his body until his ashes were picked up and carried back to the Dome. During that period, and during my times of duty the family made arrangements for private viewings. When his body was brought into the chapel of the*

funeral home prior to the family's arrival, I had the opportunity to sit with him, just him and me, while waiting for the family.

Those times were precious and gave me the opportunity to say good-bye and adjust to his passing. Being there with his body and the penetrating presence of his spirit reminded me of so many times when I was on his duty and stood by while he rested. I remembered his words from some long ago lecture when he said the 'mortal is immortal.' It was clear to me then that, though his physical body was no longer able to carry his pranas, his essence, and the power of his presence still prevailed and will continue to be there.

On the day of the funeral, I was privileged to be among those who prepared his body for the final services and to attend the casket when it was on display during the service. Many years ago he told me, after a rather scolding lecture regarding his dissatisfaction with my behavior, 'I want you to be there when my funeral pyre is lighted.' Always true to his word, I had the honor to be among those who pushed his coffin into the crematory fire.

For me, his death has not been a closure, for I feel no separation from him. In fact, I served him in death as I did in life. I am reminded of when my daughter died in 1981 and how the psychic connection with her as she passed through the blue ethers elevated me. This experience has been even greater with the Siri Singh Sahib and I will cherish that for all of my days.

Memorial Services

On the seventeenth day, in Espanola, New Mexico; Johannesburg, South Africa; Sydney, Australia; Amritsar, India – and many other places around the world – memorial services were performed to honor and celebrate the life of the Siri Singh Sahib Bhai Sahib Harbhajan Singh Khalsa Yogiji.

His timing was perfect. He left on October 6th, Guru Ram Das's birthday (the fourth Sikh Guru). Seventeen days later, the day of the memorial service, was October 23rd, Guru Gadhe Day, a very special holiday for Sikhs, when the scriptures, Siri Guru Granth Sahib was installed, becoming a living Guru (Sikhs believe that the Siri Guru Granth Sahib is a living entity. When one takes a Hukum or reading from it, the Guru is directly answering.)

The Ashes

Upon Yogi Bhajan's request, his ashes were divided into two parts, one half to be scattered at Kiratpur Sahib, India (a place where Sikhs traditionally scatter their ashes), and the other half to be over Ram Das Puri, New Mexico (the location of many 3HO events, including the annual Peace Prayer Day and Summer Solstice).

I was blessed to be able to attend both ashes ceremonies. In India, a photo of his ashes dropping from the bridge into the river has the image of Yogiji's face. In New Mexico, Guru Simran Kaur, the custodian of his ranch, who worked tirelessly to make sure the ranch was impeccable for him and his many guests, recalls that she didn't know if she could hold it together the day of the ceremony to release his last ashes in New Mexico.

> *I was having such a hard time saying goodbye. Then, at the very last minute I was asked to go on the helicopter and hold his ashes on my lap. This made it easier for me to say goodbye.*

The helicopter circled Ram Das Puri several times before his sons, Ranbir and Kulbir, and grandson, Fateh, dropped the ashes. It was a windy day, and it rained that night. Our beloved teacher is a part of the Ram Das Puri earth forever. He often said that Espanola was his home. The following is a story by Sewa Simran Siri Singh, who attended the ceremony at Ram Das Puri, April 25, 2005.

> *Being a reluctant yogi, I don't usually like going to religious events but*

finally decided to go to Yogi Bhajan's ashes ceremony. The ride up the hill was the usual washboard bumpy journey, wondering what would go wrong with the car. It was worth it, though, because Ram Das Puri was still covered in white – truly an uplifting little spot in the universe. Everyone seemed to be in a good mood. It had been awhile since the Siri Singh Sahib Yogi Bhajan's passing and acceptance was beginning to take place. My own anger and disappointment was abating. I spent the time making small talk and mostly soaking in the atmosphere. 'So when is that helicopter supposed to arrive anyway?'

Everyone was chanting and congregated outside the end of the Tantric Shelter. Finally the helicopter arrived, flying low and circling around Ram Das Puri several times. I had just begun to wonder if I had missed the release of the ashes, when the helicopter neared us again. It slowed and stopped near the location of the flagpole. Soon some form of bucket was lowered and a lot of black ashes poured out.

What happened next is hard to put into words. There was total silence, and in less than it takes to bat an eye, my whole experience within 3HO/Sikh Dharma flashed before me. It was a once-in-a-lifetime experience that I will always remember. Perhaps it was the ending of one chapter of my life and likewise in our community. After some months now, as I recall this episode, it is difficult to bring back that split second. It is not hard to feel the love and loss that I/we feel towards someone who gave his life for us. I now see the Siri Singh Sahib sitting on the Tantric stage surveying us…looking at what he has grown, like a farmer who has planted a crop and is watching it grow to fruition.

Don't Cry For Me Children of Sikh Dharma

Grieving is human. Tears flow, and there is a lot of hugging. There is something about needing human touch when one is mourning the loss of a loved one. There are many ways to grieve. Since I could not be present for the ceremonies at home, I channeled my grief by reciting 125,000 Mul Mantras ***(Ek Ong Kaar Sat Naam Karta Purkh Nirbho Nirvair Akaal Moorat Ajoonee Saibhung Gurprasad Jap Aad Sach Jugaad Sach Haibhee Sach Nanak Hosee Bhee Sach)*** in 40 days. (Refer to accompanying CD for correct pronunciation – 17.) I also gave 100 percent and more to the addicts in the SuperHealth De-Addiction Program. If I was going to sacrifice being able to go home, than I was determined to give my all to his mission, which was also my mission. Our translator for the program, Yogesh, and some of our "guys" will take Kundalini Yoga Teacher Training. Kundalini Yoga has returned to her homeland and will now continue to flourish there.

One man with us in India, Mukthiar Singh, who over the years had completed many special construction-type assignments for Yogi Bhajan was finishing his last project for him – a miniature Golden Temple made out of wood, marble and gold. He was determined to lovingly make this final project perfect.

Other people back home threw themselves into preparing for the many ceremonies. Thousands of people flocked to Espanola, New Mexico to honor him. Things had to be organized for their arrival. This was a tangible way to direct one's grief and honor The Master at the same time. Some grieved right away, some later.

One such person was Dr. Kartar Singh, who was intimately involved in organizing events that followed Yogiji's passing. He said he was so busy; he didn't have time to grieve very much. By spring, he felt himself withdrawing from the community to go inward. One morning he had a dream. Dressed in beautiful white clothes, he was at Yogi Bhajan's Ranch, curled up on a sheepskin, crying and crying and crying. He's never cried so hard. His nagging thought was, "*It's just so strange, he's really gone.*" When he woke up, he realized that he hadn't allowed himself the time and space to grieve. The dream was very cathartic – he felt released.

Don't Cry For Me Children of Sikh Dharma

Who was this man called Yogi Bhajan
Who came into our lives from 'cross the sea?
A Father, A Teacher, A Master,Servant for all humanity.

He came from the East just to teach us.
There is one God who dwells in all.
Happiness begins with commitment.
Fulfillment from answering the call.

He said, Don't cry for me Children of Sikh Dharma.
My love for you will live eternally.
Keep walking with your grace and strength and courage.
Chant the name and set your spirit free.
Chant the name and serve humanity.

In sandals in the snowdrifts of Toronto.
His mission began so humbly.
Touching the hearts of the hopeless.
He helped them regain their dignity.

Through every trial he kept on winning.
To show us that we could do it too.
With kindness, compassion, with laughter.
He said royal courage will see us through.

Don't cry for me Children of Sikh Dharma.
My love for you will live eternally.
Keep smiling with your grace and strength and courage.
Chant the name and set your spirit free.
Chant the name and serve humanity.

He sculpted every being with precision.
No matter what their status or their state.
Poking, provoking, confronting.
His only purpose to elevate.

He gave us our home as a temple.
Our marriage as a path to One.
Our wealth as a way to serve our neighbor,
Our future through our daughters and our sons.

Don't cry for me Children of Sikh Dharma.
My love for you will live eternally.
Keep singing with your grace and strength and courage.
Chant the Name and set your spirit free.
Chant the Name and serve humanity.

Don't cry to me, you are Sikh Dharma,
Let your love live eternally.
Keep walking with your grace and strength and courage.
Chant the Name and set your spirit free.
Chant the Name and serve humanity.
960 million we will be.

Sat Siri Siri Akal – Great Truth Respected Undying
Siri Akal Maha Akal – Respected Undying Great Deathless
Maha Akal Sat Nam – Great Deathless Truth Identified
Akal Moort – Deathless Image of God
Wahe Guru – Great beyond description is His wisdom

Sat Siri Siri Akal
Siri Akal Maha Akal
Maha Akal Sat Nam
Akal Moort Wahe Guru

Sat Siri Siri Akal
Siri Akal Maha Akal
Maha Akal Sat Nam
Akal Moort Wahe Guru

Written by Dev Suroop Kaur, Sangeet Kaur
and Ek Ong Kaar Kaur – Espanola, New Mexico

While attending a funeral for another member of the community, Yogiji commented about people grieving after his death. As Guruka Singh remembers it, he said something like, "If you grieve for me when I leave, it will be a great insult. Grieve now before I die. The day the soul goes home is a celebration. It is the greatest of days."

In keeping with this theme he asked that a song be written – *Don't Cry For Me Sikh Dharma.*

How Do We Relate To Him Now?

Yogi Bhajan was an exceptional human being with superhuman capabilities. His soul now resides in the etheric world. Living in his subtle and radiant bodies, he travels to all the five ethers as is needed. We can experience him in a very real and tangible way. We just need to tune in to him and allow it to happen. It is important that we not try to relate to him as a "man," because then we will be relating to personality and ego, which is limited and personal. But, if we relate to his teachings, his legacy, then our experience will be limitless.

Everyone has a different relationship and way of relating to him. Some people see him in dreams, some feel him in a room, and others hear his voice give them messages, while others feel him creating through them. Some have said that since his passing, the power in their teaching of Kundalini Yoga classes has intensified, as though his wisdom and knowledge is flowing through them. Many report that their deepest issues have surfaced, forcing them to heal and grow. Some

---

Hari Jiwan Kaur, an artist from New York, felt Yogi Bhajan guide her with the following poem:

I am here,
I am here,
I am your hand,
I am your brush,
I am your hush,
I am here...

Paint, paint, like there's no tomorrow –
The truth is now
So stop your sorrow.

Feel me with each breath,
Fully take me in,
Relax the tension,
Relax the brain,

Your work should be as your breath,
In and out,
In and out,
Nothing more,
Nothing more,
Or less.

I am your breath,
I am your brush,
I am your hush,
Paint, don't stop to think!

As a student, you are a very noble and sacred trust to me. I have no option but to forgive you for your mistakes and keep on trying to uplift your soul, I have tried to correct your projectivity, and if fate takes you away and you do not listen to my voice, I shall always listen to the voice of your soul. And keep your memories. And pray that in the hand of time and Infinity, you may wake up to some crossing of life and may study with my student.
YOGI BHAJAN

have experienced great expansion in their career, in business and in other practical matters. No one experience is right or wrong. Keep in mind that when someone is having one of these experiences, it is actually their Higher Consciousness that is responding. It is absolutely not a personality thing. It doesn't matter if you knew him personally or only through the teachings. If you practice Kundalini Yoga and Meditation and allow yourself to be open to Yogi Bhajan as your spiritual teacher, he will be there for you in life as well as in death. It is the teacher's obligation.

Sat Kartar Kaur, a musician from Phoenix, began developing a strong subtle connection to Yogi Bhajan even as early as in the 1980's. At that time, White Tantric Yoga shifted from Yogi Bhajan teaching in person to him teaching by video with a facilitator.

> *It was a sharp contrast from the interaction with his physical personality, and charisma. 'Video' Tantric was my first chance to practice tuning in to him beyond the confines of his body and was good preparation for communication with him beyond this earth plane.*
>
> *On the evening of his passing, I began to grasp what he had said many times—that when his physical body no longer bound him, he could be everywhere and could be with us much more. When I went to Espanola for his cremation, I experienced his subtle body around me again and could hear the sound of his voice telling me exactly what to do. The whole day of the cremation's events, I could hear him telling me repeatedly to go write a very important email to someone. It was as if he didn't really die at all.*
>
> *Was I crazy? Did my imagination/fantasy life, just kick in, big time? I didn't know, but to this day, it is not unusual for me to feel him by my bed when I first wake up in the morning, telling me something—to practice pratyahar (to substitute an unwanted thought which*

doesn't serve me) or to not go to work because I'm sicker than I think, or stop drinking coffee. I have heard his voice say everything from, 'Don't go back to sleep; get up and meditate,' to 'What about that guy in so-and-so city? He's a good man,' and so much more. If I look across the room at his Tratakum picture I'll hear his voice start, even before I sit down to meditate on it.

I perceive this two ways — that it is really him, or that it is the voice of my intuition. And many years back I learned that when my intuition or my spiritual teacher tell me something, I should listen very carefully and heed the message. The same is still true today – listen and heed the message.

Guru Simran Kaur, the custodian of Yogi Bhajan's ranch in Espanola was wondering what her relationship would be with him after his passing. "*Will he really be there for me?*" One rainy day after the cremation, she was driving to Santa Fe and noticed that something was wrong with her car. She pulled over to the side of the road and recounts what happened.

I said, 'Sir, you said you'd be here for me. Well, you'd better be here now.' Almost instantly, two women pulled up, one of which was the electrician for our Golden Temple Inc. in Eugene, Oregon. It was raining hard by then, and there was this woman on her back on the ground changing my flat tire. All I could say was, 'Thank you, Sir,' and I keep the feeling of that experience in my heart all the time.

As a part of Guru Simran Kaur's job as the custodian of Yogi Bhajan's ranch, she takes care of the gifts people have given to him over the years. When a student gives a Master a gift, it is customary for the master to pray for the student. She recalls,

Each gift carries a history behind it. They are not just things. They represent the sacred relationship between student and teacher and the depth of prayer attached to each. One time a couple came to give Yogi Bhajan a beautiful necklace. They had been married many years and had never been able to have a child. When Yogi Bhajan came out of his Dome to go teach a class, they presented the necklace to him. He immediately put it on and said that it would have to wait to go on his altar. Shortly after, the couple was pregnant. I love to tell the stories of these gifts. It helps me to keep him alive.

MEDITATIONS TO AID CONNECTING TO THE MASTER

Meditating on the Tratakum picture as described in the beginning of the chapter, is one way to keep your connection to Yogi Bhajan. The following two meditations are also tools to develop your relationship with him and all Masters of Kundalini Yoga.

Lie on your back. Breathe long and deep and feel the Siri Singh Sahib Yogi Bhajan within you. Put your hands over your forehead and run your fingers down your face and say, ***"Aad Such, Jugaad Such, Haibhee Such, Naanak Hosee Bhee Such, Aad Such, Jugaad Such, Haibhay Such, Naanak Hosee Bhay Such."*** (True in the beginning; True through all time; True even now; Nanak says Truth shall ever be) Then continue with – "God bless the Siri Singh Sahib Yogi Bhajan. And God, rotate the earth, so I will relax and let You manage my life." (Refer to accompanying CD for correct pronunciation – 18.)

THE COMPLETE ADI MANTRA FOR INDIVIDUAL MEDIATION

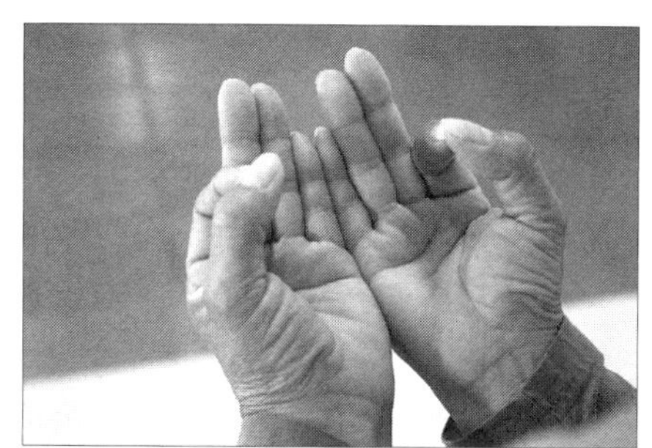

We have used the Adi Mantra to Tune In all throughout this book. The Adi Mantra centers us before we practice or teach Kundalini Yoga. It is the linking mantra for the Golden Chain of all of the teachers of Kundalini Yoga throughout time. It is a mantra of service and is not to be used as an individual mantra.

If you need a personal spiritual connection and guidance then the *Complete Adi Mantra* can be used. It establishes a link between your finite self and your Higher Consciousness.

Sit with a straight spine, with a slight Jalandhar Bandh.

Eye Position: Focus your eyes on the tip of the nose.

Mudra: Bring both palms in front of the Heart Center facing upward. Touch the sides of the palms along the little fingers together, as if you will receive something in them. Form Gyan Mudra with each hand.

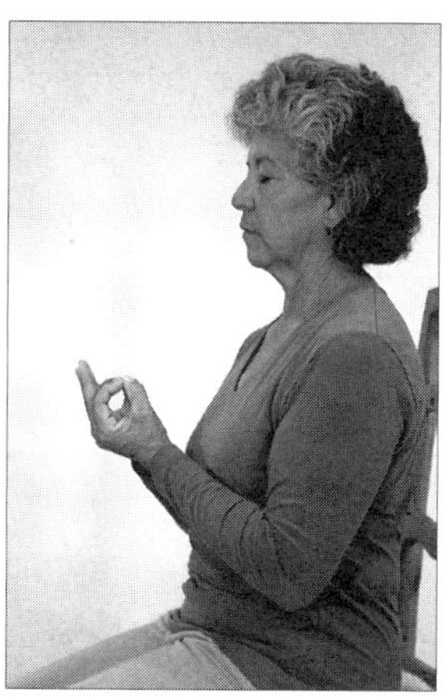

Breath Pattern and Mantra: Chant the entire mantra 3 to 5 times on one breath. Keep the number of repetitions per breath constant. The sound "***Dayv***" is chanted a minor third higher than the other sounds. The sound of "***Dayvaa***" carries slightly on the "***aa***" sound.

> ***Ong Namo, Guroo Dayv Namo***
> ***Guroo Dayv Namo, Guroo Dayvaa***

The sound of "***Ong***" is carried in the inner chambers of the sinuses and upper palate. It is the "***ng***" sound that is emphasized. The first part of "***Namo***" is short and rhymes with "***Hum.***" The syllable "***Gu***" is pronounced as in the word good. The syllable "***Roo***" rhymes with the word true. The word "***Dayv***" rhymes with save. The "***aa***" in "***Dayvaa***" is chanted with the mouth open and the sound vibrating from an open throat. (Refer to accompanying CD for correct pronunciation – 19.)

Time: Continue for 11–31 minutes for a powerful meditation and guidance. It can also be done for longer periods of practice.

With the grace of Guru Ram Das, when this mantra is chanted five times on one breath, the total spiritual knowledge of all teachers who have ever existed or who will ever exist on this Earth, is beseated in that person.

YOGI BHAJAN

Become Ten Times Greater Than Me

Yogi Bhajan has left his earthly throne for his heavenly one. He completed his mission and has bestowed his legacy to the world. Part of his legacy was to create teachers and leaders for the Aquarian Age, not disciples or followers. In this way, all people of consciousness are a part of that legacy…all of us. What's required is a choice. Each of us can choose to sit on our earthly throne to deliver something beneficial to this world. It is not a position or status but a commitment, a contract to which we agreed – a mission in life. It is a passion that gives us a purpose for being. Each of us can meditate on our contract and then live it the best we can with love.

Yogi Bhajan use to say, "*Become ten times greater then me.*" We'd all look at each other, like "Wow, how is that possible?" It seems way too daunting a task. And, it will be impossible if our consciousnesses remain individually oriented. To become ten times greater than he, requires a three-part process. First, it is important that we begin individually, by developing our consciousness by sincerely pursuing a spiritual practice; – second, we need to live our mission in life; and third – a crucial step – we must live in "group consciousness." If we consciously unite, working together for the betterment of humanity – together we can be ten times greater than he. In this way, we become a part of his legacy – like a million jewels casting their radiance upon all – until the darkness gives way to the light.

Knowing that we fulfilled our earthly job, we will go to our heavenly throne with a knowing smile of contentment and victory on our lips.

You have to understand the purpose of life. The purpose of life is to do something which will live forever.
YOGI BHAJAN

In between birth and death, you have time to emit light so you leave behind a legacy.
YOGI BHAJAN

APPENDIX I

KIRTAN SOHILA – SONG OF PRAISE

English translation by MSS Guruka Singh Khalsa

To be recited at the time of death. As a daily practice, it can be recited before bed.

I Know that God and Me are One.
This is My Guru's Gift To Me

In that house where people meditate on God and chant His praises — in that house, sing God's praises and ever remember Him.

Sing the Praises of the Fearless One. I am devoted to singing God's praises, which bring lasting peace. Pause

God takes care of all His creatures twenty-four hours a day. The Giver of everything watches over all of them. God's Gifts are priceless. No one can give the way God gives.

The day of my wedding has been set. Come, my friends – gather together and pour the blessing oil over the threshold. O friends, bless me that I may merge with God. This call comes to all homes. Such calls come every day. Meditate on the One who calls. O Nanak, the day draws near!

RAG ASA, FIRST CHANNEL OF LIGHT:

There are six paths, six teachers, and six teachings. But the Teacher of all teachers is the One who appears as many. O Baba: follow that path in which God's Praises are sung. Following it you will become great. Pause

The seconds, minutes and hours – the four watches of each day, the weeks, the months and the four seasons of the year all come from our single sun. In the same way, all the ten thousand forms of creation spring from the One Creator, O Nanak.

RAG DHANASRI, FIRST CHANNEL OF LIGHT:

The evening sky is the offering plate, the sun and moon are the oil lamps. The stars and planets are the shining pearls. The fragrance of sandalwood growing nearby is the temple incense, and the wind is the fan. The night blooming Jasmine are the flowers laid upon the altar in offering to Thee, O Lord of Light.

The vibration of the Universe is the sound of the temple drums. O, what a beautiful evening prayer this is! This is Thy true prayer, O Destroyer of Fear. Pause

Thou hast thousands of eyes and Thou hast no eyes. Thou hast thousands of forms and Thou art formless. Thou hast thousands of Lotus Feet and Thou hast no feet at all. Thou hast thousands of noses and Thou hast no nose.

Thy Play enchants me.

Everything is filled with Light — the Light is Thee. The Light that shines in all beings is Thee. One sees the Light through the Guru's Teachings. God's True prayer is what pleases Him. My mind is enchanted by God's sweet Lotus Feet. I long for them day and night. Rain Thy kindness upon Nanak, the thirsty cuckoo, so that he may find happiness in Thy Name.

RAG GAURI PURBI, FOURTH CHANNEL OF LIGHT:

The village of my body was filled to overflowing with anger and sexual desire. I broke them both to bits when I met the Saintly one. By great destiny, I met the Saint and became filled with God's Love. Greet the Holy Saint with your palms together. This brings grace. Bow to Him, this brings honor. Pause

Those who worship wealth and possessions cannot taste the sweetness of God within themselves. They are stuck by the thorn of their own self-importance. The further their minds stray from God, the deeper it pierces them, and the more pain they suffer, until finally the club of the Messenger of Death smashes their heads.

People of God are filled with God's Name. They fear neither birth nor death They have merged with God, and are honored in all the worlds and realms.

O God, I am low and poor, but I belong to Thee. Save me! Save me, O Greatest of the Great! Servant Nanak eats and drinks Thy Name and he is filled with that peace that passes all understanding.

RAG GAURI PURBI, FIFTH CHANNEL OF LIGHT:

O, my friends, listen to me, I pray you. Now is the time to serve the Saints. In this world, earn the profit of God's Name, and when you leave this world you shall be honored. Night and day, this life is wasting away. Meeting the Guru in your own mind and your affairs will all be put in order. Pause

This world is caught up in corruption and skepticism. Only those who know God are free. Only those who are awake in the constant awareness of God and who drink the Nectar of the Name can tell that story which can never be told.

You only came here to purchase the precious Name of God. Now, by Guru's grace, your mind is full of God, and within the home of your own body you easily and joyfully merge with God. You shall not be reborn again.

O Lord who knows all Hearts. . . O Primal One. . . O Maker of Destinies, grant my dearest wish.

Nanak, Thy slave, begs for this one joy: let me be the dust on the feet of Thy Saints.

***If you would like to learn how to recite Kirtan Sohila in Gurmukhi, go to the Resource Page and contact Ancient Healing Ways or Spirit Voyage. They have books, tapes and CDs of Kirtan Sohila in English and Gurmukhi.*

APPENDIX II

GURU NANAK'S JAPJI

Guru Nanak's most beloved song was *Japji*. It is the first prayer in the Sikh Scriptures, *The Siri Guru Granth Sahib*, which Sikhs believe is their living Guru. *Japji* is universal in nature and can be enjoyed by anyone of any religion or path.

Japji is a description of God's nature and the nature of man and the universe. *Japji* relates to the element ether and is the poetic meditation that links the mind with one's soul or infinite nature. Whenever you cannot feel your soul or when the radiance of your soul is weak, recite *Japji*. The whole purpose of reciting *Japji* is to give the devotee the experience of God within. Our pain and "bondage" in life is felt when we forget Infinity.

It is made up of forty *paurees* or stanzas, which can liberate one from the cycles of birth and death. Each *pauree* addresses different aspects of the relationship between man and God and each has a specific instruction, power and gift that come with it. The particular power of each *pauree* lies in the combination of pure sounds of the words themselves, which without any intellectual understanding have the capacity to transform physical, mental, emotional and spiritual reality through the chemical and magnetic change in and around the being who recites it. This is the power of the *Shabd Guru* (Sound Current), and it is accessible and useful to anyone.

It is beneficial to recite the whole *Japji* in the early hours of the morning. Reciting it will balance your brain and set you for the day. Try it for forty days and feel the results for yourself.

For the purposes of this book, I have chosen a few specific *paurees,* which you will find especially powerful on your spiritual journey. Choose one and recite it eleven times a day for forty days to feel its full effect.

If you would like more information and/or a copy of a complete *Japji*, contact Ancient Healing Ways or Spirit Voyage, (refer to the Resource Page). They have books, tapes and CDs for your enjoyment and for an accurate pronunciation.

We will begin with *Mul Mantra*, which begins *Japji* and is the foundation of its entirety. Chanting *Mul Mantra* removes the fate and changes the destiny to prosperity. (Refer to accompanying CD for correct pronunciation – 20.)

Ek Ong Kar
Sat Nam
Karta Purakh
Nirbho, Nirvair
Akal Moorit
Ajoonee
Saibhang
Gurprashad
Jap
Aad Sach
Jugaad Sach
Haibhee Sach
Naanak Hosee Bhee Sach

God and We are One
This is our True Identity.
The Doer of everything.
Beyond fear.
Beyond revenge.

Beyond death,
Image of the Infinite,
Unborn.
Full of Light
The Guru's Gift – Meditate!
Primal Truth.
True for all time
True at this instant.
O Nanak, forever true. //1//

Japji: In the 8–11 *Paurees,* we are told to listen, a type of surrendering, which becomes effortless. By listening, we become awake to all senses, so we can "hear" the Infinite speaking to us. By listening, clarity is ours and we experience "*shuniya*" or the zero point, when finite and infinite weave into one. The *Ninth Pauree* is included here, which gives expansion. (Refer to accompanying CD for correct pronunciation – 21.)

Suni-ai Eesar Barmaa Ind
Suni-ai Mukh Saalaahan Mand
Suni-ai Jog Jugat Tan Bhayd
Sunni-ai Shaast Simrit Vayd
Naanak Bhagataa Sadaa Vigaas
Suni-ai Dookh Paap Kaa Naas.

Listening...men become gods. Listening...praise comes from the mouth of the most negative person. Listening... the way of yoga and the body's secrets. Listening...all holy books and scriptures. O Nanak! God's lovers bloom forever. Listening destroys all pain and error. || 9 ||

After "listening," *Paurees* 12–15 call upon us to have faith, obey and trust. If our consciousness is clear, we will hear the Infinite command and make it into our self-command. By repeating these *Mannai Paurees* 11 times a day you can achieve self-mastery.

Japji: Fourteenth Pauree. When you cannot find your path in life, when you cannot see the direction to your destiny, when you cannot achieve fulfillment, the fourteenth pauree will show you the way. Recite it 11 times a day. (Refer to accompanying CD for correct pronunciation – 22.)

Mannai Maarag T'Haak Na Paa-i
Mannai Pat Si-o Pargat Jaa-i
Mannai Mag Na Chalai Pant'h
Mannai Dharam Saytee Sanbandh
Aisaa Naam Niranjan Ho-i
Jay Ko Mann Jaanai Man Ko-i

When you agree, your path becomes clear. When you agree, you go Home shining with honor. When you agree, you are not of this world. When you agree, you embrace the Dharma. Such is the Naam. It makes you pure. If you agree to agree, your mind becomes sure. || 14 ||

Japji: Fifteenth Pauree brings salvation. Being connected to the Infinite Consciousness, this pauree will help one swim across any difficulties at the moment of death. In life, this pauree will help one surmount any challenge. (Refer to accompanying CD for correct pronunciation – 23.)

Mannai Paveh Mokh Du-aar
Maanai Parvaarai Saadhaar
Mannai Tarai Taaray Gur Sikh
Mannai Naanak Bhaveh Na Bhikh
Aisaa Naam Niranjan Ho-i
Jay Ko Mann Jaanai Man Ko-i

When you agree, your tenth gate opens. When you agree, your family is saved. When you agree, you cross over the ocean, taking the Guru's Sikhs by your side. O Nanak! When you agree, you never wander this earth as a beggar again. Such is the Naam. It makes you pure. If you agree to agree, your mind becomes sure. || 15 ||

Japji: Twenty-Fourth Pauree breaks through all limitations with the force of a thunderbolt. It is so powerful that it affects generations; it has the power to kill misfortune. (Refer to accompanying CD for correct pronunciation – 24.)

Ant Na Sifatee Kehn Na Ant
Ant Na Karnai Dayn Na Ant
Ant Na Vaykhan Sunan Na Ant
Ant Na Jaapai Ki-aa Man Mant
Ant Na Jaapai Keetaa Aakaar
Ant Na Jaapai Paraavaar
Ant Kaaran Kaytay Bilalaa-eh
Taa Kay Ant Na Paa-ay Jaa-eh
Ayho Ant Na Jaanai Ko-i
Bahutaa Kehee-ai Bahutaa Ho-i
Vadaa Saahib Oochaa T'haa-o
Oochay Oopar Oochaa Naa-o
Ayvad Oochaa Hovai Ko-i
Tis Oochay Kau Jaanai So-i
Jayvad Aap Jaanai Aap Aap
Naanak Nadaree Karmee Daat

There is no end of good advice; no end to what is said. No end of doing, no end of giving no end of seeing, hearing and living. There is no end in sight. What mantra lies within God's mind? See the structure of the universe. There is no end in sight. See its endless expansion. There is no end in sight. Many wail in frustration, because there is no end in sight. No one can find the end. The more you try to tell, the more there is to say, God is high. The Naam is high. You must get that high to see. God knows how high He is, O Nanak! One glance can set you free. || 24 ||

Japji: Twenty-Eighth Pauree – the strongest permutation and combination of words in the world. It unites you with God, and enables you to live in a state of awareness of death. (Refer to accompanying CD for correct pronunciation – 25.)

Mundaa Santokh Saram Pat Jholee
Dhi-aan Kee Kareh Bibhoot
Khint'Haa Kaal Ku-Aaree Kaa-i-aa
Jugat Dandaa Parteet
Aa-ee Pant'hee Sagal Jamaatee
Man Jeetai Jag Jeet
Aadays Tisai Aadays
Aad Aneel Anaad Anaahat
Jug Jug Ayko Vays

Wear the earrings of patience, carry the begging bowl and wallet of humility, and smear the ashes of meditation on your body. Let your many-colored coat be death. Follow the path of purity, with the walking stick of faith. Let your sect be the family of man. Conquer your own mind and be victorious in the world. Hail! Hail! Hail! unto Him — Primal, Pure, and equal to none. There is no beginning and no end. Through all ages only the One. || 28 ||

Japji: Thirtieth Pauree places you upon the throne of divinity. It makes you into a sage and a saint. If you recite this 40 times daily, death cannot strike and karma will not hit. It can take you beyond the fear and worry of death. It can help you cross any barrier of death. (Refer to accompanying CD for correct pronunciation – 26, also Sangeet Kaur has an insturction tape available. Refer to Resource Page.)

Aykaa Maa-ee Jugat Vi-aa-ee
Tin Chaylay Parvaan
Ik Sansaaree Ik Bandhaaree
Ik Laa-ay Deebaan
Jiv Tis Bhaavai Tivai Chalaavai
Jiv Hovai Furmaan
Oho Vaykhai Onaa Nadar Na Aavai
Bahutaa Ayho Vidaan
Aadays Tisai Aadays
Aad Aneel Anaad Anaahat
Jug Jug Ayko Vays

Out of the marriage of God and Maya three worthy students are born: the Generator, Organizer and Destroyer of all life and worldly forms. As He pleases, all things move according to His order. He sees it all, but none see Him, and all are filled with wonder. Hail! Hail! Hail! unto Him. Primal, Pure, and equal to none. There is no beginning and no end. Through all ages only the One. || 30 ||

Japji: Thirty-Second Pauree pays your debts and completes your karma. (Refer to accompanying CD for correct pronunciation – 27.)

Ik Doo Jeebhaao Lakh Ho-eh
Lakh Hoveh Lakh Vees
Lakh Lakh Gayraa Aakhee-a-eh
Aykaa Naam Jagdeesh
Ayt Raa-Eh Pat Pavaree-aa
Charee-Ai Ho-I Ikees
Sun Galaa Aakaash Kee
Keetaa Aa-Ee Rees
Naanak Nadaree Paa-ee-ai
Kooree Koorai T'hees

From one tongue there came thousands more, and millions came from them. Millions of tongues are turning and churning, repeating the One Lord's Name. On the Master's Path are many steps. Climb them, and come back Home. Even worms who hear of heavenly things are longing to come back Home. O Nanak! We get to come back Home only by the One God's Grace. But the liars all boast, I did it myself! || 32 ||

Japji: Thirty-Third Pauree destroys your ego and brings home your divinity. It removes negativity and fear, neutralizes your destructive nature and prevents harm to others by your hand. (Refer to accompanying CD for correct pronunciation – 28.)

Aakhan Jor Chupai Neh Jor
Jor Na Mangan Dayn Na Jor
Jor Na Jeevan Maran Neh Jor
Jor Na Raaj Maal Man Sor
Jor Na Surtee Gi-aan Veechaar
Jor Na Jugatee Chhutai Sansaar
Jis Hat'h Jor Kar Vaykhai So-i
Nanak Utam Neech Na Ko-i

No power to be silent. No power to speak. No power to beg. No power to give. No power to die. No power to live. No power lies in worldly might. No power lies in earthly treasure. They only increase your mental chatter. No power to meditate or know the unknown. No power to leave this world and go Home. One Power. One Actor. One Doer. One Knower. O Nanak! No one is higher or lower. // 33 //

These English translations were written by my very dear friend and devotee of Truth, Guruka Singh Khalsa.

For further study and exploration, you will find included in this Appendix II the *Japji Paurees Thirty-Four* through *Thirty-Seven*, which describe the *Five Khands* or realms and correspond to the *Five Blue Ethers*. Re-read the explanation about the five blue ethers in Chapter Nine – *The Journey of Death*, and then read these original scriptures about them. As seekers of Truth, you may find these paurees insightful and enlightening in your understanding of the five blue ethers. As is the case with scriptures of all religions, they are open to personal interpretation and experience. (If you would like the proper pronunciation of these paurees, contact Ancient Healing Ways. They have numerous CDs for that purpose.)

Japji: Thirty-Fourth Pauree describes the *First Khand of Dharm* or *Realm of Duty* and *Spiritual Law*, the basis for a conscious life and death. This Pauree corresponds to the *First Blue Ether* and the evaluation each of us must make of our life's actions at the time of death. (Refer to accompanying CD for correct pronunciation – 29.)

Raatee Rutee T'hitee Vaar
Pavan Paanee Aganee Paataal
Tis Vich Dhartee T'haap Rakhee Dharam Saal
Tis Vich Jee-a Jagat Kay Rang
Tin Kay Naam Anayk Anant
Karmee Karmee Ho-i Veechaar
Sachaa Aap Sachaa Darbaar
Tit'hai Sohan Panch Parvaan
Nadaree Karam Pavai Neeshaan
Kach Pakaa-ee Ot'hai Paa-i
Naanak Ga-i-aa Jaapai Jaa-i

Nights, seasons, moon cycles, days. Wind, water, fire and the underworld. In the midst of this, the Earth was established, as a place where Spirit could evolve into Conscious Awareness of Itself, protected. For that purpose, the souls came through time and space in such a variety of colors. Those souls are so many, they are countless. There are actions upon actions, and we reflect on what we do. Thou, oh Divine One, are True and True is your Royal Court, in which all is contained. In Your Royal Court, Your devotees, the ones who have found themselves within themselves look beautiful. Their actions flow from Grace and this is the sign of You they carry. The Not-Yet-Ripe and the Ripe are both there on the Earth. Nanak, go and see it. //34//

Japji: Thirty-Fifth Pauree is the *Second Khand of Gian, Realm of Wisdom*. It corresponds to the *Second Blue Ether*, where we see the lessons of our life and what more purification is needed for the upliftment of the soul. This pauree gives us the breadth to do our duty and fulfill our responsibility in life and in preparation for death. (Refer to accompanying CD for correct pronunciation – 30.)

Dharam Khand Kaa Ayho Dharam
Gi-Ann Khand Kaa Aakhaho Karam
Kaytay Pavan Paanee Vaisantar
Kaytay Kaan Mahays
Kaytay Barmay Ghaarat Gharee-a-eh
Roop Rang Kay Vays
Kaytee-Aa Karam Bhoomee Mayr Kaytay
Kaytay Dhoo Upakays
Kaytay Ind Chand Soor Kaytay
Kaytay Mandal Days
Kaytay Sidh Budh Naat'h Kaytay
Kaytay Dayvee Vays
Kaytay Dayv Daanav Mun Kaytay
Kaytay Ratan Samund
Kaytee-aa Khaanee Kaytee-aa Baanee
Kaytay Paat Narind
Kaytee-aa Surtee Sayvak Kaytay
Nanak Ant Na Ant

In the Realm of Dharma, of Spiritual Law, we come to understand how to awaken ourselves to ourselves. In the Realm of Wisdom, we speak of how everything gets accomplished. There are so many winds, waters and fires. So many Creative Forces. So many Creations that the Creator is crafting, clothing the Spirit in Form and Color. So many actions done in so many lands and places, so many places that are not even known to us. All for learning what You want us to learn. So many Heavens, Moons and Suns. So many Galaxies with so many peoples. So many joined in Union with Thee. So many wise ones and masters. So many robed goddesses. So many gods and demons. So many persons of Honor. So many jewels of Spiritual instruction, in so many Oceans of Existences. So many ways of thinking about things. So many words that come from Thee. So many rulers of Spiritual Nobility. So many living attuned to Thee, so many of Your servants. Nanak, even Your limits are beyond limits. //35//

Japji: Thirty-Sixth Pauree – is the *Third Khand of Saram*, or *Realm of Effort*. It corresponds to the *Third Blue Ether*, where one's lessons have passed the test of time and space. One's consciousness is looking to the heavens. This Pauree brings divine realization and grants complete understanding of the heavens and the earth. (Refer to accompanying CD for correct pronunciation – 31.)

Gi-aaan Khand Meh Gi-aan Parchand
Tit'hai Naad Binod Kod Anand

Saram Khand Kee Baanee Roop
Tit'Hai Ghaarat Gharee-ai Bahut Anoop
Taa kee-aa Galaa Kat'hee'Aa Naa Jaa-eh
Jay Ko Kehai Pichhai Pachhutaa-i
Tit'hai Gharee-ai Surat Mat Man Budh
Tit'hai Gharee-ai Suraa Sidhaa Kee Sudh

In the Realm of Wisdom, Wisdom is found. There, beyond Sound, the subtle vibratory frequency of creation creates the plays and dramas. In the Realm of Effort, the Divine Word becomes form. What is crafted there are creations of Incomparable Beauty. It is impossible to speak of these matters. If someone tries to speak, afterwards, he'll only feel mournful that he couldn't describe it. What is crafted there are persons of purity, clarity and grace. Attuned to the Divine with minds that know the difference between Truth and falsehood, persons of genuine understanding and wisdom. What is crafted there are the psyches of angels and masters. //36//

Japji: Thirty-Seventh Pauree describes the *Fourth Khand of Karam* or *Realm of Action*, where sacred words are all powerful and corresponds to the *Fourth Blue Ether*, where enlightened souls reside. The Thirty-Seventh Pauree also contains the *Fifth Khand of Sach or Realm of Truth* and corresponds to the *Fifth Blue Ether*, where one merges with the Infinite and formless becomes limitless. (Refer to accompanying CD for correct pronunciation – 32.)

Karam Khand Kee Baanee Jor
Tit'hai Hor Na Ko-ee Hor
Tit'hai Jodh Mahaabal Soor
Tin Meh Raam Rehi-aa Bharpoor
Tit'hai Seeto Seetaa Mehmaa Maa-eh
Taa Kay Roop Na Kat'hanay Jaa-eh
Naa Oh Mareh Na T'haagay Jaa-eh
Jin Kai Raam Vasai Man Maa-eh
Tit'hai Bhagat Vaseh Kay Lo-a
Kareh Anand Sachaa Man Soi
Sach Khand Vasai Nirankaar
Kar Kar Vaykhai Nadar Nihaal
Tit'hai Khand Mandal Varbandh
Jay Ko Kat'hai Ta Ant Na Ant
Tit'hai Lo-a Aakaar
Jiv Jiv Hukam Tivai Tiv Kaar
Vaykhai Vigasai Kar Veechaar
Naanak Kat'hanaa Kararaa Saar

In the Realm of Action, your Sacred Words are power, and there is no other power besides it. In that Realm are brave and strong spiritual warriors filled with the presence of the Divine. There, it is a habit sewn securely inside them to honor and praise Thee. These beautiful forms are impossible to describe. The Divine dwells within their minds. There, those who have surrendered themselves in love to Thee live as lights. They enjoy sweet-tasting bliss within themselves. In the Realm of Truth, the Formless One dwells. By seeing All that is continuously done, the Divine looks kindly upon us and in that kind look, brings everything to a state of completion. There are worlds, solar systems, universes. If someone tried to describe them all, there would be no limit. There, lights upon Lights come into bodies and forms. And as the Divine Will guides them so they act.

The Divine remains in a state of contemplation seeing and enjoying it all. Nanak, describing this forges the hard steel of Truth. //37//

This beautiful English translation of Paurees Thirty-Four through Thirty-Seven was done by a dear spiritual sister, Ek Ong Kaar Kaur Khalsa. If you would like her complete translation of Japji, refer to the Resource Page for her contact information.

APPENDIX III

RITUALS AND CEREMONIES FOR A SIKH DEATH

Before Death

- Read *Sukhmani Sahib*, as it brings peace to the soul.
- *Gurbani Kirtan* is a powerful way to invoke one's feelings of trust and intimate relationship with God and Guru. Have it playing all the time.
- As the person is approaching death, encourage him or her to keep the focus on God and Guru, surrendering to His will. There is nothing to fear.

At the Time of Death

- As the soul leaves the body, recite *Japji Sahib*.
- Chanting "*Akal*" guides the soul to pass out of this worldly realm and into the *Akal Purakh*, the Undying Being.

After Death

- The body should be prepared for the funeral with a yogurt bath, including the hair, while *Mul Mantra* is recited. Let the yogurt dry on the body; do not wash it off.
- The body is then dressed in new clothes, preferably white *bana*, a new turban and the five K's, (which includes *kacheras* (Sikh underwear), *kesh* (hair with a turban), *kirpan* (Sikh dagger), *kanga* (Sikh comb), and *kara* (Sikh bangle). The body should then be wrapped in a clean white sheet in preparation for cremation.

At the Funeral

- *Ardas* is recited to start the service.
- The minister and others may offer words, recitations, stories, etc.
- *Gurbani Kirtan* can be played and other meaningful songs of the deceased and family.
- The body of a Sikh is always cremated, at least within three days of death.
- Friends and relatives should join the procession when the body is carried to the cremation. They can recite "*Sat Nam*," "*Wahe Guru*" or *Gurbani Kirtan* while proceeding.
- When the cremation begins, *Japji Sahib* is read, followed by *Kirtan Sohila*; these two *banis* should continue to be read alternately until the cremation is completed. Another *Ardas* at the completion of the cremation is appropriate, praying for the release and easy transition of the soul on its journey home to God.

After the Funeral

- The *Sangat* should gather before the Guru and recite *Rehiras* and *Gurbani Kirtan*. The Siri Singh Sahib (Yogi Bhajan) has often told us to serve a special *karah prasad* made with five seeds (See page 147), representing the five elements – poppy, cardamom, sesame, sunflower and pumpkin. A shared *lungar* is uplifting and strengthening.

- Beginning on the day of death, and for a total of seventeen days, *Kirtan Sohila* is to be read daily. This facilitates the transition of the soul from the physical body.
- An Akhand Paath should begin as soon as possible. Ten-day Sahej Paaths are an alternative. The ashes may be scattered on a river, the sea or most any body of water. The building of memorials over the remains of the dead is against the Sikh Guru's teachings.

APPENDIX IV

More Yoga Sets

KRIYA FOR DISEASE RESISTANCE

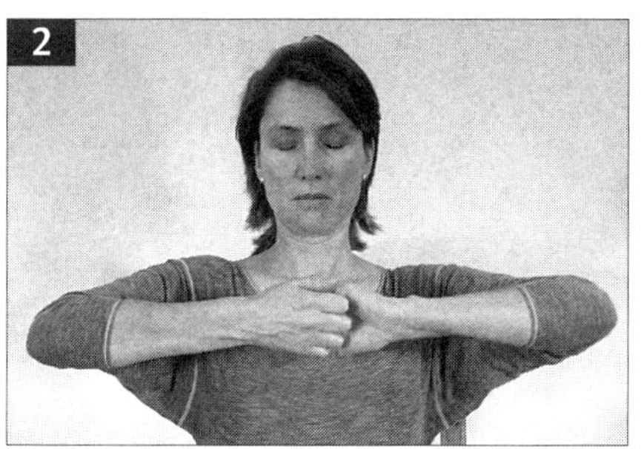

To avoid persistent colds and illness, it is essential to keep digestion and elimination functioning well. Add to this a strong metabolic balance and you will have heartiness. This *kriya* develops these capacities. It gives physical strength and builds disease resistance.

1. Pumping the Stomach. Sitting straight in your chair, stretch the arms straight up over the head with the fingers interlocked and the index fingers pointing straight up. Inhale. Pump the stomach by forcefully drawing the navel in toward the spine and then relaxing it again. Continue rhythmically until you feel the need to exhale. Then exhale. Inhale and begin again. Continue for 1–3 minutes. Then inhale, exhale and relax.

This exercise stimulates digestion and the Kundalini energy in the Third Chakra.

2. Bear Grip. Place the hands in Bear Grip (refer to hand mudras in Chapter Three) at the chest level with the forearms parallel to the ground. Inhale. Hold the breath and without separating the hands, try to pull the hands apart. Apply maximum force. Exhale. Inhale and pull again. Continue for 1–3 minutes. Then inhale, exhale and relax.

This exercise opens the Heart Center and stimulates the thymus gland.

3. Sitting Bends. Fingers are interlocked in Venus Lock behind the neck. Inhale. Exhale and bend forward reaching your torso toward the ground **(3A)**. Inhale and sit up again **(3B)**. Continue with powerful breathing for 1–3 minutes. Inhale, sit up. Exhale and relax.

This exercise improves digestion and adds flexibility to the spine.

3A

3B

4. Front Stretch. This exercise can be done with one or two chairs. If using one chair, be sitting straight in it with the legs stretched out straight in front. Bring the arms up straight in front parallel to the ground **(4A)**. Inhale lean back **(4B)**, exhale reach forward from the waist as far as you can **(4C)**, (without falling out of the chair). If available, put a second chair in front of you and place the legs on top of the chair. Do as above. Continue for 1–3 minutes. To end, inhale. Exhale and relax.

This exercise allows the glandular secretions from the previous exercises to circulate though the body and allows the body to deeply relax.

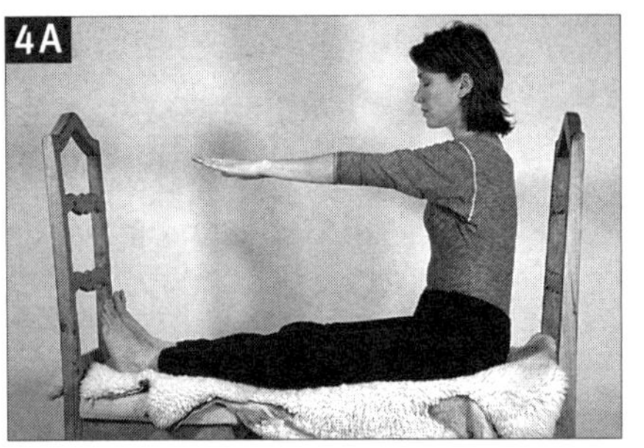

4A

4A

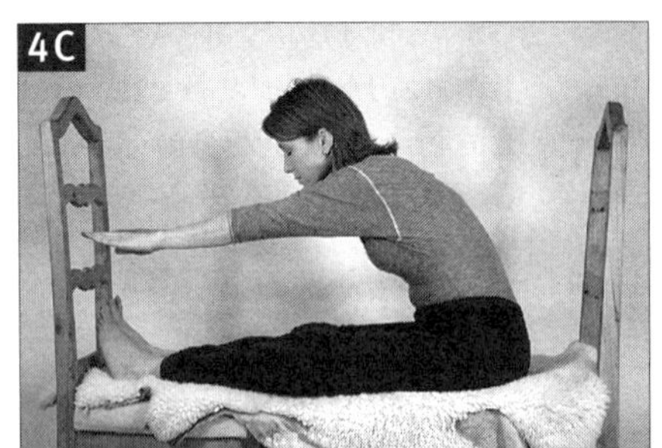

4C

5

5. Neck Rolls. Begin rolling the neck clockwise in a circular motion, bringing the right ear toward the right shoulder, the back of the head toward the back of the neck, the left ear toward the left shoulder and the chin toward the chest The shoulders remain relaxed and motionless, and the neck should be allowed to gently stretch as the head circles around. Continue for 1–2 minutes. Then reverse the direction

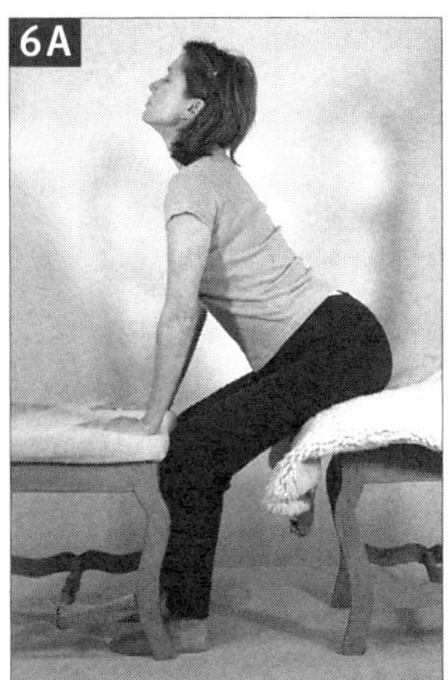

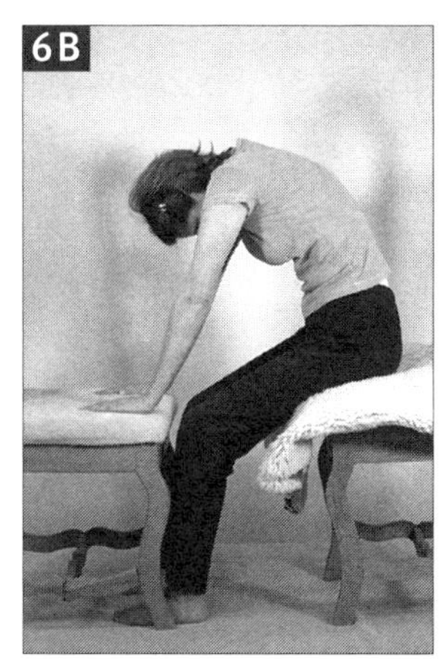

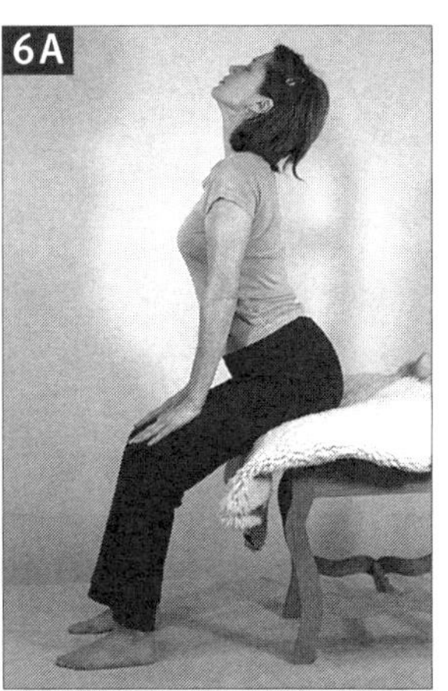

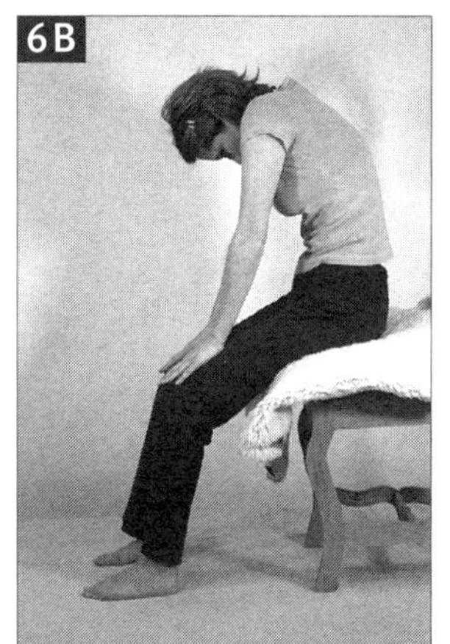

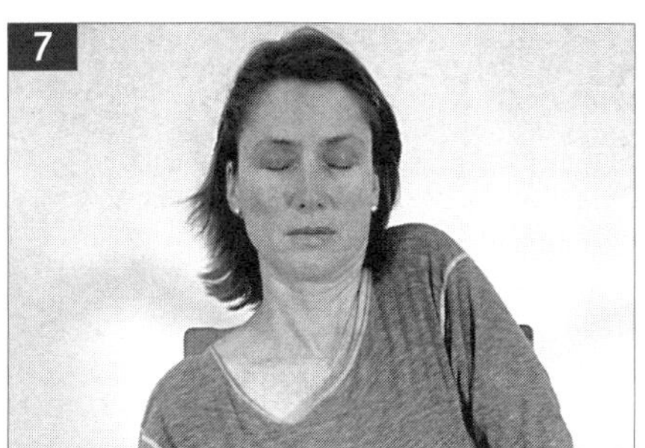

and continue for 1–2 minutes more. Bring the head to a central position and relax. Be sure to keep the spine elongated as you roll the neck around.

This exercise and the two exercises following it combine to open circulation to the brain and to stimulate the higher glands including the pituitary, parathyroid. thyroid and pineal glands, which work together to give harmony to the entire body.

6. Cat-Cow. If you have a chair in front of you, place your palms flat on the chair, shoulder width apart. Do not bend the elbows. If you do not have a chair, place the hands on the thighs near the hips. Inhale and flex the spine downward as if someone were sitting on your back **(6A)**. Stretch the neck and head back. Then exhale and flex the spine up, bringing the chin towards the chest **(6B)**. Continue rhythmically with powerful breathing for 1–3 minutes. Gradually increase your speed as you feel the spine becoming more flexible. Inhale in the original position. Exhale and relax.

This exercise, in addition to the effects mentioned above, helps to transform the sexual energy of the Second Chakra and the digestive energy of the Third Chakra while stimulating the main nerves that are regulated through the lower cervical vertebra.

7. Alternate Shoulder Shrugs. Alternately shrug your shoulders as high as possible, keeping the head still. On the inhale, lift the left shoulder, as the right shoulder goes down. On the exhale, lift the right shoulder up and the left down. Continue rhythmically with powerful breathing for 1–3 minutes. Inhale, raising both shoulders up. Exhale and relax.

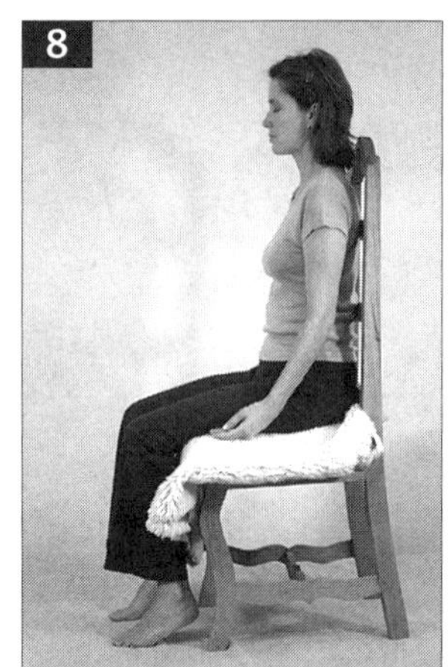

8. Corpse Pose. *Lean back in your chair and deeply relax.* Arms at the sides, palms facing up for 5–7 minutes.

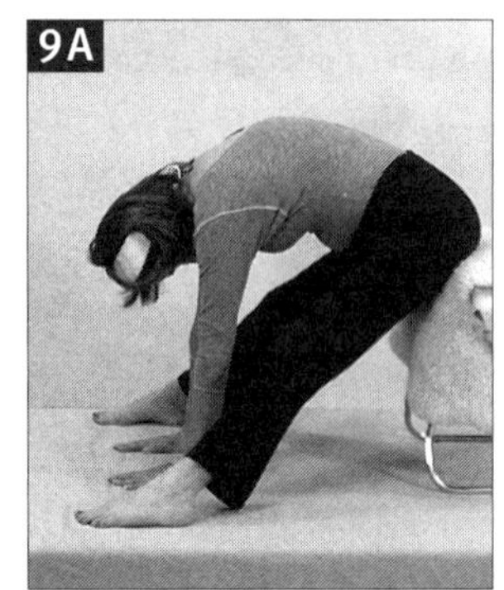

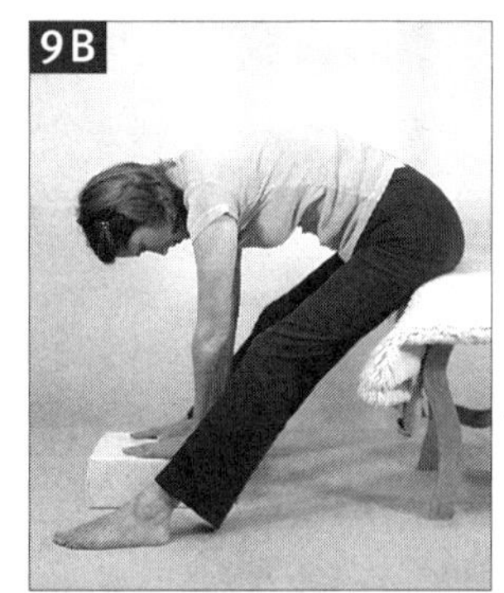

9. Chair Triangle Pose. Straighten the legs in front of you shoulder width apart **(9A)**. The best you can, place the palms on the floor between the feet. A stool can be used **(9B)**. Keeping the legs straight is very important. Breath normally. Hold this position for 1–3 minutes. Then inhale, exhale and slowly come out of the position and relax.

This exercise aids in digestion, strengthens the entire nervous system and relaxes the major muscle groups of the body.

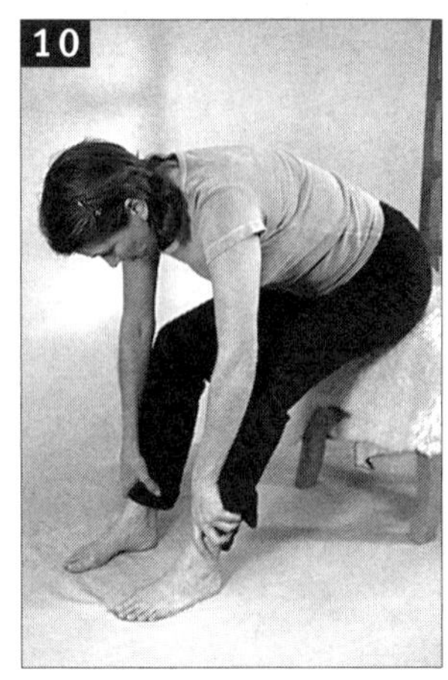

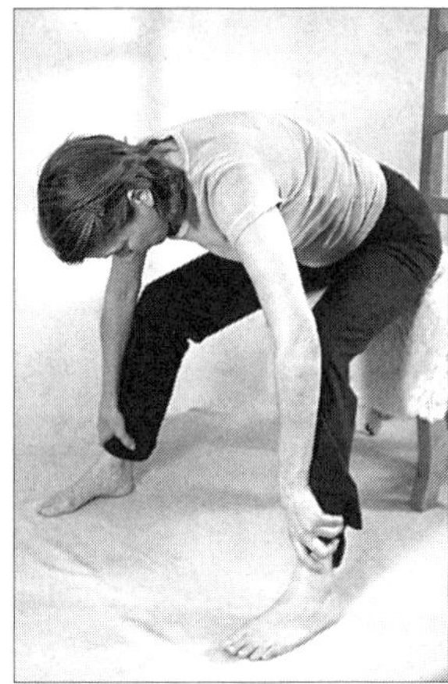

10. Chair Elephant Walk. Reach down and grab the ankles. The head is down. Walk the legs to each side and back to the center. Breathe normally. Continue for 1–3 minutes. Relax.

This exercise aids in elimination and adjusts the magnetic field to prepare you for meditation.

FOR THE BACK

(17–19 minutes)

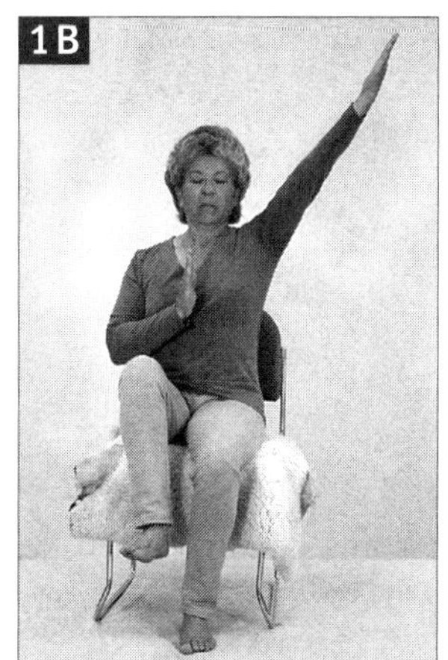

1. Sitting straight in a chair, place the hands together in the center of the chest (prayer mudra **1A**). Now bring the left arm up to a 60 degree angle, palm up, as you bring the right knee up as high as possible **(1B)** Bringing the palm back to the original position, simultaneously clap and lower the right knee. Repeat the sequence with the right arm. Continue alternating arms, inhaling as one arm goes up and exhaling as it goes down, for 1–4 minutes. Lift the knees up forcefully, make the breath heavy and powerful. Get into the rhythm of it!

This exercise is for the third vertebra and for the hip bone. Done right, it helps prevent lower back pain and develops motor coordination.

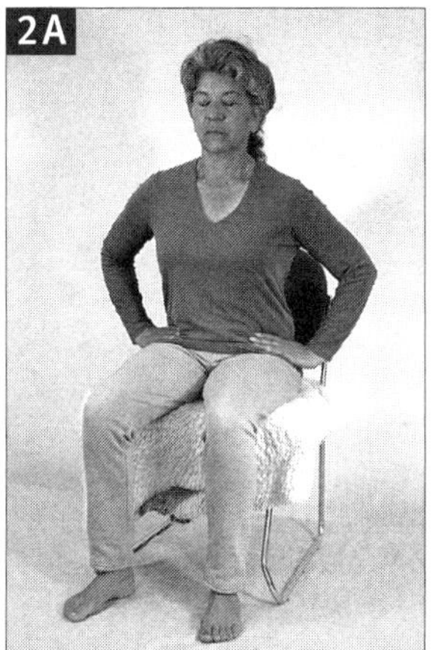

2. Place the hands on the hips (2A). Exhale as you lower the torso to one knee **(2B)**. Inhale up partially, exhale and lower the torso to the other knee. Inhale up partially, and continue. Continue for 1–4 *minutes.* "Get wild!"

3. Put the hands on the knees, inhale as you flex the spine forward **(3A)** and exhale as you flex it back **(3B)**. The breath is slightly slower than Breath of Fire. Keep the elbows straight throughout. Continue for 1–3 minutes.

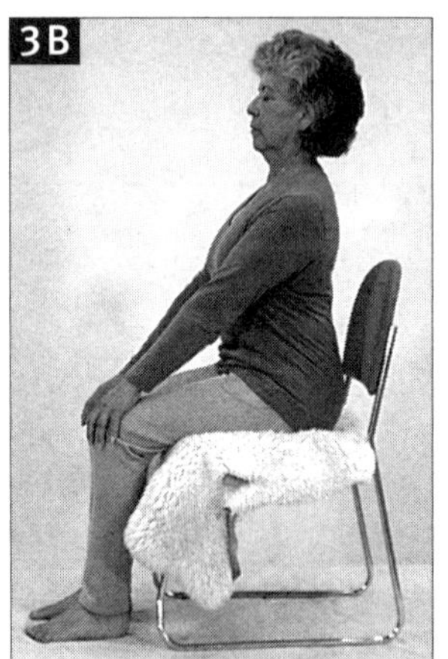

3B

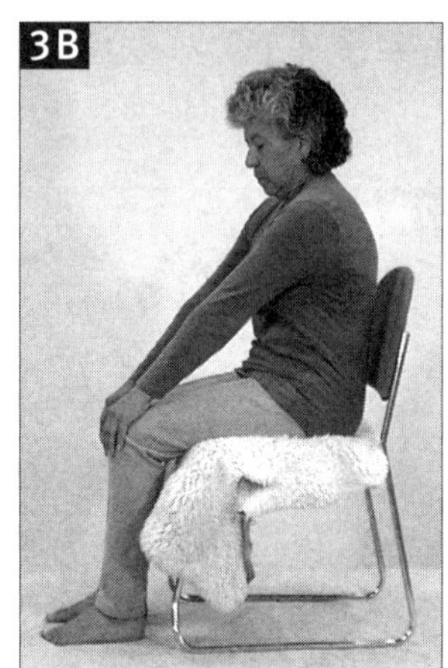

3B

4. Position arms, so upper arms are parallel to the ground and out to the sides, forearms straight up, palms straight **(4A)**. Begin twisting from side to side in a churning motion. **(4B)** Inhale left, and exhale right. The breath is slightly slower than Breath of Fire. Continue for 1–3 minutes.

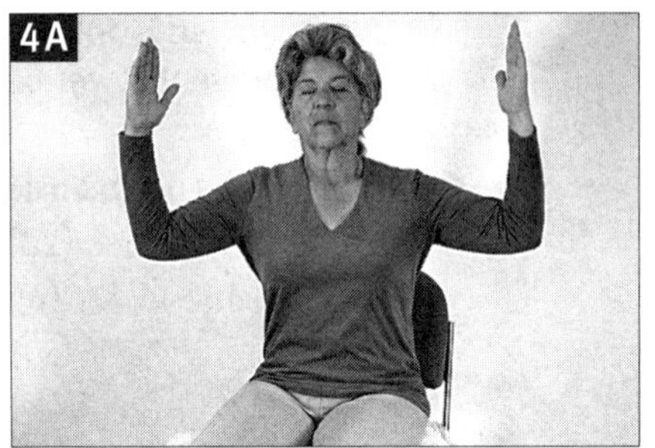

4A

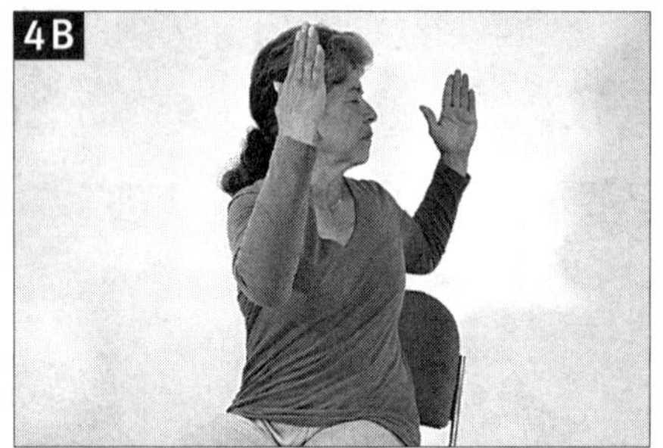

4B

5. Put the arms out straight to the side, parallel to the ground. Flap the arms up and down to the rhythm of Breath of Fire. Keep the elbows straight throughout. Continue 1–2 minutes.

This exercise is good for the lymph glands and to purify the blood.

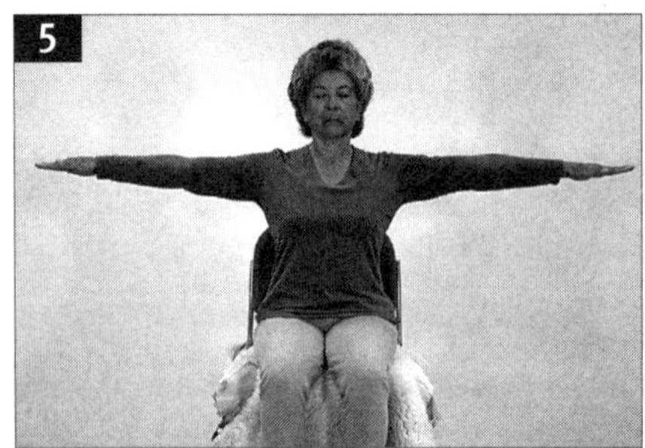

5

6. Bring the arms out straight in front, parallel to the ground. Once more begin flapping the arms up and down in rhythm with Breath of Fire. Continue 1–2 minutes.

6

7. Move the arms from front to back in large circles as if you were doing a backstroke. **(7A – C)** As you do so, chant "*Har, Har, Har*"..... in a brisk monotone. Coordinate the movement with the chant. Keep the arms straight throughout for 30 seconds.

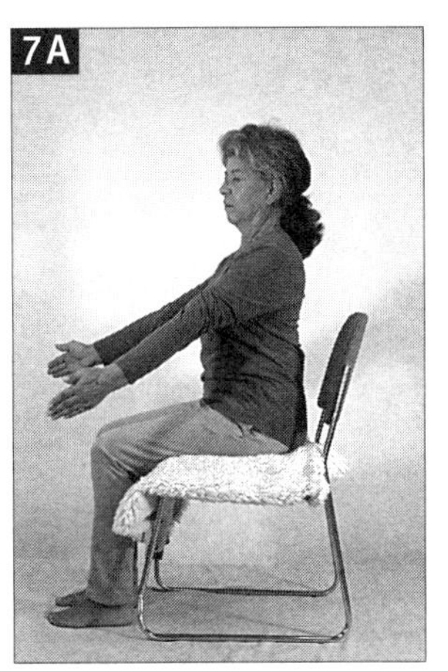

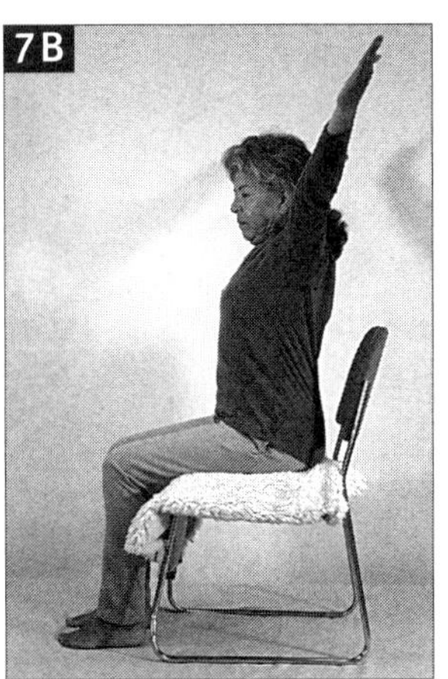

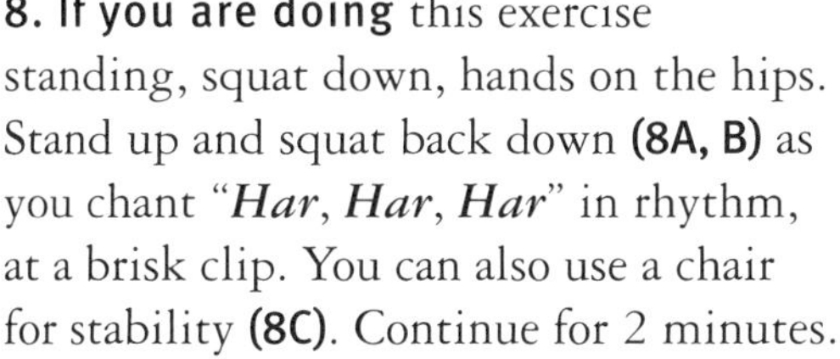

8. If you are doing this exercise standing, squat down, hands on the hips. Stand up and squat back down **(8A, B)** as you chant "*Har*, *Har*, *Har*" in rhythm, at a brisk clip. You can also use a chair for stability **(8C)**. Continue for 2 minutes.

Sitting in a chair **(8D)** – Sit straight, have the hands on the hips. Inhale lift the left knee up as far as you can, exhale lower it. Inhale lift the right knee up as far as you can, exhale lower it. It is as though you are marching. You can keep the hands on the hips or rise opposite arm and knee at the same time. Chant "Har" each time you raise the knee. Continue 1–2 minutes.

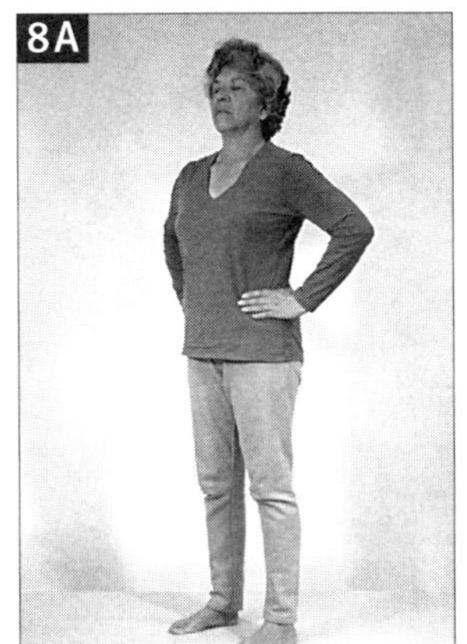

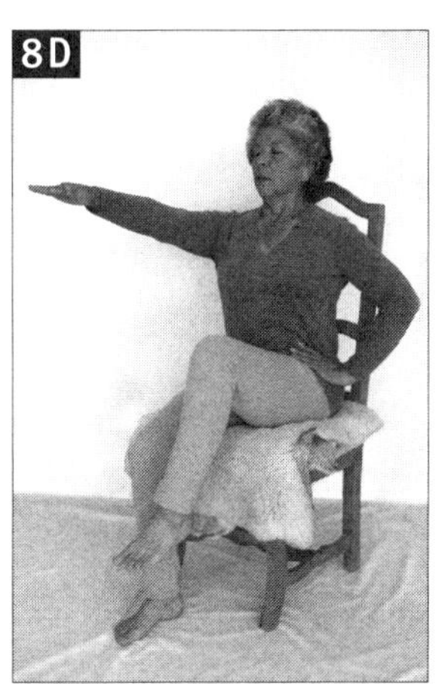

CELESTIAL COMMUNICATION

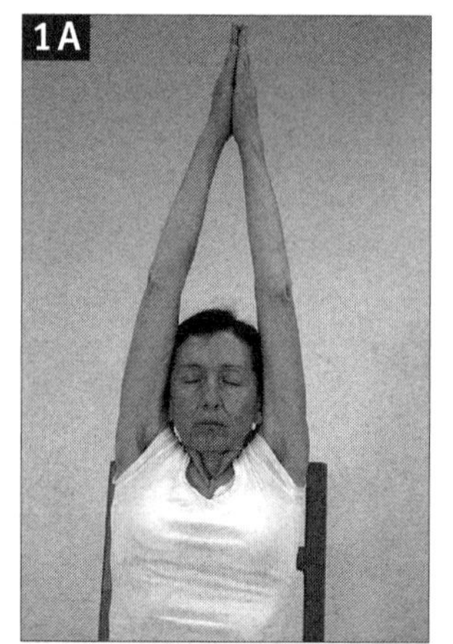

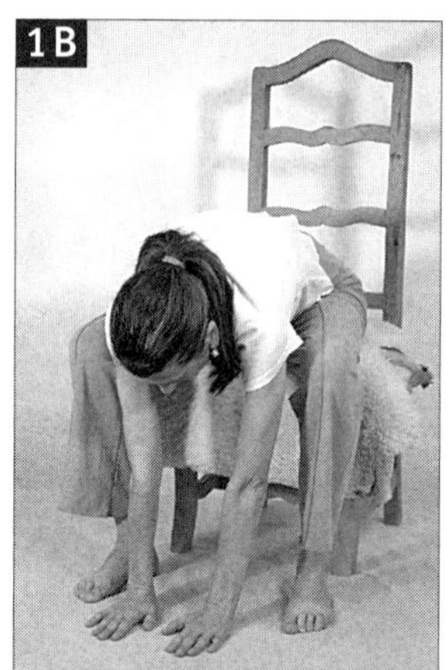

This kriya demonstrates how the combination of rhythmical movement and sound can create a state of harmony, inner strength and relaxation. Practicing these exercises will energize various internal organs, balance the glandular system and develop fearlessness in the personality.

The kriya has a three-part structure. The first part (Exercises 1, 2 & 3) energizes the lower body and tattvas, increasing aerobic capacity and circulation. The second part (Exercise 4) brings about a relaxation at the heart center through "celestial communication." The third part (Exercise 5 through 8) reinvigorates and once again balances the chakras, giving strength and clarity to your projection.

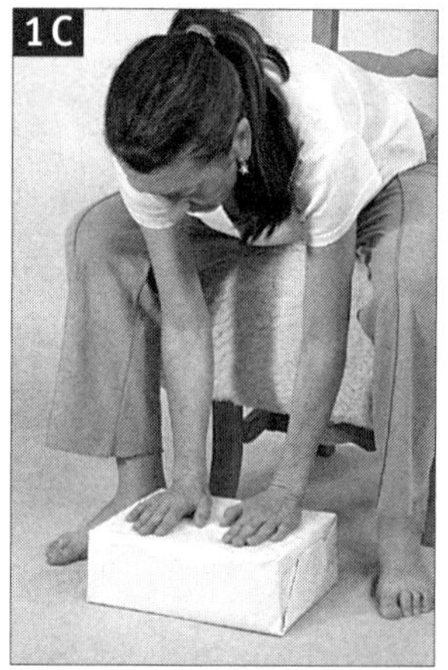

1. This is a three-part exercise with 8 beats per part. Sit with the feet shoulder-width apart and chant the mantra "*Har*" 8 times per part. (Remember to touch the palate with the tip of the tongue with every repetition of the mantra.)

A. Extend the arms straight over the head. Clap the hands 8 times so that the entire surface of the palms are firmly struck **(1A)**.

B. Immediately bend forward and strike the ground with the palms 8 times. Strike hard enough to make a noise **(1B)**. A stool can be used **(1C)**.

C. Straighten the body and extend the arms to the sides parallel to the ground, palms facing down. **(1D)** Pump the arms 30 degrees up and 30 degrees down 8 times as though you were trying to fly.

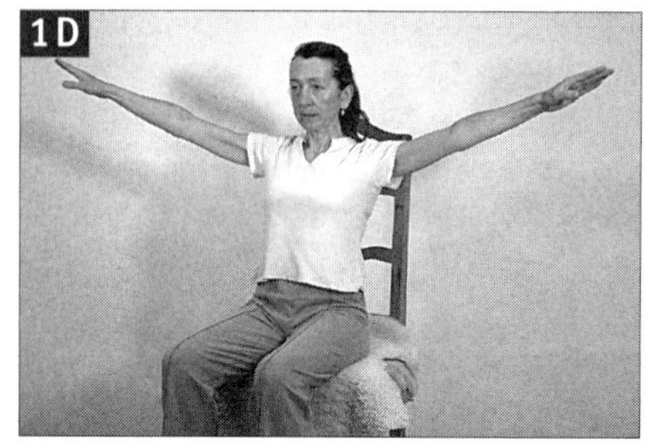

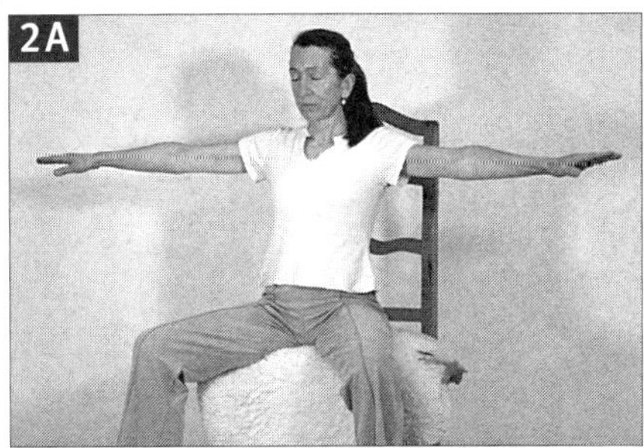

2. Be sitting with the feet shoulder-width apart and extend the arms to the sides parallel to the floor, palms facing down **(2A)**. Then cross the arms and legs **(2B)** in large movements, always coming back to the original position, arms extended to the sides and feet spread apart. Keep the arms straight and parallel to the ground and alternate the top arm and front leg. Chant "***Har***" with each cross and continue for 2 minutes at a steady pace.

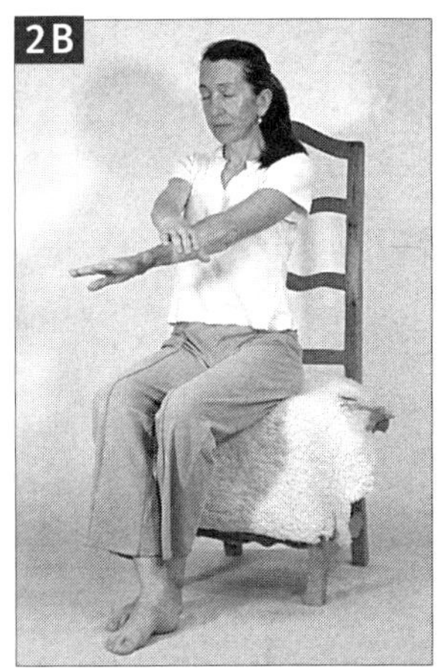

3. Remain with the feet shoulder-width apart. Repeat Exercise 1 and 2 exactly as you did previously: clap the hands over the head 8 times; beat the ground with the palms 8 times; pump the arms 8 complete cycles; and crisscross the arms and legs 8 counts (4 complete cycles). Chant "***Har***" with each count and continue for 3 minutes.

Move continuously through this series for 8 minutes.

This is an excellent exercise. Each section works on you and it also gives you a rest. Stimulating various meridians the series affects you as follows: clapping massages the brain; pumping the arms stimulates meridian points on the forearm for the colon, stomach, spleen and liver; and crisscrossing the arms and legs is a perfect brain-balancing exercise. This set is especially good for seniors who are concerned about their brain functions.

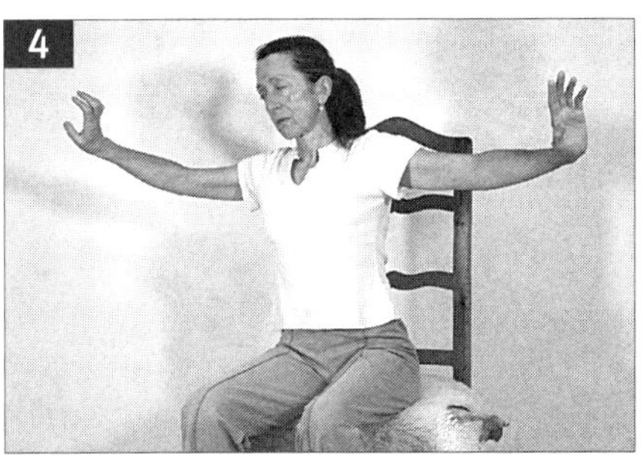

4. Sit in Easy Pose and play some beautiful and uplifting music. Close your eyes, merge with the sounds and feel very relaxed and expansive as you begin moving the arms, hands and torso to express yourself. Continue for 5–11 minutes.

This is called "Celestial Communication." It is the expression of your inner being through movement. The effect is extreme relaxation, and relaxation allows you to be truly you. It will bring you good health and happiness and will bring your entire being into perfect condition.

5. Repeat Exercise 3 for 3 minutes.

6. If possible, play the tape *Himalaya* (available at Ancient Healing Ways) or any beautiful chant and sing with an open heart.

7. Sit straight in your chair. Make a circle of claps as follows: in front of the left shoulder **(7A)**; at the center of the chest **(7B)**; in front of the right shoulder **(7C)**; and over the head. **(7D)** Continue moving the hands with the following variations:

A. As you clap, count out loud "1, 2, 3, 4" for 1 minute.

B. Concentrate at the navel point and say, "*I-do-love-you,*", one word per clap for 2 minutes.

C. Chant "*Har Har Har Hari*" for 1 minute, one word per clap.

D. Chant "*Siri Har Har Hari*" at a rapid pace for 2 minutes. Chant one word per clap.

Lean back in your chair and relax 5–10 minutes.

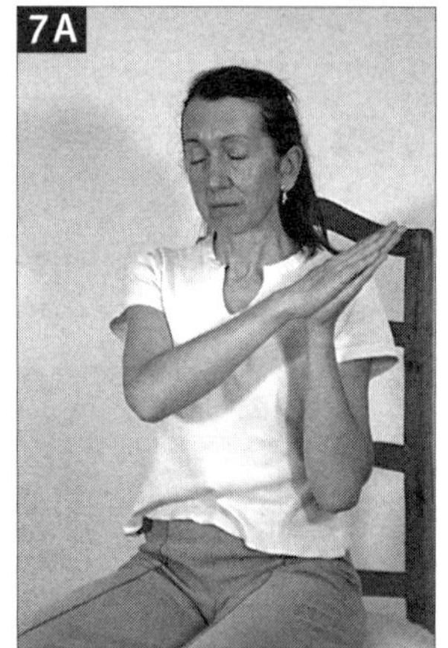
7A

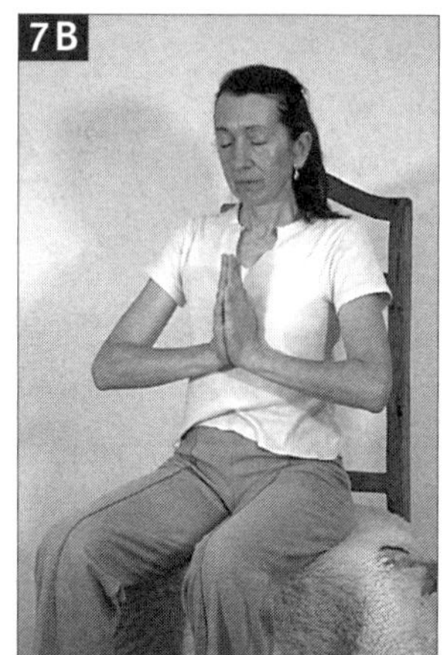
7B

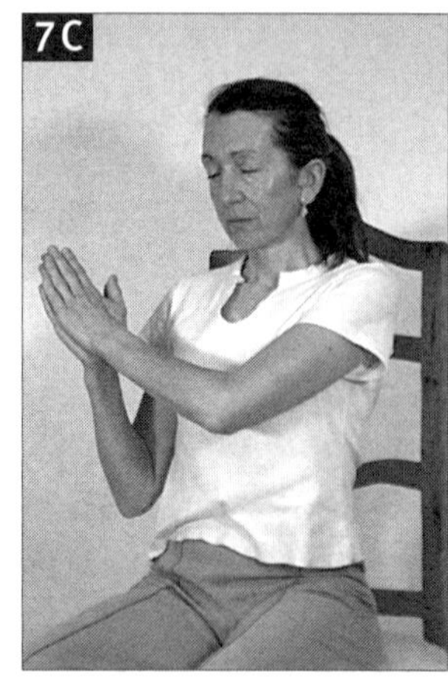
7C

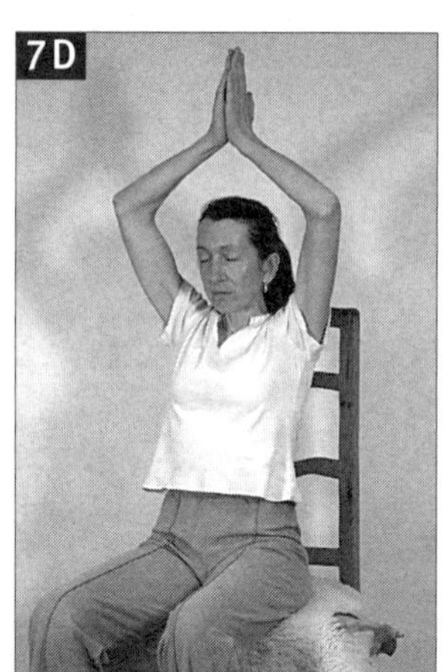
7D

RESOURCE PAGES

Guru Terath Kaur Khalsa, Ph.D.
Workshops, Phone and email consultations, Teacher Training Level I and II, Book sales for *Dying Into Life* and *The Art of Making Sex Sacred*
505-753-6241
PO Box 845, Santa Cruz, NM 87567
gtkhalsa_2000@yahoo.com
www.guruterathkaur.com

3HO Foundation
Healthy, Happy, Holy Organization
Information about Kundalini Yoga and Meditation events, Teacher Training and KY teacher directory
1-888-346-2420
www.3HO.org
YogaInfo@3HO.org

Ancient Healing Ways
Tapes, Books, Yoga Manuals, Yogi Bhajan Videos, Yogi Tea, Peace Cereals, Videos, Sunshine Oils (call for a catalog)
800-359-2940 – Retail 877-753-5351 – Wholesale
39 Shady Lane, Espanola, NM 87532
www.a-healing.com

Chavez Recording Studio
SteveChavez@valornet.com

Ek Ong Kar Kaur Khalsa
Book – beautiful English translation of Japji Sahib, Workshops on Gurmukhi scriptures
ekongkaar@sikhdharma.org

GRD Design
Print and web design.
Sopurkh Singh Khalsa
505-927-4497
www.grddesign.com
sopurkh@grddesign.com

Guru Ram Das Center for Medicine and Humanology
Shanti Shanti Kaur Khalsa
Research and educational programs, using Kundalini Yoga for health and healing
800-326-1322
PO Box 1926, Espanola, NM 87632
healthnow@grdcenter.org

Hector Jara (Muktiar Singh)
Yogic and spiritual artist. It is his energy picture in Chapter Four – Yogic Science. He will take orders.
222-245-4815
2 Sur #5948 Co. Bagambilias, Puebla, Pue, Mexico
hectorjara@lycos.com

Sangeet Kaur Khalsa
Spiritual music CDs at naad@cybermesa.com

Shakta Kaur Khalsa
1259 Bond St., Herndon, VA 20170
fax: 703-471-6553
email: yogainfo@earthlink.net
www.shaktakhalsa.com
www.childrensyoga.com for current information about
- Organizing and finding teacher training sessions in your area

- Comprehensive listing of RCYP teachers
- Yoga exercises that children can try at home
- Links to related sites, including links to ordering children's yoga books
- Teacher's Sharing Page for networking, posting ideas, ask questions, and sharing about how children's yoga is growing.

Spirit Voyage
Music for yoga, meditation and the healing arts
1-888-753-4800
www.SpiritVoyage.com

INDEX FOR YOGA SETS AND MEDITATIONS

Breathing Techniques:

Meditations:

Yoga Sets: